PASSIONATE UNCERTAINTY

The publisher gratefully acknowledges the contribution provided by the General Endowment Fund, which is supported by generous gifts from the members of the Associates of the University of California Press.

PETER MCDONOUGH / EUGENE C. BIANCHI

Passionate Uncertainty

Inside the American Jesuits

UNIVERSITY OF CALIFORNIA PRESS
Berkeley   Los Angeles   London

University of California Press
Berkeley and Los Angeles, California

University of California Press, Ltd.
London, England

© 2002 by the Regents of the
University of California

Library of Congress Cataloging-in-Publication Data

McDonough, Peter.
    Passionate uncertainty : inside the American
Jesuits / Peter McDonough and Eugene C. Bianchi.
        p.   cm.
    Includes bibliographical references (p.   ) and
index.
    ISBN 0-520-23055-8 (cloth : alk. paper)
    1. Jesuits—United States—History—20th
century.   I. Bianchi, Eugene C.   II. Title.
BX3708 .M335   2002
271'.53073'0904—dc21   2001034673

Manufactured in the United States of America
10   09   08   07   06   05   04   03   02   01
10   9   8   7   6   5   4   3   2   1

The paper used in this publication meets the
minimum requirements of ANSI/NISO Z39.48-1992
(R 1997) (*Permanence of Paper*). ∞

In memory of
BRUCE F. BIEVER, S.J.,
JOHN M. CULKIN,
and
JOSEPH H. FICHTER, S.J.

CONTENTS

Acknowledgments   ix

Prologue: Diversity without Democracy   1

1. Staying and Leaving   17
2. Becoming a Jesuit   43
3. From Innocence to Experience   64
4. Sex, Celibacy, and Identity   87
5. Ignatian Spiritualities   110
6. Eclecticism and Commitment   132
7. Life in Community   160
8. Ministry and the Meaning of Priesthood   185
9. Revitalizing the Schools   211
10. Organizational Dilemmas, Symbolic Conflicts,
        Structural Problems   237
11. Low-Profile Politics   262

Epilogue: Evening's Empire   287

Notes on Methodology   307

Notes   329

Glossary   369

List of Figures and Tables   371

Index   373

ACKNOWLEDGMENTS

We have been at this study since the middle of the 1990s, and a number of individuals and organizations have helped us along the way.

We are grateful to our wives Josefina Figueira-McDonough and Margaret Herrman for indulging our obsession through the long haul. Much of the fieldwork and data collection was supported by a grant from the Lilly Endowment. Fellowships from the National Endowment for the Humanities and the Fulbright Commission enabled Peter McDonough to devote extra time to the project. McDonough also wishes to express his thanks for the hospitality of the Jesuits and their colleagues at Milltown Park in Dublin and to the faculty and staff of the Department of Politics, University College, Dublin, where the final touches were put on the book.

The usual absolution regarding errors of fact and judgment applies. The following report, taken from an old *Irish Jesuit Directory and Year Book,* may carry a lesson for those alarmed at or hoping for mischief and iniquity in the clerical realm:

> A memorable event of the year 1921 was the invasion of Milltown Park, just before daybreak of February 21st, by some hundreds of the South Lancashire Regiment, supported by armored cars, machine guns, and field kitchens. A weekend retreat was in progress, and the object of the raid was said to be the capture of Michael Collins. After a five hour search the force departed, having found nothing more incriminatory than some books on socialism in the room of the professor of sociology.

Reed Malcolm, Jim Clark, Nicole Hayward, and Marilyn Schwartz at the University of California Press guided the book toward publication with enthusiasm and patience. Scott Norton gave invaluable advice that enabled us to tame a sprawling manuscript.

Most of all, we thank the hundreds of Jesuits and former Jesuits who took part in the study and whose words make up the best of *Passionate Uncertainty*. Epigraphs are the lawn ornaments of the book trade. But some of the statements provided by the men are so pungent that we have not been able to resist placing a few excerpts at the head of each chapter by way of preview for what's inside.

I

Catholicism is a paradoxical holdout. The Second Vatican Council (Vatican II, 1962–65)—the watershed conclave of ecclesiastical leaders held in Rome in the early 1960s—set in motion reforms that led the Roman Catholic church to support democratization in Latin America, East Asia, and Eastern and Central Europe. But on the inside, Catholicism has retained its hierarchical traditions, excluding women from the priesthood and hewing to a conservative line on issues involving what one Jesuit has called "pelvic theology"—celibacy, contraception, divorce, abortion, and the like. While its outreach has tilted leftward, the power structure of Catholicism remains confined to male clerics.

The Jesuits, the fabled group of educators and missionaries whose origins date back to the Renaissance, are caught in these crosscurrents. As the order ages and shrinks in numbers, the Society of Jesus has seen its schools and other operations increasingly staffed and run by laymen and laywomen. By and large, Jesuits have encouraged this transformation. At the same time, the shift impinges on clerical roles and priestly identity and leaves Jesuits searching for corporate purpose.

The sea-change experienced by the Jesuits has been cultural as well as institutional. Since the 1960s, and especially since the papacy made clear that it would not revisit off-limits areas such as birth control and the ordination of women, many Jesuits have lived in tacit dissent. The gap between the official teaching of the church and the practice of its middle managers—nuns as well as priests, including Jesuits—has widened.

The confluence of these organizational and cultural changes has precipitated a crisis not only among the Jesuits but also, more broadly, within the priesthood and by extension within the governing structure of Catholicism. Long-term demographics work against the replenishment of clerical ranks restricted to celibate males. The number of Catholics continues to grow as vocations to the consecrated life decline. Among Jesuits who remain, lack of conviction about once-solid moral verities is at least as common as outright polarization between defenders of a return to the old code and advocates of reform.

The sensible thing would seem to be to expand clerical numbers by relaxing the rules of membership—by abolishing restrictions regarding priestly celibacy and the ordination of women. But problems in Catholicism are rarely settled on the grounds of fairness, efficiency, or public opinion. "Men must be changed by religion," a prominent Counter-Reformation prelate argued in words that would become a rallying cry for upholders of tradition, "not religion by men." [1]

The Jesuits are in a bind. They cannot go back, insofar as that course would entail a return to clerical dominance in an age of lay ascendancy. But they cannot move forward without placing their clerical identity at risk.

Jesuits have reacted to the threat of evaporating identity by changing from a prominent if rather parochial *subcultural* presence to a *countercultural* movement. Attachments to causes and symbols that distance them from the mainstream range from adherence to religious neoconservatism, to the advocacy of radical social change, to the cultivation of a gay lifestyle, to involvement with non-Western religions. The countercultural turn—"strategy" has too purposeful a connotation—has neither boosted numbers nor contributed to the coherence of the Society. But it has kept the order from extinction by way of assimilation, and a semblance of distinctiveness has been maintained.

This is not the whole story. Another factor making for survival is that many Jesuits take genuine pleasure in their work, flying below the radar of the Vatican, and a few actually agree with the direction set by Rome. Finally, and somewhat ironically, the tendency for those in religious life to resolve their problems in personal terms, through recourse to therapy and versions of privatized spirituality, may smack of "modern individualism," but it poses little direct challenge to the Catholic hierarchy.

For all this, the steady depletion of clerical manpower jeopardizes not only the ministerial prowess but also the authority structure of the church. A thunderous contradiction exists between ministerial ambitions and clerical capacity. Something has to give.

Passionate Uncertainty looks at this drama from the perspective of key players: Jesuits who have stayed with the institution and those who have abandoned the clerical enterprise. The troubles facing the Jesuits closely resemble those afflicting the clergy in general. With the ascent of the laity, the crisis of priestly identity and purpose has become a crisis of church leadership. Insofar as the laity look toward the representatives of the church for insight into their spiritual lives, their own sense of identity is also in crisis.

The Society of Jesus stands at the terminus of a long evolution in religious life. In the heyday of the order, the versatility of the Jesuits reflected not just the culmination of the priestly ideal joined to worldly activism. In Europe, Jesuits were also the vanguard of papal ambitions for dominance in the political realm. Not until the 1960s, with the reforms of Vatican II, did ecclesiastical authorities relinquish their dream of the union of church and state. Now, having revamped its political goals, the church finds itself with less and less clerical manpower to carry out its ministerial functions. We are left with a landscape, in the words of Wallace Stevens, "like the scenery of a play that has come to an end."[2]

2

The story of the Jesuits falls into three acts. The first ended abruptly in 1773, when the pope issued an edict to suppress the Society. The Jesuits, celebrated not only for their schools and their missionary work but also for their activities as court advisers, had aroused the hostility of absolutist monarchs and the enmity of rivals within the church.[3] Except in Russia, where rulers declined to receive the papal edict, the Jesuits were disbanded, and their property was confiscated. Many became secular priests, and the superior-general of the order died in a papal prison in Rome.

After a forty-year hiatus, a papacy alarmed by upheavals attendant on the French Revolution restored the Society of Jesus. The period from 1814 until Vatican II in the 1960s constitutes the second act in the saga of the Jesuits. Once again on the upswing, the restored Society was associated with conservative, antidemocratic elements through much of the nineteenth and the first part of the twentieth century in Europe. The order was identified with "ultramontane" support for the universal, transnational supremacy of the pope.[4]

Jesuits in the United States, though growing rapidly, had a lower political profile than their counterparts in Europe. Georgetown University, the country's oldest Catholic institution of higher learning, was inaugurated in 1789 under the auspices of Bishop John Carroll, a former Jesuit who had become a secular priest with the suppression of the order. American Jesuits catered to a burgeoning clientele of Catholic immigrants and their offspring. More than Jesuits elsewhere, the American branch deployed its manpower through a network of high schools, colleges, and universities. The high schools especially became a major source of recruits. By the end of the 1930s, the Society of Jesus in the United States had overtaken Spanish Jesuits to form the largest regional contingent in the worldwide order.[5]

In the years following World War II, the energy of the Jesuits was expressed not only in their colleges and universities, expanding exponentially under the stimulus of the GI Bill, but also in the emergence of daring intellectuals. Next to the French archaeologist and mystic Pierre Teilhard de Chardin, the most celebrated of these was the theologian and political theorist John Courtney Murray, who pushed the boundaries of Catholic orthodoxy. In the late 1950s, Murray's advocacy of religious toleration and political pluralism earned him the opprobrium of reactionaries in the Vatican, and his superiors were compelled to silence him.[6]

Vatican II touched off the third act of the Jesuit drama, one whose scenario has yet to be completed. The promulgation of Vatican II's decree on religious freedom, drafted by Murray, vindicated his views.[7] Pedro Arrupe, the first Basque to head the order since its founding, was elected superior-general and undertook a program of change in line with the reformist shift in Catholicism. The training of Jesuits became less regimented, and greater priority was placed on social justice.[8] By 1965, when the council drew to a close, the Jesuits were at their peak, with more than 35,000 men around the world, about 8,500 of whom were Americans.

Even then, however, signs of trouble were detectable. As early as the mid-1950s, the number of entrants had begun to stagnate and then to drift downward in Europe and soon after in the United States. In the wake of Vatican II, which left the identity and the role of the priesthood unclear, the volume of recruits shrank practically everywhere. Jesuits left in droves. Thirty years after the council, global membership had fallen to the low-20,000 mark. Concurrently, with the drop in entrants, the average age of Jesuits soared. The decline in membership was especially sharp in advanced industrial societies. Toward the end of the 1990s, the number of American Jesuits had dropped from above 8,000 to below 4,000, and they were overtaken by the Jesuits of India as the largest regional bloc.

The dwindling and graying of the Society has prompted greater collaboration with laypeople. By the dawn of the new millennium, there were more than a million and a half alumni of Jesuit colleges and universities in the United States, and the scale of these operations surpassed the ability of the Jesuits to control them. Conscious of the secularization of universities such as Harvard, Princeton, and Yale, whose origins were bound up with Protestant denominations, Jesuits and their colleagues struggled to clarify the mission of the institutions of higher education affiliated with the order in the United States.[9] The process is not unlike decolonization, with Jesuits withdrawing from positions of leadership while leaving signs of a distinctive ethos in place.[10]

With the ascent to the papacy of Karol Wojtyla as John Paul II in 1978, the power of the Jesuits waned. The experimentalism and ecumenism of many Jesuits did not sit well with the militant centralism of the new pope.[11] In 1981, when Pedro Arrupe was immobilized by a stroke, the pope bypassed the usual rules of the Society and appointed an elderly Jesuit as caretaker.[12] Jesuits, some of whom still refer to the event as a minisuppression, were enjoined to get their house in order. In 1983, at a general congregation of the Society in Rome, the Dutch Jesuit Peter-Hans Kolvenbach was elected superior-general.

Jesuits have continued to get caught up in politics. During the 1970s and 1980s, a number of Jesuits were instrumental in the development of liberation theology in Central and South America. In 1989 in El Salvador, six members of the order were assassinated by the military for their criticism of the regime.[13] Some Jesuits, such as the peace activist Daniel Berrigan, make political statements and engage in social advocacy.[14] In 1997, a Jesuit was slain in India because of his work with untouchables; another Indian Jesuit was shot dead in 2000, probably by religious fundamentalists; and Jesuits have fallen victim to internecine warfare in Africa and Southeast Asia. The Society is a collective presence in a few areas bearing on public policy, most notably in private education. But the greater part of the politics involving Jesuits is intramural, touching on relations with the ecclesiastical hierarchy and on sensitive issues such as the role of women.

Although the Jesuits' commitment to social justice continues to receive rhetorical support, practical means for delivering on this commitment are still being thrashed out. The process is complicated by their
long-standing institutional obligations, especially in the schools. Some
of the schools serve relatively well-off clienteles, while others care for
poor people, many of them non-Catholic, in inner cities.

The onus of redirecting priorities is aggravated by manpower short-
ages. Only in India does Jesuit membership appear to be growing steadily, and even there the forecast is for decline as the country modernizes.[15]
The Society of Jesus is an understaffed conglomerate. The scope of its activities makes the corporate direction of the order uncertain, and the
continued shortfall in numbers puts its survival in jeopardy.

3

Among Jesuits, change has been massive and deep not only in numbers—the Society has lost over a third of its manpower around the
world and more than half its membership in the United States—but also
in what Jesuits believe and in what they do. The Jesuits have been transformed from a fairly unified, though far from homogeneous, organization into a much smaller, looser community with disparate goals and a
corporate identity that has turned out to be elusive.

The key to understanding this metamorphosis is to recognize, first,
what has *not* happened. The Society of Jesus has not moved from one
steady state to a new equilibrium; no overarching paradigm has replaced
the theological synthesis that prevailed in the days before the 1960s and
Vatican II.[16] Aside from the slide in numbers, the upshot has been a proliferation of agendas and lifestyles of borderline coherence within the
confines of the ecclesiastical hierarchy. The result, in other words, has
been diversity without democracy.

Jesuits are faced with dilemmas of identity, with questions of who
they are, in addition to puzzlement about what they do and how they do
it. The status of the priesthood has declined as the connection between
celibacy and good works has become doubtful. This confusion shows up
in sexual ambiguity as well as in conflict over practical, corporate goals.
As the old emblems of belonging have become tattered with the erosion
of the enclaves of immigrant Catholicism, and as certainty over clerical
purpose has given way to an assortment of ideologies and agendas—as,
in short, the security of the traditional subculture has faded—some Jesuits have found their moorings in countercultural stances shaped by

sexual orientation, social advocacy, and a variety of causes, conservative as well as radical, that in one way or another set them apart from the mainstream.[17]

The social assimilation of American Catholics and the movement toward a more ecumenical Catholicism, open to the wisdom of other religious traditions, have placed strains on Jesuits long associated with a fortress church. The problem is not inordinate attachment to the past—very few Jesuits are arch-reactionaries—but, rather, indeterminacy over what is to take its place. Mainstreaming threatens to obliterate the identity of groups like the Society of Jesus.

Instead of being absorbed by success, many Jesuits have become profoundly ambivalent about it. They have moved from subcultural certainties toward countercultural agendas. The appeal of the misfit battles with the yearning for conventional acceptance. Sometimes this takes the shape of commitment to the "faith that does justice"; sometimes it entails attachment to an outsider sexuality, as in the case of the cultivation of a gay lifestyle; sometimes the urge to define identity is subsumed in a religious neoconservatism that applauds the restorationist platform of John Paul II; and sometimes it leads to exploration of religious practices outside the Western heritage. These disparate critiques are united in little else except a renunciation of the standardization and complacency of contemporary society.[18]

This depiction of the countercultural slant of the Jesuits tells us more about the centrifugal forces operating on the Society than about how the order manages to hang together and muddle through. In order to figure this out, we need to understand the flexible nature of the hierarchy in which Jesuits are embedded.

The Society can be visualized as a three-tiered arrangement in which change proceeds faster toward the bottom than at the top. In pursuing reform, Jesuits have followed the path of least resistance. Individually, Jesuits engage in rewarding work and feel that they are doing pretty well, but the collective picture is mixed. Frustration increases the higher up the ecclesiastical ladder Jesuit operations go.[19]

In their daily lives, Jesuits have experienced significant spiritual renewal, putting new verve into the personalized religious practices associated with the first, creative days of the order. Moreover, Jesuits and former Jesuits have dropped much of the sexual restrictiveness of old-time Catholicism. A good deal of customization of spiritual and moral experience has gone on at some remove from the doctrinal propriety espoused by Rome. Not all these reforms have proceeded smoothly. Nevertheless, on the whole, Jesuits have loosened up. They are not about to go back to being "good monks." [20]

As we move farther up the line, from their personal to their ministerial activities, Jesuits are less in control, and programmatic rivalries combine with institutional drag and external pressures to produce a less clear-cut, though still significant, measure of creativity. At this intermediate level, proponents of the social justice agenda that came into vogue with Vatican II vie with the advocates of the Society's customary strengths in education and the intellectual trades. Though neither dominates, the faith-and-justice program has gained ground, abetted by the numeric decline of Jesuits in the schools.

In addition, market criteria have made themselves felt in the competition for capital and human resources. Jesuit educational operations that once catered to an almost exclusively Catholic clientele, under clerical supervision, are now more attentive to professional regulations and wider economic pulls. These secular incentives have improved their performance, even if their religious compass has been altered.

Finally, it is at the top, where the power of the Jesuits is severely circumscribed, in relations between the Society of Jesus and the Vatican, that change has been slowest. Ordinary Jesuits embrace, adapt to, finesse, or ignore prescriptions regarding, for example, the ordination of women and married people. At its apex, Catholicism remains a monarchy with few provisions for restraining one-man rule.[21] The weakness of institutional checks permits a gifted authoritarian politician like John Paul II to orchestrate a kind of populist autocracy. To classify the papal structure to which the Jesuits are bound as garden-variety conservatism—as "elitism" and the like—is to underestimate its capacity, in the hands of a media-savvy pope, for nondemocratic adaptation to mass politics.[22]

Put schematically: The politics of Jesuit-Vatican relations are less tractable than the economics of their ministries, which are in turn less malleable than what transpires at the psychosexual level of personal therapy and spiritual direction. Hollowed out though it may be, hierarchy is preserved through the tactical, local autonomy it grants.

Does this add up to anything more than a kind of protracted entropy, a drip-by-drip disintegration? The loose coupling of the bottom, middle, and upper tiers of the system keeps it going longer than might be expected. But several forces have been operating on the hierarchy, rendering it more and more anomalous.

The first of these is *therapization*. The renewal of the *Spiritual Exercises* in one-on-one fashion has been accompanied by the application of secular psychology to foster individual adjustment. The process of *cura personalis* (personal care) is two-edged. The therapeutic turn does not encourage collective mobilization against the ecclesiastical structure, but it doesn't foster loyalty to institutions either.[23]

Another big push has been toward *marketization*. Not only do Jesuits have to compete with laypeople for jobs in the apostolic infrastructure, but the ministerial institutions themselves have become more professional and deliberative in recruitment, fund-raising, asset management, and so on. Decision making by committee is the norm. Jesuit operations are more businesslike than they used to be.

A third, much weaker impulse has been toward *democratization*. Jesuits can get many of the benefits associated with such a course within a hierarchy that is fairly flexible, if somewhat arbitrary, without going to the trouble of a root-and-branch makeover. Especially in their ministerial activities, self-determination of an ad hoc variety is within reach, while reform conceived as systemwide inclusiveness and an overhaul of the rules seems costly and far off. More than a few Jesuits prefer a personal, face-to-face hierarchy than an impersonal democracy.

4

A major factor contributing to the staying power of the Jesuits, then, is the virtual compartmentalization of the tiers of religious life. The hierarchy holds together because its parts do *not* mesh tightly. The loose-jointed architecture of the ecclesiastical establishment prevents one level of the organization from getting in the way of another and, by deflecting conflict, helps keep the system from flying apart.

But because their bottom line is typically hard to pin down, Jesuits also need a shared language and a sense of common mission. This rhetoric gives Jesuits the feeling that they are all in the same boat and that the boat is pretty much on course, creaking and pitching though it may be. What is supposed to bind them together and to link the bottom to the top of the religious hierarchy is not rules and regulations, much less the threat of force, but a common culture and set of beliefs.[24]

This shared culture has come under severe strain. Since Vatican II, a sharp break has developed in the core beliefs of Catholicism, notably in the sexual code. While Jesuits exhibit some disagreement among themselves on these issues, most can be classified as liberals; and, because the sexual code is so closely bound up with the rules governing authority in the church, through an all-male celibate clergy, the progressivism of the Jesuits puts them at odds with the ecclesiastical status quo. The upshot has been enormous tension: not so much outright dissent, though this occurs, as uncertainty about the religious enterprise.[25]

The problem is aggravated by the increasing numbers of laypeople and especially women working in organizations sponsored by the Society. Even when they find the exclusionary setup distasteful and possibly dysfunctional, most of them do not press for ordination for themselves. Instead, the laicization of the schools and other apostolates works the other way around, calling into question the link between priestly ordination, celibacy, and qualification for ministry. Because the apostolates do fairly well as the clerical presence declines, the functional rationale of the priesthood is undercut. The challenge has as much to do with the need to clarify the symbolic and instrumental roles of the clergy as with virulent anticlericalism or any clamor on the part of women and married men for access to holy orders. This virtual indifference to the priesthood may help explain the lack of outrage with which revelations about this or that sexual transgression on the part of the clergy is received, but its long-term implications for vocations to religious life cannot be sanguine.

The result among Jesuits is demoralization and self-doubt as much as tooth-and-nail confrontation. The rate of departures from the priesthood has settled down from its peak during the late 1960s and early 1970s. But irresolution over the role of the priesthood has limited the attraction of the Society. The inflow of recruits is meager. The order limps along, but fresh blood is scarce.

5

So, the tightly woven subculture of the Society of Jesus has unraveled into a mélange of countercultures. What does this add up to? The ensemble reflects the wobbly situation of the Jesuits. But it doesn't lay out a master trend about where the Society is headed.

When speculating about where the Jesuits are going, two rules of thumb are worth keeping in mind. One involves a split that divides Jesuits among themselves and that, even more sharply, divides the mostly reform-minded Jesuits from cautious elements in church officialdom. The pattern originates in the gulf between men who long for unchanging principle—the adamantine core of perennial Catholicism—and those shaken by doubt and ambiguity.[26]

The irony is that although they have the numbers on their side, conflicted Jesuits are more given to equivocation than to concerted behavior. "There are the Americans," one Jesuit quipped about his colleagues, "and there are the Romans—and then there are those who can't make up their mind." A lack of appetite for in-house maneuvering also offsets the disruptive potential of dissent in the Society of Jesus. A disdain for institutions is part of the aftertaste of Vatican II. For some, the institutional church has become a necropolis of dulcet ideals. And in any event, loyal opposition lacks legitimacy in Roman Catholicism. The timorous liberalism of the reformers is not simply a temperamental flaw; it is reinforced by the penalties that vocal criticism elicits.[27]

Their conservative rivals, in contrast, see themselves as assaulted by individualism, relativism, and the like, and they appear to be less squeamish and more focused about the intramural politics of Catholicism. Hard-liners feel besieged, all the more so because of the conviction that eternal truths are subverted as much by pusillanimity as by direct challenge.

How does this imbalance between alienation and institutional leverage affect the options of the Jesuits? Besides losing a large number of men, the Society has undergone a subtle, protective restructuring. The varied and, on the whole, mutually tolerant countercultures within the order combine with an inveterate caginess regarding the larger ecclesiastical scene. There is a compartmentalization of rather than a confrontation between opinion and power. Disaffection is widespread, but it is also diffuse and largely privatized. As a result, the organizational advantage lies with the true believers. The upshot is that the official apparatus of the church and parts of the Society of Jesus persist in a kind of suspended dilapidation.[28]

A second consideration that complicates forecasts regarding religious life has to do with the fact that *Passionate Uncertainty* is about Jesuits and former Jesuits in the United States, with only side glances at the Society in other parts of the world. Ours may be a story with a spin that stresses the eclipse of yet another hierarchical anachronism by the spirit of the age. In fact, democratizing tendencies are more evident in the culture and behavior of American Jesuits than traditional images of regimentation and blind obedience suggest, and this liberalization is unlikely to come undone.

The trouble with highlighting developments in this vein is not so much that they are alien to the Jesuit style or to the structure of Catholicism or that they reflect a myopia about political customs outside North America. The problem is that such developments tend to be confined mostly to internal disputes, and they fail to specify how changes in the lines of authority within Catholicism might affect what Jesuits and the clergy in general actually do. The perspective overlooks the resemblance not between the Society and some decrepit hierarchy struggling to change its ways but between the order and nonprofit advocacy groups that have spread around the world in recent decades. Judgments about the work that such organizations do leave open the question of how representative, participatory, or accountable the organizations are. The two dominant themes of the post–Cold War era—globalization and democratization—need not unfold in tandem.[29]

The Society of Jesus is going through a dual transition. The growing flexibility of the order with regard to the needs of its members, together with a newfound emphasis on consultation, is an important facet of internal change. Another dimension—the struggle to redirect the mission of the Society—is external. The degree to which this ministerial dynamic responds to outside demand and how it flows from or affects changes in the clerical regime on the inside are difficult questions. There is no reason to assume that the various elements of the transition mesh or that they proceed at the same pace. The connection between who Jesuits are and what they do remains unsettled.

6

We draw on a variety of material, from archival sources (planning memos, minutes of meetings, and so on) to analyses and interpretations published by Jesuits themselves.[30] However, the data that we use most extensively, and by far the richest source of information, consist of personal interviews and written statements divided about equally between 430 American Jesuits and former Jesuits.[31]

Why former Jesuits? Mainly because there are so many of them. From 1960, just before Vatican II until the turn of the millennium, more men left the Society of Jesus in the United States (over 5,000) than are presently members of it (less than 4,000). For this reason alone, former Jesuits are as important a part of the story of the postconciliar Society as are Jesuits themselves.

In one instance, the contrast between Jesuits and former Jesuits goes to the heart of the matter. This occurs in chapter 1, where we examine the reasons for sticking with and leaving the order. We start with a look at this comparatively clear-cut choice (and leave the chronologically anterior question of why men become Jesuits in the first place for chapter 2) because the alternatives highlight the clerical/postclerical dynamics that inform much of *Passionate Uncertainty.*

Elsewhere, however, many of the before-and-after differences turn out to be less prominent. The attitudes of Jesuits and former Jesuits are not all that different, or they differ in rather expected ways. For example, while both have moved to the left on sexual-moral issues, former Jesuits have on the average moved farther. In this respect, the contrast between Jesuits and former Jesuits is rather like one of Alfred Hitchcock's "Macguffins." It stands as a puzzle that rivets attention and acts as an inducement to follow the story rather than a key to the meaning of the story itself.

The underlying organization of our book is not very complicated. We follow Jesuits and former Jesuits from the personal trajectories of individuals through their life and work in common to the upper reaches of church politics or at least to their perceptions of that rarefied zone. The first six chapters are devoted to the micro-level of Jesuit life: to individual Jesuits and former Jesuits as they entered the Society and decided to stay or leave and to their views on sexuality and spirituality.[32] With chapter 7, on community life, we enter the intermediate, collective level of the order. Chapters 8 and 9, on aspects of ministry, also look at the mostly corporate, institutionalized work of the Society. It is with chapters 10 and 11 that we reach the explicitly political realm of Jesuit activity, where the Society deals with Rome over questions of religious strategy.

The tiers are not hermetically separated. Chapter 9, for example, touches on the political clashes set off by the efforts of the Vatican to exert top-down control over the colleges and universities affiliated with the order. Nevertheless, the progression from the micro- through the meso- to the macro-levels of Jesuit activities unfolds more or less sequentially from the first to the later chapters.[33]

As suggested earlier, the sequence corresponds roughly to a gradient of accomplishment and satisfaction. Jesuits are fairly happy with what they have been able to achieve as individuals—in renewing their spiritual lives, for example. They are reasonably satisfied with their collective capacity for coping and innovation, even though progress in corporate ministry and community life has been spotty. They are less content with the overall directions of the institutional church and the strategy of the papacy.

7

The guarantee of confidentiality, combined with the Ignatian habit of periodic self-scrutiny, generates frank conversation. The circumspection for which Jesuits have long been known gives way to an emotional and intellectual outpouring. Jesuits and former Jesuits have been through tremendous changes since Vatican II, and much of the psychological violence and torment of this period comes out in their talk and correspondence.

The transformation of the Jesuits will strike some readers as a colossal shift away from the true-grit, hardtack, Vince Lombardi school of tough-guy religion—an extraordinarily high tolerance for pain, even an appetite for martyrdom, discipline, and zeal so colossal that they seem to drum up their own background music. These men, the salt of the earth, were supposed to take their lumps and suffer in silence. The deepest things were inexpressible, the truest eloquence was taciturn.

On the other side of this piss-and-vinegar religion is designer Catholicism: self-absorption, abounding sensitivity, arias of torment and healing, soft-boiled spirituality, and a ground bass of whining—just the sort of tedious introspection, lugubrious neediness, and bad poetry that cynics expect to gush forth when men talk about their feelings. "These guys sound more Jewish than I am!" a colleague cracked after reading through some of the Woody Allenesque transcripts. The Society of Jesus becomes the country that "may not look like much when you first get there, but once you get to know the people, it's truly awful." There is enough truth in both these stereotypes to sustain comic misunderstanding and righteous indignation for a long time, but they are stereotypes.[34]

The other impression left by the reflections of Jesuits and former Jesuits is their bluntness. In the land of absolutes, nuance is everything. Well, not everything—that would violate the law of nuance. But anyone with even a passing knowledge of the Society knows that "nuance" is a favorite Jesuit word.[35] This predilection goes with a rhetorical style favoring circumlocution or a logic that seeks to split the difference, to find some conciliatory middle ground, as if Jesuits were polite tourists in an alien world. There is plenty of oblique, polished talk here, and there is some quieter, plain-vanilla talk, for example, of prayer as "just being with God, no fireworks or epiphanies," as one Jesuit put it. But there are also many indelicate, unblinking passages, sometimes of rage or of despair or of shame at the realization of having been taken in, furious confusion over who to blame, and lacerating expletives. There is also explosive humor: "Remember what —————— of impious memory used to shriek *in extremis*, which for him was most of the time? 'Oh God, if there is a God, save my soul, if I have a soul!!!'" [36]

All this brutal intimacy takes getting use to, especially if what the reader has in mind, in what Ignatius called "spiritual conversation," is genteel discourse. Ignatius himself urged his men to write *cartas edificantes* (edifying letters) about their exploits, not only to document their trials and accomplishments but also with a view to eventual publication, to cast the Society in a favorable light. For every four Jesuits, according to the in-joke, there was a fifth registering their exploits. To their credit, even when composing under such guidelines, Jesuits often seem to have forgotten themselves and been carried away, so that they produced invaluable historical and anthropological records, and a good deal of impolitic gossip, in spite of pious convention.

Still, the eye-level observations of Jesuits and former Jesuits may sound too lacking in propriety, too squalid even, and our commentary may reflect too closely the gaze that Graham Greene traced, in noting the artist's ruthlessness, to "a sliver of ice in the heart."

There is an ampler way to put this, however. "The artist who really loves people loves them so well the way they are he sees no need to disguise their characteristics," the novelist Dawn Powell noted in her diary. "He loves them whole, without retouching. Yet the word always used for this unqualifying affection is 'cynicism.'" She goes on, commenting about different ways of depicting mourners at a funeral:

> In my satire . . . I merely add a dimension to character, a dimension which gives the person substance and life but which readers often mistake for malice. . . . Yet in giving this picture, with no malice in mind, no desire to show the grievers up as villains, no wish more than to give people their full statures, one would be accused of "satire," of "cynicism" instead of looking without blinders, blockers, ear mufflers, gags, at life. Satire is people as they are; romanticism, people as they would like to be; realism, people as they seem with their insides left out. [37]

How common is this bleak wisdom among Jesuits and former Jesuits? Something like it, a kind of rueful sympathy, is more typical than the hurling of epithets. The words of a former Jesuit from the California province, in his mid-sixties, more than three decades away from the Society, come close to being a model of ambivalent bonding and straining for impartiality. They are worth quoting at length:

> Not long back a friend back East sent on the St. Ignatius Day letter [which] a former and clearly very embittered New York Jesuit had posted both last year and this. All he had to do was excerpt some choice quotes from Loyola (his rules for thinking with the church, for instance) with appropriate headings to make his point, which was that this was not someone whose ideas most of us would want to claim as our own today. Rereading the texts, I had to remind myself that at the age of eighteen I had completely bought into all this, just as I had bought into the prevailing Catholic world view of 1952. I cringe at the thought.
>
> At the same time I remind myself that I was taken into the Society as a kid without money or family connections, given a top-flight education that has enabled me to pursue my present career [teaching and writing] for over thirty years, and all this without the slightest suggestion that there was a payback somewhere along the line if I left. Even when I did withdraw at the end of regency, my superior insisted that I should not have the feeling that I had ripped the Society off because I was not seeing through the vocation that I had thought I'd had.
>
> I've long since distanced myself from the church (which is not much like the church I grew up in) and yet I do find it hard to distance myself from the Society. It's like the traditional immigrant family with a peculiar outlook and rules that can be downright embarrassing to the next generation, yet it still is the past that can be looked at almost fondly. This is especially true for someone like myself, who really had no other family to speak of. . . . I may yet come up with a cautionary tale about intellectually challenged superiors and morally challenged scholastics . . . and there is a good chance my imaginary events will match up with real things that have happened. But I would not be where I am had it not been for the Society, and that is a debt always real in my mind.[38]

CHAPTER ONE

Staying and Leaving

Most leave because they're lonely. The deeper force is the common calling to some form of intimate company.

Men stay for two reasons: They find fulfillment in the mix of solitude and company which the Society provides, and in a measure of job satisfaction. And some are afraid to leave.

I

The bluntest fact about vocations to religious life in Catholicism is that the numbers are down. Yet Jesuits and former Jesuits are cautious about extrapolating from their own experience to an appraisal of what motivates other men to stay or leave. The crushing demographics are wrapped in mystery.

This hesitancy about causal guesswork and the fear of intrusiveness are sometimes pro forma. Once past the ritual disclaimers and protestations of ignorance, speculation flows. At the other extreme is a spurious psychology: Since every case is supposed to be unique, collective patterns are declared to be unparsable. But sometimes the claims of "who knows?" are genuine, or they are pleas to let harsh memories alone. The decision to stay with or leave the Society of Jesus may be too personal to open up about. In still other cases, the ideas burst through in a flood.

The mystery turns out to be something of an illusion. Many Jesuits and former Jesuits are sensitive anthropologists of their own kind, and some have a novelist's eye for the telling detail. Even when they're modest about venturing opinions regarding the motives of others, they are less shy about reviewing their own experiences. Men associated with the Society of Jesus are trained in self-assessment. The insights that Jesuits and former Jesuits provide reveal abundant regularities in the aggregate even if, in isolation, any single individual is liable to plead ignorance about what leads men to stick with or leave the Society.

We begin by examining the reluctance of Jesuits and former Jesuits to speculate about the reasons why others stay or leave—partly a reflection of commonsensical modesty, partly a guy's thing, and partly an admission of bewilderment and even awe before intimate journeys. Above all, the exercise throws light on a major shift in the atmosphere of religious life from a culture of blame and shame toward one of cordial if nervous tolerance. Mystery lingers because the impulse to share once-secret feelings runs up against a dread of violating privacy.

As the analysis of why men leave and stay develops, a topography of emotion and calculation emerges. It is easier to see why men leave than why they stay. This is because several things—satisfying work, supportive community, sustaining prayer, to mention a few—must come together for a man not only to persist but to find pleasure in Jesuit life. But if any one thing goes wrong, and especially if that one thing has to do with emotional deprivation and a lack of intimacy, the chances are that the man will leave. (The opportunity to exit at a reasonable cost, exemplified by the availability of a job on the outside, conditions the actual follow-up on the choice between staying and leaving.) As a result, the probability of remaining in religious life is lower than that of departing from it.

This is the starkest version of our story. An important subplot concerns the in-between cases. Some men remain not because they want to but because they cannot find a way to leave. Conversely, many of those who have departed, even if they show no desire to go back, express a profound nostalgia for their days in the order. Ambivalence of this sort reflects the difficulty of resolving, once and for all, such trade-offs as those between the longing for community and the pull of intimacy, and the demands of corporate commitment versus the desire for personal autonomy, that religious life presents in sharp relief.

2

The decision to stay or leave the Jesuits is an either-or decision; the reasons behind the choice are rarely so definitive. Different men leave or stay for different reasons, and most can muster more than one reason for their decision.

Occasionally, the reasons given by Jesuits and former Jesuits for their own decisions match their perceptions of collective trends. Some men exit not only because they conclude that Jesuit life keeps them from growing up or is not what they signed on for but also because they are convinced that staying in the order entails arrested development for those who remain and that the Society of Jesus is on the wrong side of history anyway. Likewise, some men who remain in the order believe that the path they have chosen is not only a satisfactory one for them personally but also a superior mode of life in general; and even if it is not, the motives of many who leave are suspect and unworthy. Both groups justify their choices in contrast to the doubtful motives and the sorry predicament of those who have taken the opposite course.

Unabashed conflation of individual reasons with collective trends, however, is not the rule. Among older men—a few elderly Jesuits who feel abandoned and betrayed and especially older former Jesuits who departed in the turmoil and polarization surrounding Vatican II—bitterness and outright condemnation are more common. But recrimination has generally fallen out of favor. Most Jesuits and former Jesuits acknowledge that motives for staying or leaving vary and that the reasons of the heart are practically unknowable. They recognize the hazards of extrapolating from individual anecdotes to the fate of an institution.

A decision to leave the Jesuits for doctrinal-ideological reasons—regarding the church's teaching on birth control, for example—exemplifies a motive for departure grounded on personal considerations without judgment about larger issues, such as the viability of the order itself. No honest compromise is thought to be possible between adherence to dogma and the demurral of conscience. (Interestingly, virtually none of the men who stay give doctrinal reasons for doing so.) The reasons for leaving, seen as good and liberating, overwhelm the reasons for staying, characterized as harmful to personal integrity. The alternatives in cases like these imply a parting of the ways without an explicit judgment on the fate of the organization or any special insight into the motives of others. Even if the organization is perceived as being on its last legs, this condition is cast as beyond the control of its members. Historical timing—a sort of cosmic bad luck—seems more to blame than incompetence or bad will.[1]

This outlook is popular among younger men accustomed to the idea that religious life is one option among several virtuous alternatives. They do not consider the time spent in the Jesuits as time lost, and they espouse a radical pluralism, refusing to attribute motives to others' decisions.

A second, smaller subset of men, prominent among former Jesuits who took their leave during the great exodus of the 1960s and 1970s, equate their own choice with the sweep of history. They validate their decision as part of a larger movement; they give the impression of abandoning a sinking ship. Their attitude is one of good riddance rather than fond farewell, and an element of self-justification exists in their disdain and occasional contempt for the behavior of others. For these men, organized religion itself is rather like group sex: awkward, embarrassing, and probably immoral.

A third group falls in between. They typically frame their reasons for staying or leaving as personal, but they also cast a shadow on those who take the opposite route. Men in this category are less severe in their judgments than the former Jesuits who disparage organized religious life as a futile and toxic cause. They are liable to express bafflement at, instead of outright dismissal of, those who remain or, if they are still Jesuits, to hint of skepticism about the motives of those who have left. But negative judgments tend to be muted. The men may be in separate camps—the military imagery is frequent—but they were comrades once. The code of individual choice prescribes tolerance of divergent paths, of routes taken and not taken for God knows what reasons, and it sanctions a wistful indifference. Such tender stoicism cannot escape the poignancy of loss over departed companions and the sadness of vanquished dreams. The sentiment of puzzled, separated survivors—why me? why them?—is elegiac.

3

At least as common as vocational decisions by Jesuits and former Jesuits in which the alternatives are squarely opposed are decisions reflecting ambivalence. Rather than choices between unassailable goods and unmitigated bads, men confront difficult trade-offs among equally commendable goals or rewards.

One such trade-off is between community and intimacy. As a rule, because of the vow of celibacy, religious life promises to deliver more of the first than of the second. Community and intimacy are partially at odds, difficult to maximize simultaneously.[2]

In the sphere of work, the trade-off between corporate mission and individual autonomy poses a similar dilemma. Choices between them are not zero-sum, and the circumstances under which institutional allegiance pays off for individuals and facilitates their work, as opposed to sacrificing individual goals, are so contingent that they resist generalization.[3]

Nevertheless, the hard-to-reconcile pulls of community and intimacy and of institutional commitment and personal autonomy underlie much of the unsteadiness in the vocational choices of Jesuits and former Jesuits. Moreover—and this is the important point—the balance between these goals has altered over the past decades, with the center of gravity shifting toward intimacy and autonomy.[4] Many Jesuits and former Jesuits have experienced a profound reordering of the way these values have been associated with religious and nonreligious institutions during their lifetime. Words like "autonomy" and "intimacy" were not modish in the immigrant and postimmigrant subcultures that produced squads of recruits to the Jesuits and other religious orders at a time when institutional loyalty and a sense of community were widespread ideals.[5] The values of individualism and nurturance have gained ground in the larger society, and Jesuits have proved susceptible to their appeal.[6]

The multiplicity of goals pulls Jesuits in different directions. The sacrificial culture of religious life has not evaporated; it coexists uneasily with an ethos of self-realization.[7] Efforts to absorb new values without displacing old ones make for some creativity but not a compelling new synthesis. Never unequivocal, the bottom line of the Society of Jesus has become even more multidimensional. The extraordinary difficulty of institutionalizing intimacy—for some, an oxymoron—exemplifies the quandary. Personal satisfaction of this kind was once thought to be irrelevant to religious life. Now the penchant of younger Jesuits for making friends outside the order is a telling demonstration of the Society's limitations—not of total failure but of genuine constraints—in meeting the intimacy needs of its members.[8]

The wrenching trade-offs that arise in decisions to stay with or leave the Society of Jesus help account for the nostalgia that many former Jesuits feel for the life they have left behind. They also help explain some of the uncertainty (and the occasional creative tension) in the direction that the order itself is taking as it strives to reconcile competing goals.

4

Another implication of the complex motives of Jesuits and former Jesuits looks like the reverse of this pattern of ambiguity and dissonance. It stems from the need of the men to make sense of the decisions regarding the course of their lives. The reasoning that enters into decisions to

stay or leave may be convoluted, but in the end these decisions must go
one way or the other. The urge to clear the decks and get on with life is
powerful.

If one word is evoked more than others to capture the forces behind
a decision to remain in the order, it is "grace," used rather interchange-
ably with a sense of "fit" to signify the perception of "being called." The
connotation is not only of divine intervention in human affairs but also
of the unpredictable nature of finding one's way. Such reasoning stresses
the gritty determination that characterizes a sense of vocation. The argument is not unlike that used by many who feel driven to apply themselves to nonreligious pursuits. The element of compulsion is strong.
"Why have I stayed?" a thirty-eight-year-old Jesuit asked:

> The most honest answer is because this is who I am and I could not
> leave without amputating a large portion of myself. Being a priest has
> always been my goal. I don't give up easily. Since ordination, I enjoy
> being a priest. I guess that I also believe this is who I am called to be.

This way of looking at life decisions does not rule out the possibility that
individuals may come to realize they have now and again been deluded
in reading providential action into an assortment of mundane circumstances. However, the accent remains on the ineluctably personal, mysterious genesis of the commitment to religious life.

Among those who leave, the byword is "growth." The notion is that
departure from the Society of Jesus reflects the need to move on for personal reasons. The term draws on psychology rather than traditional
spirituality, but the promise of "growth" converges substantially with
the operations of "grace" in at least two respects. Both are shorthand
for conversion experiences, and both emphasize what Jesuits and former
Jesuits alike take to be the ineradicably unique and personal nature of
discernment about things of the spirit.

Besides, a good deal of switching back and forth takes place between
"grace" and "growth." Neither Jesuits nor former Jesuits make the
terms exclusively their own. "Growth" suggests more in the way of active dedication to self-improvement and "grace" more a sense of getting
swept up in an attraction that cannot be denied.

Words like "grace" and "growth" are vastly simplifying labels for
what, in the end, most Jesuits and former Jesuits insist is an exceedingly
complex chain of events. The singularity of motives for staying or leaving resists attempts to foist airtight explanations on decisions for which

the evidence is fragmentary and partially self-serving, and it cautions us against imposing one-size-fits-all theories on individual cases. But reductionist interpretations have been pretty well discredited anyway. Our objective is simply to identify the finite but elaborate patterns behind staying with and leaving the Society of Jesus.

Men are likely to stay with the Society for multiple reasons, while a single troubling factor may be enough to set them packing. Since membership in the Jesuits entails commitment to a way of life and not just to a career or a job, a rare compound of affective as well as instrumental conditions goes into getting it right. Because the costs of leaving have gone down and the alternatives to religious life have expanded, the temptation to quit when something (when *anything*) goes wrong, when experience with the institution fails to live up to expectations, is powerful, especially among younger men.

If this logic is correct, several things have to fall into place in order for a man to remain a Jesuit, but only one thing needs to go seriously wrong to prompt him to leave.[9] While any one of a large number of reasons may precipitate departure, not all reasons are equally probable. Celibacy ranks at the top of the list, and the odds are at least fifty-fifty that "intimacy issues" more generally are behind any given decision to leave the order.

Still, leaving religious life is only one solution for those who become dissatisfied. Jesuits may hang on in varying degrees of discontent. Whether a man actually moves out depends not just on his problems with the organization but also on the availability of outside alternatives, as it plainly did during the great wave of departures in the 1960s and 1970s.[10] The momentum created by the example of others may matter as much as the dissatisfaction of individuals.

The sheer volume of misgivings expressed about vocational commitment calls attention to a widespread syndrome: the culture of complaint to which religious life seems unusually susceptible. Some frustration and a penchant for griping are built into an agenda of high expectations in which autonomy, intimacy, community, and organizational achievement jockey for priority. The demands of Jesuit life are high, but so are the expectations that men bring to it. Internal criticism—"self-loathing" would be the pejorative phrasing—may be all the more voluminous insofar as it serves as a verbal escape, like graffiti, from institutional blockages. Leaving the order is one extreme on a spectrum in which complaining is a moderate solution for the dissatisfied.

We have developed, so far, an outline of the factors contributing to decisions to remain in or leave religious life. A combination of elements, ranging from emotional gratification to satisfaction with work, goes into keeping Jesuits on board, while leaving more often comes about because one thing—usually but not always the effort to find intimacy—fails. A significant sidelight on the bifurcation of staying and leaving is that some men hang on in various states of disenchantment, complaining about the hardships of religious life without slamming the door behind them. A good part of their ambivalence, we have suggested, stems from the tortuous trade-offs between community and intimacy and between organizational commitment and personal autonomy.

Consideration of a number of specific developments helps fill in this rather schematic framework. To begin with, the ascent of intimacy and community on the agenda of religious organizations is not just a reflection of the vulnerability of these groups to trends in the larger society, important as the convergence between Vatican II and the cultural revolution of the 1960s has been.[11] Heightened sensitivity to emotional demands has coincided with growing uncertainty over the mission of the Society. Jesuits have faced an uphill battle reshaping their ministries and finding work that they feel makes a difference. As we will see, individual Jesuits do pretty well at finding fulfilling work, but the sense of collective purpose is less robust. The reduction in outlets for the order's ministerial energies and the erosion of control over commitments already in place have aggravated emotional problems, falling under the rubric of "intimacy," that were gaining prominence among Jesuits and other religious congregations anyway. This combination of functional and affective turbulence has had the impact of a one-two punch, throwing the Society of Jesus off balance.

Forms of self-abnegation that once shaped religious life have yielded to the pursuit of psychic health and happiness.[12] Self-denial has hardly given way to wild abandon. Instead, the rationales for self-sacrifice—in practice, for submission to collective goals—have gone into eclipse. The prodigies of mortification and unbounded zeal that were once rewarded as demonstrations of sanctity no longer find uncritical praise.[13] The acceptance of institutional directives that used to signify a laudable self-denial has passed out of fashion because Jesuits are more sophisticated and alternatives to self-abnegation are available to them. The religious environment that legitimized "the purgative way" as the high road to God has virtually disappeared, displaced by a discourse of psychic well-being that may or may not correspond to organizational interests.[14]

A thirty-two-year-old Jesuit combines the language of vocation as a gift, of spiritual development as personal growth, and of religious experience as the pursuit of tranquility. The tone is more steady and temperate than martyrlike. "Hardships and down times" are to be endured, but they are not sought after as badges of spiritual achievement:

> I think people stay because, after going through hardships and down times, they look themselves in the mirror and say that this is the life to which God has called them, and this is the life where they have found and will find peace and happiness. I have come to believe that for me to be . . . the person I am called to be and become, I will continue to grow in my vocation as a Jesuit priest.

So, the costs of following traditional forms of religious life have remained about the same, while some of the rewards have diminished or disappeared. In the new spiritual economy, the returns on sacrifice—certainly of the sort that bordered on self-immolation—are questionable. The incentive structure of sainthood has changed. Ascetical practice has undergone demystification and has taken on more than a whiff of the pathological, despite the persistence of idealistic impulses. This cultural transformation, together with some indecisiveness about corporate mission, undermines incentives toward institutional commitment.[15] Impromptu networks, support groups, provisional and organizationally rather haphazard odysseys, provide alternative routes.

The mixture of instrumental and affective incentives—roughly, of rational and emotional values—is not restricted to religious life, although the combination is probably more intense within groups like the Jesuits than elsewhere. Even organizations that are narrowly geared to the bottom line add a pulse of fellow-feeling to the monotone of self-interest. What makes institutions like the Jesuits distinctive is the recognition they accord, in addition to instrumental and affective imperatives, to expressive drives of a transfigurative kind—specifically, to the impulse toward "perfection of the life." For some, redemption has come to mean the construction of the self.

The individual is viewed as a work of art, to be formed over the course of a lifetime. The drive resembles, though it is not the same as, the elemental charge behind artistic production. Creativity is supposed to spill over into good works, into apostolic action, rather than into pure contemplation or the polished articulation of good intentions. Awareness of the presence of expressive drives and their cultivation in the Society of Jesus helps in understanding the uniqueness that many Jesuits attribute to their vocation and the difficulty they have in explaining it except with reference to nonrational, primal inspiration.[16]

Rediscovery of the emotional roots of Ignatian spirituality has come at a time when the outlets for expressive drives in traditional ministries have shrunk. The mystical features of the Jesuit experience remain just that—subjective, interior, and virtually incommunicable—unless they are channeled into action. Ignatius broke the introverted, monastic mold of religious organization through his stress on action—on performance and results. As we will see in the chapters on spirituality, Jesuits have tried to reinvent themselves by recovering the emotive features of the Ignatian style of contemplation. Yet, however successful they have been in this regard, they are still finding their way toward meaningful work and a reconnection of their spirituality with what they do, especially as a corporate body.

5

Why do men stick with the Society of Jesus? "Of all the questions this one may present the greatest pitfalls for the unwary," a sixty-five-year-old theologian observed:

> Self-knowledge on this matter is difficult to achieve. My impression is that during the times of upheaval, beginning in the mid-60s, there was a great deal of work to be done for which I had been adequately trained in teaching and preaching and counseling, assisting people to see how the changes in the church promoted by Vatican II made the life of faith more exciting and satisfying. One year quickly followed another, new challenges arose to be faced, and pretty soon faculty members I had hired began retiring. I suppose I should begin to think of it too.

The theologian kept busy, doing work that he cared about and was good at. He plugged away at what he was doing, and his routine turned out to have a large dose of the improvisational. He carved out various roles and set himself a varied, time-consuming schedule. Whatever problems he may have encountered with regard to personal relations go unmentioned, perhaps because they were ignored, set aside in the rush. His professional life is active, well rounded, and fulfilling. His has not been a solitary career but one that has involved "teaching and preaching and counseling," bringing him into contact with a cavalcade of people. The ideal is not that of a lone virtuoso. Versatility and sociability are the spices of this Jesuit life.

A thirty-one-year-old Jesuit in graduate studies offers a different type of response. He emphasizes a single, fundamentally mystical and highly personal reason both for staying and for leaving. This reason—a divine invitation—is unique yet pertinent, so the Jesuit believes, to each case of commitment and departure:

> It has rarely been said since the novitiate, but after thirteen years I truly believe that some men leave the order and others stay because it's the will of God. Of course, I cannot let that go without explaining that the will of God is revealed in very important human causes (e.g., desire for greater intimacy, dissatisfaction with community life, crises regarding faith, ecclesiastical authority, etc.). But fundamentally people stay because God is calling them here, often with a wicked sense of humor; likewise, people leave because God calls them elsewhere. Oddly enough, that explanation makes sense to me now in a way it did not several years ago.

In other words, while the observable causes for leaving (and staying) include the usual assortment of psychological, professional, and organizational suspects, the underlying reason is not an instrumental rationale or a social configuration at all but, rather, an amalgam of the supernatural and the circumstantial. What counts is the human response to divine prompting. Much the same kind of explanation is provided by a seventy-one-year-old Jesuit, except now the sense of compulsion is stronger and the nod to social context all but absent:

> God puts it in the heart of a person to live this life. It is something that you discover here. It is what is inside of you, you can't do otherwise and that's precisely where your freedom lies. They [fellow Jesuits] have the courage and gentleness of God's grace for the vocation.

The thread running through many of the responses given by Jesuits about commitment to their way of life is this belief in the role of divine invitation. The belief is elaborated more fully in cases of commitment to the Society than in instances of departure, even though Jesuits, the younger men especially, are willing to see the hand of God in the latter actions as well.

The language is unabashedly theological. What to the outsider may sound like pious jargon or a tall tale about hitting the celestial jackpot conveys a feeling of immersion in and belonging to a culture that is meaningful in its own terms. The interpretive mantle may or may not be penetrable to observers looking in, but it has a reassuring texture, an intuitive rightness, a "fit," as Jesuits are fond of saying, to those who know the code. It is a matter of chemistry, and that chemistry is either there or it is not.[17]

Another feature of this logic is more amenable to the uninitiated. The recourse to religious, indeed supernatural, reasoning—in particular, to insistence on the importance of the will of an engaged God—sometimes acts as a shorthand for the bafflingly complex rather than as an assertion of the inherently inexplicable. The confluence of circumstances—gratifying work, close friends, positive feedback, energizing prayer, temperamental affinity, and so on—that reinforce this commitment seems more like a fortuitous arrangement, an expression of what Henry James called "the strange irregular rhythm of life," than the product of human design or intention.[18] In this view, including the hand of God in the causal mix may seem just as reasonable as confining explanation to a passel of mundane factors and their incalculably complex interactions.

It is hard to tell when recourse to divine guidance as a key to religious decisions is a facile explanation. In some instances, because an interventionist deity is ubiquitous, God becomes a surrogate for luck in the midst of profuse happenstance. On other occasions, however, divine action is invoked as one factor, albeit the capstone, in a virtually indecipherable mélange of conditions. It is the turning point at which a myriad of contributing circumstances assumes a coherent form. The figure in the carpet takes shape. The supplicant is born again.

It is at this juncture that consideration of organizational support rather than intrapsychic imponderables and prosaic contingencies throws light on commitment to religious life. The Society of Jesus, when it succeeds, pulls together the multiple priorities and frictions of applied spirituality. It serves as a practical, many-sided support mechanism that cultivates outgoing service in men who stay the course. "Saving one's own soul in the service of others" encourages extroversion. Through vivid images and concrete programs, Ignatian prayer and the Society of Jesus affirm the reality of a spiritual motivation that might otherwise lapse into eccentricity or solipsism. The tradition is designed to give external direction to a contemplative bent, channeling desires and ideals toward a repertoire of actions that provide closure for what cannot be expressed in words and that, in any case, matters more than words alone.

Understood this way, religious life furnishes a practical outlet for urges whose origins are hard to explain and are therefore apt to be labeled, in their raw state, as irrational or atavistic. Disciplined commitment to "the call of God" becomes an alternative to pursuits that ordinarily are designated as rational and instrumental but that leave those caught up in the chase with a taste of vacancy. Divine inspiration, manic impulse—however it is construed—comes on a beneficial course of action or a commitment that is responsive to feedback from the outside world. This is the indispensable infusion of romance that some revisionary pragmatists recognize is lacking in cool, mechanistic applications of the utilitarian worldview.[19]

In emphasizing the spiritual, ultimately mysterious parameters of his world, a thirty-five-year-old vocation director summarizes the convergence of tangible conditions that enables him to get things done:

> I think that I stay in the Society because I feel happy in my vocation both as a religious and as a priest; I feel that I owe the Society tremendously for helping me to grow into the best person I could be and for leading me to God and helping me to learn how to guide others in the way of the Spirit; and I have really good friends in the Society, both peers and mentors who are wonderful companions on life's journey and who embody the ideals which first attracted me to the Society. I deeply believe in the mission of the Society and that the Society will use my gifts and talents in the service of the kingdom better than I could possibly use them in any other state of life.

The vocation director brings together three core factors—fulfilling work, "really good friends . . . companions," and a conviction in divine guidance—that sustain him as a satisfied member of the Society of Jesus. He recognizes that not all those who remain Jesuits do so for the same conjunction of reasons, even though the tenor of his remarks suggests that Jesuits who wind up being happy with the life share a very similar set of motives—and there are, he admits, a fair number who are unhappy and who stay because they cannot leave:

> I think that my experience is "representative" of about two-thirds of the Jesuits who stay. The other third would contain a few people who either think about leaving for the above reasons, or, more commonly, men who would never dream of leaving because they are not really free to leave, from either a psychological or financial point of view, yet they harbor some anger or frustrations either with the church or the Society or both, or they've been hurt along the way by some institution, or superior . . . and haven't really cast their lot back in with the common good and are not really happy.

A central message, then, in many statements about the factors that make for commitment to religious life is that professional, institutional, and affective causes form mutually reinforcing combinations. Work goes well, friendships develop, community life is supportive, prayer gives satisfaction, and ecclesiastical politics stay at the margins. Setbacks in the short term do not abolish hope in the long run, particularly if a sense of a connection with the divine develops and persists. A sixty-one-year-old Jesuit, a college professor in the humanities, gives a concise statement of this synergy. "I was happy, learned a lot, was apostolically active and well used, developed an incarnational spirituality, found the Society to be what it said it was, and was able to love and be loved both within and outside the Society."

6

The costs of leaving religious life—ostracism, spiritual jeopardy, and the like—have dropped. Ex-priests are no longer pariahs. Also, because engagement in a way of life involves multiple expectations for emotional satisfaction as well as functional accomplishment, it is easy for something to go wrong. When this happens, however, the opportunity for happiness outside the order does not automatically present itself, over and above the prospect of intermittent misery and clandestine deviance in the Society. Much depends on the capacity of individuals to negotiate a soft landing—a secure job, for example—on the outside. Without the opportunity to leave, the desire to leave turns in on itself.

The forces pushing men to leave can be divided into two: matters of intimacy and all the rest. A forty-one-year-old Jesuit rehearses a theme touched on by several others: the sense of fit in the work and ethos of the Society. He then points to the crucial importance of having confidantes on the inside, men with whom he can share his feelings:

> I've stayed because I fit in the Society. I don't pretend it's all been beer and skittles, but at the deepest level of my self, I'm happy and satisfied. I can't point to any specific circumstances and reasons for why I feel this fit, but it's there.
>
> I think many of the men who've left, especially the solid citizens whose leaving is always a surprise, left because they waited too long to talk to anyone about their difficulties. I tend to err on the side of letting everyone know how I'm doing, but I do think having friends in the Society with whom you can confide is very important. I guess there's a humility that goes with being willing to be that open to another person.

As I write this, I see the close friends I've developed within the Society are a big reason I've stayed.

A forty-eight-year-old high school teacher also focuses on the importance of the capacity to open up emotionally. It was the lack of close relationships that drove him out of the Society:

> My motivations to stay included my apostolic effectiveness, positive feedback from others, and the belief that staying in the order was a noble and appropriate thing to do with my life. It took me a very long time to be free enough to consider seriously the option of not being a Jesuit as a noble and appropriate possibility. Fear was certainly part of my motivation structure.
>
> I believe men leave the order because they conclude that there is a better life path for themselves. Certainly many men desire more intimacy than is healthily and happily available to them in the Society. Loneliness is a fundamental issue for many people who have left the Society. Emotionally and relationally, in the Society, there is less there than meets the eye.
>
> Some men stay in the Society because they are able to live integrated and healthy lives. Others remain because they are afraid to consider the alternatives.

A sixty-one-year-old former Jesuit, recalling his years in the order from 1950 to 1965, singles out the connection between the hierarchical nature of the organization and inhibitions against opening up:

> Life in the Society then did not really provide certain necessary emotional or psychological ingredients. . . . There was something in the structure of the culture of the Society that didn't allow a person to say how he really felt about an issue, for fear that it would either be reported back to a superior. Or, apart from any superior, would it not have indicated that I was unfit or in danger of losing my vocation?

Responses like these are frequent among older men whose need to express their feelings ran up against the patterns of authority and the austerity prevalent among Jesuits before and for some time after Vatican II. Fear and control fed on one another. Complaints about such organizational strictures are rarer among younger Jesuits and those who have left more recently, but traces of the limits on intimacy that religious life in community imposes never quite disappear.

Practically regardless of age, then, a core reason given for leaving the

Jesuits involves impediments to intimacy. A fifty-two-year-old Jesuit draws a parallel between separation from the Society and divorce, an analogy that is not uncommon among his colleagues, and then teases out a remarkable equivalence between the reasons for commitment to religious and conjugal vows:

> I believe men leave religious life for the same reasons that people separate and divorce from married life. They fall out of love, they grow disillusioned, they sense they are all alone. Religious life is a love affair, a love affair with the Lord. Your friends can help you, and indeed they do make God's incarnate love present in this world, but ultimately the love affair is not with other men and women but with God himself. It is the stark reality that only God's grace and graciousness can make me faithful.[20]

In this man's judgment, the supreme cause of dedication to religious life, in addition to a supportive context of work and friendship, is a capacity to sense the love of God, that is, a feeling of surpassing intimacy that is close to communion. When this goes, or if it fails to develop, religious life ceases to make sense, and the man feels abandoned, alone with his idiosyncrasies. Self-transcendence slips out of reach.

The problem pinpointed by the foregoing statements is buried sentiment. When emotions cannot come to life, a funereal solemnity and melancholy settle over the religious scene. Men leave, or they become stunted and forlorn.

These assessments also provide clues about what form intimacy might take in experiences of religious life that prove satisfying. The suggestion has to do with prayer: the regular practice of concentrated reflection that restores energy, induces peace, and gives pleasure. It is intermittent rather than constant, but so, Jesuits might point out, is sex. Also, intimacy is no more equivalent to sex than it is to prayer. Prayer is instead a channel of communion. Jesuits who find release in prayer achieve something similar to the passionate fulfillment that others encounter in sexual relationships. It is a rare occurrence even in religious life, and for this reason the Jesuit enterprise is untenable on the sole basis of prayer-as-contemplation. But when it works, the life does bring to external fruition the meditative temper that activist clerics like the Jesuits have never abandoned.[21]

Two related points make prayer or its absence central to understanding the reasons for leaving the Society of Jesus. One is the contention, more frequent among Jesuits than former Jesuits, that men leave the Society once they stop praying. Another is that for many men, even when they stick at it, prayer ceases to provide emotional fulfillment. It fails to convey an appreciation of love and its possibilities. Prayer may offer a share of the "consolation," as Ignatian spirituality calls it, that in other cases comes from intimacy on more purely human terms.[22] But mundane and mystical intimacy are different experiences.

The idea that persistence in prayer is crucial to remaining a Jesuit, and the corollary notion that letting it slide is a precursor to leaving the Society, surfaces time and again. "I don't think I ever learned how to gain spiritual sustenance from prayer," admitted the sixty-one-year-old former Jesuit quoted previously, "though I tried." A thirty-seven-year-old Jesuit high school instructor flips through a familiar catalog of reasons for staying and leaving, to conclude with the telltale symptom of laxity in prayer:

> I think men leave the order because of loneliness, struggles with celibacy, dislike of the way they see things going, too little affirmation or support, too little satisfaction, life in the Society being too different from what they have known or expected. (Those of us who have entered relatively recently experience a formation which is generally very good, but once it is over and we are put into non-formation communities, there is a shock to the system which is fatal to some.)
>
> Others stay because they are able to have their needs (such as intimacy, affirmation, support, satisfaction) met and still live as Jesuits. Prayer and a strong faith life also goes a long way in sustaining one's Jesuit life. Most Jesuits who leave, I suspect, at some point gave up on prayer.

"I'm dressed like a fireman," a sixty-two-year-old who left the Society in 1963 after eleven years said of his feelings at the time; "but I'm not a fireman. I didn't do anything spiritual."

Were the idea of a link between giving up prayer and leaving the Society confined to Jesuits, without being mentioned by those who have left, the claim would lack impartial support. But former Jesuits make the point often enough to make it plausible. What cannot be sustained is the further supposition that men who leave the Society also leave off praying, though some of them report that they have less time set aside for prayer in their post-Jesuit days. Lack of attention to prayer is a signal that a man may be moving away from the Society ("If you are not a man of prayer," a fifty-one-year-old Jesuit said flatly, "you cannot live the life"), but not all those who leave the Society stop praying. Inattention to prayer is as sure a sign as any that a man is on his way out of the Society or headed toward a state of internal exile. But it is certainly not the sole tip-off to departures, and many of those who exit keep up their prayer life.[23]

An important question of causal explanation is at issue here. Jesuits who for whatever reason stop praying or get nothing out of the practice are prime candidates for leaving the Society. But this is scarcely the only reason behind departures since many of the men who do leave continue to pray. In fact, "prayerful reflection"—meditation over the best course of action, discernment of the divine will—sometimes precedes the decision to leave.

For some men, repeated prayer becomes a renewal of the intuition of divine presence. Rather than a petition for a favor through supernatural intervention, the practice itself becomes its own reward. Divine response comes in the form of emotional restoration. The soul is replenished. Fugitive as it is, this ecstasy is sought over and over again. It offers glimpses of a self-transcendence that corresponds to the emotional lift of intimacy. When this warmth flickers out, the sense of communion diminishes, and men are liable to seek intimacy elsewhere.[24] So, prayer may provide an equivalent of the closeness that others seek in sexual relations. Where the erotic leaves off and the spiritual begins is hard to tell.[25] Prayer occasions something close to rapture, although fireworks and epiphanies, the mighty organ chords of spiritual ecstasy, appear to be rare compared to steady, disciplined meditation and petition.

Camaraderie is another source of emotional gratification that provides a surrogate for intimacy. Community furnishes a reserved style of intimacy that depends on a mostly unspoken bonding. It is male warmth-at-a-distance, a sociability that preserves a just measure of privacy. Male bonding is sometimes mentioned as a reason for staying, with corporate accomplishment secondary and in conjunction with the absence of options on the outside. A fifty-six-year-old spiritual director, less than five years out of the Society, summarized the factors this way:

> Most leave because they're lonely. The deeper force is the common calling to some form of intimate company.
>
> Men stay for two reasons: They find fulfillment in the mix of solitude and company which the Society provides, and in a measure of job satisfaction. And some are afraid to leave. They're carried along for years by

respect from students, parishioners, pride of families. But they have no marketable skills, know little about buying a house, etcetera.

"What kept me in the order for eighteen years," a fifty-seven-year-old concludes, "was a combination of close friendships with classmates and colleagues and a serious doubt about my ability to live successfully outside the order." Here, companionship was the main, indeed the only, positive feature underlying membership in the Jesuits, and even this did not suffice as a reason for staying once courage was mustered to make a go of it on the outside. As soon as the pull factors facilitating a viable exit fell into place, the man left.

By most accounts, community comes behind prayer as a reason for sticking with religious life, possibly because it tends to be seen as a kind of second-best intimacy, and without much expressly religious content besides. All the same, the argument that intimacy is the paramount factor in staying and leaving can be overworked. To consider an obvious objection: It is unrealistic to suppose that "intimacy needs" are uniform across individuals or constant over the lifetime. Some men may be less driven in this regard than others. We take up questions like these more fully in chapter 7, where we look at community life in detail.

7

Problems with intimacy, then, form the biggest cluster of reasons for leaving the Society of Jesus. A fifty-year-old former Jesuit propounds the strong version of this syndrome, one that practically rules out other factors, perhaps because his treatment of "feelings" is so broad: "Whatever notional reasons they may come up with to justify staying, I think that in the end feelings predominate and the feeling [among those who leave] is that it isn't working." For others, celibacy is the concrete roadblock against close personal interaction. It leaves these men stranded in an impalpable intimacy.

Nevertheless, some concession is made to the possibility that other troubles may cause men to leave, as in these comments by a thirty-seven-year-old expert in canon law:

> Some leave because of the celibacy stuff. While a gay Jesuit can maintain a lover while remaining a Jesuit, a straight has a harder time keeping a woman. Many if not most Jesuits genuinely have the gifts of celibacy and chastity and live their lives with integrity. A straight is more likely

to leave than a gay. [But] gays may tire of living a lie. I know at least a
dozen who have left for this reason.

I have yet to know a Jesuit who has left over poverty issues. Some
complain we're too rich. Give me a break! I know three, maybe four
who sincerely needed to leave over obedience issues. It happens that
some people cannot hand that over. Personal liberty is a tough one. . . .
Others realize they cannot minister in a church in which they have lost
any substantial confidence.

A single factor (celibacy, frustration on the job, or an unpleasant
community) is like a trip wire; it sets the alarms off. Whether men actually leave often depends on the larger mix of incentives, sanctions, and
opportunities. A thirty-eight-year-old Jesuit gives an account that, while
putting intimacy up front, stresses how cultural norms have heightened
sexuality, glamorized transient relationships, and undermined long-term
commitment:

> I suspect that they let themselves grow out of the relationships that kept
> them in. . . . You have to ask first why people leave all permanent com-
> mitments. [One set of reasons] is the lack or diminishment of negative
> reinforcement for "breakers of vows." A second reason is the deification
> of personal growth and development to the point that it eclipses com-
> mitment. A third reason is the growing assumption that makes genital
> fulfillment a right and obligation. As a culture we don't believe in "for-
> ever" any more. We also live in a culture that makes sexual fulfillment
> a right separated from any sense of commitment. Against that back-
> ground, many former Jesuits let their hearts grow out of the Society. It
> is like most marriage breakups. The key point isn't infidelity, but letting
> love die by inches each day for years.

The general notion of a cultural transformation that subverts traditional, sacrificial expectations about personal relations is sometimes
rendered with greater specificity. A fifty-three-year-old former Jesuit
starts by sketching in shifts in the Catholic subculture:

> I suspect—I don't really speak from much relevant experience here—
> that Jesuits of my generation who found their way early to meaningful
> work in a supportive social setting may have managed to bracket some
> of the questions and so remain happily enough in the order. But the
> Catholic population of the U.S. is now so swamped in the general popu-
> lation that the high-school-age potential recruit situated within the
> Catholic community, as I was [in the early 1960s], is no longer exclu-

sively "in" that community anymore. In other words, seventeen-year-olds and eighteen-year-olds begin now in the culturally integrated condition that I only reached by several highly unusual steps. . . .

When I decided to leave the Jesuits, it was because I had concluded that my decision to become a Jesuit was motivated by . . . career anxiety and sexual anxiety . . . rather than by appropriately religious motives. At this point, I was anything but full of rage at the Society. I knew that nothing had been asked of me that my superiors had not asked of themselves. I saw that they had spent hours freely attempting to help me solve my personal problems, never pushing for an earlier resolution or ever inquiring about what was going on in these therapy sessions. I knew, as well, that I had received a powerful education—one with some deficits, to be sure, but with enormous strengths.

Having laid out his ambivalence regarding the attractions and weaknesses of life in the Society, the former Jesuit launches into an eloquent coda on the limits of intimacy in religious life:

> As for personal relations, I recall, still, how the penny dropped when a thoughtful Jesuit a year or so older than I said that we Jesuits all had the same commodities in surplus and in deficit; none of us could provide what all of us needed; all of us had what none of us needed. This explained why so many of us—this was at Harvard—were so admired, welcomed, trusted among others but were so glum with each other.

In this account, it is not just the opportunities for intimacy that turned out to be deficient within Jesuit life. Disillusion also set in with what came to be seen as the extension of adolescent fantasy into a monotonous, inhumane idealism. The benefits, including the prestige, of religious life were appreciable, for a time anyway. But the costs—especially a certain emptiness that blocked off emotional maturation—became harder and harder to bear as norms about what was expected and what was permitted opened up in the larger society.

Former Jesuits, escaping what they came to perceive as the dank mausoleum of the priesthood, strive to find acceptance in the affective mainstream. In other cases, the problem is not the limits on intimacy; it has to do instead with church policy and the structure of ecclesiastical authority. Difficulties of this nature—fundamentally, with the burdens of obedience—operate at a comparatively impersonal level. A fifty-five-year-old spiritual director who has stayed on despite his disagreement with the ways of the bureaucratic church describes the predicament:

I have never seriously been tempted to leave the Society. Oh, I have had
fantasies of it at times. But the Society has not been a major issue for me
in this way. Rather, it is at times the church itself that I can contemplate
leaving. If I could remain a Jesuit while joining the Quakers, I could be
tempted!

The only reason I could imagine leaving the Society would be based
on a need to leave the church. My issues with the church concern the
present restorationism. I do not feel that women are treated equally with
men. And I find the attitude of many to be a kind of fundamentalism of
church. Catholics don't tend to be fundamentalists about scripture, but
about the church they can be fundamentalists. Church authority becomes a kind of idol to the point of giving up one's own integrity for
the sake of clarity and certainty.

Another man, a sixty-one-year-old university professor who has also
remained a Jesuit, recalls an episode that recapitulates the quandaries of
doctrinal disagreement rather than quarrels with the Society. Like the
spiritual director, his problems have been with the church, not with the
Jesuits. In the end, doctrinal dilemmas are set to the margin. Ideological
disagreements take second place to institutional belonging:

> My one "leaving" thought was prompted, perhaps curiously, not by the
> Society but by the church. In the summer of 1968 . . . while on retreat
> . . . I read with dismay of *Humanae Vitae* [the papal encyclical sustain-
> ing the ban on "artificial" contraception] and worried about its effect on
> married Catholics, including my friends and former students; wondered
> whether I could be a man of integrity and still remain in the church.
> Happily, I had enough theology (and affection for the church) to think
> my way through the theologico-moral situation in two or three days;
> I was greatly helped (theologically and humanly) by the nuanced re-
> sponses of (if I recall correctly) the Canadian, Belgian, and French bish-
> ops who asserted the ultimate freedom of an individual conscience (after
> he or she had carefully and prayerfully considered the pope's teaching)
> and who spoke out precisely as part of the teaching church. I remained
> in the church, of course—but it all made for an interesting retreat.

A seventy-five-year-old remembers a similar crisis that came to a different resolution:

> I left the Jesuits for many reasons. Perhaps the key one was my inability
> to stretch my conscience in preaching publicly against the reasonable use
> of birth control by married couples while in personal counseling, and

in confession advising the couples to do the best they could but not to worry about the use of artificial birth control. I felt torn in wearing a uniform (clerical dress) that stood for the official teaching of the church and being subversive in my actual one-on-one counseling.

8

If restrictions on intimacy are the main reason men leave the Society of Jesus, and if doctrinal and related disciplinary issues, touching mainly on obedience, form another, less common set of reasons, a third bundle of causes takes in difficulties surrounding the role of the priesthood itself.

Erosion in the prestige and utility of the priesthood differs from problems associated with intimacy and from most doctrinal controversies, for it is hard to imagine individuals doing much to change this situation on their own or organizing to remedy the deficiency. The decline in the image of the priesthood reflects a historical transformation exacerbated by official policies that are largely beyond the control of individuals. The exclusionary tenor of ecclesial conservatism conveys a message of intransigence regarding the position of women, for example, as much as an honorable commitment to upholding tradition.

A seventy-one-year-old Jesuit engaged in parish work summarizes the implications of the plummeting prestige and waning purpose of the priesthood:

> I think the relative freedom granted after Vatican II was too much to resist for many in the priesthood. And then the rejection of Vatican II and the gradual return to a dictatorship-type Vatican turned many off. Perhaps the loss of status as a priest with the emergence of the laity was/is a factor. There was not much left that only the priest could do. Many think there are far more worthwhile professions now that so much has changed. And at the present, the terrible priestly scandals hurting the church could be a factor. I avoid wearing clerics most of the time so as not to be recognized as a possible child molester.[26]

The cluster of negative signals probably acts as much to inhibit a serious look at entering the priesthood in the first place as it does to speed men on their way out. In the 1960s and 1970s, a massive exodus encouraged others to leave. Now the challenge is as much recruitment as retention. Higher costs of commitment, relative to other vocational options, and lower costs of leaving, compared to the opprobrium with which failed priests were branded in the past, have resulted in a hemorrhaging of membership and a constricted flow of entrants.

9

An important dilemma arises in understanding why men stick with or leave religious life as organized in the Society of Jesus. At critical points, the order functions as a support mechanism, assembling an array of incentives that "speak to" selected individuals. The dilemma stems from the fact that intimacy, a crucial element in the package as conceived today, is personal and not, on the face of it, deliverable by organizational means. Rather than being induced, the state is ordinarily thought of as spontaneous. Community or a semblance of community can be designed, but not so intimacy.

A partial solution devised by the Jesuits (and several other religious groups) is prayer, understood as a means of gaining intimacy with the divine and as a practice that can be taught. Contemplation does not simply happen, nor is it spirituality artless, as in popular images of sudden visions from above. Such epiphanies are cultivated through repeated observance. The foundational text for Jesuits is, after all, the *Spiritual Exercises.*[27]

The resolution is insecure. Closeness to the divine is not the same as intimacy with others, and it is the latter that institutions are not good at providing, especially organizations that require celibacy. Incentives can be put in place for tolerance, patience, and the like; these "interpersonal skills" can be learned and encouraged. But organizational efforts to implement elusive goods like intimacy may become counterproductive, as this observation on community life from a sixty-four-year-old former Jesuit indicates:

> A significant number were so confused, demoralized, or psychologically dependent that they were becoming a ministry in themselves. Too much time was spent healing the healers. The growing demands of community introspection swamped other priorities.

Skilled as they are in spiritual direction, many Jesuits acknowledge the hothouse nature of orchestrated intimacy. Sooner or later, ministerial activity is supposed to take up the slack occupied by in-house concerns. The institutional challenge is to place men in apostolic work at a time when traditional Jesuit ministries have shrunk or moved out from under the order's control.

The Society is caught in a double bind. The demand for intimacy has increased in religious life. This development has contributed not only to the excavation of a more freewheeling spirituality—to the "refounding" of religious congregations—but also to the therapeutic vogue.[28] On the other hand, the tasks facing activist religious orders like the Jesuits are instrumental and organizational as well as affective, and channels of productive work have become harder to arrange. The presumption that Jesuits are particularly well qualified for this or that task no longer holds. Together, the heightened priority given to intimacy and the sapping of roles with a recognized rationale threaten traditional versions of religious masculinity.[29] The double bind may not be insurmountable, but it is tight.

10

While it is true that the convergence of positive affective, expressive, and instrumental feedback supports commitment to religious endeavor, only a severely idealized rendition of this life presupposes that the drives toward community, intimacy, autonomy, and corporate clout work in unison or even that they are supposed to. Sometimes they function at cross-purposes. Naive theories mistake a calm invulnerability for the supreme goal of religious dedication. The real goal, following the Jesuit design, is probably more akin to a nervous, unstable tension. Individual Jesuits and indeed the Society as a whole have shown a penchant for teetering on one brink or another. Religious vibrancy seems no more a product of high-minded equipoise than does artistic or scientific creativity.[30]

What has jeopardized this institutional dynamism is a realignment of the traditional balance of objectives. Autonomy and intimacy have gained legitimacy; community and organizational loyalty have suffered by comparison.[31] Along with two other developments—the shrinking of the job market for clerics and the reduced costs of forsaking commitments to the vowed life—these changes have weakened the institutional hold of the Society of Jesus. Extended commitment has come to seem less reasonable and, after the fashion of a self-fulfilling prophecy, less feasible.

This transformation in religious life boils down to a contrast between the collective certainties of the decades before Vatican II and the indeterminacy that ensued as Jesuits struck out on their own and were left to their own devices, even as spiritual counseling became more personalized. In the old days, individual rewards—above all, salvation—were practically guaranteed by adherence to the rules, self-abnegation, and what superiors decided was the common good. Sacrifice made ultimate sense even when the veneer of regimentation occasionally came undone.[32] Now, redemption through traditional forms of self-denial and submersion of the self in communal effort is no longer taken for granted. The slippage between individual benefits, including salvation, and corporate dedication is much greater than before.

In part because it is so rare an event, remaining in religious life is more difficult to explain than leaving it. It is hard to separate the impression of the singularity of the impulse toward a religious vocation from the complex interaction of multiple causes that sustain it. Accounting for such apparently quirky phenomena is rather like trying to explain what goes into humor that succeeds in provoking hilarity; the thing itself is liable to evaporate in dry-as-dust etiologies.

Leaving, too, may be driven by a variety of factors, three of which have been singled out here: problems with intimacy, doctrinal difficulties along with bureaucratic hassles, and worries about the decline in the prestige, practical utility, and meaning of the priesthood. While they may operate jointly, any one of these factors is ordinarily enough to provoke serious reappraisal of vocational commitment.

Finally, like almost all dichotomies, staying versus leaving is a simplification. The more we try to understand the causes of commitment to and withdrawal from religious life, the clearer it becomes that the fundamental dynamic is a continuum, ranging from satisfaction with and joy in a way of life to disappointment with and withdrawal from it. The achievement of contentment in a vocational path constitutes one subset of reasons for commitment to the vowed life. Another reason for hanging on is the inability to escape. Occasionally, Jesuits describe the carping they hear among former Jesuits as the grumbling of men who have "never really left the Society"; they have failed to come to terms with their new lives. A corollary observation goes for some of those who remain: While still members of the Society, they are internal exiles.

As perceptions of the hardships of religious life and its challenges have become sharper than appreciation of its rewards, the attractions of that option diminish. Something like this has happened since Vatican II. Rates of attrition from religious vocations are probably no higher than they are for other, modestly rewarding professions.[33] But the number of applicants has dropped steadily. The central problem is no longer retention but recruitment in the first place. Why do men enter the Jesuits? This is the central question of the next chapter.

CHAPTER TWO

Becoming a Jesuit

If I was a priest, I could fulfill my father's spoiled dream and give my mother what she craved—a higher social status.

I was looking for an interesting life, and religious life seemed to offer more of a chance for that. I thought of this in religious terms: that God was inexhaustible; that life in relationship with God would never grow dull.

I

By the 1960s, economic prosperity and social mobility, together with the aggiornamento of Vatican II, had brought American Catholics as close to assimilation as they might dream. Success posed an unexpected dilemma for the Jesuits whose educational prowess had contributed so much to this assimilation. What was left of the distinctive role and appeal of religious life? What was the special identity of the priesthood now? Had it outlived its usefulness? Questions like these scarcely arose before the 1960s, or, if they did, the answers were taken for granted.

The factors that drew men to the priesthood in the 1930s and 1940s, when vocations to religious life were numerous, differed from the trade-offs that brought subsequent cohorts on board. In the days before Vatican II, men joined the Jesuits for a variety of mundane as well as idealistic reasons. This made for large numbers of recruits and a diversity of talents and for a dose of eccentricity besides. More recently, the motives behind religious commitment have become rather specialized. This change shows up in the reduced number and distinctive makeup of recruits and in the altered texture of religious life.

The narrowing of motives has resulted in the recruitment of men united in little else—certainly not a common language or social background—except the countercultural tenor of their views, which may be ideologically on the left or the right. They bring with them less of a standardized culture than their counterparts who entered in the 1930s,

1940s, and 1950s. Diversity calls forth a solidarity that is expressed not so much in corporate unity—Jesuits have had uneven results in getting their ministerial act together—or in a shared theology as in a composite of lifestyles at the margins of the mainstream. The effect has been to re-create a simulacrum of the local subcultures that once supplied legions of young men to the priesthood, now in the form of a countercultural holding area shaped by ideological leanings and sexual disposition.

The paradox, then, is that while the social background, or at least the experience, of young Jesuits seems more diverse than that of their predecessors, the range of motivations for joining the Society has probably shrunk. The rationales for entering cluster around countercultural positions, albeit of various sorts. The bread-and-butter incentives of traditional religious life, such as clerical prestige and indeed salvation after long suffering, appear to have faded by comparison.

2

What attracts men to religious life? Three sets of rationales can be discerned. One is a mélange of self-interested motives. Another involves joy in a life that Jesuits feel chooses them as much as they choose it. The third reflects the appeal of religious journeying as a countercultural statement. We will start with the first and work our way forward.

Prestige, adventure, a sense of collective mission, camaraderie, self-improvement, security, the appeal of the humanities, and salvation—all these incentives imply payoffs. Some rank ahead of others along a gradient of the edifying and the beneficent, but attached to each is the expectation of positive returns for individuals committed to these objectives. The costs—celibacy, obedience, and the like—may be high, but the perceived rewards are even higher.[1] "Heaven," a former Jesuit remarked, "would more than make up for purgatory on earth."

If there is any feature common to the disparate urges just described, it touches on the dual notion of making the best of one's talents by dedicating them to the service of God and others. The operative word is "service." While a few men embark on a religious career mainly as a solo operation (for example, to advance their scholarly ambitions), references to service suffuse the reasons given for entering the Society. Most former Jesuits wind up in the helping professions, and virtually all Jesuits work in these areas.[2] The tilt toward education, toward therapeutic activities, and toward an ethos of remediation and ministry surpasses interest in frankly gainful activities. Even if the pursuit of sanctity might be characterized as a species of spiritual greed, the guiding norm in relations with others appears not to be domination but instead to absorb a few losses and perhaps break even. Jesuits are apt to be competitive, but they rarely go for the jugular.

An exclusive cost-benefit reckoning also fails to capture another type of appeal, one that involves following a powerful attraction as much as it does calibrated ambition toward a reasonable goal. In this case, commitment reflects a vocation, a response to a call, a feeling that one fits. Like falling in love, the act involves a decision that is only partly conscious and articulate. The sense of a spontaneous, almost irresistible urge is strong, just as it may be in cases of being drawn to other walks of life: to medicine, to the arts, to business, and so forth. A vocation is both passion and métier.

Drives of this intensity have a touch of the impulsive, of the heroic, and perhaps of the reckless and extravagantly generous. Sometimes the element of choice seems minor in such behavior, as if the individual could scarcely do otherwise. A careful accounting does not take place. "I remember saying at six," a sixty-nine-year-old who left after more than twenty-five years in the Jesuits said,

> I wanted to be either a priest or a baseball player. I presumed, and everyone else close to me also presumed, that I would become a priest. Looking back, I sense that a feeling of free decision in this area just evaporated.

By comparison with the more plainly calculating motivations described at the outset, we are closer here to what is often thought of as religious commitment. But while most long-term religious engagement probably involves such drivenness, not all compulsion has a religious or altruistic expression. Powerful urges of this sort may just as well take the form of professional determination, against all odds, in one field or another, without any religious inflection. They can foster prodigies of perseverance or ruthlessness in virtually any sphere.

A couple of things should be kept in mind about such dedication. Because the expressive element is so strong, it is difficult to separate out the self-centered and unselfish components. Second, the origins of these drives seem to be just about anyone's guess.

Wherever they come from, where such drives are channeled depends on the changing salience of career alternatives throughout society. Why a particular individual chooses to follow a commitment to the priest-hood is very hard to pinpoint. But the demonstration effect of the shift-ing incidence of priestly vocations on the likelihood of further vocations is easier to grasp. A feedback loop exists between the visibility of voca-tional options and what individuals end up choosing.[3]

A third kind of motivation is prominent in, though still not unique to, religious life. The pull is countercultural or "prophetic." This adversar-ial feature is tangential in the first, more or less calculated shaping of ambition. It may or may not be present in the second, apparently fortu-itous or idiosyncratic call to dedicated professionalism.

In advanced industrial and postindustrial societies, striving to fulfill the ideals associated with religious vows stands as a countervailing wit-ness against the currents of the age.[4] Even after Jesuits have dispensed with many of the outward signs of religious life, rediscovering and af-firming the workaday world in the spirit of Vatican II, their life amounts to a partial repudiation of normalcy. Without some measure of self-abnegation that runs against the yearning for success evident in the first set of motives and that balances the drive toward self-realization and in-dividual perfection evident in the second, it is hard to see what element of the religious would remain in the vowed life.

The reasons for standing against or apart from the mainstream are themselves often at odds. Some types of renunciation have a marked al-truistic or ideological edge, and the aura of sacrifice for a cause is promi-nent. Another variant may also entail a measure of sacrifice, but the mo-tivation has more to do with identification with a group—perhaps with a minority that is perceived as put upon or with a putatively deviant sub-culture—than with abstract precepts. Men whose own identity might be sketchy can see themselves in misfits and outcasts, whose interests they take up as their own.[5]

In the heyday of immigrant Catholicism, American Jesuits were prob-ably set apart less by criticism of the national culture in which they were immersed than by the tribal mores associated with their ancestral ties—the Irish on the East Coast, the Germans in the Midwest, the Italians in California. The counterculture of the peace-and-justice and other pro-test movements came later, as subcultural identification on the basis of ethnicity waned.[6] This alteration in the environment of incentives—roughly, from the subcultural to the countercultural—helps explain why Jesuits spend so much time going over the meaning and purpose of religious life, when previously the answers to such questions seemed to flow naturally, "organically," out of the world that enfolded them.[7]

The common thread in the variety of countercultural appeals is the comparative weakness of instrumental or utilitarian justifications for religious commitment. The key issue is identity—social distinctiveness—more than ministerial effectiveness. Indeed, workaholism is often thought to be a danger to authentic personhood and community. A former vocation director offers an interpretation that is very close to this diagnosis in less sociological terms:

> What Jesuits do certainly still comes into play in vocation discernment, but it is generally not the beginning nor the end of the process. Much more typical now is a candidate who focuses on the qualitative distinctiveness of Jesuit life: the witness of Jesuits' whole lives; how they do whatever they do; in what spirit, with what attitudes—their way of proceeding—how they live and pray and relate to one another through their personal and communal life and fraternal bonds.[8]

The various motives we have outlined—the calculating, the driven, and the countercultural—are in tension but can reinforce one another. All three may be at work within a single individual. The different impulses turn up in various shadings across the membership of religious orders, and the mix imparts a resilience and adaptability that groups would not otherwise have. The strain engenders a creativity that overcomes the penchant for single-mindedness and that may enable religious organizations to bounce back and flourish.[9] In this respect, the crisis of groups like the Jesuits has as much to do with the flagging heterogeneity of membership as with falling numbers.

It is not, to put it more precisely, the social makeup of new members so much as the reasons bringing them into the Society that have become less varied. The ensemble of reasons for commitment to religious life has altered since the 1960s. The rewards associated with that life have gone down, or their clarity has been occluded, while the costs have remained high. The prestige of the priesthood is no longer what it was, and celibacy has lost much of its mystique. The practical appeal of religious life—its "normalcy"—has fallen.

In part because the vowed life has retreated to the edges of modern culture, vocations to the priesthood are less common. "Priestly vocations are calls from God," one young Jesuit observed, "but they are also historically conditioned." Just as canonization to sainthood depends on all sorts of sublunar factors, the incidence of vocations to the consecrated life depends, to some degree, on sheer demographics.[10] The fewer priests there are, the fewer priests there will be.

Finally, as the more or less self-interested rationales for joining the priesthood have peeled away and as the cultural signals favoring calls to religious life have grown fainter, what we have designated as counter-cultural rationales for signing up have gained ground. The common denominator of these newer motivations is their unconventional, anti-mainstream thrust.

Neoconservatism, bordering on fundamentalism, is one such stance. It comports well with the restorationist strategy, the doctrinal ortho-doxy, and the critique of materialism, relativism, and other assorted vices of the age espoused by John Paul II.[11] From another perspective comes a drive to ordained ministry linked with sexual orientation, specifically with homosexuality as a minority, subcultural statement. Still another cluster of rationales is bound up with the faith-and-justice movement. A welter of ecumenical or extra-Christian attractions, in-cluding a turn toward Eastern and ecological religions, makes up a fourth set of motivations.[12] Where all this leaves the old standard of the affable if slightly bibulous padre-as-man's-man is a bit of a mystery.[13] In danger of becoming a museum piece, the traditional image provides one, declining model among several alternative lifestyles.[14]

3

There is a good deal of truth to the before-and-after contrast between the world-we-left-behind portrait of immigrant, ethnic, polychrome Catholicism—enclosed, materially austere, morally restrictive, swarm-ing with priests and nuns, rich with incense and the seasonal rhythm of feast days—and the postconciliar era of the well-educated, mobile, of-ten disaffected, and, in the eyes of some critics, faintly decadent practi-tioners of "Starbucks Catholicism."[15] Consider the differences in the de-mographic and social backgrounds of the men who entered the Society of Jesus between 1930 and 1945, the oldest cohort of Jesuits and former Jesuits in our study, and the youngest, those who entered between 1981 and 1993.

Only about a third of the fathers and mothers of the older men had more than a high school education. The proportion with college and university training among the parents of men who entered in the 1980s had risen to three-quarters of the fathers and nearly two-thirds of the mothers. Similarly, only one-quarter of the older men recall that their mothers were employed outside the home during the Depression or World War II. By the 1980s and 1990s, more than half of the younger

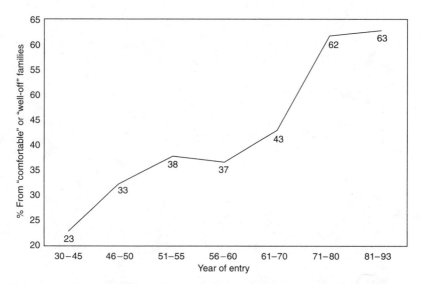

Figure 1.   Jesuits and former Jesuits from comfortable or well-off families by year of entry into the Society. Respondents were asked, "When you were growing up, would you say that in financial terms your family was very well-off? comfortable? modest? poor?"

men report that their mothers had paying jobs. Less than one-quarter of the older men describe their families as economically comfortable or well-off, while fully six out of ten of the younger men characterize the social status of their families in this way (see figure 1).

About seven out of ten of the older men graduated from Jesuit high schools. Within the most recent entrance classes, that figure had dropped to just over five out of ten. Perhaps more tellingly, just over half of the Depression-era group perceived their fathers as "devout," and 70 percent of these men saw their mothers this way. Such estimates fall dramatically among the younger men, who characterize less than one-quarter of their fathers and less than half of their mothers as devout (see figure 2).

Changes like these are consistent with what is known about the re-shaping of Catholics in the United States, with a few exceptions.[16] According to stock theories of modernization, we would expect to see a decline in the sense of community reported by the younger as compared to the older men as they were growing up. But there are no significant differences across cohorts in perceptions of the closeness of neighborhood ties. Likewise, it seems reasonable to expect that newer candidates to the

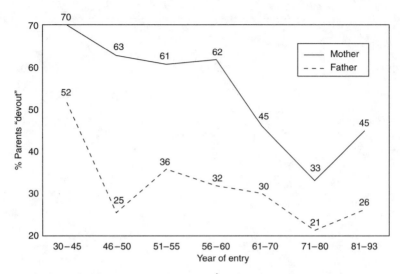

Figure 2.   Religious devotion of mothers and fathers of Jesuits and former Jesuits by year of entry into the Society. Respondents were asked, "How would you characterize your mother's/father's religious involvement? Very devout? Practicing? Occasional? Negligible? Nil?"

priesthood would come from smaller families than their predecessors, but this turns out not to be the case. In fact, candidates who entered after 1970 come from *larger* families on the average than men who entered earlier.

What is going on? While in many ways changes in the Catholic milieu have tracked changes in the larger society, in other respects—at least among Catholic families from which priests are likelier to emerge —some transformations seem to have been smaller, slower, or nonexistent. A case in point is the stability and even growth in family size. Those families from which vocations to the priesthood are likely to emerge appear to be atypical of Catholic families in general.[17]

In addition, a significant number of very recent entrants to the Society of Jesus come from families that show signs of a modest reversal in secularizing trends. These signs—the uptick in religiosity reported among the parents of the youngest entrants, for example—are not large enough to constitute a return to the old days. Nevertheless, they constitute a speed bump along what otherwise might look like a full-speed-ahead journey toward secularization.[18]

Another reason why the falloff in religious sentiment and the traditional supports for it may be less than impeccably linear has to do with the old days themselves rather than the modern era. Nostalgia suffuses the home-and-hearth imagery associated with times gone by. We need to turn from statistics to firsthand recollections to get a clearer picture of changes in the Catholic milieu from which Jesuits have emerged.

4

The men who entered the Society of Jesus during the Depression and the war years and even a bit later came from a world largely foreign to those entering after the 1960s. "When I was growing up," a sixty-two-year-old former Jesuit recalled, "everybody in the world was Irish, Catholic, and a Democrat, and I was afraid of going to hell." The ambience combined innocence and terror. The innocence grew out of a sense of protection and family stability in the midst of hard times. The fear was not so much material, though the Depression brought the parents of young men at the time close to insecurity, as imaginary. The realm of God was heavy on judgment and chastisement.[19] The ethos was as scary as it was comforting. Popular religion, with its charms against evil, its stained-glass radiance, its saints and scapulars, decked out with flower-laden shrines and warm votive candles, was inhabited by monsters, with hell-fire beneath.[20]

For some young men, the Jesuits represented an escape. The order was a cosmopolitan relief from drab if scrubbed and sheltered working-class surroundings; the Society of Jesus also offered a sophisticated alternative to the baleful theology of the era. "Everybody in my world had gray hair, false teeth, was hard of hearing, and they were always dying," a seventy-year-old former Jesuit remembered:

> Permeating life was the presence of the Catholic church: the nuns' convent right across the street, St. Bridget's school and church just around the corner. Grandmother dragged me to daily Mass. The teachings of the church were drummed into me at home and in school, mostly, as I now recall, of hell and punishment. My experience at Creighton Prep [in Omaha] changed my life forever. I acquired a profound admiration for the Jesuits, for their learning, for the quality of their lives, and for their leadership.

A fifty-year-old former Jesuit, raised in more prosperous times than the men who knew the Depression firsthand, still recalls a chill of the fear emanating from Catholicism, but he remembers mostly the engulfing magic and assuring familiarity. "I found the nuns intimidating," he remembers,

> but the two parish priests were friendly and unassuming, especially a young Italian-American priest. I was a kind of dreamy, unfocused kid who wasn't thinking of any particular future career, but if pushed on the point, I probably would've said, in eighth grade, that I was considering the priesthood. As a child I loved to go to Mass with my father. He loved the church, having attended Catholic grammar school, Catholic high school, and Catholic college. And I began to love it also. The incense, the statues, the pipe organ, the vestments, the Christmas manger, watching the nuns glide into church like penguins on a cold, early, dark weekday morning. The million laughs we had in parochial school. The certitude.[21]

A sixty-one-year-old Jesuit, growing up at the tail end of the Depression on the East Coast, expresses much the same aura of security, warmth, and continuity and adds to it what is clearly a description of the experience of being called:

> My world was stable, patriotic, and sure about things . . . I was loved, and I loved. We were comfortable: my family had known the Depression; I hadn't; and though no one made great money, an aggregate of modest salaries meant little talk about money.
>
> As I neared graduation [from high school] . . . my career interests were in law and teaching. I also had a vocation, though I didn't want to admit it to myself or anyone else. And though happy with the prospect, I felt uneasy about such a complete departure from my family. My vocation process was reasonably smooth, and I gradually came to admit that I should be, wanted to be, a Jesuit.

Far from being weird, the horror of damnation was ubiquitous. And in the emotional economy of the times, it was just about impossible to disentangle such fears from the mysterious comforts of the ritualized, operatic ceremonies and long devotions that coursed through the school year and the turning of the liturgical seasons. The neighborhoods of childhood were sprinkled with magic the way the woods were alive with hidden mysterious animals. It was a world in which the line between swearing—"Jesus, Mary, and Joseph!"—and mighty Catholic ejaculations—"and all the saints in heaven!!!" was hard to draw. The parish was the crossroads of neighborhood, the little platoons of school, and enchanted space.

One former Jesuit captures the almost claustral closeness of the neighborhoods and the schools, the intimations of what later would be called "dysfunction," and the imaginative hole that the Jesuits filled. He expresses the peculiar, tentative fusion between superstitious absolutism and the ambitious folkways of America. "Born in 1936," he notes, "I grew up in the Catholic parish world of the '40s and '50s, in the middle-class neighborhoods of Brooklyn and Long Island":

> It was a milieu of rigid certainty in the superiority of Catholicism, even though the heart of it was remote and mysterious. Everything was competitive. School work and street play were a seamless effort to be near the top, rough and fair, without cheating. Honor roll and report card averages at Our Lady Help of Christians grammar school were more important than stickball homeruns, but not by much, and both together gave you standing in the neighborhood. . . . Midway in my senior year, worried about my father's sporadic but troublesome drinking, I decided that eternal salvation was worth a kind of purgatory on earth, and I became interested in a sort of missionary life, rugged and probably gloriously brief.[22]

Another older former Jesuit, focusing on the Depression as the formative experience of his life, conjures up a world of vivid extremes and pungent characters, one close to the turn-of-the-century enclaves made famous in the Yellow Kid comics and the photographs of Jacob Riis, interlarded with some of the melancholy of *Wisconsin Death Trip*.[23] The rambling detail of his commentary punctures stylized renditions of the era:

> Born in 1920, I was ten when the Great Depression hit in 1930. It colored my whole life. We never were on relief because my father was employed, but most of our neighbors and friends were. We lived a life of meager resources. My father had a fairly good job in a bank, but having lost borrowed money in the Crash, he had to pay it back until he was 65 years of age. Consequently, we were just about able to make it. Money was a big topic of concern because we had so little. We didn't borrow, we lived very simply. My parents were hard working, very pious, proud, charitable to the poor, clean, neat, and most respectable. Neither of them was at ease expressing emotion. They were cautious and controlling.

This was the confinement of chronic austerity, of boiled food and sparse amusements, before television, that afflicted some Catholic immigrants and their subculture at least as severely as it did the poor, pinched whites photographed by Walker Evans and Mike Disfarmer during the 1930s and on into the 1940s.[24] The matter-of-fact report from memory glances at covert sins and strange rituals:

> Both parents went to novenas and put priests on the highest pedestal. I think my father, who came from an abjectly poor family, always wanted to be a priest. My mother often said she never expected to marry. . . . I truly loved my parents and tried to make them proud of me.
>
> The parish was a center of our life. We had an old grouch as pastor, Monsignor Lynch and two young curates who were our heroes. They coached us in sports and taught us how to be altar boys. They were kings of the kids. One of the curates showed signs of being a pedophile. I had a near-encounter with him in my early teens and learned to stay away from him thereafter. My parents lionized them and gave the impression that the best thing I could do was to be a priest.

The neighborhood was also a maze of chaotic lives and tenebrous passages on the brink. For many, the church and the priesthood were honorable exits from a dead end:

> If I was a priest I could fulfill my father's spoiled dream and give my mother what she craved—a higher social status. We lived in a real slum because my mother's uncle owned the house and gave it to us for $15 a month. I didn't know it was a slum until the newspaper boy who delivered our paper told my mother he couldn't deliver it any more because his mother didn't want him in that kind of a neighborhood. My mother was horrified. The police came to our neighborhood many times each week because of domestic violence and petty crime.
>
> My uncle George who lived upstairs was a wonderful man but a ne'er do well. He couldn't keep a job and drank too much but what a great friend [he was] to me! He let me drive his car in a back lot for hours when I was eleven. Also important in my life was my uncle Ernie, who later committed suicide. He was an unemployed brick layer who had been a foreman but got in trouble because he was pushing union business. He was so good to me. Both these uncles taught me how to use tools. My father was hopeless in that area. He once brought a hammer back to the hardware store because it had no directions. . . .
>
> No one in my family had ever gone to high school. We were a blue collar family, but my father attended night school for twenty-three years and really became a very educated man. My mother had the most wonderful gift of humor and social communication and an eye for art and

beauty that would have done anyone proud. She just about finished eighth grade. I had a good life at home.

Such recollections are exceptional in their depiction of harsh poverty. Most Depression-era Jesuits did not come from the lowest of the low. Nevertheless, the memories are typical in two respects. There is fondness to the description of family life. Just as vividly remembered are the overindulgence in drink, the hints of sexual misbehavior, and the absence of intimacy amid the dense networks of relatives that characterized a life with scarce resources and few distractions.

One route past the nexus of innocence and fear consisted of an alternative that combined sacrifice and security, crystallized by the Jesuits, who were paragons of virtue, academic excellence ("they seemed to know everything"), and camaraderie. Though undeniably daunting, the option of the priesthood was attractive because it had little competition during the prewar years in the eyes of those with a penchant for service who wanted not just a job but a career. The Society of Jesus looked both exotic and safe. The demands were great, but the risks were low, and the work was meaningful. Above all, the rewards were enormous. The priesthood provided not just a way out but an adventurous exit, and the end of the journey promised redemption. "Giving up sex was a big downer," one sixty-six-year-old former Jesuit put it simply. "Heaven would make up for that."

For many, the sacrifices associated with the priesthood meant virile heroism. For others, they were simply acceptable costs. This was the way the rules were set up, on a long but relatively safe road to salvation that included service to others as well as sexual martyrdom. The sacrificial ideal was connected with a flight from impurity. The Jesuits went beyond salvation by mere abnegation, however, in providing expert service, notably education. Dedication of this sort brought honor as well as holiness. The prestige of joining those who seemed to be the best and the brightest was coupled with a feeling of security that came from an understanding that sacrifice and service led to salvation.[25] One sixty-eight-year-old former Jesuit summarized the mixture of pushes and pulls that held out the priesthood as a reasonable ideal. He was magnetized by

> [the] life and convictions and power of Jesuits at Fordham Prep, my mother's desire, my desire to distinguish myself, the ideal of giving to others. My social world had in it practically no physicians, lawyers, politicians, outstanding Catholic laymen, etcetera.

The recurring theme of the recollections of the middle-aged and older men, most of whom entered the Society of Jesus before Vatican II, is this combination of push-pull factors. The Catholic neighborhoods were cozy, if fearful and restrictive. The Jesuits offered excitement and salvation. The transition to maturity and the great world was ready-made. Questions of meaning would come later. A sixty-four-year-old former Jesuit summed up his experience this way:

> Ordinary life looked boring, "quiet desperation." On the other hand, I had no great desire to convert anybody, or make people better. There was nothing pastoral about my motivation. I was religiously faithful, generally convinced of the heaven-hell sanctions for good-bad moral behavior, and afraid of going to hell. I had done some dating, gone steady, but felt no great sexual need, certainly no imperative to start a family or have children. I was afraid of marriage as a moral trap: I couldn't believe that any woman would want to live all her life with me. Unable to divorce and remarry, I would end up trapped between lifelong loneliness and mortal sin.
>
> There was, of course, a positive side to my entrance into the Jesuits: I was looking for an interesting life, and religious life seemed to offer more of a chance for that. I thought of this in religious terms: that God was inexhaustible; that life in relationship with God would never grow dull.

So, the priesthood had cultural appeal and social status on a par with other professional outlets on the Catholic horizon, and it held out the promise of attainable payoffs as well. As represented by the educated and venturesome Jesuits whom almost all the recruits met in high school, religious life was seen not just as the path to sainthood but also as a relatively clear passage to achievement and cosmopolitan glamour. It was both colorful and eminently respectable, given the alternatives. The sacrifice was great, but so was the combined sense of mystery and security. The Society of Jesus was a magnetic amalgam of idealism and pragmatism. As a fifty-three-year-old former Jesuit put it,

> Though there were no obvious positive factors actually pushing me toward the priesthood or toward the Jesuits in my community, there were some submerged negative or passive factors pushing me out of my home community toward something. Ours was a happy enough home, but the surrounding community was what I would call a working-class or decidedly lower-middle-class community. I had an uncle who [had] . . . the only college degree on my father's side of the family, and there were no

college degrees on my mother's side. There was also nothing in the way of a family business or occupational tradition (as in fire department families, police department families, construction industry families, and the like) anywhere close enough for me to see. The men had jobs, about which one knew nothing. The women were at home. The only career in full view was the clerical career.

I was not, in fact, much attracted to, though I was not repelled either by, the work of the diocesan priest: liturgy, preaching, confessions, home visiting, etcetera. Obscurely, however, I was both drawn to the notion of career and, having no models, terrified in that regard. I did not want to just have a job, but I had little idea how I would go beyond that condition—or for that matter how I would reach even that condition.

The image that the Jesuits presented was attractive because it came to me in this informational and orientational vacuum. They clearly had a work to do. They seemed enthusiastic about it. I could imagine myself doing it and being good at it. Once you joined up with them, they would decide what you should do and teach you how to do it. They were also generous, caring men. I had an idealistic side, the good boy wanting to help people. They appealed to this but combined it with an appeal to the ambitious boy, to the lonely boy, and to the poor boy clueless in the larger world.

5

In contrast to these portrayals of limited opportunities, certain aspects of the environment of the younger men—those who entered the Society from the late 1960s on—are remarkably different, while a few others show equally striking continuity. The big differences have to do, first, with the virtual disappearance of God-as-ogre and of a religious system stacked toward retribution and, second, with the expansion of career options beyond the priesthood and a handful of other traditional occupations. The culture changed; so did the structure of opportunity and incentives.[26] Becoming a Jesuit was no longer, as an older Jesuit put it, "the one great thing." A former Jesuit, on the downside of sixty, writes in a similar vein about himself as one "who entered the priesthood because he felt that being a priest was the best thing he could do with his life, and since he could, he should, and did. Never mind if he *wanted* to or not."

A major continuity involves the perpetuation of religious conviction and practice in several of the postenclave, post–Vatican II families from which priestly vocations emerge. This carryover is not a uniform or even dominant phenomenon; several younger Jesuits and former Jesuits come from single-parent or otherwise shattered families. Still, the familial and religious continuity is common enough to warrant attention. In the words of a thirty-five-year-old Jesuit vocation director,

> I grew up in a very stable upper middle class neighborhood in the same town and parish that my folks grew up in, with both grandmothers close by (within a mile) and my mom's only sister living two houses away with my seven cousins on that side of the family: lots of roots and stability going back several generations very close by. We all went to the same Catholic grade school that my dad went to, with the same order of nuns. . . . I was very involved as an altar boy, and played guitar at Mass on Sunday and at school liturgies in seventh and eighth grade. There was still some of the old "tradition" around (1967–73), but I was raised with none of the preconciliar sense of "Catholic guilt" that you hear about. Community, celebration, and concern for others were strong themes of our Catholic grade school education.

Another change, besides the dwindling image of a fearsome divinity and the proliferation of career alternatives, is the thinning of the bonds of clerical kinship in the Catholic milieu. In years past, "celebrity uncles"—priests on the father's or mother's side of the family or both—as well as aunts in religious life, came to visit, and these relations represented appealing role models. They were intimate with mystery. On holidays, primed with scotch and soda, they regaled parlors and dining rooms with church gossip. In recent times, such linkages are attenuated. A younger (thirty-eight-year-old) Jesuit recalls a few family ties to the religious life even as he stresses the spontaneous nature of his vocation:

> Ever since I can remember, I have wanted to be a priest. I am sure that the desire was reinforced by coming from a Catholic family and being a "good kid," but it is hard to track down. None of my siblings or cousins entered a seminary or religious life. One of my paternal grandfather's cousins was a Jesuit and one of my mother's cousins is a nun, but it is not part of a deep family tradition. I started grade school in the south during Vatican II, so until I entered, none of my friends or acquaintances entered religious life. This was simply what I've always wanted without a lot of connection.

The recollections of a forty-one-year-old Jesuit are similar. When he was a child, whatever clerical relatives he had seemed far away. The devotion of his parents and images of a loving God mattered more in conditioning his choice of the priesthood than any vestiges of ethnic Catholicism:

> I was raised in the usual postwar Southwestern suburb. My parents, like our neighbors, had come west after the men had been educated on the GI Bill. . . . I grew up in a very loving, caring environment with two parents who were happily married. I think their being happily married helped my vocation because I learned from the very beginning that total commitment is possible, is satisfying, and is a lot of work. The thought of being in the Society for life didn't frighten me. There aren't any priests or religious in my family, except for some distant uncle whom I've never met. Both my parents are sincere in their faith, and that certainly made an impression on me. God was never used as a threat, either. My parents wouldn't use these words, but they believed God loved them, and so taught us to live a love relationship with God, rather than a fear relationship.

As the networks of aunts and uncles in religious life thinned out,[27] as the images of hellfire and a monster God receded, and as opportunities for mobility and meaningful careers opened up, vocations to the priesthood went down. The preservation of religious feeling among parents helps stem this downward spiral, and the transformation in perceptions from a harrowing to a loving God alters one of the reasons for entering the priesthood rather than abolishing motivation altogether. But the same shift in values reduces the number of candidates by winnowing out those prompted by what might be considered mixed motives. The world in which the appeals of security, adventure, and prestige had a kind of magical naturalness, a certain transcendental pragmatism, along with the drive toward service and a sense of being called, has virtually disappeared.

A significant variation on the weakening of the customary reinforcements and cultural legitimation of religious life involves the increasing number of families of origin broken by divorce. The most frequently cited dysfunction in the old days was alcoholism. Marital breakup is the contemporary equivalent. Vocation directors and novice masters regularly report a higher incidence of men entering the Society of Jesus "from broken homes." For all this, a thread of parental, usually maternal, devotion, of keeping the faith, runs through several of the depictions of fractured marriages and families on the edge.[28] The recollections of a thirty-year-old former Jesuit paint just such a picture:

I grew up in a divorced family where we struggled to make ends meet every month. But even in this kind of situation my family, especially my mother, always told us how much she loved us and she knew that God was helping us get through the difficult times. I attended a Catholic grade school, a good education was very important to my mother. She used every bit of extra money to send her kids to Catholic school. She felt that we would learn to be better people that way.

The changes outlined here have affected both the surrounding environment and the internal dynamics of the Catholicism from which men emerge to join the Society of Jesus. The most powerful changes have been the amplification of career and vocational options and a corresponding demystification of the priesthood as one such option. Most other changes—the thinning out of the large, extended families with clerical uncles and religious aunts, for example—match this overall movement.

There is, however, a wrinkle in the downward pattern that has as much to do with differences between Jesuits and former Jesuits as it does with differences across age cohorts. The image of a terrifying deity has softened across the board, for Jesuits and former Jesuits, but the apprehension of God as a harsh father does not appear to have been so widespread, to begin with, among men who remained Jesuits. Our information is composed of recollections, so it is tricky to sort out existential differences from selective memory. Nevertheless, the fonder images held by Jesuits, as compared to former Jesuits, of their God of childhood are consistent with another difference between them. On the average, the men who have stayed in the Society report having closer relations with their parents than those who left.[29] In many instances, departures from the Society were bound up with rebellion against authority that went beyond religious hierarchy.

6

The number of Jesuits has fallen because the number of reasons for joining the Jesuits has fallen. The social and cultural conditions that draw substantial numbers of recruits to inherited forms of religious life encompass a range of motives, some idealistic, some pragmatic. Devotional rhetoric routinely makes invidious comparisons between pure and not-so-pure motives. But from a sociological point of view, and from a merely human perspective, many of these tensions are mutually reinforcing.[30] It is far from evident that such sullied drives are organizationally counterproductive in religious life, whatever psychological havoc they may wreak on individuals. The notion of spiritual endeavor as mainly the pursuit of inner harmony and psychic integration has substantial appeal in a therapeutic milieu, but whether such a view provides a realistic model of the religious complexities of the past is quite another matter.[31]

The assortment of motives that led men to the Society of Jesus in earlier times, before Vatican II, no doubt varied from man to man and shifted over the lifetime of individuals. Not all these motives can be reduced to a cost-benefit calculus. Yet it flies against the evidence to assert that the motives ordinarily labeled as "spiritual"—the main one being salvation—are immune to calculation. Some men felt that the assurance of eternal reward, or a goal close to it, made "purgatory on earth" worthwhile. In this sense, the priesthood was a paying proposition. One could do well, in the long run, by doing good.[32]

Two reminders are in order here. The previous analysis cannot do justice to the sheer quirkiness of religious vocation any more than it can explain why individuals chose *any* course of life over others. "The action of grace," as it used to be called, can no more be programmed than can a butterfly be instructed to alight on cue.[33] What we can say is that the cultural prevalence of this or that career line—the visibility and desirability of, say, the priesthood—in comparison to other occupational alternatives makes it likelier that the imagination will be seized by that particular option. The psychology of personal choice is shaped by collective, cultural profiles. To be more precise than this, we would have to know a lot more than we do about the match between the prominence of professions in the aggregate and the talents and temperaments of individuals.[34]

Second, especially since Vatican II, the instrumental incentives for joining religious life have diminished, and the payoffs are less clear. The language of Vatican II put the laity closer to par with the clergy. Theological reform coincided with long-term demographic shifts to undercut the attractions of religious life.[35] With the calculus of costs and benefits clouded or reversed, and with the demographic shrinkage in traditional forms of religious life, many of those considering ordained ministry have fewer cultural and institutional cues and reinforcements than before.[36]

A good deal of improvisation now goes into justifying religious vocations. In the absence of crisp incentives or a readily communicable set of goals and means toward these goals, investment in religious life takes on features of identification with countercultures that feel themselves under attack or marginal. Postulants seek identity, a shared sensibility, and sometimes a common sense of mission. Lacking the support they once had from the larger environment, religious congregations have taken on many of the features of support groups themselves. Members tend to adopt countercultural agendas or idioms—ideological platforms, sexual styles, and the like—that serve to set them apart and simulate a sense of collective moorings.

Jesuits have traditionally taken pride in being on the edge, and any religious organization in a pluralist setting must maintain some sort of boundary-defining mechanism that sets it apart and preserves its identity.[37] For the Society of Jesus, the difficulty comes in doing so after the collapse of subcultures that once provided off-the-shelf identities, in the aftermath of doubts about the rationale for celibacy, and in the midst of a rhetoric of inclusiveness that blurs in-group/out-group boundaries.

Decades ago, if the priesthood went beyond being one of the primary vehicles of professionalization that took men out of parochialism, "sacrifice" was the keynote of sacerdotal life, signaled by the vow of celibacy.[38] Heroism meant abandonment to God and church. Devotion above and beyond the call of duty distinguished clergy from laity, and Jesuits were the pick of the clerical elite. Today, the invocation of "service" is more common, and "sacrifice" has a vaguely weird, unhealthy tincture. The temperate ideal of service, however, fails to evoke much that is distinctively priestly, and there is not much romance to it. One way to meet the need for distinctiveness is to identify with those on the margin, as this thirty-five-year-old gay Jesuit does:

> I have a clear sense of ministry in my pastoral involvements, serving . . . the needs of particular people at particular times. I find myself increasingly connected with people on the fringe of Roman Catholicism, people whose connections are confused, strained, or almost nonexistent. And attending to them, seeing to their needs, provides me with great satisfaction.

Now that the tangible and comparatively unproblematic payoffs—the leadership status, the aura of cultivation, the problem-solving skills, the inside track to redemption, and so on—that were taken for granted in earlier times are much less the properties of a sacerdotal monopoly, solutions to the quandaries of spiritual life in which a countercultural ethos dominates have become popular. As traditional emblems of belonging have receded, the credentials of identity have become more sub-jective, ideological, and sexual—therefore touchier. Without the backup of pedestrian benefits or the old spiritual perks and clinquant arcana of religious life, informal movements and episodic membership in estab-lished organizations are more in evidence than institutionalized groups with routinized ministries. A small number of collective pathways in re-ligious life have given way to myriad byways.[39]

CHAPTER THREE

From Innocence to Experience

What are now acceptable behavior patterns for celibates in dealing with women, or for gays in dealing with each other? Women are no longer "vessels of iniquity" and threats to my priesthood . . .

The official sexual policies of the Catholic church for clergy and laity alike are inhuman and destructively unrealistic.

The church has squandered a lot of the good energy of Vatican II trying to put a chastity belt on itself.

I

The sexual magisterium of the church is the doctrinal permafrost of Catholicism. The code applies hard-and-fast principles to the deep passions and drives of the human species. "Sexuality" is an abstraction, a clinical distillate, another Latinate polysyllable. Its ramifications in Catholicism, however, are relentlessly perennial and felt in the flesh.[1]

Whatever the fixity of doctrine concerning "matters of faith and morals," actual beliefs surrounding the sexual magisterium have moved in a progressive direction since the 1960s and Vatican II, much more spectacularly than has been the case with the social teaching of the church.[2] It is the break in moral-sexual norms among Jesuits as well as former Jesuits that has shaken the ground on which the authority of the clerical edifice stands.[3]

Here we explore the extent and the nature of the transformation in thinking on sexual issues among men associated with the Society of Jesus. In addition to the focus on changes in attitudes toward sexual issues, a central motif is the persistent connection between beliefs about the sexual teaching of the church and attitudes toward ecclesiastical authority. Dissent from the sexual magisterium undermines the power structure of Catholicism. But while the flagging credibility of the sexual code serves to delegitimize ecclesiastical authority, no single set of norms has taken its place. This sets the stage for a crisis of priestly identity.

The next chapter focuses on a pair of concrete changes. One concerns attitudes toward celibacy as a condition of priesthood. Here, too, there has been a substantial shift in Catholic and Jesuit discourse away from conviction and certainty toward doubt and barely contained controversy. Then we examine perceptions of and attitudes toward sexual orientation, in particular, homosexuality. The growing visibility of a gay subculture within the Jesuit order reflects the drive to establish a distinctive identity as traditional moral guidelines and old bases of social belonging have eroded.

Several key developments underlie the diminished credibility of the church's sexual teaching within its officer corps and its near collapse among those who have left, the misgivings about the purpose and utility of celibacy, and the prominence of sexual orientation as an ingredient of clerical identity and community. A huge gap has developed between the sexual and moral principles laid down in the official teaching of the church, which has changed scarcely at all since Vatican II, and the pastoral practice of its middle managers, including Jesuits. "In many an informal setting," a fifty-eight-year-old Jesuit remarked,

> I have often said that the one survey that will never be taken (or if taken, published) is the correlation between the pastoral practice of active priests and [the] official teaching of the church, especially in sex/family issues: birth control, premarital sex, second marriages and the like.

The crumbling of time-worn certainties, especially in the sexual realm, has shaken not only doctrine but also identities.[4] As if to compensate for the vertigo, countercultural postures have gained an allure they did not have when Catholics were set apart as members of religious and ethnic minorities.

The core claim linking this chapter and the following one is that countercultural movements in the Society of Jesus (of which the gay network is a special case) are partial replacements for the distinctive bonding that prevailed under the moral fixities represented by celibacy and ethnic attachments. It is not celibacy so much as doubts about celibacy that enhance homosexual orientation as a mark of community in religious life.

2

This fifty-three-year-old Jesuit, a specialist in spiritual direction, cuts
against the grain in stating that his views about sexual issues have turned
to the right. But even he expresses doubts about the church's teaching
on birth control, and his praise of the social magisterium falls in line
with the opinion of his colleagues:

> I have become more conservative and traditional in some of my thinking
> on sexual morality and defending church teaching, the main reason be-
> ing the adolescent and abusive use of sexual life among many people.
> However, *Humanae Vitae*'s narrow view of contraceptive practice still
> seems to be wholesalely ignored by many Catholics of commitment and
> goodwill. We have to be more trusting as a church towards the married
> laity in making decisions dealing with procreation issues. I have been
> very happy with John Paul's very forthright teaching on economic justice
> in his recent writings. The Society continues to be very much engaged
> with these issues, but a finer tuning of faith and justice values in all of
> our ministries continues to occupy time and clarification. I feel very
> proud of the Society's commitment to these issues, seen concretely in the
> lives of many of our men, particularly so of those in the undeveloped
> world.

Statements like these fall way short of radicalism. The shift in beliefs
about sexual-moral issues reflects a process of growing up, the passing
of innocence, and a rejection of what came to be seen as childish ideals
and neurotic scruples.[5] The loss of virginity has been cognitive as well as
physical. The ideological conversion follows a collective chronology,
with the late 1960s to early 1970s as turning point.

For obvious reasons, Jesuits report less drastic changes than former
Jesuits. The truly striking differences, however, occur among men of different ages, whether Jesuits or former Jesuits, even though the average
outcome is in the direction of greater freedom in the sexual domain for
all age-groups. Because they grew up in a sexually sheltered environment, the older men have come a longer way toward sexual emanci-
pation and tolerance. On the average, change in the attitudes of the
younger men has been less sweeping; their historic baseline was already
further along the path away from sexual constraint.

So, while the thinking of most Jesuits and former Jesuits has altered
on sexual and, somewhat less so, on social matters, tilting in a progres-

sive direction, change has been uneven. Ideational and cultural transformations that were seismic for almost everyone seem to have been
downright traumatic for the generation composed of those men who departed from the Society in large numbers, having entered the Jesuits in
the latter part of the 1950s, near the eve of Vatican II. Sexual shock is
not so endemic among more recent cohorts.

The starting point for change in attitudes toward sexual-moral controversies is usually innocence rather than outright conservatism—a
condition even more pronounced in political and social questions than
in sexual matters. Any sweeping before-and-after contrast is thrown off
further by the fact that Jesuits and former Jesuits lean toward tolerance,
compassion, and moderation rather than the advocacy of sexual abandon. The terminology of left-versus-right captures some of this split but
misses an equally important division between the tough-minded and the
tenderhearted—between the men who stand by and cling to their certainties and those who claim to care less about absolutes and closure.[6]

Whatever its ideological characterization, the break constitutes a
rupture with the past. The new sexual ethos differs from what most of
the men were accustomed to, and the continuity in beliefs about sexual
behavior is much less secure than the carryover in social doctrine.

Even when the dominant gradualism in the shift in beliefs about sexual matters is taken into account, the transition in attitudes cannot be
called smooth. Discarded norms have not been replaced by new ones.
Clerics, including Jesuits, have been caught in a bewildering transformation. What constitutes adherence to celibacy? What makes for deviation? Uncertainty on this score, one Jesuit in his late fifties remarked,
"puts priests in a damned if you do (no coherent moral posture) and
damned if you don't (old-fashioned repression) dilemma."

> What are now acceptable behavior patterns for celibates in dealing with
> women, or for gays in dealing with each other? Women are no longer
> "vessels of iniquity" and threats to my priesthood, as they might once
> have been considered. Now everybody (with brains) realizes that the
> rules have changed. Can I work closely with a woman colleague? Go to
> lunch to discuss a common project? Go to dinner because we enjoy each
> other's company or to the theater because we share mutual interests?
> Can I kiss her good-night? Spend the night once in a while, as long it
> does not interfere with my priestly role? Vacation together? Is it differ-
> ent if she is a nun, single and lonely, has other intimate relationships,
> or is in an unhappy marriage?

Observations in this vein document the perplexities attendant on the disintegration of the old code and the rejection of perfectionism. Former Jesuits sometimes claim to have resolved the dilemma by taking leave of the Society and severing their obligation to reconcile what they saw as irreconcilable or to defend the indefensible. In the words of a forty-two-year-old,

> I am now married, and this makes the integration of sexuality easier, I suppose, insofar as the culture is concerned. This is a great relief compared with what I experienced in the Society, where there seemed to be a lot of confusion not only on my part but on many people's as to what behavior was appropriate and not. I did not see a lot of honest sharing, in the Society, regarding this topic; I saw far more secrecy, and this had a debilitating effect on all the members, in my opinion.

Among Jesuits themselves, ambiguity is reflected not only in a move from right to left but in the sheer diversity of opinion regarding the specifics of celibacy, homosexuality, and other sexual issues. The upside of all this is tolerance. Yet the variety of opinion creates an institutional anomaly. It is literally catholic: heterogeneous and eclectic but, since the sexual magisterium has stayed put, lacking the sanction of pluralism. The result is a mishmash underlying the institutional monolith of sexual teaching, without a consensual or clearly dominant alternative to the official line.

From the perspective of those who claim responsibility for upholding doctrinal integrity, a slippery slope lies just under the cultural summit of the 1960s. Underneath the appearance of common sense and moderation lurks a spirit of compromise and appeasement that is precisely the menace that has to be contained and, if possible, expunged. The enemy is no longer radicalism but the relativism evident in a lack of conviction. The irony is that creeping moderation, the fog on cat's feet, breeds polarization and ethical fragmentation.[7]

From this viewpoint, nothing seems to stand between adherence to the magisterium and an ethical maelstrom. There is no middle ground between perfectionism and permissiveness, no pluralistic via media between strict authority and anarchy. A Jesuit scholar in his early fifties captures the escalating logic of moderation and polarization:

> Clearly, married priests have got to come. I don't think there's any question. And women priests, I'm all for it as long it doesn't tear the church

apart. I'm an incrementalist and a gradualist. It may tear us apart if we *don't* do it. And it's going to tear us apart if we *do* do it.

On the one hand, then, the institutional response to changing sexual mores and attitudes toward women has been intransigence. On the other hand, forbearance regarding sexual issues has emerged in the operative beliefs and pastoral practice of Jesuits. But such moderation looks perilously close to relativism when pitted against an organizational strategy dedicated to the defense of unchanging sexual doctrine as the bedrock of absolute truth. It suggests weakness of character. Besides, some issues —a married clergy is one, divorce another—do not lend themselves to finessing; only one of two alternatives seems permissible. In either case, compromise becomes unthinkable.

One offshoot of the gap between institutional policy and the working morality of the church's middle managers, like the Jesuits, is a long-standing pattern in Catholicism but one that is probably starker today than in the past: the cultivation of a compassionate, barely subterranean culture alongside a strict official code.[8] The disconnect between preaching and practice is substantial. There is a set of official ethics, and there is a vernacular morality.

A second development is potentially more confrontational. Regardless of whether they are Jesuits or former Jesuits, men who characterize themselves as progressive on moral and sexual issues are likely to express dissatisfaction with the direction of the institutional church. Conversely, those who are more conservative on such matters are apt to be far less critical of the church.[9] The conflict is in line with the organizational dynamic that produces polarization in the midst of attitudinal moderation. Dissent on sexual matters is equated with disrespect for the authority structure of Catholicism and challenges to its credibility. Moderates come to seem as disloyal in their small delinquencies as outspoken dissidents.

3

If there is any master trend besides a conciliatory momentum that takes in the changes reported by Jesuits and former Jesuits—changes that include but are not exhausted by alterations in beliefs and behavior about sexual matters—it would be the shift from innocence to experience. Roughly, this corresponds to a movement from conservative to progressive. The accent is on "roughly" because innocence is more a state of ignorance than an ideological position. Of course, its content is colored by the norms of the historical setting in which candidates to the Society of Jesus grew up. In the case of many, especially older men, that sexual culture happened to be repressive and chilly—"colder," as one put it, "than a brass toilet seat in the Klondike!" The contrast with the younger generation of recruits is plain to see. As a Jesuit in his sixties who was once a formation director noted, new candidates have more sexual experience than was the case in the days of large numbers of entrants:

> For the most part, we're getting men six years out of college, six years in
> which most young men, gay, straight, or undecided, are sexually active.
> Can we think the ones we get have been sitting in rooms reading for six
> years? I doubt it. I know of some who've been married and divorced.
> If they say they've had *no* social life, my guess is they're likely to get
> turned down. We don't want to be a haven for recluses.

"Experience" is not equivalent to the development of what used to be called "advanced views"; it may even connote a certain loss of reformist zeal and idealism. Be that as it may, firsthand exposure to sexual realities, together with the sexualization of popular culture, has fostered skepticism about the benefits of perfectionism and bafflement at a zealous purity. It has also encouraged toleration and compassion. Jesuits and former Jesuits are less given to condemnation than they remember themselves as being. "Judgmental" has an invariably pejorative ring.

The story of this fifty-nine-year-old former Jesuit typifies the passage of many men who came to the Society in a state of innocence and who left the order during the heyday of the sexual revolution. The man looks back with puckish wisdom on the wide-eyed escapades of his youth:

> When I left the Jesuits in 1964 I went directly to New York City, expecting to meet and vanquish my demons. I had no money and no prospects.
> My parents gave me $600 from a cashed-in life insurance policy (which
> I added to the $50 I was given in the last hour of my residency at Weston College). I stayed in an $11 room at the Commodore Hotel near
> Times Square and went looking for a job in the publishing business and
> a place to live.
> My misadventures at that time would be clownish if they were not
> so dismal. My sexual naïveté was so painful and self-conscious I could
> scarcely believe it was my own body going through these paroxysms
> (not to be confused with orgasms). Gradually I found a circle of friends,
> both men and women, a few ex-Jesuits and some former nuns among

them. My sexual expectations were so idealized that I was too forward with shy women and too backward with sexually confident women. I seemed to be able to read the situation clearly and take precisely the clumsiest approach. It took me years, and a short retreat into an unwelcome celibacy, to figure out a "normal" approach to sex. It was not until the early '70s that I found a "lover" in the truest sense, and that relationship still happily endures.

The Jesuit "approach" to sexuality in the '50s and '60s was clear and "progressive" and "tolerant" and completely out of touch. I remember a psychology of sexuality class during a semester of theological studies at Weston that to this day amazes me for its infantile and repressed doctrines. Most of us had already formed sex theories (a hodgepodge of Hemingway and Camus and Roth and Wouk) as we sat and listened to "Doctor of Psychology, SJ" teach us what to say in the confessional to young men and women. If any aspect of Jesuit life in that era crystallizes their detachment from a healthy inner life, it is this stunning lack of understanding of human sexuality. At least partly to our credit, we could kick back in the rec room after dinner and laugh at it all. Little did we know how profoundly this nonsense was disorienting our real capacity for sharing love with another and how burdensome the company line would be for us as young priests.

The themes of ignorance and repression intermingle alongside a parallel universe of black humor. Prior to Vatican II, at least some Jesuits in positions of authority were struggling to break out of a doctrinal straitjacket, to develop a humane psychology for a closed theological system. In hindsight, the effort seems to have been doomed to failure. There was more than a touch of painting by numbers to the enterprise. A deductive classicism could not supply the knowledge of experience.

The retrospective evaluations of former Jesuits from this cohort, men in their fifties or older by the 1990s, run toward the negative, with a trace of fascination at the extremes and eccentricities that the subculture bred. A fifty-two-year-old former Jesuit speaks for many of his peers:

> When I compare my sexuality to that of my three sons, theirs seems much more healthy and relaxed than mine was as a youth. Being raised as a Catholic male in the 1940s and 1950s meant being taught to despise and fear sexual feelings and expressions as tickets to hell.

None of the Jesuits from this cohort want to return to the ignorance, fear, and scrupulous inhibitions of earlier times. But like several former Jesuits, they also express misgivings at what they perceive as the sexual hyperventilation and ethical fickleness of modern life. This sixty-one-year-old theologian speaks with reference to the strains on chastity, but the perspective applies to sexual mores in general:

> Since the sexual revolution of the '60s and birth control when it became institutionalized in entertainment, in the media, etcetera, there's a special strain in northern Europe and our industrial countries where there has been a split between reproduction and sexual expression that would not have been true several years ago. In the earlier period, the reasons for celibacy were pretty palatable. With no family, a priest was easily transferable from one parish to another at low cost. If you want to have a sign of the Kingdom of God or a countersign, something different from marriage, all of these things made sense, some of them practical, some of them spiritual, some of them theoretical, some of them down to earth. But with the break in that link and the diffusion of sexual imagery almost everywhere it has to affect the practice and the theory of celibacy. There has to be an erosion of that, and I think a lot of priests don't see the connection.

Some former Jesuits, particularly those with children of their own to raise, share this dismay at the sexual revolution. For a forty-three-year-old writer, leaving the order led not only to liberation but also toward fulfillment. But broader experience has alerted him to the shadowy alleys and ambiguous byways of sex:

> About eight months after leaving the Society, I married a woman I had gotten to know toward the end of my regency. We have a stable, traditional relationship; in ——— we will be married nine years. We share a satisfying sex life, making love probably twice a month, on average, with plenty of hugs and general physical contact in between. . . .
>
> My sexuality is not entirely integrated. I can still slip into sexual fantasies fairly easily, when I want to fall asleep, or upon waking too early in the morning. And I sometimes experience periods of mild fantasy-obsessions with one or another of the women at my workplace. I've grown much more aware of these patterns. Increasingly, when such notions present themselves, I am quicker to recognize them as passing fancies, more patient and gentle about acknowledging them, and then letting them quietly pass on. . . .
>
> Among my post-Jesuit experiences, I have learned that my father sexually abused my older sister. That has confirmed as difficult, if not impossible, an already difficult relationship with him. And I have been exposed to the still relatively new phenomenon of spouses leaving their

marriages for same-sex relationships. I think I have learned that issues of sexuality are, in our present culture, moving in the direction of greater confusion and uncertainty, rather than toward more positive and life-giving integration.

In broad strokes, then, most Jesuits and former Jesuits have dropped their adherence to the dour, stoic, noli me tangere pose regarding the sexual commandments that prevailed before Vatican II and the moral upheaval of the 1960s. The impression that most of the men convey is that the benefits of change have outweighed the costs. The overlay of innocence with experience has led to a rather ordinary process of growing up. "Relations with women," a sixty-five-year-old Jesuit notes,

> have gradually changed, for the better, it seems to me, partly because I was spending more and more of my life dealing with very bright and well-trained professional women and also because women themselves became more vocal in describing how they wish to be treated.

Still, costs there have been. Sometimes sexual liberation does not bring satisfaction. One of the few regularities of the new dispensation is that there are no guarantees, and it is not infrequent for former Jesuits to complain that, no matter how much intellectual assent they have given to the liberated vision emanating from the 1960s, they must strain to jettison the psychosexual baggage of their upbringing. A sixty-seven-year-old professor of political theory, who left the Jesuits at forty, describes an uphill journey:

> It has not been easy to become or to reclaim being a sexual person. There is no "how" to this, as though there were a set of procedures like a "how to" book. My experience of sexuality as a Jesuit is in a way an oxymoron. It was all deeply repressed. Sexuality was not "integrated" into my Jesuit life. I am not sure I would even have understood such a phrase. Sublimation might be more accurate. . . .
> My wife and I have helped each other to "integrate" our mutual sexualities by coming to grow and realize that sex and sexuality are not the same thing. Sexuality has something to do with simply being a person, a human being and a responsible partner and parent, if there are children. It becomes "integrated" in one's "post-Jesuit" life simply by living, communicating, working, loving, feeling, touching, making love, breathing, eating, laughing, crying, suffering, enjoying—together. It is not always automatic or spontaneous.

Twenty years in the traditional way of being a Jesuit can take an enormous toll on one's sex and sexuality. An understanding, loving and patient woman helps but eventually it is a decision to love one's self as a precondition of loving anyone else. In fact, just being a Catholic in the old traditional way can take a terrible toll on sex and sexuality. Integration of sexuality into one's broader life is a challenge for everyone, not just for Jesuits.

For others, regardless of whether they have attained personal satisfaction or not, anxiety about sexual normlessness is palpable. The demise of the old order has not resulted in a new moral equilibrium; disavowing "sublimation" has not automatically produced "integration." Like the happily married, fortyish writer, some former Jesuits complain of being stranded in an ethos of individualism, limited by the absence of restraint.[10]

A characteristic response of former Jesuits is to look back on their lives in the order not in anger but in ambivalence and to carry forward an acute sense of partial victories, regrettable but nonfatal losses, and lucky escapes in tallying up their emotional and moral careers. "I accept sexuality as a part of my life," a forty-four-year-old former Jesuit observes with supreme noncontroversiality. Then, with an almost infinitely pluralistic air that is turned on himself as well as his former colleagues, he writes,

> It is both a burden and pleasure. Very often I am dissatisfied with the role my sexuality plays in my life. I left the Society because I knew that I could never go through my entire life without eventually giving into a sexual, intimate relationship with a woman. I could not take vows, knowing that eventually I would break them. As a Jesuit, I felt this problem to be a great millstone about my neck. Despite the philosophical and spiritual contortions made by a church committed to celibacy, I believe that only a few chosen men are called to this gift of the Spirit. I, not being one, found the "sexuality" of celibate life to be an illusion. I do not believe it is an illusion for those with the gift. I have not changed my opinion since I left the Society.

4

Especially among Jesuits themselves, the big change in attitudes toward the sexual magisterium comes down not to a blanket rejection of the rules but to an embrace of flexibility and forgiveness. Many live in dissent, but they refrain from direct challenges to official policy. Their approach has become indulgent instead. "Pastoral" covers a multitude of winks and glances the other way and a good deal of sympathy, too, all grist for the B movies and guilty pleasures of Catholicism.

In other cases, however, condemnation of the sexual magisterium is vociferous, even furious. Many, though by no means all, of these critics are former Jesuits. A sixty-three-year-old academic, teaching at a Jesuit university, who left the order in 1959 dismisses the official line and laments the hardships it has foisted on clerics and the faithful generally. His story and its moral are typical of former Jesuits of his generation:

> In my years as a Jesuit, I had no sexual relations with another person. I have heard of Jesuits who have had long affairs with women and remained Jesuits, but I could not have done that. I applaud them for their ability to deal with a difficult human conflict. Others, of course, have had homosexual affairs, and some have died of AIDS. My sympathies are with them. The official sexual policies of the Catholic church for clergy and laity alike are inhuman and destructively unrealistic.

A sixty-four-year-old looks back on his time in the Society with fondness but also with horror at the costs imposed by the church's sexual strictures. In pointing up the inadvertent consequence of ecclesiastical fascination with libidinal urges, he captures a paradox stressed by many of his peers: The more that is forbidden, the greater the curiosity. So much was off limits that prurience took hold, and sexual impropriety became an obsession:

> Celibacy, in hindsight, served to exaggerate sex, to deintegrate it in a brutal way, to surround it with anxiety, prurience, curiosity, fear. Women would have always been more than humanly attractive, more than humanly dangerous. Now I enjoy the company of woman immensely, my wife, my daughter, my granddaughter, my colleagues. I enjoy women with a freedom I would probably not have had as a Jesuit.
>
> It seems very clear to me that pleasures of the body are crucial to living in a body. It is terrible to have to live in something that is a constant source of danger, temptation.
>
> Intuitively I see a whole tangle of malign influences at work in the church's attitude toward sex: Greek and Roman philosophy, Greek and Roman social attitudes . . . Jewish apocalypticism, Augustine's neurotically screwed-up sex life, the harsh life of the peasantry of premodern Europe, and the amoral sexual freedom of the courts. These all seem to

have combined to twist the church into knots of sexual misconception.
A married priesthood is not as threatening to the church as she makes it.
Ordaining women priests is not as overwhelming a threat as she makes
it. The church imagines herself threatened on all sides by nonthreats.
These may or may not distract her from the real threats, the loss of the
sense of reverence, the desacralization of all life, the loss of the capacity
to be rooted in a tradition without being enslaved to it.

When I look back, the religious tonality of my life in the Jesuits
seems dark, close, confined, like a convent parlor. I am deeply grateful
to be free of that, though there were wonderful men who inspired me
and loved me.

While sympathizing with the antipermissive thrust of the church's
doctrinal message, some Jesuits, too, demur when it comes to legal
directives. One Jesuit, a fifty-five-year-old spiritual director, distances
himself not only from the practical implications of the rules but also
from the proscriptions themselves. Insofar as the rules are binding, they
are bad or at best dubious:

> Generally, I do not feel that the church has been in practice very helpful
> to people in their sexuality. I think that the church tends toward a fun-
> damentalism in sexuality just as it tends toward a fundamentalism con-
> cerning authority in the church. The traditional idea that there is only
> grave matter when it comes to sexually sinning simply flies in the face of
> reason when it comes to understanding the developmental processes in
> humans. While on the whole I agree with the basic principles of Catho-
> lic teaching on sexuality, I find it much too literal minded. I am not basi-
> cally at home with the church's teachings on contraception, masturba-
> tion, or homosexuality.

The point of departure of another Jesuit, a theologian in his early sixties, is dissent from *Humanae Vitae*. He lambastes the prohibition of
"artificial contraception" as wrong, period. From there he goes on to a
series of ruminations about doctrine. He acknowledges the dangers of
no-fault divorce, and he upholds the church's position against abortion.
But the theologian, like the spiritual director just quoted, worries about
putting the church in bed with hard-line fundamentalists:

> Yes, I'm in disagreement with the teachings on birth control. The valid
> insight is that sexuality should be connected to procreation, but the
> point is that not every sexual act need be directed to that aim.
>   Divorce is really a difficult issue. You can't get around it; rules affect

human behavior. To make divorce difficult, while it penalizes the individuals who are affected by it, at the same time it does a service to the larger group by encouraging married couples to try to come to some kind of agreement. It also forces the impression that marriage is not simply a romantic adventure; it's a compact with two people, who will inevitably not quite live up to it but who can manage to stay together and raise their children in a responsible fashion. If you go the route of Protestant churches, you will end up presumably like that where divorce is enormously high, 50 percent of marriages in the United States. That's among Roman Catholics, too, but we shouldn't make it too easy. The problem now with the way the Catholic church has tried to deal with it is that it sees marriage that has been consummated as unbreakable, although you wonder about all the history behind it, Matthew's gospel, etcetera, which has affected it, and you have 50,000 annulments a year in this country, you're saying that there was never legally a marriage. You're also saying to the other party something dishonest. It's a legal thing, but it's also saying something that's not true.[11]

I would go along with the Orthodox church and say that anyone who divorces and wants to remarry in the church must undergo a spiritual time of penance, and the second marriage has to be celebrated in a somber way. It seems cruel, but you have to say that any marriage that fails has to be in some fashion serious. There's got to be some sanction and some upholding of the morals.

I see that abortion, from my reading among Catholics, most Catholics have as much support against abortion as against birth control, but in their hearts most Catholics have far stronger feelings against abortion. I am against abortion but would favor a law in incestuous cases. I think the Catholic church is wise to oppose it, but I think we should disengage from the fundamentalist Christians.

The theologian then turns to the issues surrounding sexual orientation. For him, the question has as much to do with changing cultural habits and lifestyles as it does with sexual practices literally construed. It is the interpretive framework of the church, not just this or that sexual ordinance, that is at odds with contemporary society:

The Catholic church is in a bit of a bind because we've tended to define sexual sin as pleasure, so I think that putting it that way, it's always been a kind of biologically oriented approach to sexuality rather than looking at the relationship. That traditional approach [to homosexuality] has led to a bit of an impasse. The Vatican has spoken with a forked tongue because some of the material has tried to be respectful, and other material

has been poor. To say the orientation is not of itself sinful but neutral
and then to say that the acting out of it leads to some problems is what's
happened. But I don't know what you do because there is a need to up-
hold family life, to encourage people who may be prematurely opting
that they're gay, there's got to be some institutional help. I'd like to
see less activity, but you'll see more because the stuff is out there. I'm
not sure that the Catholic church can say that same-sex partners can
be treated the same as heterosexual partners. I tend to encourage
monogamy and to be very critical of the gay lifestyle (the cruising,
etcetera), but there is a kind of lifestyle that rises among youth.

Another theologian, in his late fifties, also looks at the sexual magisterium as a compound of explicit rules and implicit norms that are unavoidably tied to authority and power. He begins by considering sexual
orientation but quickly takes up the sexual package in its entirety. The
counterculturalism of the church, as expressed in its ethical conservatism, is not off the mark.[12] Yet intransigence is also driven by reasons
of state. Supposedly imperishable principles of right and wrong are over-
grown with institutional tentacles like a gorgeous ruin that cannot be
dislodged:

> The tension [regarding homosexuality] is very serious; it's one example
> of where Roman Catholic teachings are very much out of cultural corre-
> lation. In some cases it's [the tension] out of whack, and that's good be-
> cause it should be critical. In other places it's hanging on to ideals and
> ways of understanding that are outmoded . . . I think it's no secret that
> the Roman Catholic church has a thing on sexuality, and it cannot get
> this subject out of its craw. . . . This is a system that cannot be cracked
> easily. It's in place and has been in place. People will change the ratio-
> nale in order to support the institution; the institution has an in-built
> desire to keep it.
>   That wouldn't be my first answer; my first answer is that sexuality
> is very, very basic. More important than sexuality, even in the church's
> consciousness, is something like the family and the structure of the fam-
> ily with sexuality being part of its continuation, the very biological sub-
> stratum that supports the family. The family is something that's much
> more deep, substantial, and anthropologically constant, something that's
> really fundamental to being a human being, of which the church, there-
> fore, is deeply concerned and of which this sexuality is a part. But it has
> taken over [a lot of other] things . . . it has become a system. There are
> questions of authority here, too, and of change and the fear of change
> and the fear of reversing; these lead into questions of power.

Specific sexual behaviors are flash points, caught between broader changes in lifestyles and the politics of institutional control. The diagnosis recalls the culture wars logic noted earlier: Polarization grows not just out of a confrontation between two diametrically opposite camps but also out of the antagonism between an incremental, relatively nonjudgmental ethic and an unswerving moral absolutism. One man's moderation becomes another's permissiveness. This is a clash not just of positions but also of temperaments and cultures.

5

All Jesuits are trained in moral theology, but only a fraction of them specialize in the subject. Most Jesuits are religious practitioners who are called on to make judgments and provide advice in a variety of circumstances, more like cops on the beat or hot-line counselors than high-powered surgeons or specialists. A good deal of what comes through as a spirit of compromise regarding the sexual magisterium reflects little more than the adjustment of theory in the light of reality and of the general to the particular: run-of-the-mill compassion, common sense. James Kelly (himself a former Jesuit) summarizes the softer side of Catholic practice regarding the church's sexual teaching:

> The moral traditionalism that sparks dissent also leads to organizational innovation. . . . While the normative moral theory of Catholicism emphasizes principles, the actual practice within Catholicism permits moral accommodation through the sacrament of reconciliation. Departures from moral teachings concerning contraception and divorce are either ignored, reinterpreted, or considered as leaving intact core and valued attitudes toward love and sexuality.[13]

But there are instances in which belief itself is at stake, when the credibility of one or another teaching, and perhaps of the whole doctrinal shebang, comes into doubt. Likewise, cases in which the implementation of the rules appears infeasible, even when the rules themselves go unchallenged, are frequently encountered. The moral terrain of Jesuits and former Jesuits would be an essentially weatherless landscape if just about all those who gave credence to doctrine actually followed the church's sexual precepts and if, conversely, most of those who no longer gave their assent had also stopped behaving as if they did. Behavior and belief would coincide in a world defined only by the right and the wrong, the good and the bad.

There are dedicated upholders of the faith, and there are those— some former Jesuits, for example—who have forsaken the faith, its colorful mythology, and most of its moral prescriptions. For both types of men, no serious gap exists between what they believe and how they behave. But there are also sinners: those who accept the moral tenets of Catholicism and the rules established for priestly status yet fail to live up to them. And there are those who, while disagreeing with some or even several doctrinal injunctions, nevertheless maintain a discreet conformity in matters of behavior. Neither type quite escapes the moral trappings of Catholicism.[14]

Take the simplest case first. The most common illustration of a close correspondence between theoretical conviction and active dedication comes from Jesuits, usually older men, who view chastity as the core expression of their sacerdotal identity and commitment to service. Attitudes toward the role of celibacy will be examined in detail in the next chapter. Here it is enough to illustrate the tie-in between commitment to celibacy as a discipline and adherence to doctrinal orthodoxy.

"Celibacy for me is an experience of being gripped by the Spirit, the Kingdom, and made incapable of marriage," a sixty-seven-year-old professor of theology observes. No qualms arise about either the theological or the practical justifications of celibacy as the sine qua non of priesthood. Mysticism and sublimation reinforce each other:

> I have been in love before and after being a Jesuit but never seriously tempted to leave the Society and get married. I am convinced that God wants me to live and die a Jesuit, giving my energies to serve God's people as a whole rather than the intimate circle of a family. In this sense celibacy is liberating.
>
> Sexuality is a powerful force, energizing me to become sensitive to others and their feelings and enabling me to communicate effectively. Part of this energy also gets channeled into productive teaching and writing.

As a vow, chastity is sacred; as a discipline, celibacy is functional. Nevertheless, a sense of duty and of pride in celibacy cannot be equated with uncritical acceptance of the magisterium. In contrast to the neoconservative zeal of some younger Jesuits, the theologian is representative of older Jesuits whose loyalty to the mission of the church is tempered by interpretive tenderness and discretion in implementation:

On moral and sexual issues, my thinking, along with that of most moral theologians, has shifted to put more importance on the personal elements of responsibility—sufficient reflection and full consent of the will—while relativizing past teaching about objective morality. We recognize the cultural conditioning of much moral teaching of the church. We are more reluctant to accuse others of mortal sin or to assign them to hell. We put far more stress on the fundamental option and the importance of love in Christian morality.

The nuanced commitment of this older theologian is typical of Jesuits who came through the 1960s and remained loyal to their vows. Even his conservatism is relativized. Tradition is now understood as a fabricated legacy, a culturally conditioned product, even as it applies to areas such as sexuality.

A look at the opposite case, in which men claim to turn away completely from the church, is instructive because it too reveals a less than absolute escape. All-out reversals of basic allegiance are rare even among former Jesuits, but they do occur. One man, fifty-nine at the time of his response, who left in 1964 after eight years in the Society recalls that he was a complete conservative on moral and sexual issues when he entered the Jesuits but has since styled himself an extreme liberal on such matters. "I'm now an atheist," he claims, "have been since 1967." He continues in a Nietzschean vein:

> I oppose all religious philosophies. I wanted to become a priest out of youthful idealism and ignorance. I possessed the typical barbaric emotions of youth—idealism and savagery go together. The Society has remained in the Dark Ages philosophically—mysticism, anti-capitalism. . . .
>
> I reject the term "spiritual." My morality is based on *this* life and *this* earth. Materiality is the only reality. Celibacy and all forms of self-denial are parts of the altruist-sacrificial morality I reject. Things which *add* to the life of a rational human being are *good* (sex, productive work, knowledge, pride . . .). Things which *take away* from the life of a rational human being are evil (poverty, chastity, obedience . . .). Obedience is the worst, where you give up your own mind and judgment.

Interestingly, this man, who makes a living teaching English to down-and-out immigrants, has not shaken off his idealism. His worldview has flip-flopped, but he still talks in terms of principles. There are cynics and skeptics, but very few utter amoralists among Jesuits and former Jesuits.

So, even the "simple" cases—the career celibate who applies sexual

teachings gingerly, when he does not bend them, and the ardently god-
less former Jesuit who takes a principled stand against superstition—are
not straightforward. More common than these are the incongruous
ones: men whose behavior does not live up to their beliefs or for whom
the connection between belief and behavior is muddled. Consider the
fifty-nine-year-old Jesuit who confesses,

> I have had a series of relationships, some aberrational, some very
> healthy. I have hurt people I loved most. Our training was sinfully lack-
> ing in honesty. We were preached a "Jesus will fill the hole" spirituality,
> and for the most part this charism is not realized in the men I've known,
> nor in me. . . . My experience of Jesuits is that most of the practice of
> celibacy is for the sake of the kingdom, that is, in order to do ministry,
> than out of an intense, satisfying, intimate relationship with God in
> Jesus, though sometimes these overlap.

Here the mystic link to the divine through prayer has snapped or is
stretched to the breaking point, and sexual transgression forms a recur-
rent pattern. But there is not much evidence of a rejection of the sexual
magisterium itself. The sense of guilt over broken vows is manifest. Behavior has gone awry, but the belief system stays intact.

The mirror image of this position is sharp criticism of, yet everyday
patience with, many elements of the sexual magisterium and the church
hierarchy. There is little hint of deviant behavior. This orientation
amounts to "critical support" of a belief system, particularly as it relates
to the discipline of celibacy and the hierarchy associated with it, that is
in need of an overhaul. In the words of a forty-two-year-old theologian,

> I think that [celibate] system is going to crash. It's in the process of
> crashing. It's going to take a long time to unfold because of the church's
> resistance to it. There're real things in the church, real tendencies in
> Roman Catholicism, towards control. I suppose that's human nature,
> but we've got deep historical roots, and it's hard to let go of that con-
> trol. That system is not working very well. If a man enters the priest-
> hood and tried to work out a vocation this day and age, out of that vi-
> sion of the church with all that control, it is not a very attractive life.

The theologian continues to castigate "the clerical system," characterizing it as a usurpation of ecclesiastical power embedded in age-old suspicion of sexuality:

The collapse of the clerical system and the collapse of the control over sexuality are intimately connected. I would relate them to an even larger issue: the emergence of historical mindedness and of a consciousness of freedom, the emergence of the individual. . . . But I think sexuality has a big part in it. What the control and guilt allow you to do is to create an organization that has an incredible uniformity throughout, and you kind of know who you are. There's a clarity there. Having that kind of clarity is very attractive; that's the totalitarian instinct. . . . What you run into is all the cul-de-sacs of the religious life, the priesthood, that this is just an unhappy life.

Having arrived at a dead end, pacing as if in a sealed room, the Jesuit comes to an exit that amounts to a fresh understanding of what the vows are about:

I think this is Ignatius's great insight, and this is what I discovered in therapy. . . . Celibacy can be a real freedom, a setting free. Of course, that's our theory, our ideology, that we do this in order to be set free to love.

This conviction, close to the classic belief that celibacy unshackles the priest for a life of service, provides a spark of hope. The theologian has undergone revival. From there, commitment entails the challenge of putting up with a tortuous short run on the hunch that prospects in the longer term are brighter:

You're never going to get that genie back in the bottle. The fact is the church is in history now in a very powerful way. Whatever else gets held up by the present dispensation trying to hold on to an old Catholic version is not going to last. It isn't going to last because the church is in history, and the tides of history are turning. What's it going to look like two or three generations down the road? I don't know, but I'm willing to be part of a generation that's a transition generation.

In fact, the short run, rather than being a mere purgatory, turns out not to be all bad. The alternative, caving in to the fashions of the times, would be even worse:

John Paul II is really right on this, that there's a lot of modernity to be distrusted, and there's a lot about secularism that's been disastrous. There is something to his notion of a culture of death. . . . I think the last thing we ought to do is baptize everything that's going on in our

own culture. Look at our culture and ask yourself, "Does this culture
have sexuality figured out?" A culture that's having one and a half million abortions a year hasn't figured out sexuality. A culture that has the
incidence of child abuse and the violence and the images on the media—
that's a mess. John Paul II isn't wrong about that. What I think he's
wrong about is that you can't just control people through the old mechanisms of shame.

At the end of the day, the theologian opts for a discrete solidarity with
the church, reserving his right to disagree, quietly, on selected doctrines.
The idea of distinctions and gradations among sexual behaviors is crucial to his argument, as is the notion that sexual issues are not as important to the emerging Catholic worldview as they were in earlier
times:

> Across the board on sexual issues, the tradition is much more open to
> other interpretations, multiple interpretations, than some people would
> say. . . . [But] I'm not going to take on some of this stuff in a bitter pub-
> lic fight because I don't think that's our best way of dealing with the
> stuff. I'm not going to try and shame the local bishop or John Paul II or
> play out some of this stuff in a public forum, but at the same time I'm
> not going to be dishonest. I think that the basic Catholic insight about
> sexuality is that sexuality is to be put at the service of love, and these in-
> stinctual energies need to be integrated. I don't think most people would
> agree with just acting out sexual impulses. Does that mean that you toe
> the line in terms of all those other issues, such as birth control? I think
> there's a big difference between artificial birth control and abortion.
> Earlier it was as if you were going to get into heaven or not based on
> whether you had committed a mortal sin over against a larger sense of
> what does it mean to be a human being with this freedom in creating
> a world.
>   The whole issue of justice is part of this shift, the sea-change. There
> are huge issues of justice far more relevant than what fantasies I had last
> night.

The dead end has given way to hope. A juridical reading of the sexual magisterium has given way to a psychology of motivations ("these
instinctual energies need to be integrated"), to a feel for gradations
("there's a big difference between artificial birth control and abortion"),
and to an embrace of the church's social justice agenda as a collective
program for overcoming tortured, self-centered sexuality. But the the-

ologian is also perched on a fence, scanning an open-ended future, without inevitabilities:

> I am open to women priests and the whole possibility of change; I don't find any of that bizarre. The thing that's probably hardest to think is that three centuries from now the Catholic church will look pretty much like it looks now with a celibate male clergy and everything centralized in Rome. . . . That's the most unlikely scenario. . . . In the meantime, do I want to stay a Jesuit and play out my life within these more or less traditional structures that are fairly well-defined by a very clerical and traditional understanding of priesthood? There's some discomfort with that, there's some sadness at missed opportunities. I feel sad about the past twenty years largely because of missed opportunities because the church has squandered a lot of the good energy of Vatican II trying to put a chastity belt on itself.

6

Most Jesuits and former Jesuits convey a self-understanding of their transformation on sexual matters that places them to the left of the institutional church. Many of those who leave the Society do so on account of disagreement with the sexual magisterium or because, even if they accept most of its tenets, they cannot live up to the vow of chastity and feel deprived of intimacy; and many, indeed most, of those who stay express reservations about the official line.[15]

Experience and some outright experimentation have engendered a feel for ambiguity and contingency. Jesuits and former Jesuits appear to be similar in this tentative, middle-of-the-road outcome. Where they differ is less in their open-mindedness than in the inclination of some former Jesuits to blast away at orthodoxy. Jesuits typically take a more accommodating tack.

Even here, however, the contrast is not crystal clear. Among Jesuits are men who quarrel with the public stance of the church, mainly in private or in restricted circles, while remaining loyal to their vows and in general to the mission of the church. There are also a few who go through the motions, keeping a low profile on verbal dissent while failing to live up to their vows. Then, too, many former Jesuits have second thoughts about the perils and excesses of sexual liberation. Rejection of the old ways has led a few to complain of perpetual improvisation in ethics and relationships as they steer clear of a return to the certainties of innocence.

A crucial irony remains. Attitudes are one thing, institutional imperatives another. Apart from the difficulty of developing new norms to fill in for discredited rules, compromise on sexual issues flies against the organizational logic of a Catholicism that views sexual prohibitions as beyond repeal. Compassion and forgiveness are possible under the traditional dispensation but not straight-out tolerance. In the eyes of the stalwarts of orthodoxy, inchoate pluralism may be more insidious and corrupting than quitting and leaving. The via media is a false trail.

In sum, two perspectives are evident in the split between the official teaching of the church and the beliefs of Jesuits, and of course former Jesuits, about sexual morality. One is the perpetuation of a compartmentalized culture that does not openly defy juridical prescriptions but that goes its own way. The polite phrase for this strategy is pastoral compassion. The negative term would be internal migration. Bending the rules goes back a long way in Catholicism. But the strategy has almost certainly spread since the 1960s. For conservatives, it raises the specter of a relativism that is scandalous by the standards of the reigning absolutism. For liberals, the problem continues to be repression and hypocrisy.

The second viewpoint may be more divisive. The more progressive Jesuits (and former Jesuits) make themselves out to be on matters of sexual ethics, the angrier they are with the habits of the institutional church and vice versa. There is strong link between where Jesuits (and former Jesuits) stand on sexual ethics and how they feel about the ecclesial hierarchy. Norms about sexuality are bound up with structures of authority.[16]

It is not just a certain sponginess in opinion among religious professionals like the Jesuits that proves bothersome from the standpoint of official policy and that becomes the object of anxiety about relativism. There are also substantive differences between doctrine and opinion, and these differences challenge organizational control. Rather than confront authority, however, such doubts sap its legitimacy. The institutional logic of restorationist Catholicism, together with the remnants of the traditional rule that there are no light matters when it comes to sex, makes temperate "deviation" as much grounds for condemnation as the latter, more openly divergent position. In both cases, dissent is conflated with disloyalty.

CHAPTER FOUR

Sex, Celibacy, and Identity

I quickly discovered that I had fallen head over heels in love with her. This scared the hell out of me since every last one of my best friends had left the priesthood to marry.

I entered as a way to cope with being gay, although that would not have been the way I put it then.

I

The era when sexuality was, in the sly Irish phrasing, "something about hemlines" is just about over among those who take part in Catholic religious life. Discussion of sexuality is more open now, and different views about sexual morality exist alongside official doctrine.[1]

Jesuits are not uniformly conservative in matters of sexual ethics, and former Jesuits are not exactly libertines. Similarly, the correspondence between clerical and lay status and attitudes toward celibacy—the opening theme of this chapter—is far from perfect. A fundamental property of attitudes regarding celibacy is that Jesuits themselves are divided, and a few are indifferent, about its significance and usefulness. Some Jesuits, and of course numerous former Jesuits, regard celibacy as dispensable for the priestly vocation, and both express doubt about its religious value in general.

The second topic treated in the following pages is homosexuality. Neither we nor anyone else have firm estimates of how common the orientation might be among Jesuits and other Catholic religious.[2] Nor can we tell for sure how much of the apparent spread of the gay subculture within the Society represents a growth in homosexual numbers or, alternatively, a holding steady of the number of homosexual Jesuits, assuming that heterosexuals today are less likely to enter or stay the course. The demographic outcomes of the differential growth and the differential attrition hypotheses are indistinguishable. And the assumption of lower attrition among homosexual Jesuits is more a surmise than an established trend.

At any rate, in the view of most Jesuits and former Jesuits themselves, homosexual orientation is more visible in the Society of Jesus than it used to be and more salient in religious life than in society at large.[3] Our focus is less on the personal roots of sexual orientation than on the causes and consequences of the ascent of a sexually defined subculture in religious groups like the Jesuits. The emphasis is on the collective manifestations rather than the individual dynamics of the gay subculture in religious life.[4] Why is it so prominent? What functions does it perform?

Answering these questions about the gay subculture in the Society of Jesus depends on our analysis of celibacy. The conventional wisdom in anticlerical quarters has been that celibacy has traditionally served as a cover-up for sexual miscreance, including homosexual behavior. We make a different, counterintuitive claim. It is when the practice of celibacy *loses* its value as a basis of clerical community that homosexual identification gains ground as a sign of priestly identity. The decline of celibacy is itself associated with the erosion of other demarcators of Catholic distinctiveness—with the fading of ethnic subcultures, for example. Along with these changes, the delegitimation of celibacy reveals the moral and cultural fracture that has created a crisis of identity in the priesthood. The gay subculture heals part of this break in the Society of Jesus.

2

In trying to make sense of the opinions volunteered by Jesuits and former Jesuits about celibacy, it is more common to come across misgivings or complaints about the practice than strenuous defenses of it. Part of the imbalance, one Jesuit observed, "stands to reason." Some, mostly older Jesuits are reluctant to hold forth on their personal lives and on what they consider doctrinally settled matters. The sharing of reflections on their spiritual, not to mention their sexual, lives strikes them as absurd, redolent of a 1960s/California hot-tub-and-white-wine ambience rather than a dark mahogany confessional. Others, former Jesuits included, insist that the whole topic has been blown out of proportion.[5]

On the whimsical side, a few Jesuits delight in celibacy and are quite willing to chat about sexuality since both are mysterious and ripe with foibles. The accent is more Chestertonian than Thomist. "I'm so happy as a Jesuit," a brother in his early forties observed, "that I would not give up this life or the freedom that celibacy brings to me." He continues tongue in cheek:

> I'm afraid I'm a nerd at heart. So when other people do radical things to their lives, for good or evil, on the basis of sexual desire, I am left sort of puzzled. My biggest problem with sexuality, frankly, is understanding why it is so important to other people. I get a lot of such people coming to me, telling me about their lives and loves and problems, because I am such a "good listener." The reason I listen is because I haven't the slightest idea what to say!

The next thing to notice, besides the fact that celibacy may be a non-topic for a few Jesuits and former Jesuits, is the split between conservatives and progressives on the matter. The division is of course clearest between former Jesuits (liberal) and Jesuits (less liberal). There is also a complex interaction between age and Jesuit/former Jesuit status. Older former Jesuits—in particular, those who left the Society before the 1980s, before kinder, gentler methods of religious formation set in—carry some very harsh memories of mandatory celibacy, waxing apoplectic about "the diabolical encrustation of hierarchical triumphalism," and they extend their criticism of the practice to "deep disagreement with the magisterium in the area of sexual morality," as one former Jesuit in his seventies contended:

> I am in good company, for the vast majority of Catholics now, sadly, find Rome irrelevant. . . . Who can rationally defend traditional teaching on contraception? Since Augustine, the church has built a house of cards of its doctrine on human sexuality and now is terrified that if any card is removed the whole structure will tumble. . . . Someday, I fear, Catholics will look at Rome as having some quaint nostalgic value, like the guards at Buckingham Palace. The Vatican will just be a splendid museum.[6]

Not all aging former Jesuits are jaundiced radicals, nor are all younger Jesuits full-scale reactionaries. Among younger Jesuits, some polarization exists between hard-liners and experimentalists. In the conservative camp, a certain fraying of patience with what is perceived as a liberal old guard and their epigones can be detected. A youngish canon lawyer betrays the exasperation characteristic of neoconservative Jesuits and indeed of a scattering of men across the ideological spectrum:

> Sometimes I feel *very* different on this spectrum. First, I have not sexu-
> ally acted out since entrance. I certainly struggle with masturbation, of
> course, but I have never engaged in any sexual act with another person
> since the day I entered the novitiate. Perhaps the primary reason for this
> is that I had plenty of sexual escapades in high school and college. Fur-
> ther, I have not frankly *wanted* sexual activity. I've got my friends and
> family to meet my intimacy needs. I have a fantasy life just like any
> other male in his thirties, but it's controlled easily enough. In short,
> for me personally this is all a nonissue, not a suppressed issue, just a
> nonissue.
>
>   I think this puts me in a Jesuit minority. . . . I feel quite alone when
> Jesuits of my generation talk about sex and sexuality. Straights complain
> about being in the minority in the "younger Society" and about being
> held to stricter norms of conduct. Gays want shoulders to cry on as they
> struggle with coming out and are unduly sensitive to any detail of a re-
> sponse which they can interpret as nonacceptance.

A third pattern is no less important than either the relatively tepid defenses of celibacy or the polarization over the issue between Jesuits and former Jesuits. Often, the shades-of-gray perspective on moral theology noted in the last chapter, and about celibacy in particular, glides from an all-or-nothing view of the vow of chastity toward a position that weighs the pros and cons of celibacy and comes up with a conclusion very close to indifference.[7] Devotion to the maturational postulates of developmental psychology has crowded out reliance on timeless precepts.[8] The stance is one of puzzlement rather than hostility toward the practice.

Thus, for example, one factor contributing to doubts about celibacy has less do with whatever cultural stigma are attached to sexual abnegation than with the exigencies of career advancement. As far as ministerial performance goes, celibacy has become just about superfluous. The transformation of the religious job market has undermined the links not only between celibacy and sacerdotal mystique but also between celibacy and professional competence. The increasingly market-driven nature of job searches for Jesuits doesn't punish them for being celibate, but neither does it reward them. There may be some appreciation for the practice as a symbolic witness, even on the part of those who are inclined to view celibates as sexually suspect, but it is not a qualification with which to garnish résumés.[9]

3

In religious life, either-or alternatives regarding celibacy are the extremes of a lumpy spectrum along which about half a dozen intermediate positions can be detected: celibacy as an imitation of Christ and a pathway to salvation; celibacy as part of a fulfilling integration of work and socializing; celibacy as conducive to a rather more specialized, pastoral sensitivity; celibacy as a useful discipline that has become confounded with the priesthood and the exercise of ecclesiastical power; celibacy as an extremely difficult and often damaging discipline that is sometimes honored in the breach; and celibacy as a minor feature of ministry for Jesuits who find most of their emotional sustenance outside the Society of Jesus.[10]

The stalwart defense of the celibate life reflects a vigorous investment of energy in work, often of a kind, like administration and fund-raising, that demands wide and constant social contact. The élan is hearty, athletic, and gregarious, close to what used to be called "masculine Christianity." It is a declaration of commitment often made by older, active Jesuits, like this high school administrator in his late sixties. His is a winding tale of pivotal choices, of command decisions and paths not taken, that have kept a firm identity busy socially as well as professionally. The spiritual and practical rationales of the discipline reinforce each other:

> I had struggled so much over leaving an engagement that it led me to believe more deeply in my choice. I left that behind. I moved ahead. While I still loved her, I did not make any overtures to go back. The goal of the priesthood didn't leave me that room because celibacy was the rule of the church for priests. . . . I've always felt that, if I left the Society for a woman, it would have to be a better one than the one I left. I haven't found that better one.
>
> On top of what I have just said, I believe my vows, maturely taken, remained with me in temptations. To me a vow is a vow, a covenant of permanence. . . . I have found the way of life of the vows peaceful and energizing for my relationships and work.
>
> I have a lot of women friends. I'm close to many, intimate with them, but practice the "affective renunciation" taught me. . . . My deepest

sharing is with some [Jesuits] within, but I have a nun friend who is a
great confidante and guide. I've had three different women direct my
eight-day retreat, and I'm in prayer groups with women. . . . My relationship to women is mature and easy.

I felt my sexuality from adolescence on. It was a fire in my heart in
the college years when I looked ahead at possible celibacy. But now
forty-eight years after the decision to enter, I feel that my sexuality is
alive, active, under control, and it makes me the successful and fulfilled
person I am. The fire has been turned into apostolic work.

This is what-you-see-is-what-you-get plain talk. The tone is four-
square, unabashedly heterosexual, with pride in accomplishment and an
old-fashioned my-word-is-my-bond sense of the vows. There is not a
glimmer of irony in the acknowledgment that a full schedule and a
round of friends make up for what celibacy cannot offer. There may be
a touch of irritation that, with Jesuit numbers down, so few others see
celibacy in a positive light. There is also a glint of a suspicion that those
who break their vows took them immaturely and were wimpish in
forsaking them. But little of this surfaces. Recrimination is kept to a
minimum.

A slightly different perspective is that celibacy is not so much a vehicle
for organizational leadership as a credential that facilitates pastoral
counseling and spiritual direction. The emphasis is on personal relationships and caring more than institution building. The connection between sexual abstinence and emotional proximity is direct and functional. Celibacy pays off in bringing the priest closer to those he works
with. The androgynous manner fosters sexual impartiality. "My celibacy helps me develop a love that people can trust," a vocation director
in his mid-thirties wrote:

> The whole witness of my vowed life enables me to function for people as
> a touchstone of the divine. I'm sure that I've been welcomed or invited
> into the sacred center of the lives of more people because of all three of
> my vows. In some ways, my celibacy has allowed me to touch the lives
> of some married women more intimately precisely because they trust
> my love and care, because of my vow of celibacy. I think that there is an
> eschatological, prophetic witness to all of our vows, and especially our
> celibacy, which helps us minister more effectively to people.

The consciously therapeutic style encourages people to let their hair
down on matters they might be reluctant to talk about with their sexual

partners. It overcomes shyness but refrains from physical intimacy. Though from somewhat different angles, the institutional and interpersonal channels for celibacy share mystical and symbolic overtones, and both see the discipline in instrumental terms as well.

A significant variation on praise for the virtue and utility of celibacy involves admission of occasional failure with belief in the rightness of the code and commitment to it as a liberating discipline. This is equivalent to the combination of sustained belief and uneven behavior noted in the preceding chapter. The road is narrow and not very straight. The problem stems from the difficulty of living chastely without abandoning the ideal.

Jesuits often struggle back from transgression. One sixty-four-year-old wittily considers the good and the bad, with a stress on the positive. He admits that he has slipped up—"I sometimes dealt with my sexuality by sinning"—then goes on to argue that, in the end, celibacy has helped him devote himself to others:

> Was it curiosity or desperation or a throwback to the hunter-gatherer my ancestor once was? I'm not sure. For one thing, I learned more of God's kindness. For another, I was skeptical that, other than through marriage and children, sex was some elixir for personal growth. The biggest pain of celibacy was having to put up with people's projections of their own often bizarre sexuality on you. The biggest advantage, for a run-of-the-mill person like me, was I could care more in terms of time and energy for others than I think I ever would have were I married.

Once past the stalwart defense and the pastoral rationale, we enter a realm where things are probably not what they seem. Sometimes Jesuits work through their crises of affectivity without violating the vow of chastity. Sometimes, after a lapse or two, they recommit themselves to celibacy, as the older Jesuit just quoted did. In other instances, the hint of clandestine sex is strong.

The next case comes close to something in between the first and second alternatives. The one after that looks very much like the third course.

A sixty-six-year-old spiritual director recounts how, at the age of forty-five, after a decade of teaching and towing the line, his life changed:

> I began to say Mass at a nearby convent. I began to do some spiritual direction and retreat work during that time, and one of the people who came to me was a sister from that convent. I quickly discovered that I

had fallen head over heels in love with her. This scared the hell out of me since every last one of my best friends had left the priesthood to marry. At the same time, I had my first true, personally chosen spiritual director to whom I went for help. After I had explained my situation at length, he asked me what seemed like a complete non sequitur. "Do you remember those old guys at ———?" Back in my scholastic years, I had taught at ———, which doubled as a retirement home for Jesuits. The old guys in question were the most petty, nosy, angry, bitter bunch of old bastards ever gathered under one roof. . . . We used to say, "I'll never grow up to be like them." I said it too, but inside I was really scared because I didn't know how they got that way; and if I didn't understand it, I didn't know how to avoid it. So, says I to my spiritual director, "Of course I remember them!" And he to me, "Well then, you have a choice. Either love this woman or wind up like them!"

Two developments converge here: the self-doubt and demoralization that followed on the exodus from the priesthood during the 1970s and the opportunities for personal relationships that had not existed before that time in religious life. The Jesuit came to his decision in consultation with his spiritual director; his change of heart and behavior was not entirely hidden from his colleagues. In addition, the priest worked out a modus vivendi as much through experience as through normative deduction. "Trial and error" is a favorite term among Jesuits, as "nuance" still is:

I knew immediately he had identified precisely what had happened to the old Jesuits—they had no one to love; but I was still afraid to open myself to any real intimacy with a woman. In my mind, and in the mind of most Jesuits in the early '70s, intimacy was not distinguishable from sexual intimacy. And couples who were close, who were spending a lot of time together, were obviously sexually involved. It took me agonizing months to arrive at the possibility of keeping the two separate. I finally asked her to risk a friendship with me; she agreed, and we have been intimate and celibate friends for the last twenty years. This friendship proves to be the most salutary single factor in my life.

This Jesuit appears to have come across a physically neutral ground, with an indefinite sexual charge, where close friendship prevails over erotic urges. He has passed through what seems to have been a period of intense, romantic love toward the discovery and possession of a confidante. The nun and he are close friends; it looks as if she has taken the place of the "best friends who had left . . . to marry."

Hell is conceived of no longer as damnation to fire and brimstone but as the ultimate loneliness of never having loved and being loved in return. This man's problem was not resentment against the dependence and lack of autonomy that afflicted many of his peers but fear of something like the opposite: a self-sufficiency that would leave him isolated. It was a travesty of stoicism that he rejected.[11]

A fifty-seven-year-old Jesuit college professor has followed a bumpier road. He leads a double life. He has remained in the Society but continues to fall off the sexual wagon:

> In high school I went out some, but I did not have any deep love or sexual experiences. I was just starting out in this when I entered the Society, and I did not miss anything at first. In regency I taught in an all-boys high school with no female teachers in it. However, through interschool events—a retreat and a film seminar with a girls' school—I met some women . . . and became a close friend and lover of a sister. This was an exhilarating experience, though fraught with secrecy. I got positive support in this relationship from a Jesuit friend who also had women friends. We tried to define the term "date" in a way that would be acceptable to our way of life. One thing we came up with was activity— it was best, and not threatening to chastity, to make sure some activity was planned—a movie, tennis, bike riding, canoeing, etcetera. This helped, but it didn't always work. There were intimate scenes, which I feel guilty about.

The pattern of companionship and sporadic sexual intimacy has continued through the Jesuit's career. To all appearances, it is equivalent to the option of "the third way," neither marriage nor celibacy, that was much talked about during the 1960s and 1970s and finally forbidden by the general superior of the Jesuits. An informal guideline among Jesuits in positions of responsibility is that once a Jesuit fails to live up to his vow of chastity on a regular basis, "he's on his way out." But the furtive sex continues:

> While in theology and after ordination, I associated with women both in groups and one on one. I usually was fortunate to have one woman friend who was special. Most of the time, but not always, she was known and accepted by my Jesuit community. . . . I think it helps to be open about the fact I see these women for pleasure. I would worry if I was doing, say, spiritual direction and had to get pleasure indirectly or secretly by directing a woman. In my present community . . . both I and another man have long-lasting and close individual women friends,

although we never talk about that with each other. I met my present
friend right after ordination. . . . I have known her for twenty-five years,
six years of which we have lived in the same city. We did not become intimate for over ten years. She is in the convent and content with her vocation. This has been the most workable relationship with a women that
I've had. Others have ended by moving or by our acknowledging that
we can't give one another what we want. But this [one] has lasted despite moving and travel. Although we don't have sexual intercourse, we
do express our love physically and feel guilty about it but also thank
God for small favors. I am in favor of optional celibacy but would probably not get married myself.

Made out for neither marriage nor celibacy, the Jesuit has settled on
an equivocal though not wholly exploitative strategy. He is frank in not
hiding the pleasure he takes in the company of women, though it is unclear how many of his affairs are known to his colleagues. He has maintained at least one long-term relationship with a woman, another religious, who accepts the makeshift arrangement on her own as well as his
terms. The bending of the rules is mutual.

Situations in which a Jesuit engages in sexual activity on the side are
rarely talked about within the order. When extramural flings and affairs
do come up for discussion, the response inclines toward the negative.
From an organizational standpoint, the obvious danger is scandal. Besides, sensitivity has grown about the consequences of sexual escapades
for the civilians who get involved. One Jesuit, a writer in his early fifties,
stresses the damage such behavior does to women:

> Be a Jesuit and have some kind of relationship? I think that's just so self-
> centered. It's like if the woman is there for *you* to fulfill *your* needs. I
> remember being in a sharing group one time, and one Jesuit said he's
> developed this real warm and intimate relationship with a woman and
> how this is helping him to grow and develop, and I just wanted to say,
> "Bullshit!" What about the *woman?* I'm not hearing you say you love
> this woman or how fantastic this woman is. You're talking about what
> it's doing to help *you* grow. Give me a break!

He goes on to emphasize the pain that such episodes foist on women:

> I think it used to be mortal sin would keep me away from this kind
> of thing. Now I think it's a respect for the other person, and so many

women have been hurt through this kind of nonsense with priests. You hear it in confessional, you hear it in counseling. They are even starting support groups for these poor women.

Comments such as these highlight several quandaries regarding chastity. Fidelity to the vow is not only difficult; one assumes that it always has been so. The trouble is that what constitutes infidelity is no longer clear-cut. Ruling out "the third way" is not equivalent to a ringing endorsement of celibacy. The tendency is to cope humanely with individual temptation and transgression rather than to take on its juridical or systemic determinants, which look intractable.[12] Explicit rules go one way, informal norms in various other directions.

The hazards associated with keeping the vow of chastity are analogous to cases of marital infidelity. Couples work out their problems, or one or the other partner or both conceal their sorties, or they sustain a union of convenience, or they go their separate ways. Yet divorce has not undone the institution of marriage. By extension, it can be argued that violations of chastity need not entail the collapse of the priesthood. Unlike marriage, however, taking a priestly vow of chastity involves a vocational commitment and is a step toward a position of institutional authority. Hence, murkiness about celibacy is liable to detract from clerical legitimacy.

Another analogy may be still closer to the mark. Just as uncertainty has infiltrated thinking about sexuality and celibacy among Jesuits and, for that matter, among former Jesuits, so too has an understanding of sexual identity-as-spectrum entered the talk about sexual orientation. Now we are in a position to examine changes such as these.

4

In the decades after Vatican II, Jesuits have struggled with a pair of questions: who they are and what they do. One source of identity among American Jesuits used to be their ethnic origins, mostly Irish or German or Italian, with a scattering of the Eastern European and the occasional French, together with mixtures of these elements. Ethnicity reinforced Catholic distinctiveness vis-à-vis the Protestant mainstream.[13] With assimilation, these traditional badges of belonging lost their luster. The old enclaves lost their standing as outposts of simultaneous attraction and tension before the American way.[14]

In addition, with the social ascent of Catholics, Jesuits began to lose the edge they had forged as specialists in secondary and higher education. Many of the schools retained a Jesuit aura, even though the qualifications of individual Jesuits began to look less competitive relative to those of other candidates judged on merit or promise, and after a while some colleagues began to wonder what "Jesuit identity" signified without a critical mass of Jesuits on the spot. The hold of the Jesuits on the schools began to slip and with it the set of defined roles and guaranteed jobs for members of the Society.

These demographic and institutional developments sapped the Jesuits' sense of corporate identity and purpose. Neither ethnic allegiance nor educational prowess set them apart as conspicuously as they once did.

One other, cultural shift induced anxiety about the meaning and functions of religious life. The search for intimacy that gained momentum in the 1960s and 1970s had reached a point of diminishing returns for many Jesuits by the 1980s and 1990s. The pursuit of autonomy and self-realization did not sustain community. The limits of this journey, poignantly expressed in the longing for the fellowship they remember from their days in the Society, come up time and again among former Jesuits. But disenchantment with individualism was also visible among those who remained. Insofar as personal identity depends on a sense of communal belonging, and insofar as this belonging depends on a stake in corporate mission and accomplishment, Jesuits and some former Jesuits found themselves at a loss for companionship. A solidarity deficit developed.[15]

The fading of the postimmigrant enclaves, the erosion of control over the ministerial infrastructure of the Society, and the outburst of and then the second thoughts about the individualism released by the cultural revolution of the 1960s coincided with a major religious change: the rejection of parts of the sexual magisterium and in particular the drop in support for priestly celibacy. Together, these developments cut into the Jesuits' sense of who they were and what they were about.

Sexual orientation offers a partial demarcator of identity for Jesuits, especially younger Jesuits, now that the old landmarks of social identity have crumbled. It makes up for some of the loss of traditional moral and cultural moorings.[16] The sense of selfhood supplied by homosexual orientation is almost always less than complete, varying from the incidental to the assertive. In the old days, with a few drinks in him, a Jesuit might get his colleagues to join in a chorus of "Ireland Must Be Heaven, for My Mother Came from There," but the intensity of this attachment usually did not survive through the light of dawn. The same goes for the prominence given to sexual orientation. It varies from man to man and over time as well.

Notice, too, that a gay lifestyle is far from being the only countercultural statement available to Jesuits. In different ways, advocacy of the faith-and-justice agenda and neoconservative condemnation of mainstream materialism place men in countercultural orbits; so does engagement with non-Western spiritual practices. In addition to being critiques of the status quo, they are expressions of solidarity; they help supply a bit of the fellow-feeling that ethnic bonds or the values associated with beleaguered, ambitious communities once did. It would be absurd to reduce the content of these perspectives to mere compensation for lost subcultural ties. The point is that, whatever their validity on substantive grounds, they also serve the social function of restoring sentiments of community.

Once the socially and historically contingent nature of countercultures in the Society of Jesus is understood, the risk of trivializing the faith-and-justice movement, say, or the gay enclave as mere manifestations of insecurity over a fraying sense of self is reduced. Anxiety of this sort contributes to but does not exhaust the appeal of countercultures within the order. The clue to the causal puzzle lies in the timing of their rise to prominence. Why now? After all, though the terminology differed, faith-and-justice was on the agenda of Catholicism long before it assumed the proportions of a social movement in the aftermath of Vatican II.[17] By the same token, homosexuality is hardly new to the Catholic clergy, even if its function as a basis of group support has become more visible.

The line of explanation set forth here—that the emergent countercultures help compensate for the erosion of traditional social and moral shibboleths in religious life—takes us beyond accounts based purely on the evolution of ideas. The trick is to account for the popularity, not just the intellectual origins, of once minor undercurrents as well as for the passion that can transform such upwellings into "identities."

The best evidence for our argument is that the timing is right: The countercultures really began to gain ground once the old props of social identity and moral judgment began to collapse. The social dynamic behind the countercultural turn is that, whatever else they do, such networks fill part of a psychic vacuum. Phenomena like the gay counter-culture in religious life are fashions, but they are customized rather than off-the-rack, in large measure because the hand-me-down models are threadbare.

A gay counterculture, then, has replaced a portion of the eclectic mix of provincialism and cosmopolitanism once fortified by traditional sub-cultures. Homosexual orientation provides something of the cultural glue and a touch of adversarial tension with regard to the larger society, as well as a bit of the ambivalence regarding assimilation, that the mi-nority tinge of Catholicism used to offer. Members of the immigrant subcultures did not strike anti-American poses—on the contrary, many Catholics at the time seem to have been superpatriots—but they did feel themselves to be different.[18] A comparably ambivalent mixture of de-tachment from and fascination with the mainstream, of an outsider sen-sibility and attraction to the rewards of inclusion, obtains among gay Jesuits.

Religious groups have to set themselves apart.[19] Activist religious or-ders want to feel that they *make* a difference, and they need to *be* dif-ferent, too, if they are to cohere as communities. Some tension between them and the larger social order seems to be necessary to foster group solidarity. The credibility of one traditional bonding mechanism, celi-bacy, has declined, as has the distinctiveness imparted by ethnicity, and there is less clarity about the corporate direction of the Society of Jesus and less certainty about career lines for its members. Faute de mieux, sexual orientation becomes a mechanism of social identity. Even if it does not contribute to ministerial action, it helps define who some Je-suits are.

It has to be kept in mind that just as ethnic identity was only a par-tial and for many just a minor sign of identity, sexual orientation is vari-ably important as a source of social identity for gay Jesuits. Homosexu-ality may be a defining but rarely a consuming stamp of identity. Only in a few cases is the gay lifestyle advocated as a corrective to the op-pressive conventions of the straight world.[20] Many gay Jesuits them-selves are of two minds about the promotion of a gay subculture.

Moreover, among Jesuits and former Jesuits alike, the recognition that sexual identity may not be hard and fast, that a continuum is in-volved, parallels the belief that sexual behavior is a matter of gradations rather than an either-or judgment. In this respect, sexual orientation of-fers a slippery though still significant hold on group identity.[21]

5

Distrust of institutions was the grand motif of the 1960s and 1970s, and an anti-institutional edge continues to agitate religious adepts under the Catholic hierarchy.[22] Struggles for individual autonomy and intimacy were hallmarks of these decades, and the themes remain current in religious life. What is missing is community. A sense of the fraying of the social fabric has accompanied the priority accorded to self-realization. The paradox of individualism in America is that it ends up in social acceptance and assimilation because it is the dominant ideology. This is its undoing. Individualism is chic; it is also oddly anonymous. Mainstreaming, even in the guise of doing your own thing, jeopardizes subcultural identities.[23]

The partially adversarial, partially assimilative ambience of the gay enclave fulfills some of the same functions that the local subcultures of the past carried out, fostering a modicum of solidarity and rootedness among those at the social margin. And, while Catholic doctrine is not receptive to or even particularly tolerant of gays, the conciliatory atmosphere of Vatican II is pretty accepting of what were once condemned as aberrant or alien lifestyles, and the promotion of a countercultural stance coincides with the church's need to safeguard its own ambiguously countercultural posture after the "updating" and accommodation of the 1960s.[24]

The hypothesis of selective attraction to religious life among gays, drawn in part by the pull of community, does not imply that homosexuals in the Society of Jesus form a homogeneous bloc. Homosexual Jesuits are divided about advancing a gay subculture within the Society. One position favors assimilation in what is taken to be a nonhostile, mostly nonsexualized environment. A second option favors the assertive cultivation of a queer lifestyle among gay Jesuits.

Consider the prudential option. A fifty-three-year-old midwestern Jesuit looks back on the evolution of his sexual awareness, explaining his current reservations about homosexual militancy:

> In my adolescence I discovered my homosexuality. It took several
> decades to become comfortable and accepting of this fact. Life in an
> all-male Society was difficult but manageable. There were numerous in-
> cidents of homosexual "crushes" on Jesuits I lived with. I dealt with my
> sexual orientation, in time, in a therapeutic setting. Over the years I

have rarely referred to myself as "gay." That is basically a political term for me. The various political, social, and cultural issues for gays have not been of much interest to me. I am upset with the church's general lack of understanding of homosexuality and the injustices and stereotypes people in the church have inflicted on homosexuals. [But] over time my homosexuality has simply become one more bit of biographical data of who I am.

A former Jesuit, about the same age (fifty), who left in the early 1970s after just over a decade in the order recounts a tale that also captures the gradualism of an earlier generation:

> Only in recent years have I come to accept myself as gay. The Jesuit years delayed that acceptance—not because Jesuits were homophobic (they weren't at all) but because the Jesuit days reinforced my pattern of submerging my needs to others. It's real easy for an ultrasincere person to fall into this trap, and it can take a long time to escape. The Jesuit years also delayed my "achieving gayness" by taking away a lot of traditional social experiences (college roommates, bars, etc.) of men in their late teens, twenties, and early thirties. In the same way, straight classmates of mine who left the Jesuits after years felt they had a lot of catching up to do in social skills. They had to take "Remedial Dating 101." But most of the barriers I had to facing my gayness were family constructs from my background [emotionally reserved upbringing], so it took me long after my Jesuit days to recognize them and cast them aside.
>
> If being gay impacted on my life as a Jesuit, it was entirely obliquely. I never thought of myself then as gay and certainly never acted on it. Being gay may have made me unconsciously more likely to join a religious order. In recent years, a fifth of the gay men I know seem to be current or former priests and religious.[25] Of course, gays are overrepresented in many other service professions too. But gay considerations played no conscious part in my actions as a Jesuit or in any of my deliberations whether to enter or leave.

Since leaving the Society, this man has engaged in a variety of volunteer services, besides holding down a full-time job, and is active as a lector in his parish and as a member of Dignity, the support group for gay Catholics.[26] Along the way, his advocacy of gay rights has grown, as has his sexual understanding, which he talks about in quasi-therapeutic, cryptospiritual terms:

I've learned that our deepest need is intimacy: the need to know and be known by, appreciate, and be appreciated by another. One of the attractions of sex is that it is the ultimate symbol of intimate, naked vulnerability to each other. Practice may be disappointing, but the symbol remains powerful. Sex may seem an avenue to deepen a relationship but can as easily create barriers of miscommunication. True intimacy doesn't require sexual attraction. Most of our intimate relationships, beginning with our family of origin, don't involve it.

For gay people, the question is a little more complex: Did God make us this way, and how does He expect us to act? . . . As a left-hander I can appreciate too well the crippling effect of a majority society blithely imposing its own, right-handed practices on a minority. I think God intends for gay people to find morally right, loving unions too.

What these men have in common is individual adjustment to their homosexuality. Social acceptance does not mean sexual segregation or the emergence of protective subgroups set apart by sexual orientation. Sometimes the strategy involves tacit acceptance by a handful of peers; in other cases, acceptance involves more widespread but still relatively subdued adjustment. The admission of sexual orientation is forthright but stays clear of collective mobilization or confrontation.

On the other side are assertive, predominantly younger gays who find emotional support in belonging to a subculture within the Society. Today, in deference to the counterattacks that came in the aftermath of the more provocative expressions of collective identity, the ethos they cultivate may be tamer than during the early days of gay pride. But expressions of solidarity come through loud and clear.

The ruminations of a thirty-six-year-old scholastic, finishing his theological studies, on his motives for becoming a Jesuit bear out the importance of the attractions of community and highlight the significance of age bonding. The man also expresses doubts about the viability of community, no matter how much emotional investment is made in it, without ministerial purpose and direction:

Consciously, I entered the Society because I wanted to be associated with the church and her work, and I wanted to live in a religious community. Subsequently, I've also come to realize that issues of "belonging" and sexual identity were tied up with my attraction to the Society. . . . A book about celibacy by Keith Clark was also influential in that it presented celibacy in a way which suggested that I might be able to live it.

So I guess I entered with a combination of idealism, based on my early church experiences, and a measure of personal/sexual longing which I hoped would be fulfilled in the Society. . . .

What I found in the Society was a collection of men, some of whom were extraordinarily generous and deep-hearted, others of whom were practically crazy, and everything in between! I quickly discovered that our sense of mission is the dominant motif in our life and that community often takes a backseat.

Generally speaking, I've found it easier to live in community with at least a few Jesuit peers around my own age. There have been some very graced experiences . . . when one or two of us have "clicked" and have been on the same wavelength. That experience of solidarity and companionship is just what I was looking for in the Society.

The theology student throws into relief connections and tensions between the multiple ideals of celibacy, intimacy, and community. He also acknowledges the drawbacks of the "lavender Mafia" model:

I entered as a way to cope with being gay, although that would not have been the way I put it then. Happily, I've arrived at a much freer sense of self with regard to my sexuality. . . . Celibacy is most difficult when I want to cuddle and be affectionate with someone. I've come to realize that while many of my sexual impulses are purely physical, they can affect me on a deeper, emotional level. I am still learning the extent of the reality that no one person can make me totally happy or satisfy all my needs and wants—and that has indeed been chastening for me, especially if I've developed a crush on a friend or colleague. Masturbation is something I still deal with.

Many of my friends in the Society are also gay—and that has been a mixed bag. The positive end is that I've had the opportunity to be pretty honest about my affective self with many more people than I would have outside the Society. The challenge at times is that some of our communities can have a gay subtext which borders on the stereotypes of that subculture in general: a generally upscale lifestyle and a heightened sense of sensuality that tends to only add to my horniness.

Looking at the phenomenon from inside the Society and from inside the gay subculture within the Society, this man is aware not only of the changes in his personal evolution but also of divided opinion among gay Jesuits themselves about how far to press the boundaries of sexual identity as group belonging.

Another man, who left at age fifty to marry, after thirty-two years in the Society and after several heterosexual encounters over the course of his last two decades in the order, also recognizes the subcultural nature of sexual politics in the Society, adding that he considers it "potentially the most divisive issue for Jesuits in the United States":

> The early '80s were the beginning of gay liberation in the Society—a subculture of gay Jesuits. Some men were pretty obvious, kind of in-your-face. I was under the impression that there was a certain amount of sexual activity among Jesuits, which I found incestuous. That's the death of a religious order.
>
> Formation directors and masters of novices typically dealt with people as individuals but didn't see them as members of a social group. They didn't realize that once you get a critical mass, the group turns over. When you live in a small community of twelve, if you get seven or eight gays, then it's a gay community. The tone is different, the humor.
>
> People are finding that the church is one institution that proclaims a certain tolerance. On the other hand, the church is a surrogate parent. Since these guys couldn't work it out with their own parents, they work it out with an authority figure represented by the church . . . a lot of validation issues.[27]
>
> There's a downside, not just the possible divisiveness. There's also a kind of bourgeois lifestyle. There'll be flowers on the table, a kind of self-indulgence. Everything very nice. I think it's kind of corrupting; there are ways in which that is really demoralizing. I do get the sense that for some guys this is a wonderful refuge. It's a wonderful cover. Some of the young guys who are straight are saying I just don't want to spend my life feeling like they're part of the oppressive hetero majority. "Every victim needs a victimizer, so you guys must be victimizers."

A thirty-year-old who left after eight years in the Society pinpoints the different group dynamics of gays and heterosexuals, reflecting (though he does not refer explicitly to the pattern) the tendency for straights to discuss their sexual activities among themselves less than gays do:

> For the most part it really didn't matter if a Jesuit was gay or straight. Everyone was expected to live the same way, celibate. But there were some differences between the two groups. . . . The gay Jesuits, being a minority in the overall society at large, tended to seek one another out for support as a group in the Society of Jesus. Straight Jesuits were much less likely to network. . . . Often times gay Jesuits were persecuted by religious superiors and by other members of their community, but they

had their network of friends to rely upon in hard times. This was true in my own case. I found that being gay in the Jesuits created some unique problems while at the same time I was given access to a set network not open to straight Jesuits. We all had grown up in a relatively hostile environment . . . so the prejudice and harassment we experienced in the Society were nothing new. The only difference was that we had to actually live in the same house with outright homophobes, we couldn't "go home" and get away from them. This is why the gay networking was so essential to our survival. Once early on in my formation, our provincial gave a speech where he condemned the fact that gay Jesuits would network with one another, but it just forced us to strengthen our ties to one another and keep things even more to ourselves.

Concern about the compartmentalization of the Society along the gay-straight divide is echoed by a thirty-seven-year-old high school teacher:

> The issue of sexual orientation is important in the Society today, I think. Many older Jesuits seem not to be aware of what their orientation is; at least they often show little self-knowledge or acceptance. And many younger Jesuits are gay, certainly a far greater percentage than the population in general, and that has affected the climate of the younger Society. Several of my former Jesuit friends would mention the large number of gay Jesuits and the impact that had on community life as being a big reason they left. As a relatively young Jesuit who is heterosexual, I believe I am in the minority, and that raises questions.

In summary, a realistic account of the role of sexual orientation in the Society of Jesus has to include the multiplicity of motives that men have for joining and remaining in the order as well as the different strategies, both individual and collective, they adopt in coming to terms with their sexuality. "The case would seem to be," a former Jesuit remarked in paraphrasing our formulation, "that homosexuality is both a special instance of change in sexual mores and one that bears in a paradoxical way on the question of building and maintaining a community of celibate men."

The gay subculture in religious orders like the Jesuits appears to be concentrated among, though not restricted to, men in training. These men are comparatively young. Younger Jesuits are more likely to establish friendship and networks outside the Society. For these reasons, how durable gay communities are, beyond the formation years, once men scatter to their assignments (or leave the Society), is hard to estimate. It may be that a disproportionate number of gays in the younger cohorts will make for a predominantly gay Society in the future. This scenario stipulates an above-average retention rate among homosexual Jesuits, an assumption that is defensible but by no means certain.[28]

A second dynamic clouds the forecast. The attraction of religious life as an expression of community among homosexuals does not lead to an institutional equilibrium. One reason for this instability, aside from difficulties posed by the potential for violations of chastity, concerns the difference between community, or solidarity, and ministry. Camaraderie itself is not service or apostolic mission. Gays leave the Society not only because their drive for intimacy may eventually conflict with the vow of chastity. Like other Jesuits, they are faced with the task of finding jobs as an older, Jesuit-controlled system of assignment to mission gives way to the vagaries of the market. If they remain in the Society without forging apostolic roles, the problem of cliquishness will probably be exacerbated. Community may be a partial solution to the limitations of autonomy and intimacy, but it is not self-sustaining in the absence of mission.

6

Jesuits and, even more so, former Jesuits have come to view chastity and sexual orientation, like matters of sexual ethics generally, not as fixed categories but as attitudes and activities on a spectrum. The landmarks of purity and certainty are recognized as social and historical constructs.

Much as the motives for entering the priesthood have narrowed, so too have the sanctifying and strategic—roughly, the mystical and the instrumental—rationales for celibacy dwindled. The reforms of Vatican II made the spiritual bonus of chastity less clear-cut compared to the benefits of married life. Similarly, the practical advantages of celibacy— the ability to devote oneself to others, for example—are not so obvious relative to the competence and availability of lay ministers and relative to the psychic costs of the discipline itself. And celibacy has lost a good deal of its eminence as a precondition for office and power in Catholicism.

Besides the decline of these three dimensions—the spiritual, the ministerial, and the political—the deterioration of a fourth facet of celibacy comes into play: its role as a demarcator of community. The eclipse of the spiritual and apostolic advantages of celibacy has depleted though not quite exhausted its power as a mechanism of cohesion among Jesuits. The theological and practical convictions behind the discipline have receded, and so has its function as a defining property of religious discipleship in community. The diminished status of celibacy as a communal bond presents a particularly difficult problem for religious orders like the Jesuits because of their tradition of living in community, but it also jeopardizes received understandings of the priesthood generally. "The priest's traditional function is unraveling," one commentator has observed:

> The values that supported the medieval ecclesial order have gone . . .
> there is a real and perhaps insoluble conflict between the archaic symbol
> system that is our traditional means of worship and the modern Western
> beliefs and values by which we live.[29]

A significant corollary of this reasoning is an idea that we cannot prove but that is sufficiently counterintuitive yet plausible to merit attention. As the role of celibacy in solidifying group identity has receded, the importance of sexual orientation—that is, of homosexuality—has probably increased in same-sex religious communities. The underlying hypothesis is that both celibacy and countercultural sexual orientation have social functions, setting groups apart from the mainstream. A queer subculture furnishes some of the social distinctiveness once provided in more institutionalized fashion, during the days of immigrant Catholicism, by the observance of celibacy.

The argument is not that sexual orientation does all or even most of the work of group solidarity, anymore than celibacy alone (or ethnic or attachment alone or corporate dedication to apostolic goals alone) guaranteed cohesion in earlier times. That would boil down to a claim that homosexuality is the supreme mechanism of solidarity in the Jesuit order. After all, many Jesuits have formed close friendships in the Society that reveal a hard-earned ability for men to care about one another and to let their emotional guard down without an erotic charge. Our analysis runs counter to the casual slur that celibacy is mainly a cover for or somehow goes with homosexuality.

On the contrary, the idea is that allegiance to a gay subculture in religious life fills some of the vacuum left by the deterioration of subcultural enclaves, erratic corporate direction in apostolic work, and doubts about the utility of celibacy. The gay counterculture in contemporary religious life simulates the ambivalence toward mainstream acceptance generated not so long ago by ethnic loyalties, theological certitude, and adhesion to old-fashioned hierarchies. For some Jesuits, it provides a provisional sense of self.

Doubts about the uses of celibacy, then, probably have something to do with the growing visibility of a gay subculture in the priesthood. To some degree, the camaraderie abetted by the latter makes up for the flagging certainty once associated with the former. We will see that beneath questions of sexual orientation and beneath the wavering image of celibacy lies a set of emerging dilemmas about the spiritual and practical functions of the priesthood in Jesuit life and about some of the core beliefs of Catholicism. Ambiguous sexuality is a sign of clerical uncertainty.

CHAPTER FIVE

Ignatian Spiritualities

My spirituality has moved more toward creation theology—Thomas Berry,
the oneness of the universe and our place in the evolutionary whole. I live
by the ocean. I have a wonderful life. I garden. I have a cat. I am very close
to God.

As I get older, I find myself less church centered. Church can be helpful in
finding and responding to God. But the church is not God. I am more interested in finding who (or what) God is and finding and responding to God
wherever God is found. In this task I find church less helpful these days.

I

Imagine a large-format camera, too heavy to use without a tripod. A
dark cloth is draped over the head of the photographer and the ground
glass at the back of the camera, shielding them from the ambient light,
so that the scene can be framed and brought into focus. The image appears upside down and backward. Flipped and reversed in this way, lines
and colors become abstract, a calm pool of Platonic shapes.

The ponderousness of the apparatus makes for formalism. Portraits
taken with these cameras are liable to make people look solemn. The air
of psychological penetration and fugitive stillness is often astonishing.
Time appears to slow down.

Imagine now a 35-millimeter camera, made to be handheld—a Leica,
for instance. It too is a precision instrument. The difference is that it can
go practically anywhere. Because it is quicker to use, it is well suited to
capturing action. A certain agility is required, though not so much patience as is needed to handle the larger camera properly.

Some of the innovations in spirituality associated with the Jesuits
are analogous to the contrast between big view or studio cameras and
handier instruments modeled after the Leica. Compared to the monastic orders like the Benedictines that came before, the Society of Jesus was

mobile. Jesuits made "the world our house," and in place of a reclusive style of spirituality, the kinetic Jesuits took up the humanist ideal of engagement in the world. They were to be "contemplatives in action"—"practique monkes," as John Donne bitingly called them.[1] Celebrated for their educational accomplishments, missionary exploits, and organizational inventiveness, the Jesuits became a model for many of the activist congregations founded after them.[2]

Another breakthrough was personal rather than institutional. Before Ignatius, it is difficult to make out spiritual guidelines that take differences in temperament into account. Models of the interior life tended to be framed in templatelike terms instead of being individualized or introspective in any modern sense.[3] By and large, medieval religious manuals seem as stilted as morality plays compared to the psychological acuity of Jacobean drama or to the suppleness of spiritual direction in the Ignatian manner. The regimented training—what one Jesuit called the sausage-factory model of religious life—that came to characterize the Society in later years, together with Ignatius's own exhortations toward "corpselike" obedience, obscured the sensitivity to personal variation and unique circumstance that early Jesuit spirituality displayed. Ignatius was, in modern parlance, a good listener.[4]

This dual feature of Jesuit spirituality—the combination of *cura personalis* and adaptability—suited the emerging individualistic culture of Renaissance Europe.[5] It was also, in the years following Vatican II, an approach to spiritual deepening that came in for revival. Preached retreats in which large numbers of participants were handed edifying points to ponder yielded to conversation that privileged the give-and take between the director and retreatant. This was the format preferred by Ignatius and his companions.[6] Attention to personal idiosyncrasies and individual circumstances displaced lockstep devotion as the hallmark of Jesuit spirituality. And because the rediscovery of the Ignatian manner coincided with the vogue of psychological counseling, its popularity soared. The therapeutic turn found legitimacy in religious precedent.

The outcome of this transformation is a spiritual pluralism skeptical of doctrinal formulas and organizational frameworks. Beneath the shifts documented in the following pages—from visions of a tyrannical deity to the embrace of a compassionate savior, from cerebral appreciation of doctrine to more affective spiritualities, from acceptance of a prescribed tradition to the reconnoitering of alternative religious lineages—is an expanding respect for personal journeys, latent in Ignatian spirituality, that stretches and crashes up against the boundaries of Catholicism by the book.

2

Evidence of the variety of spiritual changes among Jesuits and former Jesuits is easy to spot. One popular transformation is the change reported from a cerebral to an affective spirituality: "from something of the intellect to something of the heart," as a seventy-three-year-old Jesuit described his experience, adding that his spiritual outlook was now "more humane, gentler." Not far from the surface here is a dismissal of the austere, rule-bound, spit-and-polish code of religious life that many older Jesuits and former Jesuits knew at firsthand during the years preceding Vatican II.

Another commonplace, especially among former Jesuits who left the Society before the conciliar reforms took hold, is the invidious comparison between "religion" (organized, therefore suspect) and "spirituality" (more voluntaristic, spontaneous, and therefore authentic). Change toward greater personal autonomy overlaps with the heightened appreciation of sentiment over the cerebral. The logic chopping of the old days gets tied in with arid dogmatism and intellectual rigidity.

Often enough, organized religion itself comes in for criticism. "I remember even as a Jesuit," a fifty-two-year-old professor of literature observed, "reading the gospels for the first time [and] being astonished by the difference between what the narratives said and what I had been taught Catholics believed. To study the religious literature of the Hebrews and Christians identifies all the religions organized under their influence as Kafkaesque nightmares." For a few Jesuits and some former ones, the system of vigilance and surveillance that prevailed under the previous dispensation produced a virulent counterreaction: from institutionalized suspicion of individual deviation to a generalized suspicion of institutions. A pervasive distrust of authority replaced a youthful idealism about collective effort. The flip side of reverence for hierarchy meant fetishizing the search for private space.

Not all the changes in spirituality go from the conservative to liberal. "I always suspected," one thirty-seven-year-old Jesuit acidly put it, expressing a view common to his cohort, "that there was something good that happened prior to 1960 in the church." Still, condemnations of an archaic spirituality and a ponderous clerical machinery surface with great frequency.

Another typical movement replaces "complexity" with "simplicity." The heavy flamboyance of a Renaissance Latinity is so much burdensome luggage, a pile of colorful steamer trunks and incomprehensible rigging built for a slower age, in contrast to an assortment of lighter bags and sleeker equipment designed for quick trips. "The idea," a fifty-three-year-old Jesuit noted, "is to keep prayer simple. What happens in prayer is more the doing of the Spirit than mine. This is different from the little-engine-that-could model of my novitiate days."

All the transitions mentioned so far—the skepticism about institutionalized forms of religious affiliation, the thirst for simplicity, the priority assigned to emotion over intellect, and so on—are familiar to observers of the religious scene in the United States.[7] Rather than going against the grain of this broad transformation, the experience of Jesuits and former Jesuits confirms it. If there is any surprise here, it is that men identified with the Counter-Reformation and with the church militant sound so much like enlightened Protestants.

When it comes to such matters as informality in religious observance, for example, ex-Jesuits have on the average moved further along than Jesuits. Yet the difference between them is more of degree than of kind. A sixty-year-old former Jesuit, a social activist whose move to California after leaving the Society was as much symbolic as geographic, notes that his spirituality has become

> less pietistic, with fewer and fewer overt practices or liturgical events, and more grounded in nature and quiet reflection. My spirituality has moved more toward creation theology—Thomas Berry, the oneness of the universe and our place in the evolutionary whole. I live by the ocean. I have a wonderful life. I garden. I have a cat. I am very close to God.[8]

This former Jesuit has devised a de facto syncretism, a homey clutter of ecumenical odds and ends. Yet even Jesuits are more eclectic in their religious practices than they used to be. The emphasis on the virtues of the personal and the experiential all but ensures spiritual customization and the appearance of diversity. The paradoxical uniformity is the reluctance of Jesuits and certainly former Jesuits to conform. It is this polymorphous nature of spiritual change that makes their experience difficult to encapsulate.

3

Once the variety of changes in spiritual outlook is acknowledged, it is worth standing back to consider whether any core dynamics emerge amid the myriad changes. Two patterns stand out.

The most dramatic change is a flight away from a stern, tyrannical deity to one that is comforting, forgiving, less distant, even in some sense intimate. God as implacable judge is the awesome father of childhood, especially of the nightmares of the older men in their youth during the Depression. Noting that he entered the Society with "a largely rosary Catholicism," a sixty-six-year-old Jesuit remembers that he "kept a low profile before God the father whom I saw as unpredictably violent."

This forbidding figure corresponds to depictions of the Old Testament divinity and to the dark side of family life, to its economic and emotional swings, to the father on a binge, threatening mayhem.[9] A fifty-nine-year-old Jesuit hurries through his memories of harsh, arbitrary times ("Certainly God was a stern judge, and Jesus was [just] another name for God") to dwell at length on his growing close to a compassionate God:

> Jesus became a very personal reality for me during the *Exercises* and has remained such. I feel a personal closeness to Jesus as a friend. I think the experience was basically an experience of being loved, and that's been the heart of my spirituality: that God loves me for who I am and not for what I can do or not for how I perform. . . . Like most novices in 1953 I kept the rule and was fairly rigid that way and thought observance was one way to please God as we were taught. . . . Gradually I loosened up; I feel much freer in my relationship with God. . . . Really that was in that first experience with the *Exercises,* but it was a very undigested and primordial experience, and [now it is] something I think I've grown into.

Two things are going on here, aside from the evident blossoming of self-esteem with the passing of a wintry God. As the men grow up, they usually overcome their infantile vision of God as the stern father or ogre of abuse and cultivate a mellower rendition of the deity. Some of this change reflects maturation, a function of the life cycle, and the process is likely to set in regardless of cultural setting or historical epoch. But historical, generational change also seems to be at work. It distinguishes Jesuits and former Jesuits who grew up in preconciliar times and whose image of God is shaded toward the spine chilling from those who came of age in the postwar period and afterward, when a more tender and less punitive, and to some extent feminine, God came to the fore.[10]

Whatever the balance between historical transformation and change over the life cycle, the symbolic vibrations typically turn from hellfire and the God of reproach toward imagery with a powerful resonance of *misericordia* and maternal *pietà*. A fifty-five-year-old Jesuit stresses the emotional impact that such an understanding conveys:

> The past five years . . . have been an especially rich time for me as a contemplative. I have entered into a new relationship with Mary. I do some centering prayer in her presence each day. I have come to appreciate the feminine side of God. I realize much more clearly how delighted God is in the everyday aspects of life. How forgiving God is. How deeply in love God is with everything human.

A thirty-two-year-old Jesuit captures the Christ-oriented spirituality of the younger men, placing it in continuity with more traditional Catholicism:

> I grew up with some of the traditional, devotional piety of the church, and I am grateful for the ways my spirit was nourished through it. The biggest change is that my spirituality is more Christocentric. . . . I relate more now to Jesus as Lord and Teacher, as well as my brother and friend. My spirituality is that of the Second Week of the *Spiritual Exercises*, trying to know and love Jesus better, so as to follow him more closely.[11]

God the Father has become the least popular manifestation of the deity, certainly among former Jesuits and probably among Jesuits themselves. When this transformation is set alongside the enhanced appreciation of the Son and the Holy Spirit that emerges among Jesuits and former Jesuits alike, it is a safe bet that the movement implies a rebuke to authority seen as arbitrary or illegitimate. The decline of the gruff father; the rise of talk of Jesus as a brother, humane, dependable, and almost always on call; and characterizations of the third person of the Trinity as a free spirit flitting about the battlements of the church add up to criticisms of authoritarian remoteness and caprice. "My earliest Jesuit spirituality was Trinitarian," a sixty-one-year-old Jesuit observed:

> In the last few years I have grown more Christocentric, especially as the God we call "Father" becomes for me more baffling, mysterious, and in

many ways unknowable. The last few years, I more and more think of
Christ as an older brother.

By contrast, for some relatively more conservative younger Jesuits,
the fascination with Jesus serves as a path, an accessible approach, on a
nearly human scale, to a higher, distant authority:

> Jesus Christ is my one great love. I am his without reservation. Every
> time I put "SJ" after my name I am proud to make my identity one
> with his. Slowly he is leading me to the Father, or what I call the God
> beyond.

Former Jesuits are in accord with Jesuits in downplaying God as a
fearsome paternal figure. Where they diverge is in their treatment of God
the Son. Among most Jesuits themselves, Jesus remains a central figure.
"I have grown tremendously in intimacy with Christ as a Jesuit," a
thirty-five-year-old Jesuit stated:

> When I entered the Society, I felt very connected to God as Father and
> God as Spirit, but as I moved through the Second Week of the *Exercises,*
> the person of Jesus felt like a stranger to me that I was just getting to
> know for the first time.

This alertness to the sacredness of creation—the knack for "finding
God in all things," throughout creation—sticks with many former Jesuits as well. What some of them leave behind is the Christ-centered
emphasis, the conviction that Jesus is Christ. Jesus is the plumb line in
the incarnational field of Ignatian spirituality. For most of those who remain, there appears to be something unfocused in a Christian ethos
without a divine Christ. For some who have departed, the person of
Jesus as Christ tends to be figurative, an enormously appealing metaphor of the divine in all of nature, including human nature, or perhaps
the supreme expression of humanitarianism. Belief in the divinity of
Jesus thins out.[12]

Like the transformation taken up next—the shift from clinging to
fixed beliefs toward a kind of discriminating fluidity—the significance
of Jesus as a divine figure is not an either-or, categorical construct. Even
among Jesuits themselves, there is something of what might be called a
high Christology and a low Christology.[13] The difference is that some
former Jesuits have moved farther along this sliding scale toward the loss
of belief in redemption through a divinized Jesus.

4

Another major shift in spirituality seems less sharply defined than the movement away from the God of dread and reprobation. This is partly because it runs counter to the movement from the complex to the simple and partly because the trend itself mirrors shades of gray. The change-over accords priority to a feel for ambiguity, in comparison to the moral rigidity and theological polarization that most Jesuits and former Jesuits claim to have abandoned. It pits a nonjudgmental religiosity against the implacable tenets of a Grand Inquisitor. Absolutes are out; ambiguity is in.

This newfound tolerance sets itself against dogmatism and against what the men designate as "perfectionism." In the eyes of most of those who claim to have given up on it, the marathon pursuit of a transcendent ideal turns into a grotesque ambition—"religious capitalism," as one man put it—a parody of the importance of "works" over "faith." A seventy-five-year-old former Jesuit captures this rejection of the superhuman code of the Society he left in the studiously relaxed manner typical of men of his cohort who dropped out:

> I wish the Jesuits had broadened their approach to spirituality to include the arts, yoga, nature, etcetera. I always felt that our asceticism was no better than our psychological basis. We stressed "will" to the exclusion of other important aspects. I now see the advantages of a spirituality of imperfection.

"Happily," one man who has stayed the course, a college professor in his mid-sixties, remarks, "we Jesuits now think of ourselves as a community of sinners called by God."

Like the rejection of a minatory God, the movement away from crisp certainties and solid absolutes is not confined to the younger men, and it often demonstrates subtle connections with traditional beliefs rather than a wholesale dismissal of received wisdom. What falls by the wayside is the paraphernalia of denominational rivalries. Ecumenism and eclecticism are the watchwords. A fifty-nine-year-old professor of theology proclaims an uninhibited reformism. In his view, doctrine resembles what Marxists call "the superstructure," a nearly incidental epiphenomenon on top of passions and experiences that make up a common religious source.[14] He delivers a paean to ecumenism:

Outside right now the image is not great, not only [on account of] the
pedophilia thing but [also because of] the exclusion of women. Those
are issues where I would be on the opposite side of the question from
the pope. I think we should ordain women. I feel a kind of freedom in
that regard.

I am not more theocentric or Christocentric; I'm more Trinitarian,
but certainly Jesus is the focus for me. . . . My prayer is often to the Father, to the Son, and to the Spirit. The Spirit is very important to me,
which I understand as the Spirit of Jesus, the Spirit of Jesus which leads
me through Jesus to the Father in a Trinitarian sense. I not only see the
Spirit working in other religious traditions, I teach that. That's the way
I experience the Spirit, through Jesus. . . . We don't have any control of
the Spirit; Jesus didn't try to control the Spirit. The Spirit lives in other
religious traditions. I think like Cardinal Newman said, "there's no
people that has been denied a revelation from God." Every legitimate
quest for truth and for goodness and for beauty is a revelation of God,
and the Spirit is at work. I think what William James said on the varieties of religious experience is quite true; you look at the conduct and
you look at the ethical concerns, and you look at the contemplative or
prayer-type concerns, and most religions are very similar. Where they
tend to diverge is in doctrine, how they articulate intellectually.

A fifty-nine-year-old former Jesuit takes this openness still further.
Like many of his peers and former colleagues, he stresses that his journey has incorporated a conversion from the primitive either-ors of youth
to the indulgent temper of maturity. Not only denominational but also
Jesuit/former Jesuit differences seem superficial. He is reluctant to rele-
gate the milieu left behind to the retrograde or simply inferior, and his
is not quite a happily-ever-after story of an unimpeded opening toward
the light. A touch of melancholy enters toward the end. Branching out
on one's own and reaching toward an American brand of gnosticism has
brought reasonable satisfaction, but there has been some loss as well.

The former Jesuit begins with an almost excruciatingly fair-minded
overview of his spiritual development in balance with the experiences of
his former companions:

> I believe my spirituality is more eclectic, more free of the bonds of "reli-
> gion" and more open to finding inspiration and a relationship to my
> God outside the normal styles of worship or prayer. However, I also be-
> lieve that those who remained Jesuits may have had the same type of
> spiritual experiences. I believe a person's early spirituality requires rules
> and guidelines in order to understand a body of knowledge and appreci-

ate the direction of spirituality. That is the early experience of religion as the protector of a formal religious belief and the historical archive of history and its single line of evolution.

All this is by way of exordium to the main story. It is a tale of development away from bureaucratic manipulation and into the warmth of family life and a discovery of the wisdom not of tradition but of a younger generation. Almost until the end, the path is an ascent toward unblemished happiness:

> As I tried to raise my children to spirituality, I found that the process of education within the church seems to be built on the premise that control of the mind and freezing it in that early stage of development is "spirituality." Fortunately, our children accepted some of the historical stuff but then moved on to other forms of spirituality and values and norms by which to lead their lives. They listened to us and our spirituality as it grew for us in our relationship with each other and them, and they were able to reach a higher level of insight much quicker than either my wife or I had at their age. After several Christmas Eve Masses that were terrible (in our most modern church), my oldest daughter said, "Dad, why don't you say Mass at home? It would be so much better with our friends." My spirituality is more free flowing: I celebrate the breaking of bread in less formal ways. Yet I wish for a meaningful liturgy that shares community. There seem to be no good upper rooms.

The regret that creeps in here comes from the erosion of common bonds and a sense of corporate effort in collectivities larger than the family. Free-flowing autonomy is also ethereal and a bit lonely (the man is a freelance consultant), and there is a premonition of those barely tangible "upper rooms" that exist beyond the presumably lower, less sophisticated but perhaps collectively thicker levels of piety. The faint melancholy reverberates with a tenderness for a sense of belonging, a social spirituality.[15]

A young, thirty-eight-year-old Jesuit in graduate studies expresses different reservations. His difficulty is not with isolation from community (he treasures the company of his fellow Jesuits), and he shows no desire to reconstruct a past of marmoreal verities. "Over the years my spirituality has become less idealistic and more gray," he says:

> I am scandalized less by the human condition and deal with hypocrisy better. My prayer is less regular. My concern for rules is far less. I believe more in the love of God. I now look at the main religious mystery

as not being Trinity or Incarnation but death and pain. I no longer believe that I will reason out the answers.

The note is one of big mysteries and partial truths. The focus is at least
as much on the puzzle of suffering and of awe before the ways of God as
on self-realization. The young Jesuit shies away from ambitious theologizing. The hope of piecemeal affection dominates aspirations toward
system building. The idea is to relax a bit and enjoy life's small en-
chantments. In the words of a forty-five-year-old Jesuit,

> Becoming our truest self should be liberating and exhilarating. I used to
> believe [that] being a really good Christian meant suffering and doing
> really hard things and experiencing life as hard. There will be crosses in
> our Christian lives. We shouldn't be out there shopping for the biggest
> and heaviest ones.

Indifference to theological niceties might amount to nothing more
than a bland incrementalism but for the tendency to associate a lower-
ing of the intellectual stakes with an increase in emotional ardor. A
sixty-four-year-old Jesuit, denying that he has made progress in coming
to terms intellectually with his faith, shows a degree of self-acceptance
that stops short of complacence. Modest affection rather than intellectual ambition suffuses his remarks.

> I don't think I understand my spirituality a lot better now than when I
> was young. I think it's there, it feeds me, it holds me up. I've made peace
> with the fact that I don't seem to be able to be as sure of it as others
> sound. I like communal liturgies, I like mixed liturgies, I like the parish
> scene. I'm not big on the sacrament of reconciliation. I learned to like
> directed retreats, but only with a woman director. God must have had
> a hard time being my friend, so I have a lot of gratitude in my heart.

A sixty-eight-year-old former Jesuit and retired college professor emphasizes even more his transition to the comforts of a religious faith
founded on affective support. Now his spirituality is

> more dominated by God as Wholly Mysterious Love whom I struggle to
> trust and imitate. Our main union with the Divine is in all our genuine
> human loving and being loved. I follow the Catholic feminist stress on
> elements of embodiedness (especially the emotions) and mutuality in the
> best love. It centers on my experience and struggle and treasuring in lov-

ing and being loved by those in various contact with me: wife, daughter, grandchildren, students, colleagues, fellow AA members, other friends.

Hesitancy to push the doctrinal side of Catholicism comes through in a minihistory of spiritual development provided by a sixty-five-year-old Jesuit who teaches theology on the East Coast. "This is not easy to describe," he begins, and then goes on to talk of his growing interest in spiritual direction and pastoral, quasi-evangelical approaches, sidestepping confrontational apologetics. These are skills that he has consciously practiced rather than come to spontaneously. He has earned his transfiguration:

> Much of the early instruction in the spiritual life ceased to be very meaningful, and over the years many of the religious practices I once engaged in were dropped. I became much more intrigued by study and prayer that was biblically based. I also spent considerable time in learning how to give the *Spiritual Exercises* of St. Ignatius first to groups, then later to individual retreatants. Regular homily preparation has been a major stimulus for spiritual reading. Authors studied in various courses have also at times been very influential in reconfiguring my sense of God's activity in this world.

A seventy-year-old Jesuit, rector of a retirement community, describes a broadly similar transformation. He attends less to the intellectual fine points of Catholicism than to its emotional riches:

> I became very enthusiastic in the early 1960s when the documents of the Second Vatican Council began to appear. I recall racing to my theology classes with the *New York Times* to read to my students from the front page the latest revision of their textbooks.[16] I expected at the time that the entire church would catch the same fire as I had, but matters actually began to take a downward turn, and after a few years my morale was at an all-time low. Gradually it began to dawn on me that the council was not so much about a new theology but rather about a new Pentecost for the church. The examples of two friends led me to attend a charismatic prayer meeting on campus, and a year later my spiritual life caught on fire. The decision I made about my life at that time will always stand out for me as important a decision as any I have ever made. And it was perhaps the most crucial. Charismatic prayer meetings, which I no longer attend, depress me now with their biblical fundamentalism and conser-

vative agenda, but I know the enthusiasm of those good people. God bless them.

Statements like these are not so much attempts to explain faith, certainly not in theoretical language, as they are efforts to clarify how individuals come to terms with or reject the limitations of official religion. In most instances, a fond awareness of human foibles, a pastoral compassion, subverts or simply displaces doctrinal strictures. The allure of sweet complexity and contrary passions overcomes dogmatic rigor. People who were once stick figures in a theological drama now come alive as rounded characters.

In one way or another, these men highlight the supremacy of the affections over categorical understanding. In the case of former Jesuits, this change frequently involves leaving the church as well as the order, criticizing both (as one seventy-two-year-old former Jesuit furiously did) as a "clerical club trying to monopolize ministry." Jesuits themselves cannot afford to burn bridges. Some, like this sixty-two-year-old college professor, distance themselves from the ecclesiastical apparatus to cultivate their own garden:

> As I get older, I find myself less church centered. Church can be helpful in finding and responding to God. But the church is not God. I am more interested in finding who (or what) God is and finding and responding to God wherever God is found. In this task I find church less helpful these days.

A forty-two-year-old Jesuit expresses a nearly identical skepticism about the workings of the institutional church:

> Dumb battles over birth control, etcetera, miss the great theological issues. . . . God saves people outside Christianity; this is Rahner's anonymous Christian, a brilliant theological move.[17] . . . Does the legal system ever get in the way of justice? Does medicine ever get in the way of health? Art museums in the way of art? We institutionalize certain images of God. The core of my spirituality: God is and God loves. The one thing I can really hang onto . . . is that there is a God, and that God loves us, and God wants us to be life and wants there to be hope.

For both these men, a taste for the mystical-intimate bypasses reverence for ecclesiastical formalism and institutions. They go with their gut. In a pinch, a forty-seven-year-old Jesuit writer asserts, "You have to follow what God wants, regardless of superiors."

This taste for the informal puts the free spirit on a collision course with clerical authority. Ordinarily, however, the strategy is simply to treat the party line with a grain of salt. Tolerance comes down to a détente, a modus operandi of live and let live. Widespread among former Jesuits, the orientation is also common among Jesuits themselves. For all its warts, the institutional church is judged to be serviceable.

On occasion, greater enthusiasm for the ways of officialdom can be detected, especially among some younger Jesuits. The thirty-five-year-old vocation director quoted earlier is as mystical ("I think that my appreciation of the Eucharist is the most distinctively Catholic aspect of my spirituality") as his colleagues. Yet his appreciation for institutional loyalty is keener:

> That, and the sense that I feel obligated to stay in communion with my fellow Catholics by respecting and listening to authority in the church and the Society. I have a strong sense that truth is mediated through these bodies, even if at times it seems that God is drawing straight with crooked lines.

Of the pair of trends we have highlighted, the shunning of a punitive God is the more transparent. The thing rejected, an object of terror, is clear, though there is great variety in spiritual destinations from that point of departure. The passage from granitic dogma to doctrinal tolerance and ecumenism follows close along. But the psychological and institutional consequences of the latter movement are harder to discern. There is some disillusion with the very idea of doctrine, just as there is with institutional authority of any ilk. The affinity of many Jesuits and ex-Jesuits with musicians at play, or artists doodling, is striking. They are spiritual professionals who now seem more at ease or want desperately to be so.

Ambiguity makes for tolerance, not commitment or even coherent opposition. The jam sessions end, the sketches are set aside. Open-endedness implies an insecurity that can be lived with, especially if accompanied by an emotional touch that thrives on the lack of intellectual closure by ignoring it. After all, the problem from which so many Jesuits and former Jesuits have tried to escape was not only a terrifying deity but a chilly stoicism, a hyperbolically male remoteness that treated its convictions much too rigidly.

5

The notion of ambiguity covers a lot among Jesuits and former Jesuits. Compounding this diversity is a movement favoring emotional vulnerability over intellectual rigor. The amplitude of affective and cognitive transformation is so vast that it risks getting lost in its own diffuseness. The pluriform, though not quite amorphous, climate builds on a Jesuit tradition of curiosity—"based on the fact that we're educated in Renaissance humanism," a Jesuit in his mid-sixties added, "and not just (as in many diocesan seminaries) in churchy stuff." It expresses a voracious eclecticism, drawing from a variety of religious sources.[18] Vatican II released a good deal of pent-up ecumenism. This collective cosmopolitanism is an important feature of the postconciliar Jesuit experience. Such eclecticism becomes all the more interesting when it surfaces within individuals themselves. Summarizing his daily routine and then reflecting on his recent experience, a fifty-year-old Jesuit brings in a mélange of practices and influences that amount to a homegrown syncretism. Notice the ideological smorgasbord:

> Prayer is necessary for me. I sit outside every morning for half-hour. It's a prayer of silence: Nothing happens in a satisfying way. Sunday Eucharist in the parish where I help, that's when Christ is most deeply felt.
>
> Since the thirty-day retreat of tertianship, my relationship with the Lord had deepened. I've taken up the examen again. The discernment of spirits has been a major breakthrough.[19] There's a certain aggressiveness to this spirituality. Catholicism: supported by its depth. Zen: notion of nothingness, breathing. Evangelical preaching and its unencumbered spirituality have been a good check on what's essential to faith. Helping with Engaged Encounter, I've learned how to give a homily not based on solitary spirituality.
>
> On abortion I used to be more liberal. I changed after my arrest in a civil action, after the murder of the Salvador Jesuits. The arrest along with many others was a sort of baptism.

Instead of corresponding to an identifiable band along an ideological continuum, this amounts to a patchwork of practical and creedal jump cuts, assembled out of experience, certainly not deduced. It is the equivalent of a spiritual room of one's own.

The men—especially former Jesuits—have moved beyond what they consider the enclosed, ignorant piety of their youth toward a broader sampling of religious traditions. Among Jesuits, it is common for change to take the form of a rediscovery of a less impersonal devotional style, based on the *Spiritual Exercises,* accompanied by skepticism regarding organizational hierarchies and doubts about doctrinal injunctions. When Jesuits claim to be more comfortable and fulfilled in their spiritual lives, they usually mean that they have gotten used to sharing their experiences with a few friends, not that they have a firmer grasp of the theological canon. Finally, tolerance of and curiosity about other religious traditions appears to be more common than extensive experimentation with them.[20]

The balance of attention to inside-versus-outside religious traditions tends to be the reverse among former Jesuits. The older men especially, those who left before the reforms ensuant on Vatican II took hold, have little experience with the renewed format of presenting the *Spiritual Exercises.* Yet several of them remain attached to practices, many of them foreign to traditional Catholicism, that they picked up in the 1960s and 1970s.

Among Jesuits and former Jesuits, then, what prevails is no single or even dominant trajectory of change but instead a multiplicity of paths for which tolerance is the watchword. For all the sense of pluralism and ambiguity, however, most individuals do not mix their spiritual tastes to the point of syncretism. The fifty-year-old Jesuit who incorporates elements of Eastern and evangelical practices is exceptional. More typical is the tendency to favor one or the other spiritual approach—for example, a variety of evangelicalism or some form of Buddhism—but not a random concoction of multiple elements.

Many former Jesuits retain an off-again/on-again attachment to Catholicism. In the words of a fifty-one-year-old,

> I don't go regularly to church, though I welcome receiving communion
> at weddings and funeral masses. The old rituals and language still move
> me. I entertain some loose and sloppy sacramental theories about inner
> grace. I haven't entirely given up on the survival of consciousness,
> though I would agree with Walt Whitman that "it will not be what I
> expect, and it will be more surprising."

It is "the old rituals and language," not the doctrinal theories, that resonate.

Others have moved over to mainstream Protestant denominations. The contours of tradition stay in place in more accommodating form. Still others engage with alternative paths—varieties of evangelical and

Eastern religions, for example. Interest in forms of Buddhist meditation is prominent; its stress on unadorned meditation is respectable in the intellectual and professional circles that most former Jesuits (and Jesuits) inhabit.[21] Evangelical-charismatic alternatives, by contrast, have a down-market tinge. Such options share a highly provisional or intermittent sense of organizational attachment and a penchant for a deintellectualized, stripped-down communion with the transcendental. Both impulses set the men apart from the old world of institutional Jesuit life that prized logic over the expression of emotions and organizational loyalty over personal autonomy.

The exploration of alternative spiritualities by Jesuits as well as former Jesuits cannot be reduced to the flirtation of the jaded with exotic practices. Some of this is bound to be going on. But as one middle-aged Jesuit pointed out with regard to one manifestation of the countercultural appeal,

> This same turn to the East might be defended as one of the oldest things Jesuits have done, for example, back to Valignano, Ricci, and de Nobili. The difference today would be in the shift in rationality and the differing standards for estimating what we are to learn from the East. Interreligious encounter could be a kind of ecclesial resistance, but it is also a perfectly ecclesial post–Vatican II move, repeatedly applauded by church authorities and even by the pope, who as recently as *Fides et Ratio* urged Catholics to learn from India.[22] . . . The Society's newfound interest in interreligious dialogue at the [General] Congregation in 1995 wasn't directly instigated by the North American Jesuits . . . but by the Society in Asia, particularly India—and, as you can guess, this is a rather different Society in many ways, which doesn't engage in dialogue due to the mentality or aim that Americans have when we explore "the East" etcetera.

6

Nearly everything we have said so far about variations in the spirituality of Jesuits and former Jesuits is founded on two suppositions. The before-and-after terminology seems a natural enough way to cast the discussion, for the objective is to figure out how men have changed since entering the Society of Jesus. Implicit in this framework is the notion that the before-after dichotomy sets the boundaries of what has transpired. The second premise is that, no matter how much they change, the men retain some interest in matters of the spirit.

Neither of these assumptions is unreasonable, but they tie up loose ends a bit too peremptorily. For some men, former Jesuits more often than Jesuits themselves, the experience of change looks patchy and discontinuous, more like a disconnected string of volcanic islands that erupt and vanish than a path that is headed somewhere. The experience is one of sporadic epiphanies and abrupt caesurae that appear in an otherwise desultory or simply secular life, in a career that is rewarding and meaningful or less than that on its own terms. The momentary illuminations leave memories to be cherished, with long ellipses in between, rather than lessons or revelations that somehow change the course of life. The learning curve is full of corkscrew turns. There is no sign that one is "on the way to God." There is no plain and simple moral to the story.

So, for example, after making the unexceptionable point that "churchgoing is different from spirituality," a sixty-one-year-old former Jesuit recalls his participation in a get-together of former Jesuits:

> The electricity in the *aula* was palpable, everybody there was touched by the evident hand of the spirit. The feeling was indescribable. Now, whether that occasion was evidence of the presence of the tongues of fire, or a theological dove, or the traditional Third Person of the Blessed Trinity, or simply the shared emotional and spiritual feeling of so many of the faithful, it doesn't make any difference. It was real. And it worked.

The power of happenings like these comes from the experience of solidarity and not from a sense of growth in self-knowledge from which prescriptions for how to live can be read off. It is the amphitheater of collective ritual, more than articulate insight into the self, that resounds. The narrative of the individual self is replete with blank spaces interspersed with occurrences that may just as well represent zigzags and random byways as cumulative steps along an upward trail. It is awareness of the adventitious, momentary connection of fragmented lives with the spectacle of reunion that makes these episodes so piquant.

The message is that genuine ethics resist formal articulation. The skepticism latent in ambiguity, the reasoned moderation, is transformed into mystery and overflowing compassion. Here are the words of a fifty-nine-year-old former Jesuit:

> The greatest spiritual lesson I was ever given in the Jesuits was one I didn't appreciate until years after I left the Jesuits. A Jesuit classmate

whom I saw as dull and childish and irredeemably annoying had for many years only one real friend in the Society, a man so completely his opposite that many of us interpreted his kind actions as a minor martyrdom. This man's kindness persisted through the years to his death in 1991; it included having himself assigned to the same schools, and it ultimately led to a transformation in the work and personality of the "friendless" Jesuit. Reflecting on the life of that good man, an artist and a philosopher, I now know that early on he had found "the least brother" and merely treated him for the rest of his life as though he was Christ. That's all I need to remember about "spirituality" as I enter my sixties, and I still so often forget.

Both of these experiences are epiphanies—the first more clearly than the second perhaps—similar in that they trigger realizations that expand consciousness but that would wither if expressed at length in words. Drawing lessons and codifying rules, analyzing the encounters at length, as if religious experience were a kind of art appreciation, destroys the power of the anecdotes. They are cherished minutiae whose accidental magic resists translation.

Another type of shift entails not only the standard claim that organized religion has lost interest and the further admission that the sense of coherence across time in one's own spiritual development has diminished as well. It is also an admission that the things of the spirit, as understood by most people, no longer matter. This perspective constitutes a flight from what was endured as a suffocating piety or injustice at the hands of religious superiors. In addition, it stands as a rebuke against the competitive sensitivity, the duel of fine feelings, that sometimes sets in among former Jesuits. It is a reaction against the habit of drawing conclusions from the routine and the chaos of everyday life.

Here we have a sixty-two-year-old former Jesuit as *l'homme moyen sensuel,* evidently beyond caring about impressing others with what usually pass as thoughtful remarks:

> When I'm on my deathbed and I have the opportunity, I would probably call for a priest and run everything by him. . . . I sort of believe in that system, but on the other hand I look around and say I've done the things I ought to do, so if this is going to put me in hell, then hell is going to be a pretty crowded place.
>
> I don't really pray. I put in time. Religion doesn't mean very much to me. That doesn't mean that I'm immoral.[23]

In a small number of cases (but perhaps larger than even former Jesuits are willing to admit), this take on the Jesuit experience amounts simply to walking away from it. That part of the man's life recedes and fades away. Elegies for what is gone and forgotten seem forced.

A slightly different dynamic emerges when former Jesuits reminisce. In a group of any size, there are usually a few ready to deflate whatever pretension creeps into the edifying anecdotes provided by others. A studied loutishness rises to challenge the quivering sensitivity and obeisance to healing. At a reunion of former Jesuits on the West Coast, the drink was flowing so freely and the expletives were flying so thickly that one man paused and said, "I'm no prude myself but the Lord would be more present among us if we cleaned up our language." The chief offender went on his knees beside the man and pleaded, "I beg your fucking forgiveness!"

Male banter alternates with halting commentary and tears. The men are like combat veterans, some of whom do not recall having visions or hallucinations in battle or who remain silent about them for fear of releasing the wraiths of memory. They go over the stories and prosaic memories, their own and others', stunned at how comrades remember different parts of the same tale, without pretending to know what they mean. They are in awe of the bits and pieces of memory scattered about as if from a ruined mosaic. "I forget," an older former Jesuit remarked when his turn came to share. "I don't remember a thing."

7

Both former Jesuits (almost by definition) and Jesuits (to a lesser degree) have undergone a certain religious dissociation. In the days before Vatican II, doctrinal orthodoxy and organizational activity disciplined and gave direction to devotional meanderings, and the relative scarcity of alternatives imparted status and provided community support to the priesthood. The us-versus-them style of theological manuals, the round-the-clock energy needed for Jesuit ministries, and the prestige of religious life kept most Jesuits within a complex yet understandable universe. Varied recruits were inducted into a common culture; answers were clear and memorizable.

More apostolates collapsed than is sometimes supposed, and there is a rich oral tradition of subterranean joking about the folly of superiors—"those medieval despots"—under the former system. Religious life was neither wholly predictable nor entirely reasonable. In the end, however, the balance sheet of the life came out in the black. The parts of the clerical system fit together, and the Society retained its mystique.

What happened? The combination of incentives that bolstered individual adherence to corporate purpose has diminished or no longer exists. It is not simply that Jesuits have become more individualistic. Eccentricity thrived in the niches of the inherited hierarchy; "the characters" were familiar and almost all nonthreatening.[24] Rather, religious drives have come to lack the exceptional cohesiveness of idealistic and practical incentives that directed mystical ambitions toward institutionally viable channels of service. Religious dissociation entails the loss of structured outlets for transcendent drives. The landscape of spiritual creativity is not barren, but its architecture has yet to be redesigned and constructed.[25]

The peculiarity of the consecrated life in Catholicism is not the claim of standing toward the top of the religious hierarchy. Vestiges of this pecking order linger, of course. Former priests who seek dispensation from their vows are still branded as petitioners for "reduction to the lay state." However, the real distinctiveness of groups like the Jesuits lies in their insistence on combining multiple ideals that are usually compartmentalized outside religious life. The Society of Jesus aims to provide meaning, fellowship, and work that, its members feel, makes a difference. ("We never just say the words," one Jesuit insists, "or go through the motions; we want *effects.*") Any one of these goals is difficult enough to ensure in isolation. In conjunction, they suggest the pull of a utopian enterprise or, somewhat less grandly, the magnetism of a way of life. It is a rare combination of ingredients under any circumstances.[26]

In recent years, attainment of these ideals in unison has slipped out of reach. The context of Jesuit spirituality has been radically altered. The inherited system of beliefs has been shaken, the ties of community have been stretched thin, and Jesuits barely control ministries bent on going their own way. "The Society of Jesus," one thirty-nine-year-old former Jesuit observed, "seems to have moved from the model of religious community as an army to one as a professional association, à la American Medical Association. Other than for professional reasons, it is not clear why Jesuits remain."

The pursuit of intimacy and emotional satisfaction can be understood as a reaction to the difficulty of providing meaning, comradeship, and a sense of effective corporate mission. The wandering propelled by the collapse of the old monuments and landmarks sometimes proceeds in a miasma of subjectivity and solipsism, as if the dust had still not settled in the aftermath of an enormous demolition.

The imagery of confused stumbling is at odds with depictions of religious life after Vatican II that reduce it to a passage from a uniform tradition to the advent of a new paradigm. A premodern theology of "two planes," with a sempiternal heaven above and a perishable earth below, is supposed to have given way to a unitary, incarnational ethos; mundane existence becomes more than a trial or a fleeting vale of tears. This virtually inevitable, happy outcome does not square with the experience of many Jesuits and former Jesuits.[27]

Once this sort of dichotomous thinking is set aside, the temptation is to render spiritual change as its opposite: a series of idiosyncratic, almost random journeys away from the past. A featureless "individualism," with a pejorative spin, is frequently used as the master label for this centrifugal movement. Loss of respect for authority is often cited as the main accompanying pathology.[28]

Less apocalyptic scenarios can be envisioned, however. "I did decide years ago to see religious pluralism as the providential situation given to us," one Jesuit in his fifties commented,

> the only one there will be in our lifetimes. We could spend our lives figuring out how to get out of it, but I think it better to see it as a source of energy. The God we say we find in all things is the God who moves about in this pluralistic world.

CHAPTER SIX

Eclecticism and Commitment

I find rules and hierarchy irrelevant except in so far as they contribute to one's personal fulfillment. While I remain a member of the church (and other temporal institutions), I only "belong" to myself and to humanity.

I now find great inspiration and meaning and wisdom in the life of Buddha, Zen Buddhism, the I Ching, the Tao Te Ching and the Upanishads. I think of Buddha as the Eastern counterpart to Jesus. I probably follow the Dalai Lama with more interest than I do the pope.

I

Twenty years after Vatican II, the Jesuit historian John O'Malley challenged the idea that the council represented a clean sweep of tradition. Following the new theology propounded by the German Jesuit Karl Rahner, O'Malley began by noting that Vatican II signaled a move away from belief in timeless verities toward an appreciation of historical contingency. The council acknowledged the developmental nature of doctrine and prepared the way for the demystification of absolutes.[1]

O'Malley's second and more novel insight is that in contrast to the confrontational discourse surrounding earlier turning points like the Reformation, the language of Vatican II was remarkably conciliatory. "The 'rhetoric of reproach,'" he observes, "is replaced by a 'rhetoric of congratulation.' The stance is religiously admirable but rhetorically problematic, for it induces a vagueness and indeterminacy into language that deprives it of dramatic force."[2] Trying to update the church without casting aside Catholic tradition or alarming conservatives and bystanders among the faithful produced, along with genuine (and sometimes unanticipated) change, legislative muddle and oracular murk.

O'Malley stresses how open to interpretation the intent and especially the impact of the council were. "Nothing is more characteristic of Vatican II," he argues, "than the breadth of its concerns, never neatly packaged in a central issue."[3] It is not just the texts themselves but the institutional follow-up of the council that are open ended. This is O'Malley's third idea, that the council's theological fuzziness was compounded by shortcomings in organizational consolidation.

O'Malley's diagnosis proved to be prescient. When the reaction to what were perceived as the excesses of Vatican II set in, intermediary and potentially representative organizations like the national conferences of bishops and international synods lost influence. Catholicism went back to being a vast magnificent architecture with terrible acoustics.

The reflections of Jesuits and former Jesuits are shot through with the ambiguity that struck O'Malley in the council documents. The turn from generally conservative to liberal positions is unmistakable. But the shift is just as much in a way of thinking, from the ideational and heroic to the mundane and pragmatic, as it is from right to left.[4] The entire universe of discourse underwent ideological deflation. This is what the respect for gradations signifies: moderation, tentativeness, nuance, low-intensity toleration, a suspicion of grand narratives. Muddle and coping appear to be all.[5]

Or so it would seem. Out of this mellowing of a heroic ideal, there occasionally arises a different identity—or a different set of identities—and renewed dedication to religious life, more on the individual's own terms. Jesuits and former Jesuits are subject to what many of them would call a dialectic—a pair of impulses that are difficult to resolve. The ecumenism fostered by Vatican II has prompted them to explore various religious traditions. At the same time, some of the men are in search not only of diversity but of commitment as well. A few feel drawn toward those in whom they see the person of a God at the margins of human suffering. While this restlessness is easier to spot among Jesuits than former Jesuits, the quest for identity by way of dedication to service goes on in both groups. The drive is to forge a useful belonging, a kind of redemption, in the midst of transiency.

2

There is another aspect of the abandonment of classicism and canonical truths among Jesuits and former Jesuits besides a heightened feel for the contingent. This is the movement from classicism to a latter-day version of romanticism. Unencumbered by traditional constraints, the individual becomes an object of absorbing interest, sometimes to the point of narcissism.[6] More often than not, however, the extravagant style of the

romantic protagonist of literary legend gives way among Jesuits and former Jesuits to a low-key, less rhapsodic manner. Healing becomes a
modest form of redemption.

The resurgence of individualism, we have suggested, is the result of
the breakup of the social supports that once converged in a religion-
saturated environment. The fracturing of this cultural ecosystem altered
the experience of anxiety. In the days of the immigrant church, Catholics
worried about social acceptance; they wanted to assimilate and excel.[7]
Today, many Jesuits and former Jesuits worry about self-acceptance.[8]

The remarks of a fifty-six-year-old novice master capture the lower-
ing of the theological temperature and the focus on incremental psychic
adjustment characteristic of the postclassical mood. Institutional loyalty
and even ideals, understood as possibly immature enthusiasms, take second place to coming to terms with ordinary life. He is like a man who
has walked out of a huge, intimidating cathedral; now he has found a
chapel closer to human scale:

> It occurs to me that in the beginning I was more religious and less spiri-
> tual. I still need the religious. I think I would be dead meat without it.
> But I think "spiritual" has come to mean for me two things: The first
> is that I have come to know more of what I am and also that I have
> learned to be present to and accepting of what I am, both good and bad;
> the second is that I have come to accept what is on my plate each day
> and trust that God can be present to it and work through it even if it is
> just shopping or talking to the mailman or counseling or playing soli-
> taire. I find that I am getting better at the first, and I have prayer times
> when I really just take myself as I am (at least as far as I can see myself
> at the moment) and call God into whatever it is (loving someone, being
> angry at someone, feeling horny and unfulfilled—I often say to God,
> "Hey You, get in here and feel this stuff: feel how wonderful it is or how
> painful and frustrating it is"). When I do this I find I can handle it better
> and be more at peace with it all. The second part I find I'm almost just
> beginning. I still have some pretty big (and pretty vague) ideas of what
> "I *really* ought to be." They dominate me a lot and are very discourag-
> ing. But I am beginning to learn to distrust them and question them.
> Ignatius knew how the bad spirit could torment him with very holy
> ideas. This stuff is very hard to learn in the concrete.

The tone of a fifty-year-old former Jesuit, a systems analyst, is more
forthrightly psychological, but the lesson is similar: Self-acceptance,
combined with a suspicion of idealistic posturing, takes priority. With-

out regret but with some pathos, the analyst traces his evolving taste for pluralism to the collapse of the old moral order and to the absence of any single replacement for it:

> The community which functioned so well in the unreal climate of forma-
> tion fell apart in the face of the new real world which we entered in the
> late 60s. The old paradigm didn't work any more, and we had not found
> a new one. The new world demanded a social context for our endeav-
> ors, but there was no new infrastructure that integrated this with com-
> munity life. I think that many who stayed had a hope that a new para-
> digm would evolve eventually.

The old fantasy of self-contained, impregnable community has dis-solved before "the new real world." Yet this world is not pervasively de-sacralized. It opens up opportunities, some of which could be called re-ligious, where holy restrictions and forbidden things existed before. Drawing on the construct of a hierarchy of needs, widespread in psy-chological circles since the 1960s, according to which a kind of spiritual hunger increases rather than recedes with material abundance, the for-mer Jesuit describes a way of thinking and being that challenges ab-solutes and hierarchy.[9] What changes is the form, not the amount, of re-ligious searching. The tone is more evenhanded than a secularizing, anticlerical rant and, therefore, less vulnerable to attack by a traditional mind-set that equates prosperity with runaway decadence. The man has not abandoned or turned on Catholicism, but he does not give it su-preme allegiance either. The church has become one part of his spiritual tool kit:

> I see spirituality not as a separate, "supernatural" aspect of life but an
> essential part of each individual's evolution as a person. Once an indi-
> vidual has the opportunity for reflection (because his basic survival
> needs are met), his life experiences prompt a metaphysical analysis lead-
> ing to an outlook that goes beyond the material and superficial. In this
> context, the church offers its answers. Other religions and even secular
> philosophies offer different solutions. None of these has absolute validity
> or intrinsic value. The only value is the set of solutions that works for
> each to help the person become the best and most fulfilled individual
> possible and a contributing member of society. Thus I find rules and
> hierarchy irrelevant except insofar as they contribute to one's personal
> fulfillment. While I remain a member of the church (and other temporal
> institutions), I only "belong" to myself and to humanity.[10]

The former Jesuit's remarks are neither euphoric nor nihilistic. Instead, he is a deadpan pluralist. His posture is that of the autonomous individual, the sovereign pragmatist scanning the marketplace of ideas:[11]

> It is not surprising that I look at the church's teaching as just one input into moral issues. I think of rules and authority as an aid to what is ultimately an individual's right and duty to make responsible decisions.
> I am suspicious of absolutes, and I think that ethics are always situational. I do respect the church as a guide and teacher in ethical and social matters but not as an absolute authority. As with many crusading individuals and organizations, I find that the church focuses on certain isolated issues without considering the dynamics of the whole situation (e.g., birth control but not overpopulation).

Individual choice rules. But "individualism" is shorthand for a composite and not altogether consistent trend. The phenomenon is as much an outcome by default, emerging from the collapse of demographic, cultural, and institutional supports that used to buttress corporate purpose and group solidarity, as it is a set of principles. Individualism is not a ready-made identity.[12] Nowhere is this complexity more thoroughly expressed than in the catalog of changes undergone by a fifty-five-year-old Jesuit university administrator:

> I have moved in a variety of ways in the last forty years: (a) from rigid adherence to and minute observation of rules to a recognition of the relative unimportance of most such rules; (b) from relying upon external direction to a more internal self-determination under the guidance of the Spirit; (c) from a very high regard for and overdependence on the official teaching of the Vatican to a place where the Vatican plays a little role in my life; (d) from a high valuation of intellectual doctrine and conceptual insight into God to a more nonconceptual apprehension of God through love and a greater awareness on the vast limitations of the human intellect to attain to a knowledge of God; (e) from a highly imaginative and romantic notion of God to a God who is found in the everyday circumstance and work but beyond the grasp of the senses; (f) from a high evaluation of orthodoxy (being correct) to a high evaluation of charity (being kind); (g) from regarding myself always as being imperfect and less than good if anything remains to be accomplished to being happy with my human if imperfect state and on track and okay if today I am better than last week or last year; (h) from a need to be perfect to a desire to grow; (i) from a view that the job of making myself perfect belonged principally to me to the view that all growth is initiated and car-

ried on by God and is principally his work in me to carry on according to God's own good pleasure; (j) from the need to buy love and earn salvation to a belief in God's unconditional love for me and the reality of grace (as free gift) everywhere; (k) from self-rejection to a real acceptance of myself.

All the antiheroic mantras are here, from skepticism about the workings of the institutional church to disillusionment with airs of grandeur and the pursuit of perfection, culminating in the refrain of self-acceptance. The result is not quite solipsism, however. There is still the belief in a providential world, one in which a personal God intervenes and salvation comes within reach. The outcome is provisional and syncretic. The individual is a cork, happy to be afloat, drifting in the right direction, or so he hopes—not in control but not quite alone.[13]

3

The spiritual life of many of the men who remain Jesuits is no less of a struggle than it is for some of those who leave. Jesuits who are reasonably satisfied with religious life, however, frequently display two characteristics. One is the sense of a developing bond with the figure of Jesus and the image of a compassionate God. Another is involvement with their mission or their work that yields something close to the satisfactions of intimacy. Self-realization is not enough, but neither is abject sacrifice or the immolation of the self.

The story of a sixty-two-year-old Jesuit, now a parish priest after decades as a high school teacher, combines these elements and adds a few new ones. He begins by noting the move, usual among Jesuits of his generation, from formalism to an improvisational spiritual style. He stresses the almost slapdash manner that has come to dominate his prayer life over the years. He does not regret the passing of the monster God of his youth:

> My spirituality over the years? From naive to growing up. My family was strong on rules and regulations (I still have a hard time going through a red light even at some ungodly hour of the morning when no one is around). . . . I followed the rules but never got into the spirit of the Spirit.
>
> Prayer for me now is disorganized, sporadic, and heartfelt. It is a real part of my life, even if it doesn't come in regular hour or half-hour doses. And my spirituality is a strong relationship I have with Jesus,

with his God. I have no Greek need to categorize or understand; I am quite Jewish in my acceptance of what I experience: a loving Father, a forgiving Father, an infinite power, a sinner here who is picked up by the loving, infinite person who is indefinable but is there. I love to think theologically and come to understand parts of Scripture, but my spirituality seems to be getting simpler in the face of it all, not more complex.

Also prominent is the familiar rejection of doctrinal fixities, especially in matters of sexual ethics—"from black and white to a million shades of gray," as the Jesuit puts it. Dogma is irrelevant to this man's work as a parish priest. An affective conversion with collective overtones matters far more. None of this deviates from post-1960s enlightened Catholicism.[14]

The same Jesuit came to realize that he was homosexual. Struggle with the spiritual and social implications of his sexual orientation led not only to emotional release but also to an attachment to marginal people of various sorts. At the heart of his spiritual evolution is a cathexis that went beyond self-absorption toward the development of an identity related to others and drawn toward service. He is attracted more by empathy than ideology to the groups he ministers to because he feels like one of them:[15]

> When I was forty-two or so, I began to believe that I was gay. I wavered between acceptance and rejection of the concept for a couple of years until finally I was talking with another, younger Jesuit who seemed so knowledgeable about homosexuality; I asked him how that was so, and he answered simply that it was because he was gay. I paused not more than ten seconds before I was able to answer, "I am too." I had had no models I could identify with, but he was normal, and his admission permitted me to admit.

Initially, the dawning of a new identity brought on sexual misadventures, and the Jesuit's erotic drive continues to run up against his calling to the priesthood. But recognition of his sexual identity has also opened up reservoirs of compassion. Identification with losers and the despised overcomes self-hatred.[16] Awareness of mutual marginality mitigates the priest's sense of isolation:

> I was once told that the problem with admitting sexually undetermined young men into the Society is that if they finally come to understand that they are gay, they would inevitably experiment with their newfound

awareness. This happened to me, an experience that was particularly wonderful and finally destructive. I decided to leave a job that I had rather than risk the possibility of public exposure.

Today I am not so sure that I have integrated my sexuality into my life. There are too many moments of confusion, too many anxieties, too much jealousy of people that I consider to have developed in a normal way. But it has helped me to be able to relate closely to both men and women, something I had not been able to do well. And another nice thing about all of this is that I certainly have a lot of compassion for people who come to me in confession with sexual sins on their minds. I have come to believe that there is far less sin in our sexual world than a simple, black-and-white rendering of church doctrine would have us believe. Our parish is quite open to gays and gay couples, I have become very active in AIDS work, I know many gays who are happier people because they have come in contact with the kind of theology I teach and preach.

Little by little, a forlorn sensitivity gets inserted into a context of patterned, if slightly eccentric, social relationships. The self finds acceptance and a sense of mission among sinners. Like flags no one bothers to salute, doctrine and opinion flutter off to the side of emotions and identity:

> I am also able to relate on a near-intimate basis with many of the men I work with who are living with AIDS. I am not afraid of close touch, physical touch, which is something so often they lack and so need.

This is not a pristine, stand-alone spirituality, though prayer in the conventional sense takes place. Nor does it involve the application of classroom skills, customarily associated with Jesuits, or for that matter the use of expertise of any easily discernible kind. Spiritual development takes the form of a sensibility that might be free-floating poetry, exquisite and evanescent, were it not mediated through identification with the sufferings of others and through action on behalf of them. What could have remained a refined sorrow culminates in compassionate involvement. The condition sounds like the happiness of intimacy, of silent empathy and unspoken communion, that depends on but is not the same as physical contact:

> Long ago . . . I realized that there are only two things that a parish priest does: respond to the felt needs of the people and lead them to a new

level of religious or spiritual reality that they are not aware of yet, the "unfelt" needs. The former (pastoral work) is inevitable, the latter means "missionary" qualifications and exciting moments of Christian apostolate. For the most part, most of us are involved in the former, as am I. Avery Dulles talked of five or six models of the church.[17] I am very aware that we spend most of our time on his sacramental model, with energy going towards community forming. But I find that working with people living with AIDS gives me a sense of going beyond mere felt needs and sacrament, for there are moments of deep spirituality among these men, and it is a challenge for me to try to help them understand what they are experiencing, without leading them where they are not able to go. And this is true of non-Catholics, and even non-Christians, as well as of the baptized.

The Jesuit acknowledges the limits of his strategy. While he has come a long way from his pre-Jesuit days ("I never had any goals or ideals, except being happy") and from his rule-guided first years as a Jesuit, he does not confuse his customized style of religious dedication with a general program. It works for him, he gets satisfaction out of consoling others, but his pastoral manner may be a bit too polished for a broader audience or for other folks on the margin. Nevertheless, without a sense of identification with some type of outsiders and without the gratification this affords, the will to persist would probably evaporate:

> One thing disturbs me here in this parish: We simply do not respond to the neighborhood we live in. It is downtown skid row, full of druggies, the homeless both men and women, wandering kids with spiked hairdos, the poor, the spiritually unwashed. I don't think I have the energy or ability to reach them, but I sure would support a priest here who could. . . .
>
> Imagine the irony when I discovered that I, who was working for years in one way or another on behalf of the poor, of minorities, of the discriminated against, finally understood that I was one of those discriminated against. This didn't make my work any more zealous, but it sure helped me become more sensitive.

"There's nothing else I can think of," the man concludes, "except that I rather like being a priest, and a Jesuit."

It should be clear that this mode of spirituality draws not on sexual orientation exclusively but on identification with groups that for one reason or another call forth a shock of recognition as well as altruistic commitment. Empathy for homosexuals in the role of outsiders is widespread in the Society, among other reasons, because an appreciable fraction of Jesuits themselves are gay and feel on the fringe for this reason.[18] Similarly, many Jesuits who are turned off by the ways of the ecclesiastical hierarchy and the restorationist program of the papacy look warmly on borderline cases in the social and moral landscape because they feel closer to them than to their own fraternity. They see some of their own doubtful status and repressed dissent reflected back at them through misfits. Customized commitment as identification with peripheral communities often goes hand in hand with alienation from the clericalism of the institutional church. Self-doubt and a failure to fit in, whether with the church and with the social mainstream, are transformed into productive compassion.

A sixty-six-year-old Jesuit expresses this perspective with fervor. Some of the phrasing—the reliance on the "ordinary," the "real," and the like—is gauzy, but the conviction is nevertheless sincere. He talks as if he sees himself as a dedicated layman rather than as an ordained minister with the traditional baggage of clerical status:

> When you use the term "spiritual life" . . . I pick up overtones of "spiritual-life-as-spiritual-practices," which is not my way of looking at it. Let me try it this way. Things which may have been more central to my self-identification in earlier years are less so today, while others have moved more to the center. I am convinced, for example, that we gave much too much focus in earlier years, both in the church and in the Society, to ordained priesthood and too little to our identity in Baptism; my prayer now is that the Lord will keep me closely integrated into the "ordinary" people, where holiness resides and is blessed.

After decades in the priesthood, this Jesuit has lost much of whatever admiration he may have had for clerical bureaucracy. By now he sees himself as a free-spirited populist. The pleasures he gets from his ministry are pastoral—hands-on, people-to-people service. Despite the fact that his work involves giving policy advice and not just therapeutic counseling, he avoids any mention of a strategic calculus. The explanation may be that his consulting activities involve small-scale church programs. He sounds more like a parish priest than most Jesuits would admit to being years ago.

> As a result of the kind of ministry I have been engaged in for twenty-three years (church organizational consultant), I have been brought face to face with more of the unsavory or even evil dimensions of our sinful church than others may face—pomposity, pettiness, venality, fear, de-

ceitfulness, etcetera—but also the incredible transformation that the message of Jesus and the action of his Spirit works in many, many people. The real church is my home. I have worshiped in my local black-white parish as an ordinary parishioner for twenty years. Its people nurture me and ground me.

Formal sacramental action is less central, as are religious "practices," than they had been in earlier years—but frequently much more engaging. To celebrate daily Mass, simply because it's there or expected, is no longer part of my way of thinking. It would be like an every-night-is-sex approach to a marital relationship.

I have been tremendously enriched and supported by the communities I have been privileged to work with or to preside over liturgically. That's a great store of spiritual energy to be transformed into joyful service.

In summary, Jesuits who attain some spiritual balance tend to cultivate two things: an intense relationship with the person of Christ and a feeling of identification with those they serve. The former pertains to the contemplative side, the latter to the apostolic thrust of Jesuit life. Psychic identification is not only a matter of "finding God in all things"; this is something all Jesuits are encouraged to do. It also involves an effort to steady a drifting self in an alien community. Sometimes this identification takes the form of special sensitivity to homosexuals as partial outcasts; in other cases it has more of a social justice connotation or favors simply "the people of God" over against the hierarchical church. In one way or another, the process acts as something of a replacement for the crusades and certainties of the church militant and the sense of being besieged that appeared to come naturally when Catholics formed a minority at the margins of "the new real world."

The balance between the contemplative and ministerial facets of the Jesuit enterprise, expressed through Christ-centered prayer and energies directed toward out-groups in which the Jesuit self finds collective moorings, is tense. The approach is sometimes confounded with an invidious split between the prophetic and the pragmatic. The combination helps sustain perseverance, and by providing a measure of emotional release as well as professional satisfaction, it may help prevent burnout.[19] In addition, the mixture of contemplative focus and apostolic strategy jibes with the Jesuit tradition of *cura personalis*. But it also leaves the door open to amateurism and a contempt for what are taken to be the routine, traditional or heavily institutional ministries of the order, particularly education. And the psychological economy of the motivational mix is such that dedication to the causes of out-groups often carries with it, like a badge of honor, a certain alienation from the clerical establishment. The rhetoric of sacrificial identification with outcasts and adherence to a cause that borders on the righteous stands or falls not on self-awareness and heightened sensitivity but on the capacity to transform psychic wounds and ideology into good works.

4

The equilibrium between devotion to the figure of Christ and dedication to the objects of ministry is delicate because both involve perceptions that may be more or less vivid or elusive. The contemplative side is even harder to pin down than the apostolic, which can at least make claim to a tangible point of reference.

Many Jesuits channel their otherwise inapprehensible yearning for the divine toward the sacramental system of Catholicism, focusing on the Eucharist. Their feeling of intimacy with Christ is tied up with their identity as priests empowered to consecrate. A fifty-seven-year-old retreat director recalls his early experience of such communion:

> One striking event that happened during my two-year novitiate as a Jesuit seminarian was on a day I was assisting a priest who was presiding at Mass. I experienced such a profound longing to give to God what I sensed God deserved; that the goodness of God warranted everything imaginable, everything possible for touching and moving the heart of God so that God knew He had been heard and appreciated and loved, that God had been responded to with the fullness of everything that ever existed; I felt like I was going to explode with this desire to touch God that deeply, to communicate and commune with God this deeply. While kneeling there behind and off to the side of the priest, I had such a strong sense that there is only one avenue possible for human beings who want to communicate that deeply with the Divine, and it is the Eucharist; it is in the action of lifting up to God His Son and everything that is good, every man, woman and child, all of creation in its joys and pains and presenting such to this gracious God. Somehow I intuited the joy of God and the gratitude of God, an intimacy that I have never experienced anywhere else or with anyone else in my entire life.

The tale might be dismissed as a mystical effusion of youth or an experience of what used to be called "the sublime" except that the intimation of Christ in the Eucharist has carried the Jesuit through desperate hours.[20] It is at the core of his sacerdotal identity, and it provides a sense of intimacy or abounding love. The retreat director describes a bleak period he entered while finishing his training overseas. He tells of his identification with the deprived, his sexual turmoil, and the consolidation of his sense of self and the attainment of affective resolution. Doctrinal and intellectual curlicues are absent. What matters are the emotions and their expression as attention to others:

> I met in a three-year-old Filipino boy with polio-stricken legs some part of my unhealed self. I became angry with God and with this boy's parents about his situation. This theme continued into therapy for some months later when I returned to the States. While there in the Philippines, I had a serious pinch of nerves in the upper neck, and it led to partial nerve numbness on the left side of my body. Without anyone able to diagnose the problem for a number of months and with a great loss of weight, I feared I was dying. All of this was combined with a crisis in a relationship with a good woman back in the States. I had come to love her a lot. Upon coming back to the States I told my provincial that I wasn't sure I wanted to continue as a Jesuit. All of these physical and emotional factors precipitated a vocation crisis and left me in a no-man's land of knowing what to do with my life, some days thinking I wanted to leave to marry my friend, other days feeling not so clear.

Until this point, the Jesuit's story might be bracketed as the tale of a psychologically and socially accident-prone neurotic. Misery and domestic worries, all of them painful, none of them lethal, spread around him like broken glass. Then he starts to grow up:

> After a three- to four-month period of not knowing who I was before God and what I wanted to do with the rest of my life, slowly there reemerged the desire to be a Jesuit priest. What emerged as the reference point in my discernment was the unbearable thought of no longer being able to preside as a priest at the Eucharist. I felt that to deny me that would be to rip the soul out of me; to leave the Society would mean that I was no longer me. As I look back on that experience, something I could describe much better in person than in front of a typewriter, I see a great grace given to me by God: a much deeper choice of my identity and my life as a Jesuit than what I was able to do many years earlier in my early twenties. I was much more free, much more my own person at the age of forty-eight than when I was twenty. To have been in that spiritual limbo forced me to choose in a radical way. Going through that dark night opened me up to me an awareness and sensitivities out of

which I minister to this day. It certainly cured a lot of judgmental attitudes in me and made me much more compassionate toward people who go through times of ambiguity and darkness.

The respect for ambiguity and moral distinctions echoes the refrain enunciated by numerous Jesuits and former Jesuits. But a feel for gradations—put differently, a skepticism about doctrinal categories received de haut en bas—is not enough for spiritual fulfillment, though it may be indispensable to a well-tempered maturity. It lacks an affective charge, and there is not much mystery to it. Similarly, attachment to marginalized groups alone, though more important than theological orthodoxy, does not suffice. The retreat director returns to the centrality of the figure of Jesus, not just as an ethical symbol but also as the power behind emotional transfiguration, when he speculates about the factors that contribute to staying with and leaving the Society:

> In the long run Jesuits stay because for the most part they have experienced the friendship of God. Those who stay for healthy reasons, not for fear of insecurity, stay because the friendship of Jesus and the God Jesus reveals makes the decisive difference. In other words, these men have developed to a significant degree the habit of spending some quiet time each day or most days with this divine friend, both in private prayer and in communal prayer, particularly the Eucharist. The inevitable periods or stages of being tested, encountering some failure, suffering, or loneliness cannot be survived with meaning unless that relationship, that friendship, has some depth.

There is something here of the fiery stream, an intuition of passion smashing against mortality, that restores a miraculous, occasional peace powerful enough to stick in memory and to call the man back again:[21]

> Why do some men leave the Society? I suspect that many leave, just as one of my best friends left, because the celibate life was impossible to live. Such people did not have that gift and call, and their experience over a lengthy period of time brought them to that inevitable conclusion. They experienced a longing for a lifelong relationship with a woman; they really wanted to be a father of children. They wanted family and the kind of intimacy that offers. While some seemingly threw away their call, I sense many, maybe most, came in time to an awakening of their deeper self, and that required them, if they were to live in fidelity to God and the true self, to leave the Society and seek a life partner.

Here the search for a sustaining glimpse of God, for an intermittent
mysticism that makes up for the restrictions on human intimacy, is fundamental to overcoming severe doubt and despair.[22] In other cases, the
resolution of spiritual crisis is shakier. No breakthrough occurs. For
some men, desolation is clearly emotional, but the way out is at least
partially intellectual, even if doctrine in the narrow sense plays practically no part.

One Jesuit, a fifty-seven-year-old university professor, describes a
journey in which flagging belief does not quite catch up with his sense
of love for the divine. Meaning—some plausibility and a measure of
hope—rather than intimacy or conviction has been recovered. The rejection of a style of spirituality heavy on prohibitions has cleared the air,
but no full-blown worldview has replaced it. In the absence of a new
cosmology, the Jesuit is grateful for the significant but rather more modest vision formulated by the general congregations, the central gather-
ings, of the order. Hope and meaning, not the transcendence of uncertainty or even the achievement of intimacy, are the keynotes. There are
no large harmonies, no epiphanies:

> I think I have grown, with difficulty, in intimacy with Christ. . . . Up to
> my forty-second birthday I practiced daily contemplation and was ordi-
> narily not without a consoling relation to God. After that point I went
> through a long and major crisis. I lost any sense of God, Christ, church,
> and even of love and friendship. This psychological/spiritual desolation
> lasted more than a year in its most acute sense.
>
> The way back has been slow. Before this crisis, I had read a book by
> John Haught called *Religion and Self-Acceptance,* with the theme that if
> you do really want to know God you should prepare for a period of un-
> belief, vertigo, darkness.[23] He thought that the very horizon from which
> one's questions and beliefs emerge has to be stretched and opened and
> that one need not expect those questions and beliefs to remain calm dur-
> ing that time. I held on to that theory during my crisis. I could no longer
> pray in private, no longer hope that there even was a God who would
> hear. I had an indubitable experience of love for God during this time,
> but when it ended I was back in the middle of unbelief.
>
> Part of my journey through darkness took place during my doctoral
> studies. I went deep into a theology/spirituality of the Trinity in the
> world, especially as related to liturgy. . . . This semi-intellectual basis
> gave me a map for my spiritual life, a new land to let my spirit range
> about in. I am very grateful to Ignatius and his principles of discern-
> ment, his strong sense of what the world looks like when it is right-

side up. Also, the documents from the latest General Congregation give me great hope.

The Jesuit hit bottom and saw no way out. He then came round to investing his emotional longings in the figure of Jesus and to reviving his call as a priest, a man with a special relationship with Christ. This is both ministry and identity. The link between spirituality and action is stripped to its essentials. Finally, through the documents and mission statements of the Society, he comes across a working guide, a "semi-intellectual basis," for his life as a Jesuit. He holds on because of his terrible memories of the alternative—the failing, then extinguished sense of God.

For other men, no resolution of their spiritual striving is at hand. There is neither mystical closeness to the divine nor identification with those to whom Jesuits minister. The gemlike flame burns low. Men like this fifty-three-year-old parish priest, for whom humane endurance is a better description than failure, exhibit a dogged, wry self-acceptance. Jesus is God, but he is not a close friend. The road is an arduous climb. The priest persists:

> Intimacy with Christ is a constant thorn. It is probably my greatest problem today. I am totally aware of God's presence and work in my life. But I'm not aware of God as a close, personal friend. Some of it is my own stubbornness. But I think right now God is just present in my life and not making much of a fuss about it. My prayer is okay, sometimes great, other times not. Sacramental life is spotty. I tend to let work take the lead here, and I don't always make the effort. Ignatian prayer in sacramental life has enabled me to have a positive outlook in homilies. I've faced crises a number of times during my whole priesthood. In the beginning my crises were spectacular. I believe I'm in a crisis now, one called middle age, but I'm seeing it more with open eyes, and I'm not so worried about it. Conversion is an ongoing experience. I've never been struck by lightning. I have brilliant insights here and there, but I've never been thrown from a horse.

5

The deconstruction of creedal absolutes has gone farther among former Jesuits than Jesuits. Yet the magnitude of this change should not obscure two other, qualitative transformations. One is the spiritual eclecticism that flourishes in both camps. Former Jesuits have an edge here, too, but the fact that Jesuits are more apt than former Jesuits to place the person of Christ at the center of their spiritual world scarcely rules out the importation of religious practices once thought exotic, much less the adaptation of a variety of psychological remedies. The syncretism of "the new individualism" is hard to overemphasize.[24]

A second change is also one that distinguishes Jesuits and former Jesuits but, again, not very sharply. It involves a second-guessing of individualism. Jesuits are a bit more likely than former Jesuits to apply the adjective "rampant" to the syndrome. Nevertheless, in gaining personal autonomy with their departure from the Society, many former Jesuits have come to miss the sense of community and corporate purpose that the order gave them. "One of the losses I felt after I left the Jesuits," a sixty-four-year old university professor admits, "was the loss of a larger context with which to place my own life and doings." The downside of spiritual eclecticism has been a fluid solitariness, even if the effect is not always or even usually catastrophic. "This has continued," the former Jesuit goes on coolly, "though without distress."

This same former Jesuit, who now teaches theology to college students, remarks that like most of his colleagues and former colleagues he has become much more open ended regarding the dogmatic legacy of Catholicism. By the standards of a restorationist church, the theologian displays insufficient reverence for authority:

> It is strange, having been through theology, read Rahner, studied the Bible, to try to locate oneself within the church. The church doesn't like people who pick and choose; and yet I see no other way to live my spiritual life. It would be, I think, immoral to do otherwise: If the pope says black is white, the pope is wrong.

Acceptance of the chancy nature of religious exploration stands as a preface to a rough-and-ready philosophy in which rushes of emotion partly make up for the loss of doctrinal certitude:

> My spirituality is not anxious. I go to Mass regularly and am a lector, but I also teach a university course in the Bible as literature, and I am not unaffected by the shifting perceptions engendered by biblical scholarship. . . .
>
> I pray the "Our Father" often or less often, as I am moved or touched by sudden moments of self-perception. My first wife's death caused sudden bursts of angry skepticism; I experienced a kind of materialist "illumination" which made even love seem like a trick played by evolution.

On the other hand, any sudden memory of her would hit me with a lightning bolt of reverence, and I would cross myself. My present wife looks upon her as our guardian angel (my granddaughter was born on her birthday), and I confess that I share a profound hope that she is.

I go to church because I believe in the value of ritual to nourish faith: *lex orandi, lex credendi* [loosely, "praying gets us believing"]. It is also the one place in this repulsive human world where human beings are spoken of with respect. I very much need to be periodically subjected to words of respect for human beings, I am so deeply repelled by almost every thing I read in the newspapers, hear on television and radio.

For this man, the spiritual lessons of experience are indirect and the longing for community understated. His claim that "my spirituality is not anxious" is partially belied by his attachment to collective ritual as a protection against the chaos and cruelty of the world beyond the church. While he has made a settlement with his spiritual craving, he cannot quite go it alone. True to his countercultural ambivalence, he is halfway in, halfway outside the church.

For another former Jesuit, now an attorney, the accent on community is just as countercultural but more forceful and explicit. As a rule, former Jesuits stress "God in relationships" more than a vision of Jesus as divinity. In this case, however, the issue does not concern the theological status of Christ; the main distinction concerns the institutional ramifications of spirituality. The spirit of Ignatius is alive even if its corporate expression in the Society of Jesus has dimmed.

"How has my spirituality changed?" the lawyer asks himself. "I have a stronger belief that the presence of God is found in community. I am much more critical of our cultural bent to find self-actualization by developing autonomy." He goes on to the elevated assertion that "community is only possible when each of us is fully engaged in a passionate embrace of the earth" and then, sensing the danger of grandiosity, draws back to consider the specific instance of reading his father's correspondence:

My father writes about his faith in God's providence, prayer, the Eucharist, example, community, help for others and the simple things of life. It is hard to explain because he doesn't talk about these as abstract concepts, but they emerge in the course of ordinary events in our lives. They are woven into the very pattern of meaning of life. As these concepts suddenly take on flesh, the so-called "Jesuit tradition and way of proceeding" suddenly takes on new meaning. As this process continues,

I find not only more connections with my own vocation, but it also helps me to be more aware of how God's presence is only found in others, enfleshed in their stories and the need to listen and pay attention to these stories. In writing this now I recall how Ignatius said that the best way to find God is to observe the example of others. One of the biggest surprises of the last few years has been how the Ignatian charism has reemerged as an important sense of vocation and call in my life. I've discovered that the Ignatian charism is larger than the Jesuit institution.

The lawyer's perspective is exceptional less because of the separation between the Society of Jesus and the Ignatian tradition—a distinction by now commonplace among Jesuits themselves—than because of his sophistication in not counterpoising "institutions" and "individualism." He gives us a glimpse of the small communities where, he feels, the future of Catholicism lies:

> Community for me now starts with my life companion, my spouse. . . . We share everything and especially our searching in our spiritual journey. . . . Both of us brought to our marriage many experiences of living in communities. Now we are blessed to be able to have an old farmhouse home in the country where we can celebrate family gatherings and invite friends and others for long weekends. For us it is a place of renewal, community, and simplicity. While we are both committed to our respective professions and work goals, it is our home that calls us back to a spirituality of the ordinary everyday events, which keeps us in touch with our best selves.

There is no sweeping theology here. The invocation of simplicity may smack of protesting too much, suggesting an upscale, whole-wheat-and-granola sensibility that makes such an alternative tasteful and attractive, in silent contrast to the old extravagantly sacrificial ethos. Nevertheless, the lawyer's notion of community implies a via media between the antithesis of individuals and institutions as models of spirituality.

Usually, however, when former Jesuits mention community in discussing their spiritual life, the reference is in a minor key, with the ritual warmth of liturgy displacing insistence on the pursuit of intimacy. The tone of this sixty-six-year-old writer and consultant, gone from the Society for nearly twenty years, is casual and commonsensical:

> I feel at peace with a much less formal spiritual agenda and am content to seek God in the developing circumstances of my life. My prayer life retains vital importance for me, though I do not adhere to a definite

schedule. The Sunday liturgy still means much to me, despite my constant dissatisfaction with preaching, music, and other aspects of it, and I take pleasure in association with fellow worshipers.

This is spirituality as consolation and the expression of bonding—with latent consequences, perhaps, for action on behalf of belief or commitment to a cause. The enigmatic, sensual experience of collective worship is primary.

6

There is eclecticism, and there is eclecticism. One former Jesuit, a computer specialist, spends his spare time reading spiritual texts outside the Christian canon. He alludes to dozens of sources from multiple traditions, quoting various writers directly and at length, putting together his own recipe of precepts and apothegms that, paradoxically, rejects the notion of dogma. Even his attitude toward sex might be called bookish. "The main thing," he feels, "is to make sure you have a healthy attitude":

> I'm fifty-one, single, never married, with no current lover, but I agree with Thaddeus Golas, the author of *The Lazy Man's Guide to Enlightenment:* "In truth, a satisfying orgasm is a spiritual realization more than a technical accomplishment. The flesh is not apart from the spirit. The body is an ecstatic creation of many beings vibrating on other levels of consciousness. A deep orgasm is a realization of love on many levels, including those which many of us now think of as 'animal.' Love, getting into the same space or on the same vibration with others, is the ground of our being, and takes an infinity of forms. As in all other experiences, we always have the sexual experiences we deserve, depending on our loving kindness towards ourselves and others."

As for the Catholicism he grew up with, he looks on it as childish lore, though he admires "its championing of the poor and the thousands of genuinely holy people it has produced, like St. John of the Cross, the German Dominican mystic Meister Eckhart, St. Bernard, St. Theresa of Avila, and St. Francis." Not only is Jesus just one among other religious geniuses, but the impulse to divinize charismatic figures is a fallacy that mars the Western tradition. It is anthropomorphic mythology, not spirituality:

I still believe that Jesus brings one of the most "sublime and benevolent codes of morals which has ever been offered to man" (Thomas Jefferson), but I no longer believe that Jesus thought of himself as God. . . . Jesus was a spiritual athlete. That his words were "added to, deleted, altered, and otherwise tampered with as the Gospels were put together" (again Thomas Jefferson) is something we have to accept, but his large-heartedness shines through. . . .

From reading Joseph Campbell, I can see how the Middle Eastern credo religions (Judaism, Christianity, Islam) have gotten the inflection wrong. They are based on an anthology of ethnocentric historicist fictions (I wish I had heard this in theology class at Shrub Oak!)[25] In the Orient, where they've read the symbols correctly, the ultimate divine mystery is found immanent within you. It is not "out there" somewhere. It is within you. "In the Orient the ultimate divine mystery is sought beyond all human categories of thought and feeling, beyond names and forms, and absolutely beyond any such concept as of a merciful or wrathful personality, chooser of one people over another, comforter of folk who pray, and destroyer of those who do not. Such anthropomorphic attributions of human sentiments and thought to a mystery beyond thought is—from the point of view of Indian thought—a style of religion for children" (Joseph Campbell, *Myths to Live By: The Confrontation of East and West in Religion*).

The former Jesuit has cultivated a catholicism with a small "c." His spirituality is an assemblage of wisdom traditions that release him from a theological cul-de-sac:

There is nothing you have to believe, and there is nothing you have to do. I remember feeling such enormous relief when I realized that Jung says your chief obligation in life is to find yourself and live accordingly. You don't have to torment yourself wondering what Catholic dogma means! Or Jewish dogma. Or Muslim dogma.

I now find great inspiration and meaning and wisdom in the life of Buddha, Zen Buddhism, the I Ching, the Tao de Ching and the Upanishads. I think of Buddha as the Eastern counterpart to Jesus. I probably follow the Dalai Lama with more interest than I do the pope.

The odyssey of another, sixty-six-year-old former Jesuit is also intellectual, with trips to other religious traditions, but it does not take him nearly so far from Catholicism. Even so, it is no less venturesome or sinuous.

As a Jesuit, the man had taught at one of the major theologates of the order, only to leave in a crisis of faith less than a decade after Vatican II; now he is an administrator at a Jesuit university. His departure from the Society had its origins in the controversy surrounding *Humanae Vitae,* the "birth control encyclical." His story highlights the conjunction of two sea-changes: the collapse of doctrine as timeless classicism in the face of historical scholarship and the crisis over the sexual magisterium in particular:

> Partially because of what was happening at the council but more as a maturing of what had begun to happen to me at Woodstock,[26] I became increasingly conscious of the *historicity* of Scripture and of church teaching, that is, of the grounding of each and every doctrine, and especially of church pronouncements, in a historical context of presuppositions, assumptions, etcetera, which a different age (ours) might or might not be able to share. As a result of this historicity, it seemed to me that church authority could never define anything "once and for all" and that the *de fide* pronouncements which had had such weight even in my own earlier studies could not settle questions of faith in the future.

Intellectual doubts were inseparable from institutional politics. Top-down decision making lost legitimacy. Submission to authority crumbled:

> What bothered me about the encyclical was the process by which the decision had been reached—in effect, by papal fiat for the sake of ecclesiastical consistency. I knew that many, if not most, theologians were saying that the encyclical was not "infallible" and that the teaching could therefore be changed at some later date. If anything, that made the encyclical almost scandalous to me since I knew of historical instances in which "noninfallible teaching" had been changed only after its victims had suffered and died for the "fallible" teaching of the church. Most of all, I had come to believe that the whole Christian community, including the believing Protestant community, ought to have been consulted in the decision. For all these reasons, I believed that I could not go into class again and teach what I was teaching on the nature of dogma.

At one level, the story is almost banal in its typicality. It is also ironic. The credibility of the "deposit of faith" disintegrates with the progress of biblical scholarship that the papacy had sanctioned two decades prior to Vatican II. The cumulative evidence generated by textual research precipitates turmoil among men entrusted with defending tradition while having to keep abreast of scholarly advances in order to maintain intellectual respectability.

At another level, however, the impasse amounts to more than a collision of religious authority and academic logic. An ecstatic current wells up in the midst of the intellectual confusion:

> I had long been interested in the Christian mystical tradition. As far back as my early studies in philosophy, I had learned under the inspiration of the great Dominican philosopher-theologian, M-D Sertillanges, to speak of a Thomist tradition of "Christian agnosticism." ("We know that God is," says Aquinas, "not what He is." Thomas's Latin is, in this case, gender neutral, but I expect he would say "He" if he had been writing in English.) . . . I came to know Meister Eckhart and John of the Cross, as I had not known them before and had to go back to a study of St. Augustine and even of Aquinas. . . . Living with the mystics, one also grapples with the deep suspicions of "religion" one finds in such noted "atheists" as Freud and Nietzsche. For now, I will just say that the faith in whose defense I write is more groping than its official presentations suggest, but not for that reason less Christian, and that I often look to the mystics for guides in that faith.

It turned out to be a small step from immersion in the mystical and largely undogmatic waters of Christian mysticism toward the East:

> Not long after leaving the Jesuits, I had also begun to meditate each day, not after the fashion of Ignatius Loyola's contemplations, but in a loosely Zen Buddhist style. Three years ago I joined a Buddhist zendo . . . with a membership drawn from many religious traditions. I have begun to study the Buddhist dharma (teachings) and to participate in Buddhist-Christian conversations. Once again, I find that sharing in the Buddhist tradition has not made me less Christian but, if anything, more sensitive to the mystical side (*mysterium fidei!*) of the Catholic Christian tradition. I have not lost interest in the need to reconcile Catholic and Protestant theologies, but now I see our family arguments in the larger context of a very different spirituality.[27]

The former Jesuit's cosmopolitanism differs from the magpie habits of the collector; he is a voyager who may lose his way but not his identity. His explorations outside Christianity have not entailed shedding his Catholicism, but they are not mere side trips either.[28] His reconnoitering has failed to bring him toward the simplicity that many of his peers almost routinely claim as the direction of the path they have taken. Sophistication has replaced innocence. There is also a recognition of ineluctable mystery in his view of the figure of Jesus:

> I have continued over these last twenty years to read everything I could find on the Scriptural description of Jesus' resurrection. . . . I have been concerned to know how I could, in good conscience, affirm Jesus' resurrection, given what I believed to be the at best fragmentary and in some ways contradictory evidence of the New Testament. I am now more and more content that I do know what I mean by Jesus' resurrection and that these [comments] will not "take away" the resurrection, even though they may require some rethinking of the event and its doctrinal expression.[29]

The former Jesuit has joined a hard-to-pin-down community of reverent skeptics and qualified believers; his is a pensive, complex piety:

> My faith is more and more in the present. The God in whom I believe is known in T. S. Eliot's "hints and guesses, hints followed by guesses," and the Eucharist in which I share has its own "present" sacramental power, even apart from its importance as a memorial of Jesus' own life and death. The Word is in our midst, and, whatever else must be said about the resurrection, I believe with Rudolph Bultmann that "Jesus has risen into the *kerygma*" and with St. Paul that we must not be too much attached to "Jesus according to the flesh" since "we live, now not we, but Christ lives in us."

The components of this declaration of faith are indistinguishable from what most Jesuits cling to. The faith and curiosity of the former Jesuit have metamorphosed into an ongoing ambivalence that is characteristic of Jesuits themselves, with its center of gravity still in the tradition with which they are most familiar and comfortable:

> I know that the weekly Eucharist keeps me focused, challenges me, reminds me of a Christian heritage, which has formed me. My weekly session in the Buddhist zendo is a time of important silence. The weekly Eucharist is a time when I hear not the sermon but the Word and, however imperfectly, say "Amen" to the Word. In short, while I envy the spontaneous and genuine goodness that I think many of us sense in nonchurchgoers, I have no reason to think I would be any better, and some reason for thinking I would probably be a little worse, for not being a regular churchgoer. "*Sacramenta propter peccatum,*" I believe St. Augustine said. "The sacraments have been instituted as a remedy for our fallen-ness."

The 1960s scarred the university administrator, but the effect of that decade was not, as it was for several of his peers, to encourage bitter rebellion against the ways of Catholic officialdom. Troublesome yet ultimately loyal theologians such as Karl Rahner, the Jesuit who along with John Courtney Murray represented the liberating promise of Vatican II, are as alive to him as Protestant thinkers and Eastern mystics:[30]

> My theological training would also make it difficult for me to be an honestly disaffected Catholic. I know the intellectual richness of the Catholic tradition, and I am convinced that even seemingly meaningless doctrines, when read in their own context, can become stepping-stones to meaningful "faith." So I am often impatient with ex-Catholics who write off doctrines they have not even understood, and, having been trained in the exciting '60s, I am not hesitant nor do I feel disloyal in questioning the received understanding of any and every doctrine. ("Chalcedon, an end or a beginning?" asked Karl Rahner in those heady days.) I am also sensitive to what I experience as "Catholic bashing" by parts of the cultural elite, and I am often as bewildered by the illogic of the irreligious as I am frustrated by the abstract logic of the religious.

The former Jesuit's coda is a refutation of the conservative view of the preceding decades as years of religious deterioration. Here again it would be impossible to separate this perspective from that of most of the men who have actually remained in the Society of Jesus:

> Ecclesiastics have sometimes described the '60s and '70s exodus of clergy and religious as a "loss of faith." I will not presume to speak for others in that exodus, but in my own case I would say that it came with something like a discovery of the mystery of "faith," even with some questioning of "belief." In the years since then, I have become increasingly convinced that God's active presence in the world is often missed when we assume that the presence will conform to our beliefs or when we begin our search in dogma rather than in our own experience.

7

We have seen repeatedly that for many Jesuits and former Jesuits, the rejection of absolutes has encouraged a keener sense of gradations in spiritual life. The image of a fluid continuum fits much of their experience. The change has promoted the humanization of spirituality, and from this perspective the appeal of the psychological vocabulary and techniques that, some argue, have displaced "the truly religious" seems straightforward. Evidently, religion has been naturalized.

Modern jargon is not the only discourse suited to understanding the psychic transformation of Jesuits and former Jesuits, however. The insistence on moderation, on sensible balance, on savoring small delights and simple pleasures as they come, is redolent of pre-Christian epicureanism, and the heady fascination of a few former Jesuits with an assortment of refined and occasionally occult ideas is reminiscent of old-fashioned gnosticism.[31] In restorationist circles, all this looks distressingly like neopaganism and old-time religion gone soft on relativism.

Whether the conceptual framework is modern or premodern, the metaphor of a gradient or of a spiritual glide path away from the icy peaks of religious heroism toward the humid plains of mere humanity is appealing because it captures a common point of departure: the abandonment of the tortuous climb toward perfection, triumphalism, and sublime transcendence. The imagery of a continuum and the idea of moderation, of a convergence toward the mean, make sense, up to a point. The via media incorporates the almost universal adherence to a protocol of mutual forbearance and toleration—the pluralist code— that in turn mirrors the need for self-acceptance. Just as civility is supposed to prevail over militancy, the calm of an adjusted self seems preferable to the chronically agonistic soul and the collective perturbations that it brings.[32]

But the gradient metaphor and the primacy of moderation also fall short in important respects. Insofar as it implies that reasonable approaches to religious life cluster toward the middle of a spectrum, the imagery slights extremes and depths and liminal experience, ignoring hellish night sweats, transports, and mystical states that cannot all be dismissed as baroque hysteria. Rapture is traded in for tranquility.

In addition, the notion of a gradient running from stratospheric certitude toward the rolling countryside of moderation overlooks some qualitative distinctions in religious style. Religious experience can be classified into types as well as gauged according to intensity. Furthermore, few Jesuits and former Jesuits treat these types as equally worthy. The temptation to rank them, if not by intensity then in terms of some sort of evolutionary hierarchy, is practically irresistible.

At the top of this hierarchy is an engagement, more prominent among former Jesuits but also prevalent among Jesuits, with Eastern religious traditions. These explorations may venture off the Christ-centered charts, but often they build on a traditional Jesuit cosmopolitanism. They mesh with the ecumenism associated with Vatican II, the disenchantment with logic-chopping doctrine, and the demographic dewesternization of Catholicism. Finally, the Eastern turn represents a maneuver around the hedonism of the 1960s. Some versions cultivate not the liberation *of* the senses but liberation *from* the senses. And the orientation strives to leave behind what many of the men see as the puerile idolatry and gaudiness of operatic Catholicism. Its emphasis on simplicity is redolent of an updated iconoclasm.[33]

Toward the bottom is an evangelical or charismatic impulse. This provides a less cerebral, more affective release from the ideal of chilly stoicism that almost all Jesuits and former Jesuits have forsaken. The style tends to be relatively inarticulate, reminiscent of the raucous ecstasy of gospel music, more schmaltzy and honky-tonk than meditative, even violent, as these properties are understood among educated men. There is an emotional bravura to the evangelical manner that runs counter to the earth-toned, reflective sensibilities of those who have taken the Eastern route. It combines the expression of feelings with a moral and biblical conservatism that many of the men have pulled away from. Several men report having been drawn to and helped by the charismatic option in the disarray following Vatican II. On the whole, the evangelical-charismatic alternative has a demotic tinge, relative to the upscale, more broadly traveled air surrounding the Eastern turn.[34]

There is a third stratum, between the two just mentioned. For want of a better term, we describe this as ordinary Catholic practice, with a renovating twist. It has two defining characteristics. Its adherents do not usually wander far outside the church for spiritual sustenance; their ecumenism is passive and tolerant rather than a matter of strenuous outreach. Second, proponents of this strategy have concentrated on retrieving what has come to be considered the original Jesuit charism, founded on the early form of administering the *Spiritual Exercises,* and other streams of the Catholic legacy. Rather than range widely across traditions, they have tried to go deep, into the past. The accent is on refounding Catholic identity. Emphasis falls on the creativity of Jesuits before their suppression in the late eighteenth century and their revival as a conservative arm of the papacy.[35]

These categories—call them the cosmopolitan, the charismatic, and the Catholic—form a significant pattern. The point of departure—impatience with doctrinal embellishment and affective distance—is very much the same for Jesuits and former Jesuits. But the paths traveled from this baseline have not just been longer or shorter; they have also diverged. These minicultures differ in kind, among one another, in addition to varying in intensity, within themselves.

Another way of putting this is that spiritual change runs along multiple dimensions. Warnings about reducing "the truly religious" to some baser phenomenon commonly presuppose a singular spiritual reality, some unmeltable core of universal truth. Our quarrel is not with the reality but with the singularity of it. We need not rely on the divisions among cosmopolitan, charismatic, and Catholic paths from tradition in order to be struck by differences in apprehending spiritual experience. Other terms might do. Some men emphasize the social action side of their faith; others are attuned to religion as a pharmacopoeia of psychological remedies; still others reveal an aesthetic appreciation of spiritual life; yet others talk of mystical union. Some mix these approaches. All of them are probably related to temperamental variations that are irreducible to a singular, "truly religious" experience.

None of the spiritual styles or strategies is plainly dominant, nor are they mutually exclusive. The variations are not infinite—indeed, the major patterns are small in number—and in that respect, a picture of relativism run amok would be overdrawn. But the overall configuration is polycentric. Steep hierarchies and fixed meanings have given way to a motley spirituality.

CHAPTER SEVEN

Life in Community

The Lone Ranger mentality is still all too prevalent among Ours. So for me the most difficult aspect of working within the Society is that I can sometimes feel like we're all working alone—together.

Clearly today's Jesuits have and are supported in having more outside relationships and engaging friendships, with women as well as men. There are few today whose life is identical to and exhausted by the life "in the house."

I

Just as happens with the spiritual experience of Jesuits and former Jesuits, it is easier to depict a shared beginning—the citadel-like, us-versus-them, subcultural redoubt of 1940s and 1950s Catholicism—than it is to chart the variations in communal arrangements that have taken shape since that time.[1] The men have fanned out in different directions.

Assessments of Jesuit community life vary enormously, and so do the expectations brought to it. In one instance, however, accounting for positive and negative evaluations of religious community is easy. Both Jesuits and former Jesuits regularly give higher marks to the experience of living together during their years of formation than to their life together in ministry.[2] Bonding is powerful among men undergoing the rigors of training, and it slackens as men move on to communities that are sometimes little more than holding areas for busy professionals engaged in disparate activities in scattered venues. "In the novitiate, community life was intense and intentional," a thirty-eight-year-old Jesuit mathematician in university teaching observes:

> After formation it is more chaotic and less organized. My best current description is that it is a fabric that allows and encourages friendship and fidelity to a mission. I don't know if it can be expected to be more. We are all busy people, and we expect community to be a base from which we go out to do our work. It is not to be our preoccupation.

Religious training is a collective enterprise—a heady mix of introspection, ritual, and sharing.[3] Later, as many Jesuits go their separate
ways, the collective cadence grows fainter. The community of memory—
of youthful solidarity, irretrievable energy, and promising vistas—exerts
a powerful appeal as men get older. They long for a world that preceded
the diaspora of adulthood.[4]

Another pattern is more complicated. Former Jesuits are likely to report that since leaving the Society they have rarely developed friendships
of the intensity and depth they had while they were Jesuits. Yet men who
remain Jesuits often claim that many of their closest friendships have
been formed outside the Society.

One clue to solving the puzzle can be found in the differences between community and friendship. In religious life, communities are like
the weather. However much they complain, Jesuits can do little about
the communities, or at least about the composition of the communities,
they are thrust into. Their main buffer consists of friendships, some of
which may be formed on the inside, others outside the Society. In either
case, friendships are chosen, not arranged.

Religious life establishes a context for the development of powerful
bonds. At the same time, traditional religious communities are inherited
constructions that require upkeep over the long haul, and they have a
more institutional flavor than the one-on-one relationships that constitute friendship. On balance, religious communities tend to be more un-
wieldy and less satisfying than the extraordinary friendships they breed.

How, then, do Jesuits deal with the challenges of life in community that
have emerged since Vatican II? In addition to making friends on the outside, they have challenged the "given" nature of religious community and
have forged customized networks defined in terms of age, mission, or
sexual orientation. These subgroups might not stay within the Society at
all, however, were it not for two other variations on togetherness, one
practical and the other ideal: the persistence of a neutral community, a
common ground, that serves as a logistical backup to everyday ministry,
and attachment to a vision of Jesuit brotherhood as a worldwide companionship. These are the key permutations of Jesuit communal life.

2

We are interested in perceptions about Jesuit communities that separate
one generation from another rather than in shifts over the life cycle, such
as those reflected in the perennial difference between evaluations of for-

mation and apostolic communities, that occur regardless of historical period. A pair of these historical, intergenerational transformations runs broad and deep. One is the movement toward looser, open communities. To take a concrete example: Laypeople, women as well as men, are much more frequently guests at lunch or dinner in Jesuit houses than would have been the case before Vatican II.[5]

The other change is a not altogether consistent combination of heightened expectations about the significance of the community ideal in Jesuit life and a realistic sophistication about what religious community can actually deliver in the way of intimacy and personal fulfillment. Quips to the effect that "he shows up for breakfast, doesn't he?" no longer suffice as guides to the common life among male religious. Jesuits are freer to admit their need for intimacy and are more alert to the body language of maladjustment in groups. But they are also less convinced that community as lived in a physical locale can be either useful or emotionally sustaining, and they are apt to look for life's satisfactions elsewhere.

The origins of the change from closed to porous communities lie in the abandonment, sanctioned by Vatican II, of the monastic solemnities that came to encumber the mobile, extroverted Jesuits of the order's creative days. Many of the old formalisms—the ringing of bells calling to prayer, the reciting of litanies in unison after the evening meal, the slow psalmic rhythm of burnished liturgies, the smell of melting candles, the "long black line" wending its solemn way through an ordered, mysterious world—have gone.

Reforms in community life have been especially visible in the training of Jesuits. The new approach, developed to form Jesuits in a less sheltered environment, not only gives them greater contact with the outside world but also is supposed to foster psychosexual maturity.[6] Despite the prohibition against "particular friendships," the traditional regimen did not often impede deep bonding among Jesuits. What it did block, and what has changed massively with the reform of Jesuit training, was access to the world outside, as this comment by a fifty-nine-year-old former Jesuit makes clear:

> Community life in the '50s and '60s encouraged many close friendships, though very few of us had formed significant friendships outside the order. "Externs" were still received in parlors, and only rarely did a secular guest show up at dinner. "Visitors Days" were part of an annual calendar and were a disruption of normal routine.

While men destined for the diocesan clergy have reverted to being trained in relatively cloistered seminaries, their contact with women severely restricted, the openness of Jesuit communities follows the spirit of Vatican II and the rules for contemporary religious orders.[7] Still, remnants of the claustral mode linger, for example, in reservations expressed by some of the older fathers about possible laxness in dealing with women. "What did he think I was going to do?" said one middle-aged Jesuit miffed at the success of an elderly colleague, renowned for his prayer life and love for the Society, in having women barred from the dinner table. "What did he think I was going to do with her? Throw her down on the floor and have my way with her?"

Accounting for the growth of seemingly contradictory expectations surrounding Jesuit community—the heightened importance assigned to it, together with a certain realism about its capacity to satisfy longings for personal fulfillment—is more complicated. Religious communities are subject to competing pulls. One factor placing strains on religious communities is the importance accorded to the search for intimacy. Another is the professionalization and market-driven nature of the work that Jesuits do.

If religious communities are not very good at nurturing close personal relationships without requiring men to put up with boring and annoying peers, Jesuits are apt to search elsewhere rather than question the ideal of intimacy itself. The religious community is liable to become a looking glass reminding its members of unresolved longings.

In addition, the more that Jesuits—especially but not exclusively those in higher education—get caught up in national job markets, the stronger their professional loyalties may be than their ties to local institutions. Even those in secondary education and other, less high-powered fields are busier than ever because of the scarcity of Jesuits and the demands on the time of those who remain. A thirty-six-year-old Jesuit finishing his theological studies, about to go on the market, catches some of the effects of professional specialization on the solidarity associated with the vanishing traditional communities:

> For me, the challenges of work within the Society usually have to do with community—or lack of it. Most of us are pretty good at our fields of specialization. The difficulty we too often have is genuinely collaborating with one another, planning things we want to do *together as Jesuits*. The Lone Ranger mentality is still all too prevalent among Ours.

So for me, the most difficult aspect of working within the Society is that
I can sometimes feel like we're all working alone—together.

All this affects how Jesuits define community: whether in local, brick-
and-mortar terms or metaphorically, as the *communitas ad disper-
sionem*, the far-flung ideational union of men who are supposed to make
their home anywhere. The latter construction—more like a reference
group with which Jesuits identify, a "union of hearts and minds," than
a community as physical habitat—is usually thought to be closer to
what Jesuits were originally about. But the ideal leaves open the question of the operative model for Jesuit communities here and now, in
everyday life.[8]

3

"I entered in 1953." The speaker is a Jesuit theologian in his sixties. He
is talking about his days in the splendid, Spartan novitiate of the New
England province:

> Shadowbrook [in the Massachusetts countryside] was a world that con-
> tinued the adolescence that I had been living already. People lived very
> close to each other in Shadowbrook, a big Carnegie mansion, and that
> meant that it was close for the sixty of us. We slept dormitory style, so
> we were only two or three feet from each other, and we had classroom
> space, which was your desk in a room with twenty other desks. There
> was cold water and individual sinks. It was a very regulated life. I was
> used to it actually, having six siblings, so the issue of privacy was not a
> problem. The regimented life made sense. It tended to organize your life
> for you rather than allow you or invite you to organize your life.

For men who entered the Jesuits before Vatican II, religious life was
both an adventure and an extension of the "urban villages" they came
from. Formation communities—the novitiates, the philosophates, and
so on up the line, to the theologates—were large, and at least in the early
years of training the setting was Arcadian and manorial. In a single
province—Maryland, say, or California or New York—from thirty to
forty young men (across the country, over 300), most of them fresh out
of Jesuit prep schools, would enter toward the summer and early fall of
each year, and they would be housed in the countryside with an equivalent number who had entered the year before.[9] They were close in age

and background, but because there were so many of them, the groups were fairly diverse in talent and temperament.

The pulse of the traditional formation communities carried over from the celebratory density of Catholic neighborhoods; scarcely a beat was lost in the move from prep school to seminary. The semimonastic model of Jesuit formation enjoyed the support of the Catholic immigrant and early postimmigrant enclaves. The seminaries were peaceful islands in the riptide of tradition and social mobility.[10] The recollections of a fifty-year-old accountant, who entered the Society at eighteen in 1964 and left five years later, swept up in the massive exodus of the time, focus on the enveloping subculture of his youth, and he cherishes his memories of that vanished community:

> I recall growing up in a very Catholic world which included parochial grammar school almost completely staffed by nuns, being an altar boy, faithful Mass attendance, often daily, all boys' Catholic high school with a significant number of Christian Brothers, parents who sang in the choir as I also did eventually. Most of the neighborhood was also Catholic, and that culture was assumed. . . .
>
> Certainly the best aspect of my years in the Society was community life. Perhaps it resulted from the compatibility, at a very basic level, of the types of people who chose to enter or a sense of a common goal, akin to teamwork. Perhaps it is the shared experience of formation. Perhaps it is the shared sense of values and ideals, but I have never since shared friendships like those I made in the Society.

The sense of excitement and of being part of a collective venture so vast and so certain of itself that it made space for individual differences also comes through in the reflections of Jesuits, especially older Jesuits, who stayed the course. These remarks by a sixty-seven-year-old theologian capture the communal exuberance of the old days, affirming that camaraderie reached its peak during formation and hinting that collegiality has worn thinner in his professional milieu, as the academic scene has segmented and factionalized:

> I was basically happy all along. The workload was very heavy, and not everyone shared my ideas or values, but there were always kindred souls. My companions were very patient with me. I truly enjoyed celebrating Mass, hearing confessions, visiting the sick, counseling, teaching, writing. Being a Jesuit is fundamental to my identity.
>
> I have had good friendships all through the Society, more so perhaps

in formation, men whose companionship I enjoyed, with whom I could talk about prayer and work, despite many restrictions in the early years of formation. Classes were very large throughout formation, which provided opportunities to find people with similar tastes. The teaching communities were also large. I have always felt enriched and challenged by diversity.

In regency we learned to rely on one another, building on strengths, compensating for weaknesses. This has remained true on the university level, making the theology department an apostolic team—until the last five years.

The old days were not halcyon. A major factor propelling men out of the Society was the clockwork rigidity of Jesuit life. Some of these tensions surface in the reminiscences of a fifty-four-year-old high school English teacher who left the Society after thirteen years in the early 1970s. He tells of his experience over a tumultuous decade, when conventions came to seem robotic, revealing cross-purposes in the traditional mores, while new standards struggled to emerge. "As I look back on it now," he begins, setting the stage for the great transformation,

> I feel I was poised on the border between the old, almost monastic tradition and the new (though certainly firmly rooted in the basic Ignatian tradition), more apostolic approach adapted to the people and culture of the twentieth century. I began my life in the Society when there was strength in numbers; by the time I left, the numbers were drastically reduced.

Monotony does not seem to have been the chief failing of pre–Vatican II religious community. The life conveyed a reassuring sense of stability and the quirks unavoidable with large numbers lightened the atmosphere. The high school teacher points instead to a couple of traits that were latent in the manorial communities and that were released with a vengeance as the 1960s spilled over into the 1970s. One was a jockeying for individual distinction among males, or simply the ambition to make a difference:

> In my day, many of my contemporaries looked upon the spiritual formation of the novitiate and tertianship merely as something to be endured; the work itself was all important. On the whole, we were a very gifted lot, fairly intellectual and usually successful at whatever we attempted. Self-confidence was a given. A subtle form of competitiveness crept in, and there was an unwritten law that each of us was destined to put his

individual mark on the apostolate of the Society and the destiny of the
church.

As the 1970s gave way to the 1980s and 1990s, job-focused Jesuits became more keenly attuned to the promptings of the market. For some,
choosing professional advancement meant cutting back on commitment
to community. Simultaneously, a desire for intimacy took hold as the
traditional communities decayed and were dismissed as gloomy bachelor clubs. The scramble for jobs and affection pushed and pulled at the
traditional boundaries of community:

> In the course of my stay in the Jesuits, friendships were very important.
> In the earlier years, it seemed we were more reluctant to share our deep-
> est thoughts and feelings, part of which was due to certain formational
> emphases; but in the course of my training, sensitivity groups of one
> sort or another came into vogue, and perhaps thanks to the charismatic
> movement and a new emphasis on the way of giving the *Exercises,*
> a greater depth of sharing deepened friendships a great deal. Unfortu-
> nately many of my closest friends left before I did, and contact after-
> ward was somewhat limited. When I left, I felt community life in the
> Society was on the wane, and much more emphasis was placed on be-
> coming a very strong individual and making it on your own with a very
> strong personal relationship with the Lord or on developing deep friend-
> ships, support groups of a sort, outside the Society.

Jesuits could see what was going on, complained about it, and struggled to correct it. The substance of what one Jesuit, a fifty-nine-year-old
spiritual director, has to say about the ups and downs of community life
is the same as the diagnosis made by many of his comrades, but he expresses his views with exceptional poignancy. Instead of concentrated
pain, there is a diffuse fondness and melancholy. Jesuits have learned to
put up with and support one another, and if this falls short of intimacy,
civility is nonetheless an improvement over incessant feuding:

> I have had wonderful communities, and awful ones, and have lived
> alone or with 150 people. Personally the loss of most of my best friends
> found me without close Jesuit friends, at least historical ones for many
> years, and not easily letting others in. . . . It hurt too much to say good-
> bye. I have had lots of very good but superficial relationships with those
> with whom I worked. A few have crashed through; a couple have stayed
> constant, though they (two) live in other provinces. I think Jesuits, in

general, really try to support, nurture, share with each other. We do it awkwardly, but honestly. . . . We try to share our faith, to pray together, to challenge and support each other. We are better at it than most men I know. Strangely I find people forty-five to sixty-five better at it than some younger men, perhaps because we know how much we need it. I have lots of friends outside the Society, few intimate ones; sadly, many more people who would call me their friend, than vice versa.

4

Community as an exercise in civility is the backup option in Jesuit life. What it lacks in vibrancy it makes up for in pragmatic acceptance and polite evasion of emotional entanglements. It allows men to get on with their work. "By and large, I find community life to be enjoyable and nourishing," a thirty-two-year-old finishing his graduate degree observes:

> In ten full years in the Society, I have had only one year where community life was unpleasant. My family was close as I grew up, and we remain so to this day (although I am the one who is most absent). I never looked to the Society to be a surrogate family. Some Jesuits do, and I think they never fail to be disappointed. I seek a community where I can pray with others, support others and be supported in what we are doing, have some fun together, as well as some serious conversation. By and large, I have found this in community. If you were to ask others, I think people would say I enjoy community life.

Then the reservations set in. The experience of community is far from bleak, but it is not exactly fulfilling either:

> Having said all this, I also have to admit that there is a certain men's club atmosphere that can permeate our houses. In regency, I lived in a community where the school and sports were the two main topics of conversation and recreation. I fit well into this and enjoyed it. There was a lot of mutual liking and respect, we had liturgy together, we laughed together, but there was not a lot of personal sharing. We related to one another on a safe level, and given the age differences and differences in training and experience among Ours, that was not all bad. In our scholastic communities in theology, we do a better job of faith sharing and getting beyond box scores and politics. Yet there is a certain sophomoric atmosphere that we (at least I) can fall into, and we can be insen-

sitive in our remarks to and about others. We tend to fear and avoid those issues that we know can be divisive.

The neutral-to-lukewarm version of community rarely stands alone. More often it exists as a logistic convenience at the edges of which men go about devising solutions to their own needs in the form of subgroups. The community as minimalist encounter coexists with several network-like adaptations to the challenges of religious life.

These variants—there are four main ones—are not mutually exclusive. One option covers subcommunities shaped around work or the closely associated division between faith-and-justice versus humanistic approaches to ministry. Shared mission provides the social fixative. Another variation involves subcommunities built up around identities, principally those shaped by age differences or sexual orientation, that have little relation with the type of work that members perform. Their apostolic function tends to be less important than the sensibility and lifestyle their members share.

Communities formed around mission as well as communities based on identity usually have addresses and phone numbers, a tangible locale. By contrast, the borders of two other adaptations are diffuse. One is made up of networks of friends, typically non-Jesuits but also sometimes Jesuits, outside the place where men collect their mail and occasionally take their meals. Another is the imagined community of Jesuits worldwide, the ambulant fraternity that is a metaphor for the Ignatian ideal. "It is clear that there is a widespread shift taking place," one Jesuit observes, touching on both understandings of community:

> The quality of relationships is becoming the defining characteristic of good community, and the fact of living under the same roof with one's fellow religious—or not—is quite secondary. The old identification of community, with common life, that is, a regular *horarium* with daily presence at common exercises, is rarely invoked today.
>
> My sense, gained from times of visiting a local Jesuit community or participating in province gatherings, is that the prayer of these [new] communities is much more intense, personal, and genuinely shared; less simply the recitation of formulae than might have been the case in the past. Our men seem also to be gentler with one another, more sensitive to each other. Clearly today's Jesuits have and are supported in having more outside relationships and engaging friendships, with women as well as men. There are few today whose life is identical to and exhausted by the life "in the house."

Floating clusters of friends are not only less grounded than traditional religious communities; they are also composed of acquaintances who are chosen by rather than thrust on Jesuits. They are consistent with the fluidity of individualism.

For its part, the metaphorical community evokes the cosmopolitanism and venturesomeness of the original "companions in the Lord" who traveled far and wide. In theory, this peripatetic communion circumvents the problem of the decline in solidarity as Jesuits move from training to work. Properly formed Jesuits, so the idea goes, carry the image and ideals of the Society of Jesus with them wherever they venture.

The neutral community grew out of the ferocious confrontations of the 1960s and 1970s. The truce it embodies also preserves continuity with the bachelor habits many Jesuits feel comfortable with. Some older Jesuits are so accustomed to clubby banter and the rituals—the preprandial drinks, the respect for privacy—that there is no question of disliking the arrangement. They would no more pry into the lives of their peers than they would violate the norm of male reluctance to ask for directions when they get lost. Middle-distance pleasantries and masculine joshing are part of the fiber of their lives. Many practice unobserved kindnesses, and some will drop everything to pick a colleague up from the airport, flying from one emergency, large or small, to another. But they rarely talk about this side of their world.[11]

Not all these men are lonely geezers, curmudgeons, or tipplers. Some have found the life that suits them, one in which optimism, exercise, a blaze of mysticism, and contentment in work overcome flaws in their sociability and misgivings—after all, they are Jesuits and therefore self-critical—about what they might be missing. Beneath the affability and the problem-solving temper and the ingrained restraint against talking about their feelings, there is passion and bluntness. Here is a plain-spoken sixty-seven-year-old college professor and part-time preacher, fifty years in the Society, coolly reviewing his life:

> I have always liked the communities I have been in and have always
> made a special effort to keep community life rich and attractive. Yet I
> would have to say that I have not made many deep personal friendships.
> I seem to spend too much time thinking and working. My relationships
> with other Jesuits tend to be happy but not profound. For instance, I sel-
> dom invite a fellow Jesuit to go out to dinner with me although I note
> that other Jesuits do this. Maybe I should try it. At the same time, I have
> no tendency to avoid community meals.

Then, as if out of nowhere, fast-forwarding from storms to a radiant sky, comes the terse, traditional affirmation of the joys of the consecrated life. "I really believe," he says, "with moments of anguish, that there is a God, that God is wonderful, that to know and serve Him is splendid." The pivot of religious life, for this Jesuit, is a flickering premonition of the divine, the oceanic feeling that passes and returns.[12] Temperament, talent, and circumstance count; so does work and so does community, more or less. But all these are matters of degree, and none inspires awe.[13]

Other Jesuits accept the neutral community as a realistic compromise, but their acceptance is touched with sadness and buffered by a very pragmatic coping mechanism: the cultivation of friends outside the Society. The following story, related by a fifty-one-year-old Jesuit charged with fund-raising for his province, reinforces the idea that the neutral community is not tenable on its own. His initial observations about "decent human affective exchange" accord with numerous descriptions of the equable, supportive but reserved climate of religious groups:

> The quality of community life is changing dramatically because the Society is changing. We are mostly old men now and with diminished numbers, tend to live in groups of a dozen or so. I find that the rituals we follow ground us in a routine which is intended to attend to the quality and decent affective human exchange. Early on I experienced much more quality in terms of community, but then I was not apostolically focused as ultimately we are all expected to be.

He next recalls a turning point, an encounter toward the end of his formation, that convinced him to seek out more warmth and close contact than he knew he would be able to find in traditional Jesuit communities:

> I remember one community meeting as a theologian when a Jesuit from another country finally spoke up regarding the intense introspective nature of those formative years.[14] He spoke about who would miss him were he to die and who would really mourn his passing. No one in the room that day would likely be there and so his investment in us would remain, accordingly, cordial and friendly, but certainly not the intense relationship expected by the group. I have always remembered that meeting, and to some extent I think he is correct. So, I have maintained a strong relationship to those outside of the Society, especially a couple of women friends, with whom, and like Bobby McGee, I share the secrets of my soul.

5

Since Jesuits have come to do so many different things, since their work
has become more specialized, and since so many Jesuits have settled into
retirement, only a handful of large communities built around an en-
compassing corporate mission—secondary education, for example—
remain.[15] There are a few sizable, apostolically heterogeneous communities assembled partly out of budgetary considerations. For a number
of reasons, not the least of which is the expense of maintaining them,
growth in the number of small communities has subsided.

Nevertheless, de facto subcommunities or satellite communities of
the like-minded are the norm. Task-specific clusters proliferated in the
wake of the 1960s. A forty-one-year-old Jesuit, still in graduate school,
speaks glowingly of his intermittent experience with a community dedicated to helping city kids prepare for high school:

> This kind of inner-city apostolic approach is a very hopeful model,
> smaller groups of guys who have high levels of responsibility within
> their particular area of activity, and who perhaps live together in a house
> and have dialogue about their projects at that level. . . . My own experi-
> ence in a Jesuit community, some of the most intimate times, have been
> those occasions on which I was working with another Jesuit, in care of
> someone in one of our apostolates, like a kid who was in trouble, or
> something like that. There's an incredible sense of bonding I've experi-
> enced at times, when all of a sudden there is a concern about someone in
> need, and it's shared by more than one Jesuit, and more than one Jesuit
> is working to try and help this person through a difficult experience.
> That's a great feeling of camaraderie.

The Jesuit sets the intensity of his life in small, job-focused groups
against the ho-hum atmosphere that he fears enshrouds the larger communities. His agenda, however, is not simply a matter of searching for
intimacy among those who think like him or who do the same work.
He is on the lookout for intensity by way of diversity, something that re-
stricting himself to any single minicommunity cannot supply. Like many
of his peers, he gets around the limitations on close relationships within
the Society by making friends on the outside:

> The majority of my social and personal life is outside the Society, which
> I'm sure would raise questions for folks inside, but my experience has
> been that in lots of ways Jesuits are just terrible at intimacy. . . . We're
> not very capable of real intimate interaction.

This said, the Jesuit cuts against the grain by extolling the bonds forged with those who are different, by reason of age or because of their marginality. A hint of dilettantism hovers over his cosmopolitanism.

"We're men, in a masculine world, and we're insecure," he observes, launching into a criticism of generational cliques and the individualism they express. He contrasts the jockeying for advantage that ambition and competitive anxiety foster among the younger men, for all their sensitivity to the silent language of community, with the tranquility of older Jesuits who are out of the race:

> And ego is the big thing. We're worried about all this posturing sometimes. It really kind of gets in the way of any kind of exchange or any vulnerability that would allow us the freedom to care for one another at any kind of intimate level.
>
> I've had successful experiences, of gratifying friendship and intimacy with older Jesuits, because they're not being driven by issues of career and production and status in the Society. They're not interested in becoming a rector. They're not interested in doing the right thing to be noticed or not noticed. They've published whatever they're going to publish, and now all they want to do is live in the Jesuit life before they die. Those guys are fabulous. But in my own age cohort, I've found it difficult at times. I do have some Jesuit friends. I couldn't stay in the Society otherwise.

The graduate student concludes with a panegyric to "casual interaction" with people who are not one's own as a way to overcome the limits of religious community. His serendipitous journeying is an alternative lifestyle, providing glimpses of meaning amid the useful interventions, rather than reconstituted community itself. The ideal is not in fact community or commitment but the energizing promiscuity of chance connections and fugitive epiphanies that the bustle of the city and its drama permit:

> I think there's something about the structure [of the Society] which can be detrimental. There's a kind of something to the casual interaction with children and women and older people that you don't get on a day-to-day basis in a Jesuit community, like you might get if you were a family person. But a lot of people don't have that. I think it's an issue of taking responsibility for getting it. It's like the kind of opening experience of being with the poor, someone who's suffering. Any kind of contact with human suffering has a profound influence on people, changes their values, makes us look at the world in a different point of view.

And I think the same could be said in maintaining regular contact with women, with children, people outside of our age cohort.

A younger (thirty-three-year-old) Jesuit, finishing his theological studies, offers a different but equally intricate assessment of community. He too laments the gulf between younger and older Jesuits. Subcommunities tend to choose up on different sides of the generational gap. Yet he finds delight in the bonds forged among Jesuits, and he joins with former Jesuits in confirming the claim that his most abiding friendships have been those that originated within the Society:

> In many communities, the lack of peer support for the younger men is a serious problem. I've heard many a Jesuit complain about the lack of peer support. Many of the older men have had a formation radically different from the formation the younger men have. This has caused a lack of understanding in communities among the different generations. This situation has and does cause problems in communities.
>
> As for friendships, I can honestly say that I have wonderful Jesuit friends. I can't imagine finding friends like these outside the Society. I am far closer to Jesuits than I am to my friends outside the Society. This is true because I spend more time with my Jesuit friends. We share a common life and many experiences. It would be hard to leave the group of friends I have in the Society of Jesus.

The story also emphasizes the distinction between quasi-familial community and friends. The former is an institutional arrangement. The latter is a relatively amorphous network of men who may or may not be in the same place. Such ties are likely to be intense but occasional. The off-again, on-again quality of dispersed friendships lends them some of the unexpected magic that the Jesuit quoted earlier hunted for in casual encounters at work. Communities bear the onus of long-term commitment without the selective advantages of friendship. The cultivation of enduring friendship engenders a feeling of personal, willed success that the security of insertion in community cannot provide.

Friendship is not enough, however. The intimacy of love remains out of reach:

> Loneliness has frequently been an issue in my formation. In an extreme way this was true when I was [overseas], but it is also true on a daily experience. I have been blessed with many good friends, but there is no one person who loves me and whom I love. I feel this most when I am with my siblings or with married college friends.

In the end, this young Jesuit believes that there is no optimal solution to the flaws and limitations of community life. Religious life is a path, often tortuous, to be followed, and companionship is not redemption after all. In the words of another Jesuit, he is on his way to "ultimacy," not intimacy: communion with the divine rather than union with another human being.[16]

Community can be both a support and a burden; nothing new here. It is when the discussion of community spills over into a consideration of the reasons for staying the course that the assessment of benefits and drawbacks generates consequences. Talk spans the pragmatic (the good that Jesuits do is "more significant than the difficulties they experience"), a mystical understanding of intimacy ("being a companion of Jesus"), and commitment to an ever-expanding cause ("the greater glory of God"):

> The men who leave no longer believe in the *magis*. There is a desire among those who leave the Society to strive for the "glory of God," but not the "greater glory of God." As I see it the call to do "more" seems to be more difficult today than it was years ago. With that in mind, the primary reason men leave the Society has to do with celibacy and intimacy.
>
> Why do men stay? For myself, the main reason why I stay is that I still feel called to be a companion of Jesus. I still think the Ignatian vision is not only valid but a truly efficacious way of being a companion of Jesus. I should not discount the fact that most of my Jesuit friends believe this too, so I feel accompanied by good friends in religious life. Without that I can honestly say that it would be tougher to stay.
>
> Most stay because they feel called to the mission of the Society and they feel supported in what they do. They see the good of what they do as more significant than the difficulties they experience. They feel the Society has a relevant vision in the world, and they are excited by that vision. They feel the *magis* makes sense in their own life and it makes sense for the church today.

This is a spirituality of heroes, sustained by the bonhomie of heroes. Commitment to a cause, with a countercultural tinge, surpasses the costs of religious vows, including restrictions on intimacy. Community is expressed more through the grandeur of common purpose and a shared, sonorous language than in the daily routine of living together. Zeal of this intensity is not infrequent among small cohorts of younger, conservative Jesuits.

Although they are less transcendent sounding, the following remarks by a slightly older (thirty-seven-year-old) high school administrator still resonate of gravitas. He captures what has by now become a standard maneuver to find both spiritual sustenance and friendship beyond the community at hand:

> One of the most important things in my life is the faith-sharing group of Jesuits from around my time with whom I get together once a month. We call ourselves a "nongeographical community," and the support from that group keeps me going for the rest of the month.
>
> But community life, as usually understood, is in crisis. There is very little shared prayer or affective unity of any significance. All that is done in common is drinks and dinner—sometimes.
>
> I have many close Jesuit friends, although I do not live in community with any of them. But that is typical for a Jesuit of my age. I also have very good friends who are former Jesuits. I value the time spent with them because they know what I am talking about so that I can be honest with them about my frustrations. They will hear me out and often finish with, "———, I don't how you do it," "it" being stay in the Society. And for some reason that does me good.
>
> I have other friends outside the Society whose friendships I value deeply.

"Happiness," the comedian George Burns used to point out, "is having a warm, caring family—in a city nearby." The arrangement just summarized follows the Burns model and is common among Jesuits. It sidesteps the heavy remnants of monastic enclosure. It takes advantage of the shrinking of distances that telecommunications has made possible. It promises the rewards of occasional contact with friends without having to live with them around the clock. It is a fluid, voluntary association rather than the close-knit stoic community of the religious ship at sea.

6

Aside from age, sexual orientation is the major demarcator setting subcommunities in the Society of Jesus apart on the basis of social identity rather than ministerial function or ideological agenda. The gay ethos offers a sense of belonging to men in transition from outcast status. The countercultural sensibility creates an atmosphere of kindred spirits, and of receptivity to feelings and the urge for intimacy, that raises the comfort level of homosexual men. And the appeal of homosexuality seems to be greater among younger than older Jesuits. This is the challenge of "the gaying and the graying" of the Society.

The order is unwilling to accept the gay subculture as even a partial basis for community. Individually, homosexual Jesuits do not appear on the radar screen of religious superiors except perhaps as candidates for therapy. As a collective phenomenon, however, the gay network represents another cleavage that threatens to divide or distract the Society.

"One big concern I have about contemporary community life is about gay men in the Society," a fifty-one-year-old Jesuit in pastoral ministry argues:

> There are a host of problems connected with this issue, not the least of which is a subtle division between gay and straight, networking that can undermine authority for missioning the men, and problems of credibility for mission that could erode the confidence of the people of God in the Society.

Several concerns are evident or just below the surface here: worry about sexual transgression, damage to corporate image, and the dissociation of this community of identity from a sense of apostolic direction. Sexual orientation is more a component of who Jesuits are than what Jesuits do. Trouble begins when the sexual orientation of individuals turns into a pivot of collective identity and of cultural allegiance that runs up against obligations to the corporate hierarchy and the larger community. Imprecise as the demographic proportions of the gay subculture may be, the ethos is conspicuous enough to affect lifestyles and values.[17] The fear is that cultural metamorphosis is a precursor to more tangible repercussions. A senior theologian echoes these preoccupations:

> My last year as rector, I went to every house and ran a company discussion; I asked what it was like to live with gays and straights in a community. . . . There's the whole issue of people's availability for assignment, whether or not you form a society within the Society, which I've seen happen right here in the houses, where a subculture develops. If you make it too much your identifying handle, it's problematic being in the Society.

The increasing legitimacy of a once-deviant sexual orientation coexists with the traditional belief that it remains aberrant ("intrinsically disordered"). Reluctant tolerance perpetuates the shadowy aura and demimonde status that solidifies the gay community as a counterculture but that prevents it from being institutionalized.[18] Because they cannot think of much to do about it, superiors give the impression of failing to acknowledge the phenomenon. Is it a trend? Is it a social movement? The transition from scattered, closeted individuals to a visible but not quite recognized collectivity lends the gay subculture the peculiar air of a beleaguered minority that does not risk extinction but that cannot quite move forward.

Most homosexual Jesuits have little incentive to push beyond their tacit niches. As long as they are not punished for their sexual orientation, many see nothing to gain by concerted action. Gays make up an elusive community of fellow-feeling that thrives on the refinement of marginality rather than mainstreaming. The consequences of what, in the eyes of some Jesuits, is a vaguely ominous or alien ethos, a kind of surreptitious hedonism, are hard to pin down. The fate of homosexuals in the Society of Jesus has been equivocal adaptation.[19]

So, the gay subculture hovers in the crannies of Jesuit life, as one among several emblems of community—those defined by age, for example, or ideological position. It has a distinctive edge in one respect, however. Many homosexual Jesuits stress the quality of community life itself, of sensitivity to ambience and the minutiae and nuance of daily interaction, and wind up provoking carping about "the flowers on the table crowd."[20]

Once in a while, a gay Jesuit—this man is a thirty-five-year-old finishing his theological studies—challenges the assumption of a zero-sum trade-off between lifestyle and ministry:

> Despite some of the hothouse craziness that reigned in the theologate . . . my community life was the most satisfying that I have ever experienced. We weren't necessarily "pals," but we were clearly a community of people trying to live responsibly with one another. We prayed together, we shared our faith, we fought and argued and debated, we laughed through good times, we supported one another in difficult times. We were accountable to one another. We were hospitable—the mark, I think, of a group of people working at becoming a community.

After attempting to clear the air of the usual suspicions about predominantly gay communities as a cover for illicit sex, the Jesuit elaborates on the distinction not only between community and intimacy but also between community and friendship. The need, he argues, is to recognize that ministerial obligations and investment in community can enrich and reinforce one another:

> It strikes me that the distinguishing feature of religious life is the commitment to community. And I do not think we have yet understood how to begin revitalizing communities. Some measure of common work, some measure of shared prayer and community conversation, some measure of recreation, some measure of companionship . . . these things seem essential to me, yet there persists an ideology that preaches that any attention given to community life means attention taken away from the apostolate. Bullshit! This view labors under the faulty assumption that Jesuits possess X amount of energy that needs to be split among competing obligations. Closer to the truth, I think, is the notion that energy flows freely between community and apostolate, and both must be duly attended to. And this is about community, *not* about intimacy. I, and many Jesuits, have many intimate friends within and without the Society. Complaints that attention to community would seek to make the major apostolate of any local house a quest for intimacy are simply untrue.

This is about as far as discussions of trade-offs between community and ministry go. The pitfalls of the pursuit of intimacy as the basis of community are recognized. The search for a corrective turns outward, toward apostolic work. The hopefulness of the message depends on agreement about mission ("a measure of common work"). But in the job market that Jesuits are caught up in, such consensus is difficult to come by.

7

When it comes to the experience of community in the Society of Jesus, there are important exceptions to the tidiest of regularities. But even the exceptions—in this case, a sixty-year-old attorney, his life as a Jesuit nearly thirty years behind him, who looks back on the Society with analytical sangfroid rather than ostensible nostalgia—may prove the rule. Muted regret overtakes mere indifference. The cadence becomes elegiac:

> The quality of community life in the Society was wonderfully supportive for me. I never lived in a small community. I never had the formation of friendships as part of my agenda. It is not surprising, I suppose, that I have had rather little contact with my Jesuit friends from the time I left the order.

In retrospect, we may have been well served by some assistance that would help us recognize and express our feelings. I realize I am saying this as a rational statement. I do not feel any significant loss or sense of waste. I know it is true that I was together with men for seventeen years and hardly knew them. But I cannot tell you that I feel any strong sadness about that.

Almost any change from the nearly uniform strongholds of times past was bound to produce experimentation rather than a unique solution. If there is a common thread to these experiments, it is their rejection of the one-size-fits-all template of community life.

Whatever the diversity of outcomes, we know that at least two dynamics have undermined the insularity of Jesuit life: upheavals in the clerical job market, destabilizing the model of corporate ministry anchored in phalanxes of Jesuits, and the priority given to intimacy. A third change, the aging profile of the order, has also altered the texture of community life. One fifty-year-old Jesuit theologian, residing in a large community, underscores the last problem:

> Community life is tough, sometimes, and I wish we were further along in our understandings of how to live in a healthier way. Except for two years, I have lived my life in the Society in institutional houses, and it sure would be nice to live in a home! The aging process of our "older fathers" is taking too great a toll on folks my age; the community conversation is defined by the past because there are just not enough younger folks to balance it out. I feel for our few scholastics who are living with their grandfathers (and maybe even a grandmother or two).

The likelihood that a younger Jesuit will spend his career at the same place has dropped. A seventy-one-year-old Jesuit, retired from university teaching, provides graphic insight into the sea-change:

> I think it's a valid observation that there is more confusion about the work, the ministry, among the younger generation. The work and the possibilities for my generation were clearly defined. We can look back and say that they were too narrow. I can see today where younger Jesuits have so many possibilities.
>
> I remember a very young, astute Boston College student, a scholar, reminding me one day that he lived in a different world where he had about sixty choices, where I only had two, and that was true. There is so much choice compared to what it was thirty or forty years ago. Life

was more determined. Sometimes you look back and wonder about
these movies, for instance. How could a British butler be so happy for
years? His whole life is planned out for him, and if he took to it, he
could be happy in it. I took to it, and I'm happy in it, I'm not an exploratory type. Some people are. Some people of my generation who
were exploratory people probably didn't stay.

The decimation of the bridging generation of Jesuits—those men in
their late forties and fifties during the 1990s among whom departures
were very high and who left a gulf between the youngest and oldest cohorts—had made the ministerial payoff of investing in community problematic. Many Jesuits are retired or in infirmaries, handfuls are in training, and those in between are spread thin. The professionalization of
work has made Jesuits more mobile and has arguably brought them
closer to the foundational thrust of the Society. But the aging of the Society, temporary as it may be, pulls in the opposite direction, and the
spirit of intimacy goes where it will, sometimes putting pressure on community, sometimes ignoring it.

If the not-so-bad community were a case of a political transition—
away from dictatorship, for example, to some less nasty system—it
would be deemed a success. It occupies a middle zone between the dictates of ambition and intimacy. The loose tethering of Jesuits to this
commons constitutes a physical reminder of belonging. But it is not a
place in which the men put much time or energy. This dissection by a
thirty-one-year-old student of theology is representative:

> I heard a Jesuit provincial say once that each Jesuit leads three lives:
> a public life, a semiprivate life, and a private life. The public life is that
> arena wherein he does his main work, the semiprivate life is the Jesuit
> community, and the private life is his friends. On the whole I live these
> three different lives. Community life is not bad, but it certainly will
> never fill my needs. I've long accepted that. I am fortunate to have about
> five or six wonderful friends (the majority of whom are Jesuits) who are
> my life blood. Without them I could not stay in this life. It is always a
> great blessing to live with one of these, but it is not necessary, so long as
> one goes out of his way to keep in contact (phone, e-mail, visits, vaca-
> tions). I have a very good social life with people outside the Society, one
> or two of whom are extremely close friends. My concern with commu-
> nity life is that, if our private lives allow us to live fully, we can tend not
> to invest as much in our "semiprivate" lives. Sometimes I think this is
> reflected in a poverty of significant conversation in Jesuit communities.

Besides the safety valve of friendships on the outside, subcommunities, shaped mostly around ideology or more or less specific missions or around age cohorts or psychosexual identity, are the main adaptations built up at the edges of the not-so-bad community. These are truly adaptations rather than definite alternatives or frontal challenges to the status quo. They are provisional coalitions no one of which dominates the others.

With the proviso that the parts can operate in combination, this mélange of arrangements forms a rough pattern. Friendships are designed to satisfy the need for intimacy or some approximation of it. The ideological or task-centered subcommunities tend to be apostolically anchored. The subcommunities of identity provide a sense of belonging. And the raison d'être of the not-so-bad community is primarily that of practical support, with vestiges of ceremonial continuity.

At their best, such measures reach for a balance between the monastic overgrowth of preconciliar times and the utter disintegration of boundaries. Ironically, it is "particular friendships," once so vehemently discouraged, especially with non-Jesuits, that seem to have prevented Jesuit communities from turning in on themselves and imploding altogether.[21] The fifty-three-year-old spiritual director quoted earlier summarizes the lesson:

> I believe a Jesuit gets the community he deserves. It takes real effort to love all the different characters that may be given in a particular community. . . . Friendships inside and outside the Society are crucial for a Jesuit living a balanced, sane, and productive life.

A sixty-four-year-old Jesuit who has been in parish work for most of his life makes the same point more colorfully:

> As anywhere else, friendships in the Society are much a matter of luck and chemistry, and there are a lot of ups and downs. I wish I could make new friends with younger Jesuits, but that's a rarity. Our relationships are inevitably male. They are not helped by the fact that our workplace and living place is mostly the same. I think a lifetime in an all-male community is a prescription for stultification or workaholism. Maybe that's the way it has to go, but I would advise Jesuits to break up the routine of their living settings, or they'll go under. Still, people are kind and sincere. I admire the gays who have struggled with integrity but I get annoyed with those gays who seem stuck on one note—anger. With some few exceptions and for all the camaraderie, I miss that different

kind of give-and-take that you get with women. I have a lot of women friends without whom I wouldn't have made it.

These adaptations—licit, illicit, and various shadings in between—prop up rather than replenish religious life. One indicator of the limits of such coping is the correlation between age and satisfaction with religious community. Older Jesuits tend to be somewhat happier with post-formation communities, younger Jesuits more restless and less satisfied.[22] Numerous small- and midrange reforms have not reversed the slide in the attraction of religious life among upcoming generations, for whom the costs of commitment are increasingly salient.

If there is an inkling of an alternative vision, the imagined community of the Society of Jesus as an itinerant, transnational brotherhood—an inspired cosmopolitanism on the move—qualifies. The progressively international makeup of the order lends substance to this vision. But the ideal of nation-spanning harmonies—the amalgam of purpose and belonging, together with adventurous mobility—is such that it makes almost any on-the-ground setup look deficient by comparison.[23]

One Jesuit, a sixty-eight-year-old academic living in a house with eight other men, six of them in formation, has positive words for the changes that have worked their way through community life:

> Part of it is the kind of training that the younger people have had and the kind of transformation that the older people have gone through in terms of what they need and want from a community and what a community should do. The old training was a training in very privatized life with external formalities. Community was formed through litanies, through meals together, and so forth. What we've been struggling for is a deeper bond, and through a miracle, sometimes that is achieved. Some of the communities in my own province have moved very well in that direction.

The logic of group transformation on a small scale, however, does not reproduce itself readily beyond the local. The kinder, gentler communities are therapeutic productions that have enhanced interpersonal sensitivity.[24] But, as in love, gentleness is not enough, no substitute for the grip of passion:

> I don't think the Society has ever had a very sterling record as far as community is concerned. Many people of my generation, as well as the younger men, are looking for something else and have been able to find

some measure of it. I think one problem of the Society and institutional
life is that it runs on ideals; therefore, there's so much room for disappointment and disillusionment because you're actually dealing with human beings in this situation.

If Jesuit communities fail as often as they succeed, two things should
be kept in mind in evaluating them.[25] First, we have no matched comparison between religious communities and alternative networks set up
by former Jesuits. Jesuits have moved toward a variety of provisional solutions to community living, and former Jesuits typically pass not from
one community to another but from the rejection of religious community to the pursuit of intimacy. We have no systematic evidence about
the affective happiness of former Jesuits, about their talent for making
friends, or about their success in reconstituting forms of community and
social solidarity.[26] It is easier to show what does not work than to envision a model that does.

Second, as the scholar observed, the Society "runs on ideals." Brotherhood—"companionship in the Lord"—is one of them. Clinging to this
ideal perpetuates expectations that are bound to be tested severely. The
lurch toward intimacy that characterized the 1960s and the 1970s dem-
onstrated to some Jesuits that chasing after individual bliss often sapped
collective spirit. Intimacy turned out to be only one dimension of community. Another—a sense of corporate mission and organizational activity—looks toward the wider world. It is to this realm of Jesuit life that
we turn in the following chapters.

CHAPTER EIGHT

Ministry and the Meaning of Priesthood

We are engaged in massive corporate denial. We simply cannot continue running these major institutions on the scale we have been, and I see no provincial (superior) making provision. Sometimes I am a bit pissed off because I think that my generation is going to have to deal with it.

In theology a number of men suddenly confronted the fact that they could not articulate for themselves any fundamental difference between ordained ministry and lay ministry. Consequently, they began to wonder why they were making the sacrifices that ordained ministry required.

I

As they struggle to set the course of the Society, declining numbers of Jesuits argue about alternative slants on ministry. Mission-minded priorities contend with therapeutic concerns, and collaborative approaches vie with assertive faith-and-justice agendas. Underlying the skirmishes over corporate purpose, a deeper question looms. What, if any, is the connection between ministry and priesthood?

The Jesuit presence in the schools, parishes, retreat houses, and other operations affiliated with the Society has dropped precipitously. Secondary education provides as good an example as any of the decline. In the early 1960s, just before Vatican II, about half the instructors in the forty-five high schools run by the order in the United States were Jesuits. By the mid-1970s, this figure had fallen to slightly above 30 percent, by the mid-1980s to a little over 20 percent, and by the turn of the millennium into the neighborhood of single digits.[1] The result has been a partial takeover of the works by laypeople. It is no longer accurate to speak of these places as run by the Jesuits. Non-Jesuits and in some cases non-Catholics have taken up the slack.[2]

A second change has entailed the seepage of Jesuits out of the class-room and educational administration into various types of pastoral and parish work. This shift has been slower than the drop in numbers. To some extent, it flows from the aging of the Society. Jesuits have custom-arily spent their retirement years in spiritual counseling and helping out with the round of parish chores. As the membership of the order ages, the proportion of Jesuits in pastoral work grows larger. But some frac-tion of the exodus from education also stems from competition with lay professionals; it is harder for Jesuits to get tenure in what were once their institutions. The brain drain is also driven by the demand for men to carry out priestly duties and by such competing priorities as the com-mitment to social action. Altogether, the occupational profile of Jesuits makes the order look more like a network of parish priests than would have been the case a few decades ago.[3]

The impact of these trends on organizational performance and mo-rale is more complex than the changes themselves. The apostolic opera-tions of the Society look to be in reasonably good shape. With the pro-fessionalization of faculty and staff, the quality of the high schools and many of the colleges and universities has risen. If the Society of Jesus goes under, it will not be because its ministries collapse.[4]

Success in these terms raises a pair of questions. If the schools and other operations launched by the Society can do well enough on their own, what is left for Jesuits to do?[5] And what remains of the religious identity of the schools with a vestigial Jesuit presence or none at all?[6] This chapter and the next address these questions.

Apart from the professional upgrading of the schools and other ac-tivities, another development has accompanied the decline in member-ship and the reallocation of manpower in the Society. On the average, Jesuits turn out to be more satisfied with their work than former Jesuits—not by much but by a large enough margin to dash sweeping conclusions about demoralization throughout the ranks.[7]

For all their tribulations, Jesuits find it a bit easier to infuse their work with a sense of ministry than do their former peers. Men who leave the Jesuits generally do not switch fields. They usually wind up doing what they were trained to do or have an affinity for, with the result that their professional profile is similar to the distribution of jobs among those who remain. But not quite. Somewhat fewer former Jesuits work in edu-cation and the service professions than do Jesuits themselves. Earning a living to support a family sometimes forces them to take on work and follow career lines that might not represent their heart's desire.[8]

So, many operations that took shape under Jesuit auspices are now thriving or doing well enough under non-Jesuit or team direction, and most Jesuits do not seem to be frustrated on the job. Outcomes such as these, which join promising and discouraging elements, are the result of two different responses to the crisis in religious life. On the one hand, in the wake of the disorientation following Vatican II, the Society of Jesus has undergone what anthropologists call a revitalization movement.[9] The interior life of Jesuits has been made over. The rejuvenation of the *Spiritual Exercises* in one-on-one form has been the paramount demonstration of this revival. On the other hand, much of the energy of the Society of Jesus has been devoted to coping with demographic and institutional decline. This stopgap stewardship becomes apparent in efforts to manage retrenchment and the geriatric bulge in membership. But it also crops up in urgent attempts to keep the Jesuit presence alive, and occasionally to innovate, within the apostolic infrastructure.[10] The contemplative side of Jesuit life appears to have been turned around. The record on the activist side, especially as it concerns the corporate thrust of the order, is less impressive.

The numerous mission statements, issued by the Society's general congregations, redirect Jesuits toward a commitment to social justice, collaboration with the laity, and a dialogue with contemporary culture. These declarations represent an effort to supply a unifying link between renewal of the interior life and ministerial effectiveness across the various areas in which Jesuits are active, against a backdrop of falling numbers.[11]

The guidelines remain controversial, however, in part because the new direction runs up against the turf wars or sluggishness built into long-standing commitments in other quarters, such as education, and in part because they arouse principled or ideological opposition. Jesuits have succeeded in reconstituting themselves as individuals more readily than they have managed to adopt and push forward a common direction. The disjuncture between individual progress and uneven collective success is at the heart of the analysis that follows.

Our initial focus is on the motivations and satisfactions that Jesuits, and not a few former Jesuits, bring to and take from their work. Then we move from the psychological toward the strategic dimensions of ministry. We look at the main programmatic shifts—collaboration with the laity and the priority to social justice—that the Society has adopted in order to give direction to its collective ventures. The relationship between these agendas is not altogether harmonious, and the ligatures they are supposed to provide between the therapeutic and institutional goals of the Jesuit enterprise sometimes pull apart. Laying out these tensions prepares the way for the analysis of changes in Jesuit secondary and higher education presented in chapter 9.

2

Most Jesuits and many former Jesuits have no trouble understanding what they do as ministry. But what do they mean by "ministry"? Sometimes it is simply a gratifying task that stretches a man by challenging him. "Teaching high school was very demanding but I generally enjoyed my work within the Society," one former Jesuit says plainly. "I like to work and the Society had a lot of really worthwhile work to do." Paeans to fulfilling activity are interspersed with half-jocular jibes at workaholism. Even so, tasks that somehow make a difference are prized. Ministry takes many forms, but at the heart of it is a precious satisfaction that Marx would understand: a sense of nonalienating labor.[12]

The core idea of ministry is satisfaction in personal service to others. "I do what I like," a sixty-five-year-old Jesuit in campus ministry declares. "I enjoy what I do. They let me do unusual and creative projects. I do love kids." Not only do such men like what they do, but they give the impression of considerable freedom, of really doing what they like. The twin themes are service to others, with a strong person-to-person touch. The maxim that virtue, with a measure of self-esteem thrown in, is its own reward holds true for many Jesuits. Work is both expressive ("I do what I like, I like what I do") and devotional (for the greater glory of God).

Meaningful ministry, then, consists of personal service; a motivational boost that lifts work beyond the pastoral or the purely ad hoc is often present as well. Ministry is transfigured with a zeal for pitching into the sacred adventure ("building the Kingdom"). Self-satisfaction is magnified through a sense of taking part in something larger than the self.

A thirty-five-year-old theologian, soon to be ordained and about to return to high school teaching, combines these elements. He complains, as do many of his colleagues, about the theological lucubrations that pull him away from person-to-person work on the outside:

> As a full time student, my days are filled with reading and study. Although we talk about studies as an "apostolate," for most of us, I think,

this is little more than a language game designed to soften the hard fact that time spent with books, no matter how interesting, is no substitute for time spent working with people. I know only a few Jesuits who entered the Society in order to study more.

Quickly, he warms to his passion:

> The high point for me, and I imagine for most of my peers, was regency. I taught English at ———. During those three years I found myself finally doing the sort of work I had entered the Society to do. I was making a contribution to people's lives and to the life of the church that simply could not be missed. I spent myself with great joy in that work. At no point in my Jesuit life has it been clearer to me how it is that this life can make sense. The needs of the People of God were clear and obvious and "in my face" from the moment my homeroom began to fill with students at 7:30 or so each morning for three years. I loved being a regent at ———. Those are probably the three happiest years of my life so far.
>
> I stay because the love which I have for the church and the Society fires a vision or a dream in me that helps me to see this life in what many would probably call "romantic" terms. Despite the occasional setbacks, I do find Jesuit life to be a noble and ennobling endeavor. I do see Jesuit life as a project or an undertaking full of challenge and meaning which make it worth the efforts of a man's whole life.

3

Often, men who leave the Jesuits pursue careers that allow them to keep up a sense of ministry. This case of a forty-seven-year-old educator is a little exceptional only in the strength of the carryover:

> The vision I developed in the Society still burns with great ferocity today. I wanted to help the poor. I organized in the Society, left, and for the last sixteen years have worked with kids who dropped out of high school and returned in Brooklyn. . . . This career choice is terrific. I've been able to help kids who need it and I feel great about that. I've also grown a lot.

On occasion, however, the sense of ministry gets short-circuited among former Jesuits. Sometimes the problem can be traced to distasteful aspects of the job, compounded by competing personal obligations. And outside the Society, communal support for selfless dedication may be in short supply.

The frustration of this forty-nine-year-old lawyer is that he is obliged to pay the bills by working at a job that does not live up to his yearning for service. "When I left the Society [after four years, twenty-seven years ago], I went on to graduate school and obtained a Master of Social Work degree," he begins:

> I continued in youth work for eighteen years, during the last of which I went to night school for a law degree. I now work as a lawyer. I defend doctors and hospital in cases of alleged medical malpractice.
>
> I have found over the years that neither social work nor law have been fully satisfying. Both have their good points but both are mainly ways to earn enough money to support myself.

The striking feature of the lawyer's story is the persistence of his aspiration for ministry. The work he happens to do takes up "nine to twelve hours a day," but it remains a sideline compared to his appetite for the ideal of service and taking part in a larger cause:

> I try to find connections between my work and "building up the Kingdom." I do not find the connections to be strong or immediate. It takes a constant mental effort, and I fail more often than I succeed even in remembering to look for connections.
>
> The Kingdom is more accessible outside the law office. I listen to the New Testament on tape in my car nearly every day, and I find that exercise very helpful. I am active in my parish and in my [adopted] son's . . . high school, and that helps too. I find I need to be in contact with a faith community. It is very hard for me to keep on track otherwise.
>
> I continue to hear a quiet call to work for the Lord on a more full-time basis. I do not know how to do that and still support myself and my son. Perhaps when he is grown up, I will be able to do something along those lines.

In the end, however, the greater satisfaction that Jesuits report in their work is only modestly higher compared to that of former Jesuits. As a rule, because so many of them stay in the helping professions, a good many former Jesuits are apt to consider their work as ministry of some sort, even if they do not surround it with the vocabulary of religious heavy breathing. A few former Jesuits object to the terminology itself. One former Jesuit in his mid-fifties who runs a data-processing system at a government hospital prefers the word "service" to "ministry" because the latter has the note of evangelizing, "which I don't try to do." Another man, a management consultant who was with the Society for over twenty-five years, argues that

> the border around the category "ministry" has become very fuzzy. I never did like the category much. Good people contribute to the commonweal the best parts of themselves. That's it. Calling some of this ministry puts a halo on it that is inappropriate.

As with Jesuits themselves, the more directly their work brings former Jesuits into face-to-face contact with others, and the more directly it requires efforts at caretaking and remediation, the more likely they are to retain a sense of ministry and to find satisfaction on the job. *Cura personalis* and pastoral flair are at the core of the longing expressed by this forty-three-year-old former Jesuit:

> Connections between my work and a sense of ministry? Not many connections really. My "ministry" now, I suppose, is to the quality of the printed word in religious publishing. I bring to bear on this my sensitivity to the English language, my knowledge of church and theology, and the Catholic/religious market that we serve. But this more often feels quite detached and unconnected to other people. The personal contact dimension of ministry I sorely miss. I see myself as having more people skills than I can presently use. I feel drawn to some form of pastoral ministry in which I can both share/explore and counsel in terms of more personal and spiritual issues.

In short, freedom from family obligations may be advantageous in certain cases, but it also appears to heighten the need to find personal satisfaction through face-to-face interaction with others. If sociability is reduced, the sense of ministry suffers and personal satisfaction falls. Jesuits are not troglodytes.

4

Jesuits are supposed to be contemplatives in action, dedicated to ministry. For men committed to "an honorable worldliness" (as one lay colleague put it), navel gazing is no substitute for action. "Mission is after all what we are here for," a Jesuit in his late sixties insists, invoking the Society's activist bent.

Remarks like these belie an uneasiness with the self-absorption released by the cultural revolution of the 1960s. A Jesuit psychologist in
his late thirties points ruefully to the therapeutic syndrome. He worries
about the inclination of Jesuits responsible for decisions on the deploy-
ment of manpower to second-guess the value of the approach. The introspective path may lead to gossamer puzzles. By comparison, the ministerial arena at least sets up objective problems that may be solved.
After so much self-scrutiny, an extroverted pragmatism has the appeal
of engagement with reality:

> Some of the men presently in positions of authority are reacting to the
> '60s, '70s focus on interpersonal knowing, deep sharing, and so on, and
> they're investing in the apostolical. It is as if you were looking at a pen-
> dulum swinging in the other direction. "Let's keep our focus there and if
> you have problems or whatever, we can talk about it and work it out."
> Right. And the fear of navel gazing—I think they are terrified that people
> are going to get into a kind of inward focus that would be crippling.

Another young (thirty-two-year-old) Jesuit who was to leave the Society within a year distinguished between "the mission model," familiar
to Jesuits of older generations, and "the therapeutic model" prevalent
in the postconciliar era. The distinction ("an oversimplification," he
warns) is largely self-explanatory. In the old days,

> formation was structured, programs were developed, experiments were
> offered, that prepared the man to take part in the apostolic mission of
> the Society. In other words, you were trained for the apostolate. Per-
> sonal concerns and "issues" were subjugated to the apostolate (if al-
> lowed to surface at all). Today, however, I think it is clear that the thera-
> peutic has taken over. Under this model the individual's formation is
> aimed at self-knowledge, mental and physical health, emotional stability,
> and lives of intimacy.

Balancing the two—"integrating" is the preferred word in counseling
circles—proves difficult. There is a suggestion that self-awareness cannot measure up to the romance of being swept along in collective purpose. But perhaps because corporate mission has yet to be clarified, the
therapeutic model remains attractive:

> Those formed by the mission model may well look at young Jesuits and
> say (and I quote), "Your needs are all well and good, but look to the
> apostolate for meaning and vision. If you are happy in your work, you

can put up with some of the smaller stuff around community." There is wisdom here. One of my contemporaries puts it this way: "Give the men a job and they'll be fine.". . . We know that the apostolate is the focus and the reason, but no matter how good my day at work was, or how much I am nourished by the apostolate, if I come home to closed doors, unhappiness, privatization, and solitude, the previous eight hours are of little consequence.

In the end, achievement on the job, however gratifying, does not make up for the lack of human warmth. This is why so many Jesuits seek out face-to-face ministries.

Jesuits today are more willing to acknowledge the sentimental rewards and the creative rush they derive from what used to be depicted as heroic self-abnegation. In the old days, a cordon sanitaire of tight-lipped unflappability and long suffering was drawn around the Jesuit whose emotions were expressed in athletic competition or drowned in a drop too much. The therapeutic manner has heightened awareness of the desiccating effects of absorption in work and of toughing it out through self-effacement. Jesuits were supposed to care for others but to be weirdly impartial with themselves. Such severity toward the self has been rejected.[13]

Few post-Freudian Jesuits are wholly convinced of the beneficence of displacing libidinal energies into work. The jokes about workaholism are uneasy. At the same time, the talk of personal integration is very earnest. Jesuits these days favor a mix of personal contact, zeal, and professionalism—a somewhat contradictory bundle that may be at least as demanding as the traditional, harshly ascetic code surrounding ministry.

As happens with expectations for community life, aspirations about work tend to be both turbocharged and cautious regarding the possibility of contentment. What may constitute a plausible ideal of getting it together for one man may for another be a sack of competing pulls.[14] Here is a twenty-eight-year-old Jesuit describing the gratification he gets from face-to-face ministry, only to question how far it can take him toward fulfillment:

It is a struggle to integrate sexuality as a vowed celibate, and I am not convinced it is possible to do so in an entirely healthy manner. I can say that I have found that when I am engaged in a work requiring me to become involved in people's lives because they trust me, there is an intimacy present that is very satisfying. That is something that I suspect few people outside of priests and ministers get to experience very often. It is a privileged place to be present for the foundation moments of so many lives. On the other hand, this is a very lonely life at times. Having both Jesuit and lay friends, both gay and straight, helps to give vent to some sexual needs. But in the end the physical needs basically go unmet unless one breaks his vows, which happens sometimes.

While their views are slipping into the minority, some older Jesuits are inclined to dismiss such reservations as sissified. In their place, they put a massive dedication to work, suffused by an obdurate passion for the divine. Obedience, not fulfillment, is the watchword. An elderly pastor, more than half a century a Jesuit, sums up this stern, heartfelt perspective:

> I think a personal love of Jesus Christ is the only reason men stay; I think they leave because of expecting the glory and getting the cross and not being able to handle it. I am a pastor of an African-American parish. I do not have an assistant or a secretary or a bookkeeper. I am kept quite busy doing all the things that these would do, and I find all of these things to be part of my ministry to which I have been assigned and which I love deeply.

The traditional and therapeutic takes on Jesuit life converge in their somewhat parochial, on-the-ground view of ministry. Neither has much truck with abstract doctrine. The operational code of ministry is outgoing service. This is the ordinary view of ministry, and, though it is non-monastic, it does not distinguish Jesuits from parish priests. The traditional and therapeutic approaches toward ministry differ more in their expectations than in their working definitions. One carries the baggage of disciplined obedience and love expressed as zeal. The other prizes personal growth and intimacy.

In both cases it is the hands-on, practical, personal element of ministry that counts. Like troops in combat, many older Jesuits expect to receive orders. They are used to obedience, not to ruminating over grand strategy, and some of them get confused and angry when clear directions are not forthcoming and they hear repeated exhortations to be self-starters. Likewise, younger Jesuits wrapped up in concerns over intimacy are not given to contemplating the big picture. The result is the same in both instances: a focus on the here and now, with not much strategic vision.

Structural transformations—professional specialization, increased competition in the market for education and services, and the erosion of institutional control by the Society—have also contributed to the sense that ministry is what goes on locally and rather haphazardly in the midst of larger, barely comprehensible forces. It is institutional fragmentation in the apostolic agenda of the order, as much as a cultural fashion for self-indulgence, that limits horizons and simultaneously heightens anxiety about the direction of corporate change.

"The most satisfying part of my work is, by far, having the sense that I am connecting with people—a wide range of people on a fairly intimate and significant level of their lives," a thirty-one-year-old theology student and part-time teacher declares, echoing the personalist line. "The most frustrating part, I suppose, is not knowing where we are going collectively/communally." It is difficult to step back from close-up interaction and contemplate long-run strategy:

> I think that we are engaged in massive corporate denial. We simply cannot continue running these major institutions on the scale we have been, and I see no provincial making provision. Sometimes I am a bit pissed off because I think that my generation is going to have to deal with it. I am not terribly concerned with the shortage of vocations, because I do think that God will give us what we need, so long as we are not stupid ourselves.

The testimony of a thirty-nine-year-old former Jesuit, recently retired from banking and looking forward to a stint with the Peace Corps, conveys a similar message. He praises the spiritual renewal that has taken hold in Jesuit life ("the most positive feature of formation was the personal integrity and witness to our faith by individual Jesuits on a daily basis") but expresses dismay at the failure to lay out a strategy of institutional renewal:

> The most important negative feature of formation was the difficulty the novitiate team had in telling us what the Society of Jesus was going to look like in the future, even the near future. We read and studied documents of the Society's congregations but were all too aware that the documents and the lived experience were far apart. In a generation before, guys knew when they entered what they were getting into: a monastic formation, jobs at some Jesuit high school or university, probably cut off from much of the mainstream intellectual tradition of this country. When they retired, they would head to a Jesuit retreat center or a Jesuit parish. All the communities were large and institutional. Someone may like or not like this future, but they knew when they came what they were buying into.

No longer! Some guys came because they wanted the old-style Society, complete with Latin and cassocks. Others wanted to live in poor urban areas and had visions of cooking lentils and rice for their small communities for the rest of their lives. They wanted nothing to do with traditional Jesuit structures. Our formation team was unable to tell us what we would expect. They didn't know themselves. I suspect that the answer may still not be known, even now, almost twenty years after many of the most dramatic changes in Jesuit community.

In brief, two transformations have reshaped the opportunities presented by and attitudes toward Jesuit apostolates. The infrastructure of schools, not to mention other operations such as retreat houses, once under the control of the Society of Jesus, has become a loosely coordinated network that is impossible to steer in a single direction. This organizational transformation has a dynamic of its own, apart from though perfectly compatible with a second major change: the therapeutic revolution. Close to becoming the universal language of religious life, the latter change accentuates skills at individual self-discovery and rehabilitation over collective problem solving.

Together, these trends have produced a fragmented market of decentralized institutions and initiatives that preserve considerable room for maneuver but that resist coordination and planning. The myth of a synoptic, self-contained coherence in "the works" has gone the way of theological system builders and holistic paradigms.

5

Three other developments confound inherited approaches to ministry besides the slide in institutional control and the emergence of a therapeutic ethos. One is the decay of the humanistic ideal as a pedagogical model. Another is variation in the spiritual feel of ministry across different apostolates. Finally, there is puzzlement over the connection between priestly ordination and the conduct of ministry.

Historically, Jesuit identity has been bound up not only with ordained ministry but also with the humanities and the liberal arts. From the outset, the Society of Jesus became identified with educational apostolates—with what in retrospect could be called the cultivation of human capital.[15] During the postwar period, with the success of the GI Bill of Rights and then with the expansion of enrollments and professional specialization from the 1960s, as most of the twenty-eight Jesuit colleges and universities in the United States grew, the number of students in the humanities has dropped in relative as well as absolute terms.[16] Far from being distinctive to Jesuit or Catholic schools, the declension in the liberal arts reflects what has been happening in American higher education generally.[17]

The decline of the humanities has been accompanied by some curious sidebars, for example, the creation of professional schools (initiated at least as far back as the 1920s) partly as cash cows and as mechanisms for recruiting women, as paying customers, into an educational enterprise from which they otherwise would have been excluded. The exclusion of women from the liberal arts colleges was maintained (as the practice was at Yale University) for some time after the profit-making professional schools were established.[18] But, unlike some of their elite secular counterparts with ample endowments, not many Jesuit colleges and universities could afford to preserve the humanities as their intellectual flagship.[19]

More was at stake in the crisis of the humanities in Jesuit education than financial solvency. The Jesuit understanding of the humanities resembled the vision shared by Protestant ventures in higher education in the nineteenth and early twentieth centuries: The humanistic disciplines signaled the union of learning and virtue at the crux of the Renaissance ideal. Because their wisdom was supposed to shape values and build character, propagating the classics and more broadly the liberal arts was a kind of ministry.[20] The project—forming leaders, as it was called—had ethical purpose as well as a vocational payoff. The idea was to produce gentlemen. Even if the humanities were never as central to the schools as idealized renditions of Jesuit pedagogy might suggest, the liberal arts curriculum set the tone. It was the institutional signature of the Society, much as the commitment to faith and justice has striven to dominate the ethos of the order in recent years.[21]

The influence of the Society of Jesus in higher education has come in for hard times not just on account of the reduction of Jesuits in the classroom but also because the nature of the Jesuits' specialty, the humanities, has changed drastically. At least in research universities and graduate faculties, the convergence between learning and virtue has been stretched to the point of breaking.[22] In light of this dissociation, the testimony of a sixty-four-year-old former Jesuit, now a university professor, has special poignancy:

For a long time I was unable to formulate what it was I was doing in the classroom. One of the losses I felt after I left the Jesuits was the loss of a larger context within which to place my own life and doings. That has continued, though without distress. However, some years ago, as we discussed our new core curriculum, I arrived at the very clear understanding that, whereas others were in the classroom to raise consciousness, I was decidedly there to hand on the intellectual and cultural tradition of the West. I am clearly not a postmodernist; however, my Jesuit initiation into the culture of the West also made me very aware that it was, at its best, an open tradition. I hand on the tradition.

A professor of English at one of the smaller Jesuit colleges makes a case that reports of the death of the humanities may be overblown. "The general erosion of confidence in humanistic education," he admits, "[is] a major factor in shaking these guys' [the Jesuits'] confidence in the educational apostolate. . . . It's the perception of doom that's most important and that certainly is the mood of the day. But," he continues,

> I think (hope?) that the prophesies of doom for the humanities and the traditional arts and sciences are exaggerated. . . . In fact, the more I get to know faculty at other [Jesuit] institutions, the more I think that we— somehow! and at least at the undergraduate level—have retained more of a generally humanistic sense of what the university is up to (and of at least the wish for interdisciplinary synthesis) than have the secular institutions that we compete with. It may finally be nothing deeper than the survival of a core curriculum that includes philosophy and theology, so that at least the Marxist literature professor may occasionally be confronted by a student who may know something that would stand up against a glib identification of religion with opiates. But I do think there's a difference.

A second change goes with the breakup of the humanities as the union of learning and virtue. A sense of ministry is apt to be more compelling in pastoral work, spiritual direction, social advocacy, and the high schools than in research and teaching as these activities have developed in American higher education. Spiritual direction is replete with God talk. "It's easier being in pastoral or social work to see ministry and priesthood and the Society as integrated into everything I do," a fifty-six-year-old associate pastor says:

> You asked about a typical work day. Today's Ash Wednesday. I got up at 5:30 as I usually do, spent some time in prayer and finished off my

homily preparation. I presided at two Eucharists at 8:00 and 12:00. I took Eucharist and ashes to six shut-ins spread out all over the city. I met one of my three retreatants doing the seven-week parish-directed retreat. I talked with four people, out of the twenty-six I have met so far, who are doing the Lenten Journey, a parish program that gives an orientation to Lent and helps people discover an integrated approach to prayer, fasting, and almsgiving that gets them where they want to be on Easter. I returned twenty-seven phone calls and fixed up the legal papers for a marriage that was performed at ———— without proper authorization by the local government. I opened eleven pieces of mail and dashed off a few notes. Tonight I am supposed to have dinner with a parishioner and his female companion, not his wife; believe me, I'll still be on the clock. I do a lot of work with couples preparing for marriage and with people seeking annulments. I talk with a lot of angry Catholics, angry from every imaginable angle. Yesterday I had two long phone conversations with parishioners who are going to write the cardinal because [the parish] had introduced the Nicene Creed. My Annotation 19 retreatant came in right after that, and she won't recite the Gloria because it's not inclusive. I've been taking an hour a week of scripture with two Visitation novices, the only non-Americans in the community, one from Kenya and the other from Kerala. I'm active in WIN, a community organizing project for DC sponsored by the IAF [Industrial Areas Foundation], a Saul Alinski–inspired organization.[23]

In contrast to all this hands-on pastoral work, the figure of the pastor-in-the-classroom as a model of Jesuit pedagogy and scholarly achievement has not quite passed from the scene. But it has seen better days.[24]

In addition, one of the prime motivators of apostolic dedication appears to be identification with the people to whom Jesuits minister. Many Jesuits can see the face of Christ in the inner-city poor, in Native Americans, in those who suffer from AIDS, and in the materially marginalized more readily than they can in college and university students. Empathetic identification is not limited to the economically deprived. Frequently, such commitment is extended, as a form of paternal care, to "the kids" in high school. Nevertheless, the structure of spiritual incentives in the colleges and universities is a little opaque. Crudely put, there is a tension between intellectual-humanistic and humanitarian-spiritual rationales.[25]

These factors—the deterioration in the status of "the classics" (associated with the silent burial of Latin) and variations on the differential sense of ministry present in the schools as compared to other apostolates—are all developments that pertain directly to Jesuit education. One other factor affects the role of Jesuits elsewhere as well: the disconnect not between work and a sense of ministry but between ministry and ordination.

For some, mainly older Jesuits, the ministry-ordination tie-in remains as clear as can be. Their work is ministry, and ministry has a sacerdotal aura. In the words of one sixty-three-year-old professor of literature,

> I view myself as a writer and teacher who is not a hyphenated priest. St. Paul's famous [statement that] *whatever* furthers understanding, in individuals and academic fields, of God's creation—human and other— furthers understanding of the Creator. I believe that all serious learning is advanced contemplation, and I believe that my teaching and preaching often bring something new to classes and congregations.

Another Jesuit, about the same age (sixty-one) and in the same field, admits to misgivings about the sacerdotal aspects of his work. He recognizes some tension between priesthood and dedication to professionalism:

> I wonder if I'm adequately perceived *as priest* in the incarnational work I do, especially by my students. Working to be integral to my field, I do not teach from a professedly Christian "angle" (though I do choose some course material for religious or faith-justice reasons, for example, a course on the contemporary Catholic imagination in America, or a novel about race or the poor).

The concern expressed here is deeper than the spiritual equivalent of a paper cut, but it is still at a considerable distance from the dismay that emerges among younger Jesuits about the connection between their lives as priests and their ministerial activities. A thirty-one-year-old Jesuit in theological studies captures this anxiety, which comes to a head as the time for ordination nears and which he dealt with affirmatively:

> One thing that I found interesting was that in theology a number of men suddenly confronted the fact that they could not articulate for themselves any fundamental difference between ordained ministry and lay ministry. Consequently, they began to wonder why they were making the sacrifices that ordained ministry required, and some concluded that the sacrifices could not be justified so they left.
>
> In the two theologates that I attended . . . I didn't find anyone providing a cogent explanation of ordained ministry and its relation to lay ministry. I find it difficult to articulate the difference between the two,

but I have a sufficient sense of it for myself that I could see the rationale for making a commitment to the ordained ministry.

Still another younger (thirty-five-year-old) Jesuit, now ordained and working as a high school teacher, voiced frustration during his days as a student of theology at what he saw as surrender to the notion that the priesthood has become a gratuitous adornment to ministry:

> I am constantly trying to find connections between the studies I am do-
> ing and the work I will be doing once I am ordained. Some days this is
> easier to do than others. It is a task that is not made any easier by the
> fact that the world of a theology center is largely divorced from the real
> world of the church. I find much of our energy is spent fighting the
> battles of the immediate fallout of Vatican II (battles which have left
> deep scars on many professors but which are not the pressing issues for
> Jesuits of my generation) or preparing for life in an idealized, politically
> correct church that does not exist now and is not likely to exist in my
> lifetime.
>   Tellingly, the word "priesthood" is rarely mentioned in our classes.
> In fact, this year when the third year theologians . . . gathered in Boston,
> most men from all three centers reported that they had spent the last
> two years either ignoring or apologizing for the fact that they were pre-
> paring for ordination. Such is life in the ideologically insulated and
> trendy city-states on the self-proclaimed cutting edge of theology. In an
> atmosphere such as that, it can often be difficult to make connections
> between what I am doing now and what I will be doing once I am or-
> dained. For now, I play the game of political correctness and try to re-
> mind myself that life in the real world and the real church has little to
> do with life in a theology center. A sad statement, but true.

An older (seventy-one-year-old) Jesuit, still at work in university administration, also sees the declining credibility and attractiveness of the
priesthood as the noxious product of cultural fashion. But with most of
his career behind him, he sounds less caustic than the neoconservative
Jesuit who is just beginning his career. The older man writes,

> One [main problem I see is] lack of vocations not only to [the] Jesuits,
> [but] to the priesthood, to religious life in general. There seems to be no
> special dignity attached to such a vocation or way of life by society in
> general, by "good" "Catholic" parents, and schools no longer have reli-
> gious models. Emphasis on the work of the laity in the church and the
> anger of women in not being allowed to serve as priests have increased

the negative aspect of priestly vocations. I have no solution, but I am
sure the Holy Spirit is leading us somehow.

A couple of problems, then, are distinctive to Jesuit ministry in higher
education. Aside from the likelihood that the sense of ministry is less
palpable in higher education than in some other apostolates, the decline
and metamorphosis of the humanities, much of it coincident with the
decades following Vatican II, have eroded a traditional source of collective mission. The liberal arts are on the defensive not only as preparation for career choices that pay off but also normatively, vis-à-vis the
faith-and-justice thrust. But the gravest problem is almost certainly disarray over the role of the priesthood as it pertains to ministry. This is
particularly worrisome for an activist, apostolic order.[26]

6

The dispersion of organizational control has coincided with doubts
about the functions of the priesthood in ministerial work. Both the outward, apostolic operations of the Jesuit project and the interior, normative foundations of the Jesuit priesthood are in flux. Organizational decentralization realigns the institutional activities of the Society. Qualms
about the sacerdotal role reflect symbolic uncertainty and psychological
anxiety. To this might be added, in higher education specifically, the
slump in the prestige and perceived utility of the humanities.

When time-honored routines no longer hold, "ideologies" frequently
emerge to restore meaning and direction to events that seem to have
taken on their own wayward dynamic.[27] The Society of Jesus has responded with two all-embracing mission statements. One stresses collaboration with the laity, the other gives priority to "the faith that does
justice."

These broad visions capture the conciliatory and the contrarian strains
in the Jesuit tradition. One is founded on the drive toward "accultura-
tion"; the other is a "countersign." At a very general level, the two elements of the Society's agenda are complementary. The option for faith
and justice helps preserve the institutional identity that is in danger of
vanishing in the rush toward Jesuit-lay collaboration.

While it is hard to find non-Jesuit coworkers who would argue with
the benefits of collaboration, some have doubts about the faith-and-
justice program. Conversely, a few Jesuits fear an erosion of authority
and a confusion of roles in the promotion of collaboration. Neverthe-

less, the collaborative agenda, bent on compromise and inclusion, confers legitimacy on what even most diehards see as adaptation to the inevitable. The faith-and-justice program is more controversial. Even if Jesuits are sympathetic to the priority in philosophical terms, implementing it requires hard choices about the allocation of personnel and other organizational resources.

A striking formulation of the collaborative theme was laid out in 1995. In the guise of a report to his colleagues on the thirty-fourth general congregation of the Society that had completed its work earlier that year in Rome, Edward Kinerk, then provincial superior of the Missouri province, gave an address that accorded pride of place to Jesuit-lay collaboration. By then, thirty years after Vatican II, outright resistance to collaboration between Jesuits and their colleagues had all but disappeared. Father Kinerk was doing little more, he said, than naming something already in place.[28] His purpose was to harness commitment to a transformation that looked unstoppable.

"Imagine for a moment," Kinerk begins, "that I am standing on a moving sidewalk. You know what a moving sidewalk is if you have ever been in an airport; it's like a conveyor belt. Remember, too, that moving sidewalks run in only one direction, and the particular direction is not an option." The analogy with the course of the Society of Jesus is inescapable:

> Now, I am standing on the moving sidewalk, and there is no question about the direction in which the sidewalk is moving. Right now I am standing on the year 1995, and the next stop is 1996, not 1994, and not 1950. The direction is not a choice; it is not good, not bad, not liberal, not conservative—it is just the way it is. Time only moves in one direction. I think we all agree that this is true. We would also agree that the hopes we have for SLUH [Saint Louis University High School] in 2010 are great hopes and that such a SLUH would be a wonderful place in its own right.
>
> So what is the issue? The issue is that I have a choice on this moving sidewalk, only one choice really, and that is the choice about which direction I will face while the sidewalk moves from 1950 to 2010. Knowing that I am going to 2010 . . . I can still choose to move toward 2010 with my face turned to 1950. Certainly, this is understandable—and we can rightly grieve over something great which has passed—but if I remain facing in that direction, the focus of my vision will remain a past which gets dimmer and dimmer, and this is sad because I am watching what will never be. But, if I look in the other direction, facing 2010, if

I direct my energies in this way, I am looking at the school which is to
come. Now I am focusing not on what the school once was but on what
I hope it will and can be.

The task is not to analyze much less brood over the past but to get with
the program, even if a master plan for how to get from here to there is
lacking.

Objections to this strategy have less to do with issues of efficiency
than with nervousness concerning the loss of identity and authority and
the collapse of a way of life that the criteria of efficiency or fairness address only obliquely. "I guess I am one of the conservative crowd," a
sixty-seven-year-old college professor, fifty years a Jesuit, avers:

> I hate the fact that we have dropped clerical dress and are embarrassed
> to be recognized as priests. I hate the sloppy way we do liturgy, the fact
> that liturgical vessels are now cheap five-and-dime glassware. I hate the
> fact that liturgical music is just guitar music. I hate the loss of real artists
> to do liturgical art. I hate the sellout to liberal scriptural scholars who
> date the gospels in the '80s or '90s or later.[29] But I still love God and the
> church and try to say a public Mass as reverently as I can despite the
> liturgical chaos. And I love to spend time preparing sermons each week,
> and I very much like the Jesuits I live with. They could not get me out
> of this group with a shoehorn. God willing, I will be around till I die
> and keep trying to regain an atmosphere of adoration and reverence.

The aroma of nostalgia is thicker in statements like these than in most
avowals of concern over Jesuit-lay collaboration, which are rare in any
case. But the underlying worry is widespread. From the standpoint of
most Jesuits, the difficulty is not with collaboration. Instead they worry
about what the Society actually brings to the table, and it is at this point
that the priority assigned to faith and justice assumes strategic importance. It is "the faith that does justice" that is supposed to lend content
and militancy, a definitive stamp, to the Jesuit enterprise in the postconciliar years. The program is not merely a matter of strategy; it is also
bound up with corporate identity. It is a call to action that sets the
agenda of what the order is about.

Even if many of them cannot make out what it means in practice,
ordinary Jesuits tend to be receptive to the faith-and-justice agenda in
principle and out of a kind of humanitarian instinct. For this reason,
much of the friction generated by the priority given to the righting of
social wrongs stems from institutional rivalries and turf protection, not

only from ideological divisions in the abstract. The question of *who* steers the specific ministries associated with the Society of Jesus through Sartre's "disordered monotony of the everyday" has been all but settled in favor of coalitional and broadly consultative arrangements. But the question of *where* the works should be headed, giving the variety of preexisting commitments and the diversity of functional interests, is difficult to sort out. The mix of players has become more heterogeneous with collaboration.[30]

The outcome has been low-grade polarization among Jesuits and, to some extent, between Jesuits and their colleagues regarding the faith-and-justice agenda. Sometimes, as happens in higher education, this takes the form of bewilderment about what the faith-and-justice agenda could mean, short of absurdity, in a mathematics class.[31] A different criticism surfaces in reservations about the possible displacement of what many Jesuits take to be the order's foundational, spiritual goals.

Martin Tripole, a Jesuit theologian, asked more than a dozen colleagues in leadership positions what the Society's faith-and-justice mission meant and concluded that they were not sure. "The most common answer was 'I don't know.' And the second most common answer consisted of words to that same effect." Tripole goes on:

> Once a temporal work is prioritized to such an extent that it becomes the integrating dimension of all mission activity, the danger is present that work becomes the principle legitimizing that mission rather than being an action that furthers the mission's more ultimate spiritual goals. The contention of this study is that no foundational principle is legitimate for the Society, any more than it is for the church, other than the mission of evangelization, that is, the proclamation of the gospel and the promotion of God's kingdom, in this world as well as for the next. . . . We risk being . . . social workers with—at best—pious motivation . . . the promotion of justice may and should be understood as a significant and important apostolate of the Society. But it is not the one that integrates and constitutes the norm against which every apostolate in the Society is justified.[32]

The faith-and-justice agenda threatens the traditional investment of the Society of Jesus in "the intellectual apostolate." Arguments are made to the effect that, in theory, one activity reinforces the other.[33] But the trade-offs can be harsh. Pondering over what is permissible within the current ecclesiastical climate, searching for where he senses the main chance of the Society lies, one influential Jesuit expressed his position this way: "If I had to choose between an organization that provided guarantees of civil liberties, free speech, et cetera but that didn't do much for the poor, and an institution that struggled for the poor but didn't bother to defend freedom of speech and the like, I think I know which one I'd pick."

The implication is that the schools draw too much fire from Rome, that some of them are elitist, and that they are not worth standing up for, compared to investment in the good that might be done elsewhere.[34] At some point, the argument goes, the rivalry between excellence and equality takes on an either-or cast, and it is the Jesuits' intellectual tradition that has to give in light of the Society's newfound commitment to the underprivileged.

The option is a matter of prudence as well as principle. Attacks on theological exploration and academic independence stemming from the Vatican trouble the schools and raise the costs of intellectual controversy. The generally favorable reception accorded to good works within the church makes it easier, on that score, to pursue social justice.

7

The faith-and-justice agenda is a prescriptive resolution more than a blueprint for action. It imparts a countercultural, cutting-edge aura to an assortment of pastoral and meliorative activities that coexist with a scattering of challenges to the social status quo. Commitment to the "faith that does justice" evokes the militant side of the Jesuit legacy, in counterbalance to the order's equally venerable habit of collaborative, adaptive ministry. Both of these currents—the push toward collective purpose versus the pull toward piecemeal accomplishment and the tradition of a conciliatory, accommodating strategy versus the adversarial impetus toward cutting against the cultural grain—are evident among Jesuits.

Two further patterns are especially significant. Jesuits who are content with their work tend to be supportive of the institutional church and to be relatively conservative on moral and sexual issues.[35] These Jesuits keep their heads down and get on with their work without bothering about grand controversies, except to affirm their confidence in the overall direction of the church and its core teachings regarding sexuality.

The second pattern comes into view when corporate ministries rather than individual works are considered. A significant association can be detected between progressive thinking on faith-and-justice questions and approval of the performance of Jesuit ministries. Similarly, Jesuits who take advanced positions on sexual-moral controversies also express satisfaction with the apostolic agenda of the Society.[36]

What do these linkages add up to? When Jesuits try to envision the course of the Society as a whole, principles are engaged and tensions come to the surface. The faith-and-justice tenor of declarations from recent general congregations has resonated positively among Jesuits who call themselves progressives. Conversely, the minority who see themselves as conservative on such matters are less happy with the apostolic strategy of the Society. Jesuits who express enthusiasm over the social agenda of the Society are also likely to entertain liberal views on sexual-moral issues and vice versa. Differences over ministerial strategy are not just administrative quarrels over the disposition of resources. Ideological rancor is involved as well.[37]

Yet a certain compartmentalization between individual work, specific ministries, and global directives mitigates confrontation within the Society. The degree to which Jesuits claim to be satisfied or dissatisfied with their own work has *nothing* to do, one way or the other, with their perceptions of the overall performance of the Society or with their views on social and economic policy.[38] Assessments of the collective accomplishments of the order are one thing, judgments of performance closer to home another.

Some Jesuits, convinced that synoptic issues are a waste of time, ignore the managerial apparatus of the Society as best they can and plunge ahead with their own priorities. This man, a fifty-three-year-old high school administrator, has little use for those in staff positions in the Society who busy themselves, so he feels, with well-meaning directives and calming nerves. His attitude oscillates between indifference and contempt:

> The local leaders [superiors and provincials] are inexperienced managers, and too much runs on "nice guy-ism," rather than on any kind of goal-centered direction for the provinces, so the provinces don't have any goals. . . .
> The provincial comes around, or the superior comes around, and he has his annual visit, and he asks "How's it going?" and "How's your spiritual life?" and all these generalized kinds of questions. "How's your health?" and all. . . . But say "What goals did you have, Father, for this last year? What were you trying to achieve? And how did those mesh with the goals of the *institution?*" Whatever those particular goals are.

And, "Father, do you know what the goals of the institution are?" And if you're not trying to foster the goals of the institution, you should be elsewhere.

Dedication to the work at hand compensates for cynicism with regard to the powers that be. This Jesuit cultivates his garden:

> The work I do isn't for the Society. I work as a member of the Society, but the work I do is for the kids in the school, and education in general. . . . Do I like to think about the Society dying? I think no more than I like to think about me dying. I don't think about either one of them very much. I just don't find it helpful to review it on a frequent basis. I just have other positive things to do with people than to be thinking about it. So I put it out of my mind because I am not in a position to do anything concrete about it.

8

A feeling that control over the works has slipped out of the hands of the Society of Jesus is not new. During the Depression, a number of schools went under, and other operations were scaled back. Hectic scrambling and hand-to-mouth subsistence were the order of the day. On the upside, authorization was sometimes given after the fact to initiatives that grew like topsy, spurred by enterprising Jesuits acting on their own. Almost always, however, there was little doubt that ministerial operations were headed in the general direction of preestablished goals.

Three things set the current situation apart from the usual gap between ideal and actuality. One is that expectations regarding the personal fulfillment to be had from ministerial work receive at least as much attention as the organization of the ministries themselves. Second, the connection between qualification for ministry and the requirement of priestly ordination is less convincing. Both these concerns, along with a few others, are voiced by a twenty-eight-year-old Jesuit in theological studies:

> It will be harder as laypeople take more and more leadership positions in the church to justify having to give up sex and independence. The Society will have to reinterpret ministry as such in the near future. What will make us distinct from committed laity?
>
> Obviously, the whole question of priestly roles in the church has to be reexamined in the light of seeing all as being called to ministry. Com-

munity has got to change. Jesuit identity within our institutions somehow has to be guaranteed despite the shrinking number of Jesuits. Vocations have sunk to such low levels that it may well be that religious life
is dying out, and unless there are radical changes, it will disappear. I do
not see any of the leadership of the Society at present as facing honestly
up to the situation. We will be forced to react in the future because we
have not been honest in the present about what is going on.

The third new circumstance conditioning the apostolic direction of
the Society of Jesus involves the match or misfit between norms about
ministry and their actual operation. The one area in which a reasonable
congruence prevails between rhetoric and reality is in Jesuit-lay collaboration. Most Jesuits accept and many of them welcome the advent of a
"lay-centered church." A major concern of the Society is with preparing
for the transition by assuring that laypeople, whose theological literacy
may not be up to snuff, are equipped for the takeover. The strategic
question is not whether but how and when.[39]

But in two other areas, institutional arrangements are out of sync
with official rhetoric. Organizational habits have yet to catch up with
exhortations toward commitment to the poor. Conversely, no official
blessing has been given to the drift of Jesuits into parish and other forms
of pastoral work. Here, demographic and organizational changes have
outrun suppositions about what Jesuits should be doing.[40] In the first
case, it is a matter of rhetoric outstripping reality, in the second case, of
reality outrunning rhetoric. In both instances, practical incentives are
out of line with the articulation of goals.

Competition over agenda setting is the most contentious area of apostolic planning in the Society of Jesus. Claims that the rival priorities
given to faith-and-justice endeavors and educational institutions are
blendable are not just wishful thinking. But clashes about putting strategic goals into practice persist, especially when they entail decisions
about missioning scarce manpower under circumstances when manpower itself has considerable leverage for bargaining.

Underlying this conflict, however, is a pair of perhaps even less tractable dilemmas. The credibility of hierarchy itself has declined, along
with the administrative centralization of the works. The pull toward
self-realization in service and away from corporate strategizing begins to
look irresistible. The question becomes not one of which agenda or style
to adopt (the conciliatory in balance with the adversarial) but one of the
feasibility of *any* sort of collective action in religious life.

In addition, the debate over the faith-and-justice agenda versus the more traditional commitments of the Society fails to address the question of how holy orders—that is, the priesthood—bears on ministry. Once shielded in charismatic mystery, the status of the priesthood becomes all the more puzzling as its practical functions recede. "None of the men I know," a seminary official, deeply committed to social justice, observed, "care about being a priest. What matters is being a Jesuit." Such doubts reflect the declining acceptance of celibacy as a prerequisite for ordination. The problem has as much to do with the dubious link between celibacy and priesthood as with the customarily privileged connection between priesthood and ministry.[41] In either case, the sacerdotal legacy has fallen on hard ground.

CHAPTER NINE

Revitalizing the Schools

There was the feeling that the Catholic university was becoming increasingly secular—secular and not obedient to the fundamentalist teachings of the church. It made people like Cardinal Ratzinger and some of the others very, very nervous. I made four trips a year, three days each, to argue and plead and cajole and advise over there.

They've (the Jesuits) made mythical claims about their devotion to the arts and sciences, but I doubt that their devotion is all that great. What's really great is turning out Catholics who can make their way in the world, and that's still the case.

I

While they do many things, Jesuits are best known as educators. The proportion of Jesuits in pastoral activities is on the rise and will probably continue to be large. Still, considered as a whole, the Jesuit presence in secondary and higher education in the United States remains impressive. Activities in secondary and higher education cannot be taken as representative of the full range of the order's ministries, but they are sizable enough to warrant attention.

The involvement of Jesuits in education matters for one other complex of reasons. The recent history of the schools dramatizes many of the issues that run through the life of the Society: declining numbers, the pressure for collaboration, the impact of changing spiritualities on work, and bafflement about the nexus of priesthood and ministry.

It is essential to recognize from the outset that the different trajectories followed by the high schools and the colleges and universities exemplify alternative strategies of accommodation with the aftermath of the 1960s. Experiments in Jesuit secondary education have not rattled the guardians of orthodoxy in Rome. But the course followed by Jesuit higher education (and Catholic higher education as a whole in the United States) has alarmed the Vatican.

Both the forces pressing from the outside—principally, legal regulations, accreditation and funding criteria, and standards of academic freedom—and the responses to these factors on the inside, in the form of programmatic initiatives, have differed dramatically between Jesuit secondary and higher education. Since the late 1960s and early 1970s, the colleges and universities have had to operate in a political environment that has inhibited and indeed prevented them from characterizing themselves as "pervasively religious" if they are to obtain public funding. In the face of such rules, no Jesuit college or university has been tempted to style itself as the Catholic equivalent of a sectarian bunker, wholly dependent on private contributions. Even before the 1960s, with the initiation of the GI Bill, Jesuit colleges and universities felt that they were in no position to turn down federal monies if they were to swim with the sharks. The high schools, much smaller in size and privately funded, have been under no comparable restrictions.[1]

In addition, beginning in the late 1960s, the colleges and universities associated with the Society of Jesus have been "separately incorporated" from the order—technically, from the religious community resident at each of the schools. They are no longer the property of the Jesuits. The high schools operate under varied arrangements that may approach but rarely attain the legal separation prevalent at the institutions of higher education.[2]

The devolution in the control of the colleges and universities toward lay-dominated boards of trustees was prompted by aspirations to secular excellence that were never felt as powerfully in Jesuit secondary education because the high schools had much less reason than the colleges and universities to see themselves as second-rate in relation to peer institutions. From as early as the 1960s, faculty at the flagship colleges and universities of the Society were recruited on the basis of their academic credentials, without much regard to religious affiliation. Selection on the basis of religious motivation continued to count in hiring at the high schools.

So, the high schools on the one hand and the colleges and universities on the other have pursued different visions of where they were coming from and where they were headed. The direction of Catholic higher education in the United States was set in 1967, at the peak of the euphoria inspired by Vatican II, with the issuance of a manifesto, the Land

O'Lakes statement, calling for "true autonomy and academic freedom in the face of authority of any kind, lay or clerical, external to the academic community itself." This policy got its impetus from a yearning to overcome the laggard state of Catholic higher education, a predicament that had been cause for complaint among Catholic intellectuals since the 1950s. The diagnosis attributed the sorry academic standing of Catholic colleges and universities to the ghetto mentality carried over from immigrant times. The Land O'Lakes manifesto, which took its name from the retreat center in Wisconsin where the heavy hitters of Catholic higher education assembled, fixed the agenda for the vanguard colleges and universities over the next decades.[3]

The Jesuit high schools began to get their act together a few years later, in 1970, around the time that the aging umbrella organization, the Jesuit Educational Association, split into the Association of Jesuit Colleges and Universities (AJCU) and the Jesuit Secondary Education Association (JSEA). The leaders of Jesuit high schools had little reason to worry about their reputation for academic excellence. Nor was there much need at the time to be concerned about access to public funding, even if educational vouchers were to become of interest later on. The overriding goal centered around the imperative of consolidating a distinctive niche for Jesuit secondary education. "We were determined," one participant in the events of the early 1970s insisted, "to make our schools *different.*"

The directors of the Jesuit high schools articulated a vision of where the high schools should be headed, reemphasizing Ignatian spirituality and religious education. The moral content of the curriculum and the character-building ethos of the school setting were stressed to a degree barely possible in higher education.[4]

The reformers also democratized participation in the JSEA. Lay administrators and teachers were consulted and brought into decision making. If curricular content was not exactly traditional (the Latin requirement began to fall like bowling pins across the prep schools), it was still in line with a revitalized version of the Jesuit legacy, and the manner of implementing these changes was participatory, certainly in comparison with the older, almost purely hierarchical management style and in contrast to the unwieldiness of the much larger colleges and universities.

The feeling of inclusion and involvement was enhanced as the JSEA cast itself not as a lobby or accrediting agency but as a service organization, providing opportunities for pedagogical retooling through workshops and seminars. The effect of these three moves was to foster an aura of common purpose and stakeholding that transcended the ups and downs of the member schools. Downplaying its bureaucratic side, the JSEA took on the features of a social movement.

The AJCU, on the other hand, has acted primarily as an interest group vis-à-vis the federal government. The performance of its major task—making sure that Jesuits colleges and universities get a hearing in the councils of American higher education and in the maneuvering for government funding—has practically nothing to do with the religious ethos of the member schools. Even though, from time to time, the AJCU uses its resources to back one social or political cause or another—for example, protests against the School of the Americas run by the U.S. military to train officers from Latin America—members pay their dues mainly so that the Washington headquarters can take care of business: influencing federal legislation. Until the crisis over *Ex Corde Ecclesiae* broke in the 1990s, questions of collective mission stayed largely on the back burner. Finally, while the AJCU has more than a dozen lay-run satellite groups dedicated to specialized administrative and professional functions within higher education, membership in the executive committee of the organization has been restricted to the presidents of Jesuit colleges and universities, almost all of whom have been Jesuits. In contrast to the JSEA, the apex of the association has not been laicized or democratized.

The contrast between the AJCU and the JSEA, though instructive, can be overdrawn. Before the 1990s, and before the conflict over *Ex Corde Ecclesiae* put them on the defensive, a few Jesuits and their colleagues already realized that the budgetary and legislative focus of the AJCU was too narrow to handle concerns about the identity and mission of Jesuit higher education that arose independently of prodding from the Vatican. The leadership of the AJCU expressed no strong objections to taking up soft issues. Yet it was clear that the priority of the Washington office continued to be getting the member schools up to snuff by secular standards and making sure that their material interests were attended to in the corridors of power.

Hatched out of talks that began in the later part of the 1980s, the National Seminar on Jesuit Higher Education took shape to fill this vacuum. One of the founders tells the story:

> In 1985 or '86, the provincials, concerned about a sense of "malaise"
> (their word) in higher education communities, constituted a small com-

mittee and asked it to look at the Jesuit higher education scene and make some suggestions. The committee was chaired by [a Jesuit who had just stepped down as provincial] and included a rector, a president, and two faculty members [all Jesuits]. . . . We met three or four times . . . and came up with three proposals: (1) a seminar and publication based on *Studies in the Spirituality of Jesuits,* to circulate ideas and stimulate discussion; (2) a national meeting or regular series of meetings for "the troops" (our idea was that all sorts of administrators met and shared ideas about what worked and what didn't and so formed support networks—presidents, rectors, deans, financial VPs, deans of students, etcetera—but not the Jesuits doing the ordinary work of teaching and administering the universities; and (3) a discussion process in each province among Jesuits working in higher education. Number one resulted in *Conversations,* two got melded with the Georgetown bicentennial celebration and resulted in Assembly '89. My impression is that three didn't result in much.

The need was for ongoing exchange about the direction and meaning of Jesuit higher education. "I suppose this could have been [understood as] movement in anticipation of pressure from Rome," a layman who was in on the early days says. "Kolvenbach's talk at Georgetown in 1989 is part of this, of course.[5] But the spirit of it in 1988–96 or so was very much not in a spirit of compliance with authority but a recognition from within of the need to pass the baton [from Jesuits to laypeople]."

Composed of about two dozen Jesuits and laypeople, the Seminar meets periodically and produces a twice-yearly magazine, *Conversations on Jesuit Higher Education.* The format is like that of a glossy alumni publication but the contents of *Conversations* are generally weightier: "The Heart of the Matter: The Core Curriculum," "Teaching as a Vocation," "Catholic Intellectual Life," and so on. The seminar and *Conversations* constitute a forum for the exchange of ideas that the AJCU alone does not provide. Such activities form a significant subplot within the sprawling network of Jesuit higher education.[6]

2

The strategy adopted by the movers and shakers in Jesuit secondary education rested on two premises. One was an acknowledgment, shared by leaders in higher education, that the Society of Jesus could no longer go it alone. Some form of collaboration with and perhaps transition to lay management was unavoidable. The second idea—recognition of the need to resurrect and propagate a distinctively Jesuit educational vision, a strong identity—added a normative message to the practical lesson drawn from implacable demographics. Faced with a less complex legal and institutional environment, and sharing similarities in size and student and faculty composition, the high schools responded in a more coordinated fashion than the colleges and universities to the task of forging a unified agenda.[7] They developed a message and devised methods for communicating it.

By the middle of the 1970s, the JSEA had already begun to map out a vision of the "Jesuit High School of the Future" that would be refined through the following decades.[8] Anchoring these mission statements was a shrewd diagnosis of the options open to Jesuits in the high schools. The JSEA realized that the schools could not continue as they had, yet Jesuits and like-minded laypeople wanted to avoid what some perceived to be the disintegration of their hold on the colleges and universities and the secularizing dynamic let loose by the Land O'Lakes summit.

A memorandum drafted in 1975 considered ways for the high schools to avoid what was thought to have gone too far in the colleges and universities affiliated with the order—the drop in control over all facets of education, from finances to doctrinal correctness to recruitment and academic content.[9] The memorandum began by noting that according to the civil code in the United States, any tax-exempt corporation had to be governed by a board of directors or trustees. However closely customs inherited from Europe approximated the Platonic ideal of the philosopher-king, and no matter how dearly it was held as integral to the habits of the Society, one-man rule of Jesuit operations, or exclusively Jesuit governance, was open to challenge on legal grounds.

Centralized control was also imprudent because the consolidation of myriad activities under a provincial superior would render the Society all the more open to litigation. Separate incorporation buffered the order from such worries. As long as the institutions were separate in law, a provincial's office could not be held responsible for bailing out a bankrupt school or for salvaging other improvident or unlucky apostolates.[10] In the spirit of John Courtney Murray's prudential defense of pluralism as a culture that Catholics could live with because it safeguarded their own religious liberties, acceptance of the realities of power sharing in the high schools might bring unexpected advantages.

There was another reason for welcoming such a course. Laypeople could no longer be induced to dedicate their energies to the high schools without an understanding that they would exert genuine influence over the course of the schools.

Movement toward fuller lay participation, then, was advisable not only because the American legal system exerted pressure in that direction but also because a stringently hierarchical model no longer worked. Even if retention of control by stacking high school boards with Jesuits handpicked by provincials looked like the most effective fail-safe device, there were not enough hours in the day, nor was there sufficient competence among Jesuits, to run the schools by central authority. What was once a philosophical ideal had become counterproductive.

None of this differed significantly from the thinking that dominated advanced circles in Jesuit higher education. The trouble was that legal analysis was better at pinpointing an option that could no longer be defended than it was at providing an alternative showing where the schools should be headed.

What set the high schools apart was their capacity to infuse functional necessity with a motivational rationale. Members of the JSEA based their vision on a broad directive issued by the superior general of the Society. The reason for retaining administrative control over the high schools, Pedro Arrupe declared, was that "the religious formation of the high school student is an essential goal of Jesuit secondary education." [11] The JSEA made variations on religious formation and moral education a major theme for secondary education while finessing the delicate matter of control even as working arrangements moved in a democratic direction. The hope was that if members of the faculty were or were to become sufficiently imbued with the Ignatian spirit, then potential confrontation over Jesuit versus lay control would evaporate into a nonissue. A reconverted laity would carry the Ignatian torch passed on by the Jesuits.[12] Democratization on these terms would not jeopardize religious identity. Confined to organizations of manageable size, reengineering the high schools centered more on a sense of community and team spirit than on individual rights.[13]

Preoccupation with financial viability reinforced concern over the religious identity of the high schools. The argument that "academics aren't everything" drew sustenance from the cultural climate of the 1970s. The program of renewal happened to be a strong if variously interpretable selling point. Old-fashioned ethics differed from possibly radical consciousness raising. Most important, at the high school level, there was a market for the inculcation of virtue of *some* kind. Emphasis on character formation consolidated a domain that the Society had staked out long ago. Jesuits could build on their strengths. They could march forward with some confidence that the past, or what they selected as the best of the past, would not be left behind.[14] For all these reasons, importing some version of the faith-and-justice program and updating the traditional stress on character formation faced fewer obstacles in secondary than in higher education.

3

Though they soon managed to regroup, Jesuits in secondary education felt their dynamism slipping away just after Vatican II. In those days, toward the end of the 1960s and the beginning of the 1970s, just as the high schools were breaking off to form their own association, demoralization was widespread on two fronts. Financially, the high schools were in trouble, and the cultural upheaval let loose by Vatican II and the 1960s generally put corporate direction up for grabs. Business as usual was not an option. "We were talking out of a broken heart," one key player in the meeting that gave birth to the first postconciliar programmatic statement for Jesuit secondary education recalled:

> We were having some financial problems. We weren't into big-time fund-raising yet, so we were having a hard time paying all the bills. We kept having to raise tuition. These things we didn't like to do.
> The other problems were really theological. We had a split group. The mandates that we thought existed in Vatican II weren't always accepted by everyone. . . . One theology was that we should stay very classical, that we should give a very intensive academic training, and that we should keep the traditional models. And the other group said no, we've got to go into collegiality, we've got to go into personalism, we were trying to form the kid, not just inform him. And hopefully he'd be reaching spirituality. So we discussed what was going on in the religious ed department. That's where the vulnerability came; we were very vulnerable in religious ed. Some were still holding onto the very dogmatic definitions, and the courses in the four years of high school were very scripture oriented, very definition oriented. The other group said, hey, we've got to do something, so they blew up a lot of balloons and they carried them to the classrooms. They were trying to open up the individual to his own experience, and that was what they thought was important. So it was two types of theologizing, and they were not compatible. We had to get something in between.

What emerged from this free-for-all was a back-and-forth series of mission statements and workshops that drew increasing numbers of faculty and administrators from across the separate institutions. Inspirational "preambles" and "reflections" spawned, in rapid succession, how-to "instruments for self-evaluation" and detailed guidelines specifying the standards that students should measure up to by the time they graduated.[15] Feedback was quick and continuous. The process bore a striking resemblance to the dynamics of the *Spiritual Exercises*. Whatever mystical epiphanies shaped the program were embodied in specific, hands-on prescriptions:

> We wanted people to look into their own experience. At the time, we didn't know what we were looking at, so we got confused and upset. But now we know you can carry that wherever it goes—the opposite of a deductive, dogmatic approach.

A shared perception of the survival value of collaboration facilitated the reconciliation of contending positions. There were also advantages to the modest size of the high schools. The Catholic atmospherics and the sense of personal as well as professional community were thicker in the high schools than in most of the colleges and universities:

> Now you have many professors at Jesuit colleges that don't like Jesuits and that's a real problem. From the early '60s on they were just hiring academics only. This didn't hit us so soon. We had some lead time. We didn't have a lot of people on our faculties that hated us or were hostile.

Moreover, experiments that might seem radical from a pre-1960s perspective, such as heightening the attention paid to the nonacademic side of education, were justified by invoking traditional Jesuit values—for example, "educating the whole person" and *cura personalis*. The high schools offered both access to therapeutic interventions and discipline associated with the vaguely awesome appellation of "Jesuit-trained." Sharpening the focus on what used to be considered extracurricular activities fit the post-1960s educational climate and also spoke to the needs of the increasing number of students from troubled families. In sum, the break with tradition was less abrupt in secondary than in higher education, and the educational goals of the high schools were clearer.

Some ambitious features of the faith-and-justice agenda were toned down partly for pedagogical reasons, out of a recognition of the limited capacity of young teenagers to absorb the message, and partly out of political savvy about how far the message could be pushed with parents more interested in having their children make their way in the world than in righting social wrongs. Jesuits scanned their clientele and constituencies astutely:

> A high school senior is just starting to have the ability for the abstract thinking needed to understand large moral issues. We put on these dramatic workshops in all of these schools that included parents and students and provincials, and the basic concepts of justice that came out of these meetings that included kids were "Don't write on the toilet walls, don't steal and don't cheat." Practical stuff. . . .
>   We never had parents who complained about these justice-consciousness efforts. We might have been a little timid in our methods. We didn't take the kids out into scary scenes of squalor. . . . We were talking about doing something brave and bold that might upset alumni and many other constituents. Well, we did upset a few parents, and that worried me. I think our best step was to take the kids on the level they were at. I don't think that we made a lot of mistakes, but we weren't as bold as we could have been. But really we were about changing structures and not just serving soup in a kitchen.

Behind the revitalization of the Jesuit high schools, then, are several interlocking ingredients. The scale of the problem was close to manageable. Just as important was the way the problem was conceptualized. From the beginning, the task was framed as one of devising methods to reaffirm the Jesuit ethos in institutions whose academic standing was in reasonably good shape. No wrenching conflict flared up between this goal and the exigencies of fund-raising. Innovation in the name of tradition provided a strategic identity rather than another empty slogan.[16] In stressing the development of the whole person, for example, Jesuits could feel they were retrieving a legacy rather than venturing off into the unexplored territory represented by a research university. They knew, more or less, what they were doing.

4

We can entertain generalizations about the high schools not only because they are smaller on the average and less complex than the colleges and universities but also because the variation in their size is restricted, compared to the enormous diversity in scale across the twenty-eight institutions of higher education. A handful of Jesuit high schools has more in common, and is liable to be more representative of the whole, than a comparable sampling of Jesuit colleges and universities. And what Michael Lacey has called the "radical decentralization of the universities" [17] is not just a matter of differences in size; it is also reflected in their internal complexity and composition: professionally specialized faculty recruited on national markets and students drawn from a wider geographic range.

Accreditation standards, professional competitiveness, and government funding practices push Jesuit higher education in one direction, toward achievement in secular terms, while the priorities of the Vatican and the commitment of some Jesuits tend to pull the colleges and the universities toward religious ends. The high schools rely much less on public funding and are more evidently in the business of character formation, so that neither Washington nor Rome bothers very often with their internal workings.

Besides the impetus provided by the Land O' Lakes statement, the push toward professionalization in Jesuit higher education gained momentum with programs like the National Defense Education Act of 1963 and similar measures reflecting the budgetarily expansive spirit of the Great Society. Indeed, the classical curriculum modeled on the *Ratio Studiorum*, the Jesuits' "guidebook for the first international educational system," had begun to give way as early as the end of the nineteenth century, under pressure from accrediting agencies and an immigrant and postimmigrant clientele more interested in vocational advancement than humanistic polish.[18] What the postwar years, beginning with the GI Bill, added to these legal arrangements was a panoply of economic incentives that encouraged compliance with regulations designed to restrain the sectarian nature of qualifying institutions. The fact that funds became increasingly available at a time, the early 1970s, when private colleges and universities were facing mounting competition from public institutions, especially the embryonic community colleges, added to their allure. A staff member of the AJCU at the time recalls,

> The main problem (Paul Reinert's book *To Turn the Tide* tells the story) was that all private colleges were in deep financial trouble, and the problem was to get money for kids to go to college. The financial crisis must have been building up over a period of years, and the increase in the number of public institutions added to the problem; the public institu-

tions were competing with private colleges, and these public institutions
were increasing like crazy.[19]

Founded in 1970, the AJCU stayed out of the business of direct fund-
raising, probably because the twenty-eight member schools did not want
the central organization to muddy the waters by interfering with their
separate endowment campaigns, foundation contacts, and other solici-
tation drives.[20] But this did not prevent the AJCU from trying to
influence legislation that would direct the course of funds to member
schools.

During the heady period of the early 1970s, before the recession of
the Carter years and the cutbacks of the Reagan presidency, the Nixon
administration kept up the flow of support to higher education. The
AJCU entered into legislative alliances with secular and denomination-
affiliated lobbies in defense of private schools. ("The whole purpose was
to form a united front vis-à-vis the Congress.") Sometimes, as happened
with legislation that would eventually become the Pell Grant program,
tactics involved scripting application formulas that would allow lower-
income students who would otherwise attend public schools to qualify
for tuition support at private colleges and universities. Sometimes, legislative maneuvering was targeted more specifically:

> In 1979–80 Boston College asked me how they could get funding for
> their library; that was not "a facility" (eligible for funding under exist-
> ing legislation). Now they had a first-rate lobbyist who was politically
> well connected in Massachusetts. He took me to the Sheraton and asked
> me how to do that. So I said that the first step was to get three words
> into Title VII of the Higher Education Act, which is the facilities part of
> the act. I said just get "including research libraries" in there. He got it
> in, and BC got a twenty-million-dollar Tip O'Neill Library!

The political world in which the colleges and universities operate
extends beyond relations with Congress and government funding agencies.[21] Domestically, it encompasses a number of formidable alumni
groups as well as elements within the Society itself—the more aggres-
sive faith-and-justice advocates, for example—at odds with one facet or
another of the institutional obligations of the order. On a larger scale,
the Vatican has kept tabs on Jesuit higher education since the 1960s.
From its formative days, the AJCU has had to navigate through the rip
tides generated by these contending forces.

Jack Fitterer, who eventually left the Society to become an Episcopal priest, was called from the presidency of Seattle University to assume the leadership of the AJCU in 1970, a position he held until 1977. Conflicts raged on several fronts. One obstacle Fitterer faced was resistance from fellow Jesuits against the process of solidifying separate incorporation and the development of lay boards for the colleges and universities. (". . . a real dog fight; I can't tell you how much opposition there was to this; there was talk of betrayal of the Society.") Another was the distrust of younger Jesuits toward institutional commitment and toward the "elitist schools" in particular. A related difficulty was the fallout from the political activism of Jesuits, most conspicuously Daniel Berrigan. Such goings-on bewildered and angered some benefactors and longtime friends of the Society. "I knew," Fitterer stated, "that these universities could not succeed unless we had the strong support of laypeople."

But the problem that most disheartened Fitterer was the stiffening reaction of Rome to the repercussions of Vatican II. "[This] really caused me to lose my hope for the success of Jesuit ministry":

> I could see that this was going to be a very difficult period with the Holy Office and other organizations of the Vatican breathing down the necks of the theologians. It set in with *Humanae Vitae*. There was a French cardinal, I can't remember his name, who said to me, "If we breed enough children, some genius will come along and solve the problem of the population explosion." That did it for me.
>
> There was the feeling that the Catholic university was becoming increasingly secular—secular and not obedient to the fundamentalist teachings of the church. It made people like Cardinal Ratzinger and some of the others very, very nervous. I made four trips a year, three days each, to argue and plead and cajole and advise over there.

In short, the origins of the controversy over *Ex Corde Ecclesiae* can be traced back several decades, before the restoration espoused by John Paul II, as Rome marshaled its forces against the cultural revolution of the 1960s. Jesuit, and Catholic, higher education constituted altogether rockier terrain than the high schools, where academic freedom was never a major issue and the makeup of both staff and students was relatively homogeneous. To the cohort of Jesuits and their allies who spearheaded the laicizing reforms that they felt were inspired by Vatican II, retrenchment on the part of the Roman authorities brought up memories of "the generally unhappy history of the church's relations with its scholars and intellectuals." [22] One Jesuit who became involved in the negotiations over *Ex Corde Ecclesiae* during the 1990s recalled a caustic

observation made by Timothy Healy, the Jesuit who headed Georgetown University from the mid-1970s through the 1980s before going on
to direct the New York Public Library, regarding the "loyalty oath" stip-
ulation of the papal directive:

> Tim Healy was not bashful. He was so vocal, there was never any doubt
> where he stood. "They are managing to do what all of secular education
> in the United States could not do," he said, "and that is to get us to
> cease being Catholic."

5

By the time the 1990s rolled around, conflict in Jesuit higher education
had reached a crescendo. One hundred years after Leo XIII had condemned Americanism as a heresy, the colleges and universities affiliated
with the Society found themselves accused of becoming too American.[23]
Such assimilation as they had achieved ran the risk of costing them their
Catholic soul. Gloomy parallels were drawn with the secular fate of universities like Harvard, Yale, Duke, and others whose origins lay in sponsorship by Protestant denominations.[24]

As early as 1979, John Paul's first year as pope, the Vatican Congregation for Catholic Education had issued a directive spelling out norms
for pontifical institutions, like the Catholic University of America, that
were directly answerable to Rome. In 1983 came the revised code of
canon law, requiring that theologians at all Catholic colleges and universities receive "mandates"—that is, certification—from local bishops
attesting to their adherence to doctrinal orthodoxy. Nothing much happened. Then, two years later, in 1985, the Congregation for Catholic
Education published another set of norms that extended the rules directed at pontifical institutions to Catholic colleges and universities as a
whole and reinforced the guidelines laid out in the canon law. Drawn up
to bring Catholic higher education into line with the magisterium, these
documents set the terms of negotiations that lasted through the 1990s
and came to a head with the approach of the millennium.[25]

By the late 1980s, as the professionalization of their colleges and universities was cresting, Jesuits began to coordinate several initiatives,
aimed at safeguarding the religious identity of the schools, that had
sprung up more or less haphazardly in different places. Many of these
initiatives, like the Pulse program at Boston College, were variations on

service learning; some involved exposure to hardships in Central America and other impoverished areas. They were designed to sensitize participants to "the service of faith and the promotion of justice."[26]

The refrain of all such efforts has been reaffirmation of the conviction—as Frank Rhodes, then president of Cornell University put it— "that moral excellence was the ultimate goal of Jesuit education."[27] Coming from the chief executive officer of a major secular university, this sounded remarkably like Pedro Arrupe's exhortation regarding the central purpose of the high schools. Some of the programs emphasize individual spiritual renewal; others stress the sharpening of social conscience. Insofar as "moral" is understood as "spiritual" or "ethical" in a personal sense, they have taken the form of adaptations of campus ministry involving, for example, centers for Ignatian retreat and counseling. Programs of this sort have not typically entered the curricula, and they appear to reach administrative staff more than faculty.[28]

The ideal, even when espoused by such outsiders as Frank Rhodes, has been a tough sell inside Jesuit higher education. Admiration for social outreach programs coexists with uneasiness about the expansion of extra-academic goals into the classroom.[29]

A chemistry professor at a Jesuit university on the West Coast echoes the appreciation for "education of the whole person," the theme at the core of Ignatian pedagogy and one that is sounded repeatedly by instructors in the high schools. "This translates," he explains in classical humanistic fashion, "into a broad liberal education which focuses on intellectual, spiritual, and ethical development and which prepares students to become responsible leaders." He also praises improvements in Jesuit-lay collaboration, now "very good; it didn't used to be that way." However, when he considers the nitty-gritty of university policy as expressed in budgetary decisions, where financial pinch comes to shove, reservations emerge:

> When the university administration started emphasizing social justice to the point where "social justice" and "resource allocation" were used in the same sentence, many faculty in business, science, and engineering were concerned that the Jesuit administration would no longer value basic research that did not have a social justice component. Also, when resources are allocated to the core curriculum in areas where courses focus on "competence, conscience, and compassion," sometimes faculty in the more technical areas, where "educating" often equals "training," feel that they are being neglected.

Another lay faculty member (a professor of management) at the same institution comes up with a similarly divided assessment by way of a different slate of reasons. Like his colleague, he begins with a litany of Jesuit educational virtues old and new:

> Love for one's students; belief that you impact their future in ways beyond the knowledge imparted in the classroom; teaching which encompasses concern for servant leadership, social justice, ethics; a sense of community within the campus; concern with educational integration and education for the whole person—these values are in the official statements of the institution, are part of continuing dialogue at convocations, become part of the discussion in evaluation of faculty, and culturally permeate the institution during hiring, new faculty socialization, and during discussion of program initiatives.

The stress on educational values is so pervasive that a sense of community envelops campus life. There is a concerted tone to the university, an ethos equivalent or close to the school spirit characteristic of secondary education:

> Topics which might be seen as peripheral become central and gain greater attention and credibility. Within the university community, faculty politics are more gentle, students are more central, and those who find compatibility with the value structure have higher job satisfaction.

But community does not signify commitment to the party line if it diverges from professional standards of academic accomplishment. While qualms about the faith-and-justice agenda and its spin-offs surface everywhere in Jesuit colleges and universities, skeptics really seem to get their backs up in those institutions that have done much of the basic work of professionalization and are beginning to contemplate what is required to make the steep climb beyond assimilation and mere respectability toward excellence:

> The greatest tension is [the impression] that "feel good" activities and interaction with students displace serious scholarship and that the teaching emphasis keeps the Jesuit institution from engaging the scholarly vocation as opposed to the teaching vocation so that Jesuit institutions never become truly world-class, accepting a less rigorous standard of scholarship than is needed to be leaders in university-level as opposed to college-level concerns.

Two conflicts, one the flip side of the other, come to the fore. One is the rivalry between social action and academics. The other stems from a perception that, since objections to the faith-and-justice agenda from defenders of academic excellence keep recurring, the social activists, like athletes with an erratic reputation in the classroom, are liable to become appendages to the educational enterprise. The difficulty of integrating faith-and-justice programs into the academic life of the colleges and universities impels them toward ghettoization:

> I am disappointed that the majority of the energies of the Jesuits seems directed toward "social welfare" manifestations of commitment, that is, working with poor neighborhoods. By contrast, there is little discussion of developing spirituality in the core vocational sectors of the students (i.e., spirituality for business leaders, spirituality for scientists, spirituality for engineers, spirituality for psychologists). It is as if the focus is on training individuals to be social workers or community volunteers; the Jesuit influence is peripheral to the work life which will occupy the majority of time and the students' vocations to science, business, engineering, etcetera, which will shape so much of our society.

In brief, so the management professor argues, the faith-and-justice agenda is isolated, as tends to happen with women's studies and similar cause- or advocacy-driven programs in higher education generally.[30] Or, like athletic departments, such programs enjoy only second-class citizenship in the academic pecking order. The integration of the agenda into the meat-and-potato courses of the university sets up a tension between the pursuit of the academic excellence of the first rank, defined by secular criteria, and "the quest for coherence—within the disciplines, between the disciplines, in life at large."[31] The compartmentalization of the faith-and-justice offerings is a special case of the professional fragmentation and implicit stratification of academia.

However, only a very small number—probably no more than two or three—of the top-flight, best-off Jesuit universities frame their strategic dilemmas as a choice between academic specialization and the integration of knowledge.[32] Most of the schools rank as regional or comprehensive institutions, not research universities. They have not reached the stage where they feel they can afford to or should make bold gestures in the direction of intellectual breakthroughs. Developing and maintaining their physical infrastructure and meeting payrolls still take precedence over the scramble for national visibility. And for many of these schools, breaking into the top ranks of higher education is neither desirable nor feasible. Such a course might mean abandoning their niche and their primary mission, defined as undergraduate teaching.

Because many Jesuit colleges and universities are neither research nor teaching operations but hybrids in flux, ambitions clash over what priorities are to be rewarded. A professor of theology, a layman, in a midwestern Jesuit university acknowledges that the rivalry between social activism or service and academic professionalism amounts to a genuine conflict; he is skeptical about the faith-and-justice movement:

> There is a serious problem with what I would call a few anti-intellectuals (among the Jesuits). . . . To become a very serious, contributing scholar in American academic intellectual life, that has to be a lifetime's work. And the Jesuits' lifetime work is peace, justice, and the transformation of society. Some of them make it through to an academic orientation in their lives; most of them simply don't have the desire for it. They have other, competing desires. . . . Here among the faculty at the university, Jesuits who become serious scholars are relatively few. Most of them are not interested in scholarship. They're very good teachers, they care deeply about the institution, and they work hard for the institution . . . but the life of scholarship is not there.

The faculty member goes on to suggest that the faith-and-justice agenda may be less of a problem than the constraints imposed by having to attend to brick-and-mortar needs. In other words, an equally grave if possibly temporary impediment to scholarly accomplishment of the first rank, the faculty member argues, is the strategic commitment to husbanding the material resources of the university. The imperative is less intellectual than pragmatic:

> There's no indication that I can think of that they're going to forgo a building in order to hire ten or fifteen good scholars. Frontline scholarship is not the name of the game at all. You have institutions that are defining themselves in such a way that includes the hope of serious scholarship, but it's not the top priority. Their worry and concern is about undergraduate education, as Jesuits always have. They've made mythical claims about their devotion to the arts and sciences, but I doubt that their devotion is all that great. What's really great is turning out Catholics who can make their way in the world, and that's still the case.

According to this scenario, a hierarchy of needs constrains strategic choices in Jesuit higher education. Even prominent universities like

Georgetown, which has benefited enormously from its location, are undercapitalized compared to secular rivals among privates like Brown and Duke, and an institution like Boston College, which has prospered since the 1980s, has vivid memories of skirting financial disaster.[33] Furthermore, even were the economic obstacles to implementing the faith-and-justice program lifted, some faculty retain an image of Catholic higher education as an enterprise historically prone to distraction from its academic agenda by religious obligations or the dictates of Rome. In their eyes, assertive forms of the faith-and-justice program are the latest in a parade of temptations for failing to grasp the brass ring of scholarly excellence.[34]

Some faculty members at the comprehensive universities find themselves caught between those of their peers who press for a full-speed-ahead course in the race toward academic glory and those, like the bishops, who voice concern over the Catholic identity of the schools.[35] "The issue is more than how many Catholic rear ends you need in the department chairs," one English professor at a Jesuit college on the East Coast declares:

> That's not the spirit of the thing. The colleges and universities are not virgin brides. They get tons of state money, tons of defense money. We accommodate funding agencies. So let's stop acting as if the bishops didn't exist. I can't abide that stuff by Richard McBrien, all that knee-jerk bluster about refusing to seek a mandate to teach theology: "I will single-handedly uphold academic integrity!"[36] Please. The ball's in our court.
>
> Look, I have a lot of sympathy for people like Monika Hellwig [director of the Association of Catholic Colleges and Universities]. Maybe this [the bishop's assenting vote to *Ex Corde Ecclesiae*] is going to set Catholic higher education back fifty years. They're genuinely aggrieved over it. They've worked so hard, so thanklessly, for so many years.

He then considers the possibility, in the midst of financial pressure to concentrate on keeping up the physical plant and improving faculty and staff compensation, of reaching for academic excellence of a kind that prizes instructional quality rather than the pursuit of breakthroughs in research:

> There's a lot of nervousness, a lot of anxiety about money. And many of my colleagues are underwhelmed by the whole question of Jesuit identity.

I would like to see these places, colleges like this, thinking about diversity, what Jesuit education means. A potential cooperative venture. We're not *all* research universities. We are distinctive. You can ask the big questions here. How envious she was, this colleague of mine [in a state university], when we were pounding the table. "I envy you being able to have that conversation," she said. We haven't given up on the tradition of meaning and coherence at the undergraduate level.[37]

Remarks like these, praising the virtues of diversity, are notable for combining a perspective that sees beyond the individual school while keeping close to a rather traditional vision of undergraduate education in the humanities, one with an interdisciplinary thrust. The statement reflects the reality that Jesuit colleges and universities differ in size, goals, and resources. It also implies the aspiration that somehow the institutions can hang together by respecting differences in the kinds of things they do. Human nature in its academic guise makes extraordinary demands on reserves of charity and forbearance. The hope is that the temptation to rank qualitatively different kinds of institutions can be minimized.

6

The conflict that came to a head in the dispute over *Ex Corde Ecclesiae* set two ways of thinking against each other in a manner reminiscent of the rivalry between the hedgehog, who has one big idea, and the fox, who has many smaller ones.[38] While the AJCU as a whole has little unity beyond defending the legislative interests of its members, a few of these member institutions are probably more Catholic, though Catholic in different ways, than they were before Vatican II. The varied opportunities for the expression of religious devotion and social concern that have sprouted on some of the campuses are not synonymous with a single perspective.[39] They express distinct subcultures within Catholicism and different ways of relating to the non-Catholic world as much as they do degrees of churchiness.

The unity-in-diversity theme resists simple formulation. It is as hard to overcome fears of centrifugal anarchy among conservatives as it to assuage fears of clericalism among liberals. When attempts are made to formalize an inclusive, here-comes-everybody détente, more often than not the result gets watered down into bland accommodation: "Tolerance is the enemy," in the not-so-ironic phrasing of one of the principal non-Jesuit players at Georgetown University.[40] A key protagonist among the Jesuits at Boston College spots a similar flaw while recognizing that mission statements are only documents, not binding prescriptions for action:

> What we've got is a document that a lot of articulate Jesuits are not entirely happy with but it is probably a pretty good document nonetheless. One of them said that "it's a little Unitarian, it keeps asserting the importance of all religious perspectives, and the word 'Jesus' is not mentioned anywhere. It's all God, religion, and occasionally Christian and Catholic." They would also argue that religion is not just one of the things we do here, a religious vision is the *whole* reason we're here, and that therefore it ought to be part of the vision you have of undergraduate life, of the kind of research that you see faculty doing. Whereas what you actually have is the reverse of that. It's like "we are ambitious to be a really good university and we are also doing religious stuff." The latter is much more the way it comes out in the document. But I think, pragmatically, how much do you want a document like this to accomplish? The important thing is what people do.

"The fundamental issue is pluralism," the professor at Georgetown insists. "I don't think pluralism need result in a hollowing out of coherence. But it's the easy way to deal with that problem." When the lengthy presentations, colloquia, roundtables and the like are boiled down on the printed page, the product tends to get diluted into earnest resolutions rather than concrete mechanisms or incentives to action. Issues of religious diversity and identity have entered polite conversation on Jesuit campuses, and this represents a change welcome even by secular faculty grown weary of the antiseptic exclusion of such issues from academic councils. But because the range of interests is so vast, it is difficult for deliberations over purpose and identity to proceed beyond accords that agree to disagree.[41] In the eyes of a Catholic layman, a professor of English at Boston College, diplomatic caution reflects an exquisitely self-conscious adaptation to a dilemma for which there may be no definitive solution:

> There is great failure on both sides of the great divide between Catholic and non-Catholic faculty here; failure of imagination about how to incorporate the non-Catholic world into the Catholic ethos, without watering down the later, or distorting the former. The whole school is haunted by the evolutionary-decline model of religious identity in uni-

versities. But the Catholic attempt to halt this decline, without a radical incorporation of the non-Catholic faculty, is probably doomed, as the Catholic side becomes increasingly diminished and marginalized by the normal hiring practices which stress professional excellence and academic improvement.

A closely related lesson concerns the limits of pluralism as a standard of academic governance. On the one hand, the schools represent a special case of the difficulty of promoting pluralism within a traditionally hierarchical institution. Internally, whatever its behavior toward organizations on the outside, the church tries to run its affairs along autocratic lines. On the other hand, aside from this tradition, the foundations of the pluralist code itself—in particular, the premise of a common culture—have come increasingly into question. Conversation is no guarantee of consensus.[42]

John Courtney Murray, the Jesuit theorist who stressed the compatibility between Catholicism and "the American proposition," sanctioned pluralism as a necessary, and necessarily imperfect, adaptation to the realities of a cosmopolitan world. For the urbane Murray, procedural democracy was a second-best solution, an unavoidable compromise, not a theological ideal.[43] Since Murray's time, the church has accepted this understanding of democracy in dealing with states and other institutions, including other religions. Many church-affiliated organizations have adopted consultative, "dialogic" management styles.

Murray's faith in pluralism rested on an assumption, one that he always considered fragile and that he grew to suspect as the 1960s unfolded, of the discoverability of objective truth by way of open discussion. Beneath reasoned talk lay the bedrock of natural law and the reachability of a consensus on right and wrong—what used to be called shared norms. Today, as Murray feared, the playing field may be level— that is, democratic—but the ground itself has shifted. One Jesuit, writing about denominational diversity on Jesuit campuses, put the situation this way:

> Looking too deeply into pluralism might get us into trouble by raising questions we cannot handle. Since pluralism is not susceptible to coherent planning anyway, one might argue, it is better to neglect the topic altogether. Although this worry is legitimate, unpredictability and lack of clear boundaries are intrinsic to today's religious environment in America.[44]

A fifty-one-year old Jesuit, a professor of theology, elaborates on the predicament of the Society in even broader terms, questioning whether themes like pluralism and "democratization" capture what is at stake. He focuses instead on the unresolved dissonance of postmodernism:

> I have to wonder whether the problematic, democratization, cannot also be described as the end of modernity. By modernity I mean that period stretching from the sixteenth to the mid-twentieth centuries when the overarching realities of human life (political, religious, moral, etc.) were founded upon as yet unchallenged premises that lent a certain coherence to life and at least [to] the quest for meaning. The Society of Jesus was founded at the dawn of modernity, and in many ways its radical nature can be understood as a result of its investment in modernity. In a sense it placed all its eggs in the basket of modernity. However, one could argue that the modern consensus has disintegrated, pitching those institutions like the Society (and even the Tridentine church) into massive crisis. Certainly we are living in a time when, in the Western world, and particularly in the North American world, there has been a widespread loss of any sense of coherence or direction, despite all the rhetoric to the contrary. I suspect that this is not a problem peculiar to the Society of Jesus, but it is certainly one in which we share in an acute fashion.[45]

This irresolution can be put in more concrete terms. Jesuits at many of the order's colleges and universities stand at the edge of a cumulative, twofold problem. In balance with the talent and determination that qualified lay people bring to the academic job market and the marketplace of ideas, priestly ordination has lost much of its rationale as a prerequisite for ministry. Fewer reasons exist for distinguishing between clerical and lay personnel for educational assignments. Professional credentials have in many cases surpassed apostolic zeal as the criteria for hiring and promotion. As the functional link between ordination and ministry slips, so does the legitimacy of clergy-dominated management. The downward demographics of the Society of Jesus indicate that the issue of control is all but settled and that the meaningful quandary is over what role might be left for a corporate Jesuit presence in the schools.

Second, as ecumenical comity becomes routine on Jesuit campuses and in other Jesuit works, it also becomes difficult to distinguish Catholic from non-Catholic operations on the grounds of what they do. Religious presence comes to rest on icons and symbols, rituals and barely tangible meanings—the atmospherics—whose consequences for action are elusive.[46] In the pluralist bazaar toward the upper reaches of Jesuit higher education, religious presence may not be a function of control or even of signature programs but, as happens with inveterate New Yorkers, of the capacity to identify with and cheer on diversity itself.[47]

7

The moral of the story behind most accounts of the evolution of Catholic higher education in the United States is that history, left to its own devices, repeats itself. Evidently, all but a few Catholic colleges and universities are pulling away from their religious roots and are on their way to duplicating the secular trajectory blazed by their Protestant counterparts. Evidence from the past and present looks compelling enough to warrant alarm that a happy ending, in traditional religious terms, is unlikely unless forceful measures are taken to head off the process. Appeasement doesn't work. It was agreement on this pessimistic historical prognosis, along with relentless pressure from the Vatican, that led the American bishops to vote for the implementation of *Ex Corde Ecclesiae*.[48]

This leaves out a lot. For one thing, the baseline from which Catholic higher education is supposed to have departed is a mixture of the veridical and the mythical. The good old days of clerical control were times of religious indoctrination as much as theological discussion. The administration and the atmospherics of the schools back then were plainly Catholic, but the transmission of belief was neither seamless nor particularly intelligent.[49]

A comparable difficulty arises with the "after" side of before-and-after reasoning. At least a few of the twenty-eight Jesuit colleges and universities, not to mention some of the more than 200 Catholic institutions of higher education in general, are bound to lose almost all semblance of religious identity. The numbers are too large to preclude casualties.

The Vatican seems to have grasped the actuarial realities that belie the protestations of loyalty by members of the Association of Catholic Colleges and Universities. It is easier for the papacy to husband its connections, apply its fund-raising resources, and concentrate its favors on a select few institutions—the Roman houses, for example, such as the Gregorian University, and a small cluster of neofundamentalist colleges, from which an above-average number of religious vocations can be expected—than to bother with exerting serious control over all the Cath-

olic colleges and universities in the United States whose spiritual credentials appear to be in disarray.[50] If some of them fail to measure up to
the prescriptions of Ex Corde Ecclesiae, the loss would not be seen as ir-
reparable by central authorities in search of conformity. The "few good
men" strategy reflects a win-win situation for Rome. If its terms are met,
then central control would seem to be ratified. If some colleges and universities do not go along, that is acceptable too since it gets rid of dubious appendages, cafeteria Catholics, and other lukewarm members.

Yet the same statistical logic indicates that the outcome is unlikely
to be a split between one brand of orthodoxy and a singular, uniform
"relativism" or "secularism." Some of the Jesuit colleges and universities are on their way to becoming Catholic in different ways, no matter
what the bishops and the Vatican do or do not do. This model is weak
by identity-as-template standards but vibrant by reason of its diversity.
Rather than being only or mainly a matter of degree, Catholicism becomes in this view qualitatively, and perhaps incommensurably, diverse.[51] Routes like these do not converge on a steady state. The signal
trait of such a complex pattern is its unpredictability. There is no "resolution" or equilibrium point.

The drive for academic excellence, if it continues, fosters the professionalization of faculty and administrators whose expertise makes them
visible beyond the institutions where they happen to be employed. The
potential for mobility expands individual leverage at the expense of institutional loyalty, counterbalancing organizational authority and traditional hierarchy.[52] Such marketization undermines the image of the
self-contained institution and encourages a variety of contingent deals,
provisional coalitions, and fluid iterations of purpose.

Among conservatives, Jesuit colleges and universities come up looking like dubious operations in contrast to the Society's high schools.
Even if the contrast amounts to an apples-and-oranges mismatch, the
judgment indicates that for the Vatican the ideal of Catholic education
remains some hybrid of secondary and seminary education, with the research university a suspect add-on.[53] Yet the success of the high schools
can be overdrawn, for a couple of reasons.

First, there is an almost complete lack of systematic evidence to document the wished-for impact of social action, character building, and
other religious programs on the students themselves. For all the enthusiasm of some faculty and staff members for these measures, their effect
on the socialization of students is hard to verify.[54] If there is an iron law

for individual students comparable to the secularizing dynamic that is thought to afflict the schools at the institutional level, it is the tendency for students in Jesuit high schools to become *less* pious with exposure to religious education—a development that seems as attributable to maturation as to any instructional failings of the schools. Growing up subverts the hold of at least some features of religious belief.[55]

Second, the remoralizing strategy of the JSEA and its members has been necessarily selective. It has concentrated on religious education, an area in which accreditation agencies have left the Jesuits a free hand. The jury is still out on broader attempts to revamp curricula through a diffusion of "the Ignatian pedagogical method." As with the revival of Ignatian spirituality, the Jesuits have pressed forward where they have found an opening. Elsewhere, in the face of legal and institutional obstacles, progress has been problematic.

The triumph of the high schools is that they have earned what Jesuit identity they have, pooling their own resources and devising their own initiatives. Whatever its content, this is identity through self-determination, an exercise in cooperative autonomy that suits the American milieu. The attempt to protect or restore the religious identity of the colleges and the universities from the outside and from on high looks contrived by comparison.[56]

CHAPTER TEN

Organizational Dilemmas, Symbolic Conflicts, Structural Problems

The Jesuits rarely talk about the latent schism in the church but they have made an about-face in attitude—"men for others" says a great deal. Not the elite avant-garde, the pope's men—rather, service of the poor, the fringe people, an attempt to reshape the structures toward this goal.

The institutional church seems to be drifting into rigidity, uniformity and forced conformity. In the Society, our apostolates seem to be doing well but there seems to be no urgency in addressing the issue of where we should be and where we can be in light of rapidly declining numbers in the U.S.

I

In religious orders like the Society of Jesus, practical problems frequently have political undercurrents. Efforts to staff positions in the Society's apostolic infrastructure with suitable Jesuits can become test cases about the linkage between leadership, qualifications for ministry, and priestly ordination.

Of course, the ecclesiastical hierarchy allows for tacit understandings and informal settlements. Going by the book and adherence to precision are not hallmarks of the Mediterranean streak in Roman Catholicism.[1] The Society of Jesus has made a name for itself handling friction between sacred imperatives and profane exigencies—"the real politics," as the English professor in the last chapter noted, "that Jesuits are so good at." Sometimes, however, organizational designs and religious customs don't mesh. Disagreement over particular policies may turn into quarrels over the nature of religious hierarchy itself.

When Jesuits and former Jesuits ponder the challenges facing the Society, they rank issues in rough ascending order of seriousness. The first set consists mostly of inside controversies involving choices about apostolic assignments or, more broadly, strategic decisions about the social justice agenda as compared to other corporate goals. Battles over organizational priorities such as those analyzed in the last chapter can be painful and very costly, but the damage is not fatal.

A second cluster of controversies comes loaded with altogether heavier symbolic freight. These touch on one facet or another of moral theology and the sexual magisterium. Because they are so closely tied to the hierarchical traditions in which Jesuits are immured, such controversies risk putting the Society and the Vatican at loggerheads. As the institutional repercussions of change in moral rules become inescapable, tensions rise. Corporate identity is thought to be at stake.

A third set of challenges bears down almost fatalistically on both the Society and the Vatican from the outside. The rise of the laity, the feminization of the ministerial workforce, and the gaying of religious life place the traditional meaning of the priesthood and clerical dominance in jeopardy. Individual villains seem less important than systemic wear and tear. Antagonism is liable to give way to resignation.

Once we get beyond the contentious but still practical questions involving the organization of ministry and the assignment of manpower, how does this progression from the more or less manageable to the intractable operate? One scenario unfolds according to a slippery-slope logic. The fear is that a seemingly minor change—for instance, appointing a non-Jesuit to the deanship of an arts and science faculty, traditionally the centerpiece of higher education in the Jesuit mold—risks opening the floodgates of clerical supervision. The possibility of appointing a non-Jesuit as head of a college or university affiliated with the Society can assume iconic importance, even if the question has practically nothing to do with doctrine and has few practical repercussions.[2]

A judgment that the everyday pluralism and incremental problem solving that have penetrated Jesuit institutions corrode their religious mission also transforms practical issues into symbolic battles. The enemy is not the give-and-take of organizational coping itself but the absence of any deeper project. Creeping pluralism, so the perception goes, reflects and compounds confusion of purpose. Relativism lurks under the unkempt bed of Jesuit-lay collaboration. Specialization encourages a tunnel vision that loses sight of larger, spiritual goals.[3]

Another reason why many of the issues that Jesuits face need to be understood in emblematic as well as practical terms is that they are clusters of controversies rather than isolated quarrels. The clearest illustration of this interconnectedness is the bundle of issues involving the role of women in Catholicism. The supposition is that change in one area—the ordination of women—cannot help but cascade into a series of changes in other domains of belief—for example, sexual ethics—and into reforms that touch on the edifice of male clericalism. From the perspective of canonists schooled in the Roman legal tradition, the inclination to deal with such issues in piecemeal fashion is an exasperating habit of the coarsely empirical Anglo-American mind. Furthermore, as the proportion of women at work in various ministerial endeavors of the Society increases, and as the roles and competence of women expand in society at large, questions of this sort assume more than theoretical interest.[4]

The close association between convictions regarding sexual-moral issues and beliefs regarding the shape of institutional Catholicism makes it difficult to treat this welter of issues as if they were negotiable.[5] It is easier to deal with the human costs pastorally and therapeutically than to alter the legal code. Disagreement is tantamount to lèse-majesté. When John Paul II prohibited discussion about women's ordination, a substantive policy conflict got caught up in discord about the heavy-handed procedure used to quell the conflict. Two ideals dear to the American way—equality of opportunity and freedom of speech—were dashed in one stroke.[6]

The common denominator of all these cases is that something larger than a narrow ruling on particular issues is at stake. Institutional change has symbolic consequences, or, conversely, change in belief spills over into other beliefs and affects the distribution of organizational power. Tensions escalate in both instances.

There is another, rather different way in which mundane issues become serious problems in the Society of Jesus. This happens when long-term ailments pile up into a drag on the future of priestly service. The gravity of such cumulative developments—vocational attrition is the prime example—is less a matter of conflicts in opinion than a recognition of the demographic endgame in religious life. Transformations like these reflect systemic problems more than ideological conflicts.

As we will see in this and the following chapter, the convergence of all these conflicts and difficulties—the infighting over apostolic direction, the tension between the order and the hierarchical moralism of Rome, and the onslaught of structural and cultural changes that undermine traditional understandings of the priesthood—puts the Society of Jesus in an extremely tight spot.

2

Jesuits and former Jesuits, we know, have changed on moral-sexual issues.[7] They have moved farther to the left in the moral-sexual arena than they have on social-political matters. While former Jesuits have shifted even farther leftward than Jesuits, the experience of both groups has been more discontinuous in the moral-sexual domain than has been the case with the evolution of attitudes toward the social teaching of the church.

In order to grasp how the braiding of preferences on doctrinal and institutional questions intensifies ideological divisions, we first need to establish where Jesuits and former Jesuits stand with regard to the institutional church, then determine how their perceptions of the church line up with their opinions on doctrine (see figure 3). Not surprisingly, although former Jesuits are more critical of both organizations, Jesuits and former Jesuits alike have warmer feelings about "the direction that the Society of Jesus has taken over the past few years" than about "the direction that the institutional church has taken over the past few years."[8]

The average perceptions headline a fundamental split not so much between Jesuits and former Jesuits (although that is real enough) as between evaluations of the two organizations themselves. Some portion of the favorable ranking of the Society reflects a natural solidarity with companions present or in the past. The low rating of the "institutional church" captures a divergence between the order and the ecclesiastical hierarchy since Vatican II, aggravated under the papacy of John Paul II.

The gap between positive evaluations of the Society and negative assessments of the church happens to be widest among Jesuits in their fifties, within the cohort that has felt acutely the swings from Tridentine Catholicism to the euphoria of Vatican II and then the retrenchment of the 1980s and 1990s. This transitional group combines caustic criticism of the church with something approaching chauvinism about the Society of Jesus as the cutting edge of Catholicism. Older Jesuits, by comparison, tend to be more a bit sanguine about both, while younger Jesuits tend to be skeptical of the directions of the Society and the church.[9]

Jesuits are seriously divided about the agenda of the Vatican.[10] "The

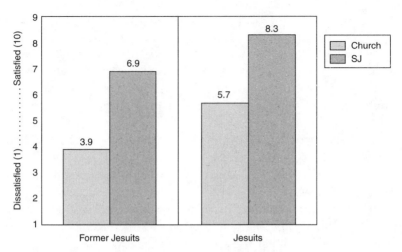

Figure 3.   Average perceptions of the church and the Society of Jesus by Jesuits and former Jesuits

Jesuits are under close scrutiny by the institutional church," a fifty-nine-year-old theologian remarks,

> and in several respects are not free to develop in the way they might otherwise. The polarized situation created by an overly conservative or restorationist papacy in matters internal to the church has resulted in polarization in the Jesuits and thus severe constraints on leaders and thinkers in the Society, especially relative to theology.

This division is aggravated by the close link between positive perceptions of the church hierarchy and conservatism on moral-sexual issues. The tie-in between liberal or conservative positions on sexual morality and correspondingly biting or supportive opinions about the authority structure of the church is strong.[11]

How do evaluations of the Society of Jesus itself relate to doctrinal preferences and institutional perceptions? Here we encounter a striking pattern. There is *no* significant connection between attitudes on moral-sexual issues and assessments of the Society on the part of either Jesuits or former Jesuits. The men abstain from linking their feelings about sexual morality with their judgments of the Society.

But a strong association does emerge between positive assessments of the Society and progressive leanings on social-political issues. In other words, Jesuits (but not former Jesuits) who express satisfaction with the way the Society has been moving do so to a significant extent because they agree with the faith-and-justice agenda, regardless of their position on questions of sexual morality. Conversely, Jesuits with misgivings about this agenda, formulated at the congregations of the Society held since Vatican II, claim to be less enamored of the corporate direction of the order.[12]

It would be erroneous to depict this as a standoff between the institutional church at one end and the Jesuits at the other of a single divide. For all the schismatic talk, the Society is not an openly mutinous "dissenting denomination."[13] Instead, Jesuits tend to visualize the Society and the ecclesiastical hierarchy as lined up along moral and social axes that are roughly at right angles to each other rather than as directly antagonistic. The church has staked out a conservative position on a scale defined mainly by views on sexual morality and, correlatively, hierarchical authority. A fifty-four-year-old formation director expresses the idea this way:

> I see the hierarchical church's direction today as different from but not antithetical to that of the Society. The hierarchical church is often concerned with orthodoxy, clerical advancement, maintenance of church power, univocal thinking, and being right. I think these concerns hurt the whole church.

The Society of Jesus, on the other hand, tends to be viewed in light of the social agenda that the general congregations of the order have adopted after Vatican II, especially since the Thirty-second General Congregation of 1974–75. The perception is that the order keeps its distance from the institutional church on matters of sexual ethics and related issues, instead of entering directly into conflict with the magisterium. Discretion veils dissent.[14]

The two domains are not exactly commensurable. The moral dimension pits traditional authority against individual discretion, specifically in matters of sexual ethics. The other, social dimension contrasts "elitism" against egalitarianism. Some overlap exists between the two. But the domains are different enough to allow for a partial division of loyalties. This helps keep the institutions off a collision course.

There is another reason why the priority given to social justice does not get the Jesuits into serious trouble with church authorities. Especially when it competes with the educational commitments of the Society, the social justice agenda stirs up resentment and controversy among Jesuits themselves, and budgetary battles can become pretty heated even when they don't have much to do with first principles. But the main reason why Jesuits can get away with promoting a radical and semiradical social platform is that the philosophy is targeted almost entirely at inequities *outside* the church. Issues of sexual-moral doctrine are touchier; they bear directly on inside matters of "faith and morals." [15]

3

Many former Jesuits and at least a few Jesuits would contend that the sexual magisterium is a thing of the past, while the social justice agenda represents the wave of the future. One Jesuit, a sixty-eight-year-old writer and artist, reviews the divisions between the Roman authorities and the Society and expresses his admiration for the priority given to social justice by the order but admits that implementation goes slowly:

> "No one should even entertain the idea of women's ordination. Not even the church can change, etcetera." Rome has made these end runs. There's strong support for conservative Catholics who seem to want Vatican I back again. . . .[16] How does this affect the Society? The Jesuits rarely talk about the latent schism in the church, but they have made an about-face in attitude—"men for others" says a great deal. Not the elite avant-garde, the pope's men—rather, service of the poor, the fringe people, an attempt to reshape the structures toward this goal. There have been massive changes in the way Jesuits shape their life and goals, but like an artist moving from one accomplished level to a deeper vision, there's a lot of mud that shows up in the paint, till form has clearly emerged. We're in the mud, period, but there's a light at the end, beginning to emerge.

The strategy is to pay as little attention as is prudent to what goes on at the command center of the church ("the direction of the institutional church is not the criterion") and to count instead on the grassroots. "There's a revolution going on in the parishes and among the laity." For this Jesuit, the grassroots consist of the parishes, which "need and express what is beyond 'institutions.'"

For others, most of whom are also content to keep their heads down and their distance from Rome, the world to be dealt with is not so starkly split between the stratospheric top and the populist bottom. It is composed instead of a jumble of middle-level institutions—principally the schools—that resist efforts to coordinate and turn them in *any* direction, toward social justice, toward evangelization, or any other single goal. While the obstacles to change may be compounded by Rome, the stubborn decentralization of these organizations is a major internal impediment to setting the Society on a unified course. One former Jesuit, a writer in his fifties, states the two-sided nature of the problem concisely. "The church under John Paul II," he argues,

> is growing more rather than less rigid, and I observe little clerical challenge, though some lay challenge, in the U.S. The Society of Jesus, which is shrinking steadily, is largely if understandably trapped by the institutions it has created.

Many Jesuits and former Jesuits take pride in the Society's push toward social justice and its agility in pressing this agenda without ruffling the Vatican. "The Society has not sold its soul," a fifty-eight-year-old Jesuit sociologist comments, "to the 'Restoration' of John Paul II." But the political obstacles to reform do not arise only or even mainly from ecclesiastical quarters outside the order. The preexisting commitments of the Jesuits, combined with declining manpower, slow the pace of redirecting the mission of the Society.

One thirty-seven-year-old Jesuit, an associate pastor on the East Coast, highlights the difference between the performance of separate ministries and the overall thrust of the Society, apart from the tensions with Rome:

> The institutional church seems to be drifting into rigidity, uniformity, and forced conformity. In the Society, our apostolates seem to be doing well, but there seems to be no urgency in addressing the issue of where we should be and where we can be in light of rapidly declining numbers in the U.S.

Much the same mixed assessment—dismay at the backtracking of the Vatican, satisfaction with the performance of separate apostolates, and impatience with the wavering direction of the Society as a corporate actor—comes through in this statement by a fifty-one-year-old Jesuit chaplain:

> Two problems: (1) the lack of subsidiarity that is evident in changes in and the application of canon law and (2) the absolute stances on a range of issues that are more ambiguous than the bishops admit point to an emerging fundamentalism that is disheartening, to say the least.

> I think that the ministries are doing well—the universities and high schools, for example—but the Society has been unable to prioritize commitments on a national level. As personnel become more scarce, the lack of clarity and collaboration across province lines will have an adverse impact on the apostolates.

Another man, a fifty-three-year-old former Jesuit who has kept close to the Society as a member of various boards, admires the order's experiments in social justice at the same time that he recoils from the bureaucratic entanglements and political constraints that afflict their institutional operations:

> I can personally witness to some very exciting efforts by the Jesuits. They are moving in many very worthwhile directions: community organizing, bringing the [Spiritual] Exercises to the people rather than bringing them to an institution, a theology experience where theologians experience the poverty of the inner city, reflect on it in their studies, and are called to be involved in internships to put that insight into action. The real rub and discontent is that this is engaged in by too few and thus has too little impact.
>
> The institutions of the Jesuits, by their size and constitution, demand great financial expertise that disallows them to be reflective of the kind of independence and freedom to commit their resources at a moment's notice to a pressing enterprise. They have become institutionally bound. They are in the business of feeding the monster, the large universities and high schools that are dependent upon donor support and thus are too sensitively tied to the agenda of those supporters.

The social agenda of the Jesuits has recast the terms of discourse about the direction of ministry. And, especially in some new undertakings, such as the innovative high schools dedicated to minority students, the social thrust has been consolidated in action.[17] But, aside from the sheer weight of institutional attachments, two other factors thwart the drive toward social outreach.

One of these roadblocks is cultural or ideological rather than purely organizational. The priority given to social justice threatens not only to deprive the high schools, colleges, and universities of scarce manpower but also to displace the traditional self-definition of the schools as bastions of the humanities and purveyors of literary and intellectual standards in which ethical values are not equivalent to social policies. A sixty-one-year-old Jesuit professor of English worries about the risk that dedication to social justice poses to this academic tradition:

I'm delighted that we stay so well in contact with the *real* needs of the church and world. I regret only that, in higher education, the justice/ service dimension seems sometimes to *prevail* over education of the "full human" instead of being a significant part of it.

Another man, a seventy-two-year-old former Jesuit who continues to teach theology at a private college, has similar reservations. In the old days, when education was indisputably the premier activity of the Society, social activism was a sideshow, often looked on as the pastime of a few difficult men.[18] Now, the situation approaches the reverse. The ascendancy of the faith-and-justice agenda and skepticism about the reputed torpor of the inherited ministerial infrastructure have come to threaten the primacy of the schools:

> While I admire the commitment to social justice and [the Jesuits'] involvement in various justice ministries, I worry a bit about what seems to be diminishing attention to the large-scale institutions (like universities) where they (and perhaps only they) can provide a community effort at creating a deeper Christian impact on today's cultures and dealing with many-faceted issues like inculturation.

The other roadblock to redirecting the Society as a corporate entity is neither organizational nor ideological but personal. As a rule, superiors can no longer assign Jesuits to apostolic jobs without checking with a variety of interested parties. Younger Jesuits find themselves on a job market where they have to fend for themselves and where their own choices, which may or may not match up with thematic priorities like social justice, are frequently decisive. They are close to being free agents.

One Jesuit, nearing retirement, spots a serious slippage between the Society's renewed interest in planning and its capacity to implement changed priorities. In his view, market signals, the therapeutic turn, and the impulse toward organizational slot filling act more forcefully than central direction on the allocation of Jesuit manpower:

> The provincial could no longer effectively assign ministers if they were no longer acceptable to the ministries they were assigned to. With that came gradually an unforeseen diminution in the corporate identity of the Society. The irony was that this was happening at the same time in the early '70s . . . when we began to engage in planning programs and we adopted the Arthur D. Little model, which was a highly rational model based upon management by objectives. And yet we were developing

a model for planning based upon objectives and strategies at the same time that even though we were not realizing this, the power of anyone in the congregation to manage this was being diminished by the structural changes we were experiencing.

So what happens is that the provincial's role ultimately devolves into a personnel management office. It becomes rhetorical to call any Jesuits to be missionaries somewhere in terms of our major apostolates. What does that mean? We're in massive denial; we still believe that this has some reality.

If I'm your provincial and I say to you, "Peter, you want to change your job, well, go out there and see what's out there and get back to me," and you go, like anybody else out there, and you look for a job and then you come back and say, "I've looked around and"—our standard catchword—"I've prayed about this, and I would like to go to X and they are willing to accept me and even though I've had other offers this is the one that I want." I say to you, "Peter, this is great! It fits your talents. I will mission you there."

By this time the Jesuit's fuse has grown short. He loses patience with the gap between the talk of missioning and the reality of job hunting:

Well, what the hell does that mean? The rhetoric still carries meaning. But in the old days the missioning *meant* something because you were missioned to the apostolate and you were missioned to achieve the goals that the Society had. Sometimes, even though you wanted to ask whether a place was suitable for you or not, you had to go there because you were sent. You could console yourself by saying, well, "I'm under obedience, and this is what the Society wants me to do." What meaning does that have today?

The judgment of some Jesuits and former Jesuits is that all this makes for a dispersion of energies. "My general impression is that there is too much individualism in the choice of ministries," says one fifty-five-year-old Jesuit, a parish priest:

We have lost or are losing a sense of corporate identity and corporate effectiveness. Jesuits frequently do not support other Jesuits in the name of "professionalism."

Another Jesuit, a sixty-four-year-old professor of business, chimes in with a similar evaluation. Like many others, he directs his criticism not at the corporate rhetoric and the declaration of principles but at what he sees as a failure to follow through on the hortatory talk:

> I am satisfied with the general directions, universal directives and pro-posals, as well as outcomes, *postulata,* and documents and resolutions that come from very well-planned and executed meetings and congre-gations, *but* I'm more than disillusioned, bordering on cynicism. . . . Months and years are spent on examining, consulting, and discerning on areas such as "The Formation of Ours," "Choice of Apostolates," etcetera, but very little is really implemented or enforced. Individuals will still choose their own "niche" or favorite "job," in or out of any Jesuit institution or structure—and live an independent life beyond the control or supervision of the superiors. . . .
>
> Some of the new apostolates are performing very well, but the use of personnel is very much dependent on the "likes and dislikes" of individ-ual members. . . . It is a common practice to see individuals who person-ally decide when, where, and what to do—and *not* to do—while the superiors seem to accept it as part of personal discernment and individu-als rights.

This sort of diagnosis, distinguishing among institutional propa-ganda, the limits of corporate coordination, and the comparative success of individual and midlevel operations, is widespread. It recognizes that the incentives driving Jesuits today differ from the sanctions that guided them in a previous era. The Society is no longer the sovereign monolith of heroic memory. Decentralization has clearly taken place. The Jesuits have changed from being a rule-directed to a role-driven organization. But there are no handy criteria for computing the effect of such a trans-formation on the delivery of services. It is simpler to gauge the satisfac-tion of Jesuits with their work than to assess the ministerial impact of what they do.

Arguably, individual autonomy makes for effective performance, at least in the short run. There is no reason to suppose that decentraliza-tion does not improve organizational effectiveness. What is lost is the sense of corporate control. The change mirrors an increase in the bar-gaining power of individual Jesuits as total Jesuit manpower becomes scarce. The process reflects incipient democratization. It also leaves the apostolic direction of the Society at some distance from its overarching program.

It is not just an uncertain future but memories of an idealized past that throw a shadow over the Society. The air of melancholy comes from nostalgia, among middle-aged and older Jesuits and former Jesuits, for a time when collective direction seemed unshakable and when solidarity in corporate accomplishment, a colossal esprit de corps, suffused "the Jebbies." Then, the Society had an aura of disciplined power. "Jesuits priests needed frequently to check themselves," a former student recalled, "to guard against the sin of pride because Jesuits were in fact very proud of the Jesuit order and very happy in it. One inevitably wonders whether that pride is quite whole after the strains of the 1960s." [19]

With the mixed feelings of a movie buff assessing the glories and pitfalls of the bygone studio system, this sixty-one-year-old former Jesuit, now a philosophy professor, considers the passing of the golden age of the order, when (so he remembers) hoards of talented men labored in unison. As it happened, he left the Society because he felt that the demands on his own freedom had become unbearable; he is acutely sensitive to the trade-offs between organizational purpose and individual autonomy:

> [As for Jesuit apostolates] much seems better, but what gave the Society its strength before was an ability to pour resources into a relatively few high-profile operations (universities, for instance). Today I read about programs that reflect the energy of particular individuals.
>
> Jesuits seem less concerned about leveraging their work (the old idea of training future leaders, for instance). The focus is more "Christian" possibly, but this may mean the return on the training of a Jesuit is now much less. If I were to evaluate the Society as an organization, I would have to mark it as less successful today than it was forty years ago. On the other hand, there may be a far greater degree of personal fulfillment, but that's like a general noting that his troops are happier soldiers even if it's less likely they could win a war for him.
>
> Am I being inconsistent? Do I sound too nostalgic for the long black line?

4

Institutional sluggishness, the hold of the order's traditional strength in the humanities, the diminished capacity to move men around the ongoing operations of the Society, the professionalization of work and the ascendancy of personal incentives as criteria for tackling jobs—all these things condition the Jesuits' ability to translate a newfound mission, with the accent on social justice, into corporate impact. Most such handicaps are matters of internal politics in which budgets tend to be more important than beliefs. Within the order there is little dissent, though there is considerable skepticism, about the ideal of corporate élan itself.

Nor does the Society's passion for social justice arouse as much consternation in the Vatican as do doctrinally combustible matters of faith and morals. The fight between advocates of the social justice agenda and defenders of a traditional humanistic pedagogy reflects as much a set of logistical problems and battles over turf—how best to deploy manpower—as a standoff between philosophical positions.

The sting involved in these conflicts is further reduced by the tendency, abetted by falling numbers, adherence to a therapeutic manner, and a sense of tedium with institutional baggage, for Jesuits to pursue ministries on their own, as a means of personal fulfillment. Talk of "left versus right" or "progressive versus conservative" is tangential to this maneuvering.

Squabbles over resources also deflect the potential for confrontation in the particularly spiny links between certain clusters of controversies— for example, moral-sexual teachings—and attitudes toward the hierarchical church. Ideological tensions originating in this area have more to do with Jesuit-Vatican relations than with administrative quandaries internal to the Society. Jesuits have to maintain the appearance of fidelity to the Holy See, and many of them also believe that controversies like these rarely affect their everyday work anyway. Most of them are busy dealing with managerial dustups and pastoral emergencies. No matter what they think, Jesuits usually get on with their work.

A forty-year-old high school teacher takes the long view, one that is prominent among Jesuits outside the colleges and universities:

> Unlike some others I do not worry very much about these things. I take the view that the recent changes in the church need to be considered against the broader scope of church history. I see recent moves (the statement about women's ordination, for example) as efforts of those in authority now trying to consolidate and insure the permanence of directions taken during this pontificate. I think these efforts are unfortunate, but I wonder about their long-term effect on the life of the church. I don't see these directions affecting the Society very much. . . . This is not my experience of the church. I find Catholics in my part of the world less preoccupied with these questions than I did when I lived in the North. In a recent conversation with a Jesuit director of one of our apostolates, I happened to mention a resource I was using in my teaching an evening morality course to adult catechists in the diocese. I referred to

this summary of *Veritatis Splendor;* the Jesuit did not even seem to recognize the title of the recent encyclical. This may say something about
lack of interest at the grassroots level.[20]

The story is particularly interesting for what does not happen. Even the
potential for polarization around moral-sexual issues is just that—a latent conflict—rather than a predetermined explosion. Sometimes the
missiles exchanged between antagonists on widely publicized controversies fly over the heads of Jesuits in the trenches. The issues make for
lively coverage in the house organs of the Catholic left and right, but on
a day-to-day basis they get put on hold. A Jesuit in his mid-sixties, teaching at a university on the East Coast, registers dismay at what he takes
to be the bishops' connivance in promoting *Ex Corde Ecclesiae,* then
quickly dismisses the importance of the affair for his own work:

> How could the bishops have begun a process that they've not at all
> thought out? Alas, they (it seems) jump when the Vatican says "jump!"
> or they're so tired of the mess that they just want to do *something.*
> Luckily, my focus is on God and Christ and the deeper (and wider)
> church and less on this gang.

There is another way, however, besides ideological polarization in
which challenges and difficulties come to a head. This happens when
routine problems accumulate and converge around the worsening
shortage of manpower, throwing into relief the question of the viability
of ordained, celibate ministry. After a while, for some Jesuits, the perennial annoyances of working through and around a sprawling enterprise
fuel the suspicion that something fundamental might be amiss. Tactical
patching and hauling no longer seem enough. A steady diet of bad news
wears Jesuits down.

A fifty-seven-year-old pastor states the difficulty plainly: "How we
practice our Jesuit priesthood in a church that is in the midst of a crisis
over ministerial priesthood—not admitting married clergy or women—
is taking its toll on priests in the trenches. I am loyal to the institutional
church," he continues,

> but find the directives so inflexible and seemingly lacking in insight into
> people's lives. What we have is a pluralistic grassroots Catholic church,
> trying to be governed by a hierarchical, monolithic Roman church. The
> biggest issue still facing us is "inculturation," from America to Africa.
> I think many of us in the Society find ourselves caught not knowing

what to do but trying to be loyal to the hierarchical church because of the need for unity.

Though it may eventually take on ideological coloring, the problem here arises not from a clash of beliefs but from the drain imposed on the daily life of ordinary Jesuits by a systematic refusal on the part of higher-ups to contemplate institutional reform. The dilemma feeds on itself. The long-term diminution in numbers depresses morale and raises questions about the wisdom of official policy. For its part, chronic low-grade irritation with institutional inertia escalates toward a fixation with churchy issues and intramural gossip. "I worry," a fifty-nine-year-old Jesuit sociologist says,

> that too many people in the church have become obsessed with internal problems of church order (women priests, married clergy), and we spend far too little time thinking about how our faith and our church have impact on the world. I am a bit concerned about the long-term effects of a growing conservatism among both hierarchy and clergy, more because it seems out of step with the pastoral needs of our people, especially those under fifty. For younger Catholics, it is clear that, in many instances, their institutional loyalty is weak and their belief patterns are different from their elders. I am also disturbed by the remnants of the Catholic left, especially the more radical groups (such as "Call to Action," *National Catholic Reporter,* etcetera) who seem narcissistic and intellectually bankrupt. The moderating group hovering around the "radical center" seems to be diminishing, and I find this very worrying.

In many cases, then, dismay with the institutional church flows only indirectly from abstract questions of faith. More typically, Jesuits get overwhelmed by the weight of falling vocations to religious life, and this shakes their confidence in received notions of priestly identity. Priests are both increasingly rare and less distinctive. Their reason for being is hard to specify, compared to the motivations of competent laypeople. "Our greatest problem is the lack of vocations," a seventy-four-year-old hospital chaplain laments, echoing the majority of his colleagues. Then he relates a touching vignette:

> We have one scholastic at our school, and I feel for his sense of being quite alone in some ways. We had so many, and our esprit de corps was high. Surrounded by lay teachers who are able and with great spiritual strength, one would think the temptation is to wonder what special quality Ours have in doing the same work.

Again, numerical decline triggers questions about the causes of decline. This breeds concern not just about systemic forces impinging on the priesthood from the outside but about problems internal to the Society and frictions between the Society and the hierarchical church. Attributions of blame fly in several directions. Exasperation can produce a gruff, cut-the-crap style of assessment that crosses back and forth between a list of the Society's troubles—some of them self-inflicted, some of them the inescapable consequences of a changing world—to complaints about a hidebound Vatican.

These are the reflections of a seventy-one-year-old parish priest, expressed in a brisk, thinking-out-loud manner. He begins by claiming that the main challenge facing the Society is "attracting candidates in an entirely new world":

> Eventually we will have a married clergy (with a new pope!). That will put added pressure on recruiting by the Society. I have difficulty in seeing how Jesuits could be married and still have a community lifestyle, but I suppose that could be worked out. In any event, young men attracted to the priesthood and marriage in the future will opt for the diocesan clergy unless ordained [religious order] priests are also permitted to marry. That could be a serious obstacle as celibacy is viewed with less favor with each passing year. Jesuits still inspire enormous respect in and out of the church. We must keep our standards high; I fear the admittance of gay men as a serious threat to the Jesuits, as it has become to the diocesan clergy. It will be a long time before the average Catholic layman/-woman will accept a gay clergy, let alone an openly active gay clergy. This is a problem that has to be studied carefully. Perhaps a much smaller order is in the cards, sort of a "remnant" to be the fermentation in the dough.
>
> I guess what I am saying is this: A married clergy could be a real threat to the existence of all religious orders unless they were willing to have a married, community lifestyle. Secondly, the gay lifestyle is another serious threat to the clergy in general. Our lifestyle at present attracts gay-oriented men, and I cannot see a gay clergy being accepted by the majority of married Catholic laypersons. Perhaps the whole idea of a nonmarried clergy should be scrapped and we should emulate the practice of our Protestant brethren. Psychologically and spiritually in today's world, celibacy cannot work. Too bad the Vatican has ears but does not hear!

Flipping through interviews and statements like these produces no master explanation of what has gone wrong. What does emerge are three broad types of causal reasoning. One focuses on conflicts internal to the Society—for instance, the low-grade friction between humanistic and faith-and-justice strains in the order or (to take a somewhat outmoded example) upholders of large communities versus fans of smaller ones. Though rarely fratricidal, all these conflicts constitute specific demonstrations of the failure of the Society to get its act together.

Another explanation lays most of the troubles on the Vatican, especially (as does the Jesuit just quoted) but not solely on its intransigence in matters of pelvic theology. The priesthood could be saved, even if the Society might not, were Rome to grow up about sex and gender roles.

A third diagnosis stresses the long-term tangle of structural and cultural transformations before which both the Vatican and the Jesuits seem defenseless. The fault lies with the juggernaut of historical change that crushes traditional religious life in Catholicism, regardless of what Rome and the Society do.

These renderings, as we will see, vary among Jesuits and former Jesuits according to their ideological positions.

5

The apprehension of cataclysm brought on by declining numbers is not confined to left-of-center Jesuits. Conservatives are also disturbed by the drop in recruits. The difference is that they are more likely to blame the downsizing of the Society on internal decay and caving in to cultural fashion than on impersonal structural forces or on the meddling of the Vatican. One such man, a seventy-two-year-old high school counselor, calls himself a "cockeyed optimist about the Society." Things are so bad in and outside the church, he reasons, that they can only get better:

> Lack of moral absolutes, loss of a sense of sin or taking responsibility for one's own actions, constant blaming of others, society, my parents, my peer group, etcetera, etcetera, loss of direction among the young, unbonded kids from broken homes, trash culture of MTV, distrust of all institutions, church, schools, corporations, government, older generation: My optimism comes from how bad things are. We are due for a turnaround.[21]

Most Jesuits share the judgment that political feuding between the papacy and the Society is nothing new. From the perspective of the man just quoted, the larger cultural and institutional downturn that afflicts

Jesuits is part of a cyclical process from which the order can rebound by thriving on adversity. The Jesuit tells a story to lighten the funereal mood, then launches into an upbeat forecast that depends on maintaining a countercultural posture:

> I recall a statement while in theology that was attributed to a general of the Society, truthfully or not. He is supposed to have said at that time, 1950 or so, that "there were too many Jesuits for effective administration, that one in five could leave, or die, and it would be good for the Society." We gleefully went through the alphabetical list of our province catalog and arbitrarily eliminated every fifth person, thereby losing some eminent men.

The lesson to be drawn from the woes of the Society is that just as prosperity weakens character, hard times strengthen resolve. The enemies are not the pope and the Vatican but cultural decline on the outside and a crepe-hanging pessimism on the inside of the Society:

> The church does better when it is persecuted and the clergy do better under persecution than when they have the illusion that they "have it made." Complacency is one of the most deadly enemies of the church. Because of the glaring and unfriendly light of the media, the constant and legitimate challenges of the laity, the stress of modern living, the powerful leadership of John Paul II, and diminishing numbers of the priests, the kitchen has gotten rather hot. . . .
>
> The loss and gradual diminishment of our numbers is not a catastrophic problem but represents a purification process. We were suppressed almost entirely at one time and came back. The Society is at the service of the church, and the church must increase, and perhaps the Society must decrease. The rebellion of the '60s against all forms of institutions is still having its effect in the culture at large. How long it will be at work among us no one can say. Also, the culture of "self-improvement" and exaggerated pursuit of my own personal happiness is still having an impact. . . . In the meantime I think our Jesuit communities are being renewed, we are getting bonded to one another much more in the ordinary life of the Society, and there is an increased desire to work among the poor and homeless, and there are healthy signs of more vigorous apostolic energy among us.

A younger (thirty-seven-year-old) Jesuit offers a pessimistic variant of this reading of cultural deterioration. Like many other conservatives, he argues that efforts at reform, however well intentioned, speed up the downward spiral. According to him, the Society is collapsing through its own fault, not because of exogenous forces. It has drifted toward an adversarial role for which there is no space within the church:

> The Society of Jesus is rotting spiritually, I fear, and this, I think, is the single greatest problem facing us as we enter the next century. It also, I think, is why we are dying as an order within the church. We are dying slowly, of course, but dying nonetheless. Many women's congregations have simply "shot themselves in the charism," thus insuring a quicker, cleaner death. Sometimes I feel that we Jesuits are shooting ourselves with a hammer: somewhat silly to look at, very long and painful in the experience, but ultimately effective.

There is little question here of "reading the signs of the time." The tonic has to be steadfast resistance against political correctness, in solidarity with Rome.

> The church's direction is *our* direction: As goes the church, goes the Society of Jesus. This is foundational to who we are! It is so very sad for me to see so many of Ours place themselves outside the Roman Catholic church. They criticize "it" without realizing that our order, by its very constitution, cannot ever separate itself from the Catholic church. I have heard some of Ours joke about being former Catholics; unfortunately, I suspect there are many who would not joke about it nor admit to it but who have no less drifted outside the Catholic communion. . . . Even if in loyal opposition, the Society of Jesus must be unquestionably in union with Rome, in theory *and* in practice. The church's direction must be our direction. We cannot be a "church inside a church." We cannot be an alternative church. I fear again that I am a minority Jesuit in holding this opinion.

Conservative Jesuits, then, see the Society's own efforts at reform as contributing to its demise. Some centrists and progressives too have soured on the double-edged character of reforms, exemplified by the reliance on therapy, that may impede corporate solidarity by privileging personal autonomy and encouraging narcissism. Whatever positive impact personal care has on apostolic effectiveness seems circuitous or may have reached a point of diminishing returns.

Conservatives and progressives have discrepant ideas about the consequences as well as the causes of the order's decline. For conservatives, the prospect of continued downsizing represents a lamentable and at least partly avoidable loss, a lingering, exquisitely self-conscious death. Progressives accept the prospect of decline with greater equanimity. They look on diminishment as contributing to an inevitable laicization of the church.

Beyond their differences, however, most Jesuits would almost certainly agree that the toughest problem facing the Society is not papal policies, troublesome as these may be, or even the steady downward pressure on vocations to religious life exerted by modernization and the career alternatives it opens up, or self-inflicted wounds, destructive as they are. The root challenge is the task of devising a credible model of the priesthood. Fixing blame for the failure to come up with a readily understandable design for the clergy is difficult; it is not as if there is an abundance of bright ideas or positive models.

Sometimes this dilemma is expressed as the upshot of a lack of doctrinal conviction that eats away at respect for institutional authority. "There are many conflicted people in the Society," a thirty-five-year-old theology student observes, "conflicted in that they don't believe what they are necessarily supposed to teach and preach." On other occasions, discouragement with a slew of both workaday and strategic problems piles up, depleting confidence in the functions and the future of the priesthood. Like an officer embattled on multiple fronts, a fifty-three-year-old director of public relations for his province scans the crucial challenges. Ripples of hope and an undertow of self-doubt are both evident:

> Loss of membership for one. Relationship to the hierarchical church for another. Maintaining a sense of mission for a third. The only avenue I see for meeting these challenges is to just keep trying and stay the course. I think we also need to deepen our prayer and revitalize our own individual spirituality. I am somewhat appalled by my own and others' lack of faith in community. In general, I am positive about the church today. I certainly am not put off by the church's direction. I believe God is in charge and that the Holy Spirit is with us. I believe it is our task to do our best and then leave it in His hands. In particular, I believe the laity have the advantage in terms of faith and enthusiasm. There is more hope there than in the priesthood or religious life. These directions in the church seem to be discouraging some of us while energizing others. It's not any one thing.

6

The diversity of perspectives that Jesuits and former Jesuits bring to their assessments of the Society of Jesus is symptomatic of a real complexity in the situation of the order, hence the pain involved in thinking through tortuous choices for dilemmas that may be insoluble no matter how they are attacked.

Jesuits can and do adopt opposing positions and advocate different policies on issues involving, for example, the sexual magisterium, and these conflicts may assume an ideological, even intractable, cast. This schematic way of framing issues at least provides a map of what might otherwise be unbearable confusion. Some degree of tension has always lent a certain vibrancy to Jesuit life. A thirty-five-year-old Jesuit in theological studies provides a good illustration of this mode of understanding the political realities in which the order moves:

> Honestly, I think badly about the direction in which the church seems to be moving. In fact, the gallop toward conservatism often prompts me to reflect on how much longer I can stand to be associated with an institution that is often so at odds (officially) with what I and many others understand to be the more egalitarian claims of the gospel. The recent reaffirmation of the exclusion of women from the ordained priesthood affected me quite badly.
>
> The Society must respond to these movements with its own spirituality, defined more by "finding God in all things" than "following blindly." There remain many young, conservative Jesuits . . . and this is wonderful (I guess). The variety of this organization remains one of its most precious gifts. However, Jesuits rooted in the U.S. experience cannot deny the issues, concerns, problems that legitimately surface in this democratic milieu. The equality of all people and the empowerment of women *is* a real concern for the world and not a chimera conjured by liberal Americans. Can we live, effectively, the tension?

When are such tensions energizing? When are they enervating? The issues that bother Jesuits, like the controversy over the ordination of women, are doubly difficult because they are stuck to a thick mat of correlative conflicts over the prerogatives of hierarchy. They are not just about sex; they are also about authority.

Nevertheless, the lines of conflict are not quite reducible to a single, sweeping division between progressives and conservatives. The institutional ramifications of divided opinions in the sexual and the social domains are different. The faith-and-justice program has created divisions *within* the Society, but it has set Jesuits against one another more in a struggle for divisible resources than out of differences in principle.[22] The struggle has not, on the whole, made for confrontation *between* the Society and the Vatican.

The profile of opinion on sexual morality within the Society is generally liberal, though not consensually so. Regardless of the distribution of opinion, however, differences on moral-sexual issues look to be more fiercely ideological than practical; they carry a huge symbolic charge. Because they bear directly on questions of authority and habits of control, these are the issues that heat up tensions between the Society and Rome.

Besides "conflicts," however, there are "problems and challenges." These entail issues in a psychological, cultural, or structural rather than doctrinal sense. "Troubles and worries" are difficult to resolve not because Jesuits and/or former Jesuits have clashing opinions on them but because useful alternatives to such trends are extremely hard to come up with, regardless of whatever bias is brought to bear on them. They constitute developments for which workable responses, whether progressive or conservative, have yet to be formulated.[23] Rather than being a contest between sharply defined antagonists, the struggle is a game against nature, in which "nature" is a series of virtually unyielding constraints on resources and historical openings. These systemic problems weigh on conventional forms of religious life, especially on the traditional priesthood. They produce frustration rather than an adversarial standoff.

The reflections of a thirty-five-year-old high school teacher are directed at just such worries. This Jesuit explores a pair of "problems and challenges" that affect the culture of religious life and that resist resolution by administrative ingenuity or theological debate:

> I suppose I see two major problems facing the Society, at least the Society in the United States, today. The first is indicative of not only the Society but also of the Catholic church in the United States and even of American culture in general. I would describe it as the gradual displacement of religion and spirituality by psychology. More and more of our purportedly religious language and thinking is couched in terms of self-fulfillment, dealing with my issues, empowering myself, claiming and owning my weakness, getting in touch with who I am, etcetera. I don't have any hard statistical evidence, but after almost ten years in the Soci-

ety I would be willing to bet the farm that the vast majority of scholastics have been in therapy for at least one extended period during their
time in the Society. In fact I think it is fair to say that therapy is an
expected part of Jesuit formation these days. Therapists are accorded
a kind of authority and deference that was once reserved for spiritual
directors and superiors. The number of scholastics who have been on
medication for one kind of psychological difficulty or another during
their time in the Society is astounding and, to me anyway, troubling.
I sometimes think that Prozac and Zoloft are for my generation what
scotch was for the generations before mine.[24]

    Perhaps most troubling to me is the fact that we have entrusted our-
selves and our future to the world of psychology without, as far as I can
tell, any systematic or corporate effort to ask the seemingly logical question, "What are we getting in return for all of the time, energy and
money we spend on therapy and medication for our men? Are we more
effective as an apostolic order in the church? Are we better, more effective Jesuits after our time spent in therapy and on medication?" My suspicion is that the answer to these questions would be "No," but I am
ready and willing to be proved wrong. I just wish we would ask the
question.

The young Jesuit moves from classifying the disease—therapization—
to diagnosing its causes and suggesting a remedy. He suspects that the
cure for the ailment lies not in more psychological treatment but at a
structural or organizational level, in a renewed emphasis on ministry.
Ironically, as the Society has become more open to outside influences,
deliberately undoing its corporate shields, many Jesuits have turned
inward:

> The primary reason why I see this "psychologization" of religious life as
> a problem for the Society is that the psychological ethos and its faithful
> handmaid, the "therapeutic model," with their unmitigated and uncon-
> textualized focus on the "human development" of the individual, under-
> cut the very self-understanding of an apostolic group of men whose very
> reason for being is outwardly focused, other oriented, and group based.

The new escapism of marathon introspection doesn't work. It fails to
enhance the sense of organizational purpose. Yet corporate identity or
collective self-understanding does not automatically flow out of an extroverted activism. Rather than being "group based," such behavior
may just as well be carried out by lone Jesuits or by laypeople.

    This leads the young Jesuit to consider a second development. The gay subculture provides a de facto support network that relieves the isolation of the therapeutic individual even if it does not advance a ministerial program. It helps resolve the deficiencies of community without addressing the question of corporate effectiveness:

> The second problem which I see facing the Society in the United States today is our unwillingness or inability to come to terms with the fact that a majority of Jesuits under forty are not heterosexual. Until we assimilate this fact into our corporate self-understanding and into the way we incorporate men into the Society and our way of proceeding, we will be operating out of an artificial and delusional mind-set. I'm not sure exactly how we go about doing that, but I do see it as a major problem facing us today.

Such "worries" have no quick fix. Unlike conflicts, they do not generate clear-cut policy options. In these cases, even if positions more precise and practical than generalized approval or distaste can be formulated, constructive courses of action—policies that might bring in recruits or improve organizational effectiveness—are not obvious. The temptation is to handle such challenges at the micro- and meso-levels, through therapeutic massage and adjustment to the market, and to leave the equivalent of major surgery on the rhetorical plane. With or without intervention on a grand scale, the risk of losing the patient is high.

"Problems and difficulties" have a momentum of their own. It is awareness of the possibility that trends like these may have no remedy consistent with tradition that makes contemplating the prospects of the Society with the expectation of a turnaround in its fortunes painful to men accustomed to decisive action. They remind Jesuits of the mortality of religious life.

CHAPTER ELEVEN

Low-Profile Politics

If the stance of the Society is widely perceived as anti-institutional hierarchy, anti-Vatican, anti-pope, and if political and politically correct norms are used to select candidates for the Society, most of those who wish to serve Christ's church will go elsewhere.

I think the pope is, in many ways, a magnificent world leader. He stands for certain things; he's clear about them; he has a certain magnetic personality, and he's a very genuine, upright person. . . . Inside the church, though, he's a disaster. He's not one of the worst popes; he's *the* worst; don't misquote me. There's a cutting off of dialogue, a listening to one side, at least that's the impression he gives. Control, not listening.

The single most difficult thing about being a Jesuit today for myself, and for many whom I know best, is that we are instantly and unavoidably perceived to be representatives of the institutional church, which is a constantly compromising position to be in.

I

At the dawn of the third millennium of the Christian era, on the verge of half a millennium of existence itself, the Society of Jesus could be depicted as a triumph of durability, unstable but long-lived all the same. Yet the Jesuits show signs of having reached an impasse.

Confusion stems from the clash of priorities within the order and from directives of the kind represented by *Ex Corde Ecclesiae*. Add to this the tendency of Jesuits to be at odds with the sexual magisterium, and the Society begins to look hamstrung. Put schematically: Differences over the implementation of the social justice agenda divide Jesuits themselves, and differences with regard to moral and sexual doctrine separate Jesuits from Roman orthodoxy.

None of this might be unmanageable if the confluence of problems and conflicts did not raise further questions about the nexus of ministry, ordained priesthood, and the consecrated life. Self-doubt among Jesuits surfaces in their anxiety about sacerdotal roles as well as in their wavering about the corporate thrust of their ministries. The work that Jesuits do continues to be valued, but the same cannot be said for the priesthood itself.

Jesuits are at a critical juncture in the evolution of Catholicism. Starting in the nineteenth century, with the curtailment of the temporal power of the church in Europe, and culminating with the Decree on Religious Liberty issued at Vatican II, the ecclesiastical hierarchy gave up trying to exercise political dominance in pluralist democracies.[1] Though the church acts vigorously as an interest group, it has retreated from the Counter-Reformation ideal of promoting religious conformity, and it has become one actor among several pressing for influence over public policy.[2]

A second threat to the power of the church has gained momentum more recently, this time from the inside. Since Vatican II, with the rise of the laity, clerical control over the ministerial agencies associated with the church has plummeted. Improved communications may make the surveillance of renegade theologians easier and enhance the magnetism of a telegenic pontiff. But the depletion of clerical manpower renders one-sided management of the educational, social, and pastoral activities associated with the church impossible. Though it hits activist orders like the Jesuits particularly hard, this shearing away of apostolic functions throws the clergy generally into crisis.

In addition to these institutional difficulties, a hollowing out of traditional beliefs and customs is apparent. Prohibitions against discussing possible alternatives and solutions—the ordination of women, the authorization of a married clergy, and the like—compound the problem of organizational debility. Since Jesuits, in more or less circumspect fashion, and of course former Jesuits talk about such options anyway, the back-and-forth of suppression and dissent undermines authority without relieving the pressure on human resources or removing obstacles to reform. The process resembles the peeling away of concentric layers, from the externals of organizational hierarchy toward core convictions about the status of the priesthood and on to the inner sanctum surrounding the divinity of the historical Jesus.[3]

By getting on with the work at hand, many Jesuits ignore such dilemmas. Time and again, conflicts of the sort generated by rival priorities within the order or by divisions between Rome and the Society echo only faintly in the daily grind of Jesuits. Nevertheless, the beat of these conflicts joins with the attrition in numbers to call into question received understandings of priestly ministry and the wisdom of ecclesiastical authority. Cumulative pressures raise strategic issues. Where will change occur? And who will control it?

2

For Jesuits, the price of dealing seriously with complex strategic and theological issues, which tend to look insoluble from almost any perspective, is daunting. Frustration is written all over them, relative to the satisfactions of getting on with the work at hand. Prudence counsels waiting out the dysfunctions, rather than outright resistance or visionary innovation.[4]

Some Jesuits look on the bright side, sustained by a realism of the sort that brackets the remote scuffles among those in authority as nuisances that are so much court politics and background noise, distant thunder. "The church is more than the institution," one Jesuit, a fifty-six-year-old parish priest in Washington remarks:

> People in administration get those jobs to keep things together, and they're just doing what they have been chosen to do. I, obviously, don't have to deal with church or Society authorities, so they have little immediate effect on my life. I think Father Kolvenbach has done what he was appointed to do by keeping a low profile.

The Jesuit mixes optimism about the luxuriant diversity of the grass-roots church with a fatalism and indifference toward politicking in the upper echelons. The split-level formula has practical appeal. The priest is too busy to be demoralized. He stays focused on the pastoral here and now, glancing only occasionally at megatrends and matters of grand strategy:

> I am excited about the changes that will have to come from the internationalizing of the Society. I believe God's grace is powerfully moving in our ministries and our lives. Our future depends on that, not our cleverness or our plans. The church appears to be in one place today, but time passes, and the church will be in another place. There are lots of great things happening in the church all around the world. I'm sure I would think differently if I had a different background or personality or ministry. "What, me worry?"

What the Jesuit knows of the larger church tells him that it is bubbling with diversity. He has no time for stratospheric abstractions:

> It's the thirteenth, and I have to finish this letter and get back to the chaos on my desk. I was at our Lutheran-Catholic dialogue this afternoon, and Joe Fitzmyer referred to the difference between Ratzinger Junior and Ratzinger Senior. I don't have to deal with Ratzinger, but the way I see it is that he has a job from the church which he interprets to be a watchdog. I think excommunicating that Oblate in Sri Lanka was screwy, but I guess they think they're just doing their jobs. There's so much more to the church than that stuff for me. In fact, for all practical purposes, the Holy Office doesn't exist. I still resent the way they hassled Pedro Arrupe, but the Society survived.[5]

So stalemate stops short of collapse. Jesuits lower down the hierarchy are less powerful than those, like bishops and curial officials, toward the top. They are also further out of reach and, as they shrewdly perceive, difficult to supervise. For this reason, Jesuits are apt to more satisfied with operations close to the ground than with the doings of those higher up. "I would say the higher the level (pope, Congregations for Faith and Doctrine), the lesser the satisfaction," a fifty-six-year-old Jesuit who teaches English at the university level argues neatly, "the lower (lay participation and collaboration), the more; the bishops are somewhere in the middle."

The system avoids a good deal of confrontation, but it also fails to provide channels for change. There are almost no mechanisms for processing conflict. If behavior is discreet, officialdom will not be aroused. Because ecclesiastical authority is diluted at the lower, less visible levels of the system, a measure of operational autonomy is sustained. Jesuits act rationally within their circumscribed purview, cutting their losses. Some of this is equivalent to a cat-and-mouse game. In other cases—in some of the faith-and-justice initiatives, which do not present doctrinal difficulties, or in educational areas far from theology—a spirit of adventure stills prevails.

3

Besides compartmentalization, another mode of reacting to the air of looming crisis follows a traditionalist line, specifically with regard to the differences between the Vatican and the Society. Some Jesuits see themselves not as dissenters from the teaching of the church or the directions of the papacy but, on the contrary, as members of a minority opposed to the prevailing liberalism of their colleagues. In their hearts, the intensity of faith outweighs any head count of opinion. They are the passionate nucleus whose zeal matters more than democracy by the numbers.

A seventy-nine-year-old Jesuit, retired from university teaching, works as an assistant pastor at a largely Spanish-speaking parish. His take on the predicament of the Society is that too many Jesuits have abandoned the old ways. Traditional values, from corporate solidarity to sexual probity, have gone by the wayside. The fundamental menace, he suggests, has less to do with the attrition of manpower than with the erosion of respect for hierarchy and a traditional personal code:

> The major problems today in the Society as I see them are losses in great Jesuit traditional values: (a) the lack of respect, especially among theologians, for papal positions and doctrines; (b) the seeming rejection by some younger Jesuits of the "all-for-all" principle and the tendency to divide a community into separate groups of the like-minded; and (c) a seeming lack of caution in many younger Jesuits in dealing with the opposite sex.

"I have liked everything coming from the pope," he concludes, "and most things coming from the Vatican."

For this man, cracks in institutional loyalty and slipping adherence to core precepts are worse than the falloff in numbers. Whatever pain accompanies the demographic diminution of the Society may be a call to "embrace the cross." Statistical bad news does not capture the even graver spiritual peril and corporate disarray in which Jesuits have become ensnared. "I am not in dissent from any teachings of the church," a thirty-six-year-old student of theology, about to be ordained after twelve years in the Society, says:

> I entered to help support the direction that Pope John Paul II has given the church. The Society has a mixed response to this direction, and the confusion it causes will ultimately hurt the effectiveness of the Society.

Not all conservative diagnoses of the plight of the Society are pessimistic or unconcerned about downsizing. A sixty-one-year-old Jesuit, working in parish ministry, finds consolation in discipline and adversity. "I want to live the celibate life I am living. I hunger to know God through the peculiar emptiness it provides":

My prayer life needs to be much more alive than it is. I want to be on fire for Christ, filled with gratitude, but I simply continue with a firm effort. . . .

We must be convinced of our call to serve Christ as Jesuits. In a way, we must forget our past, at least insofar as we try to continue past achievements into the future which have seen their day. I see the future as a great springtime. I see the future possibly so alive in Christ in the next century or so that people may begin to wonder if Teilhard's omega point might soon be reached and the Lord lift it all up in his parousia.[6] [But] the sufferings and crosses will also be great and terrible.

This Jesuit arrives at his conservatism out of periodic stress and a sense of modesty about his own capacities. His conversion combines doctrinal orthodoxy with a desire for belonging and group support. The man is not a strict authoritarian. Within the church at least, he just doesn't see much point to a liberalism that puts a premium on individual rights. The well-ordered household of Catholicism is his community:

During the late '70s and early '80s, I lived in a Jesuit parish where the pastor was loyal in an extreme way to the pope and the tradition of the church as he understood it. I learned through this man to be deeply attached to the church. I hope with less rigidity than he had but, nevertheless, attachment to the church, its bishops and other leaders, its teachings is my—and I believe our—Jesuit way to glory.

It is the group that counts, not so much in the abstract but as personal, meaningful hierarchy, a cause. The sentimental bond with this institutional image overwhelms strict calculation of the losses expressed in numbers. The decline in manpower is a refining fire. Perseverance is the supreme demonstration of hope.

4

Support for the status quo, then, originates not only in the inclination of some Jesuits to focus their energies on the work at hand (*age quod agis*—"do what you're doing," in the Ignatian phrasing) and to consider most efforts at reform as a morass of tedious politics and feckless utopianism. In a smaller number of cases, commitment is founded on a belief in the rightness of the restorationist agenda.

Another element of hesitation—of ambivalence more properly than steadfast resistance to change—derives from skepticism directed at the proponents of change instead of from unstinting loyalty to tradition. This Jesuit, a sixty-seven-year-old professor of theology, is far from being a reactionary zealot. But reservations about the motives and political acumen of reformers in the Society pervade his astringent view of their limited success:

> The Society of Jesus today is caught up in nostalgia for the Second Vatican Council, Popes John XXIII and Paul VI, and Father General Arrupe. Almost all of its leaders were shaped by those experiences and values. A small minority are enthusiastic about the vision and values of Pope John Paul II and Cardinal Ratzinger; the rest are waiting for a new pope, who they hope will restore the dynamism and direction of the council. They are not convinced that the pope really is committed to the listening necessary for any fruitful dialogue—with other Christian churches, with other religions, with scholarly disciplines, with economic, political, and technological forces shaping contemporary cultures. Instead of dialogue there are various forms of monologue—encyclicals, apostolic constitutions, declarations by curial congregations, the *Catechism of the Catholic Church.*

Although the theologian is out of sympathy with the high-handedness of the papacy, he does not reject the idea of reconciling papal accomplishments and criticism of what many Jesuits judge to be a repudiation of the spirit of Vatican II:

> In this context the Society is challenged to recognize the positive achievements and talents of the pope, to stand up for his decisions, to be loyal to the pope while being loyal to God and God's people. This is fairly easy in the areas of social justice, fairly difficult in areas of church management.
>
> The decrees of the recent Congregation [GC 34] reflect well the priorities of the council and Popes John and Paul, as well as sensitivity to the emerging importance of the laity and social issues like feminism and ecology.

"These enthusiasms," the theologian adds dryly, "are not equally shared by all in the Roman curia."[7]

The theologian's head is with the reformers, but he cannot resist chastising his colleagues for a certain self-absorption. He is put off by the epicene lifestyle and the paucity of rough-and-tumble credentials that he sees among younger Jesuits:

Another major challenge is to move beyond the rhetoric about poverty and the option for the poor into a modification of the excessively comfortable lifestyles of communities and individuals, particularly Jesuits under fifty. Younger men have had no experience of the Great Depression; only black and Asian Jesuits have experienced severe poverty and destitution over long periods other than novitiate or regency experiments. This affects Americans but also Western European and Australian Jesuits.

Another Jesuit, this man a thirty-year-old student of theology, eight years a member of the Society, also feels caught in the middle. He is much less taken than some conservatives are with the notion that the drop in numbers represents a purifying ordeal. For him, failure in recruitment is a real problem. In addition, he worries about the split developing among younger Jesuits. This polarization, he contends, arises from insecurity about where the Society is going and the future of oncoming cohorts in the institutional apparatus of the church:

> A lot of younger Jesuits lack clarity on the question of their position vis-à-vis the institutional church. They have a great sense of being spiritual and religiously oriented men. However, a significant percentage stand at two extremes in relation to the hierarchical church that they are ordained into: either they are '50s romantics and highly clerical, or they are shocked that they have to represent an organization and ideology bigger than and different from themselves. The latter is the bigger problem.

The quandary about the direction of the Society results both from internal muddle and from the restrictions placed on it by Rome. It has been easier, argues the theology student, for the leadership of the Society to identify what Jesuits needed to jettison in the received model of religious life than to clear a path along which the order should be headed:

> In the face of decreasing numbers in the Society, I think superiors need to do a better job of articulating a vision to the younger ones of us who will be taking over in a couple of decades, as things (hopefully) have leveled off. Superiors are doing a good job of confronting the current management (Jesuits in their fifties and sixties) with the fact that the Society doesn't have the institutional control it had as these guys entered. My generation is much more used to this reality, but we still need a vision from our superiors as to what might be, rather than simply what clearly won't be.

Because the Society has had uneven success in formulating a vision of priesthood and corporate purpose, many Jesuits find themselves at a psychological remove from the restorationist camp while at the same time drifting, in default of a positive alternative, toward pastoral duties. The young Jesuit maps his colleagues onto an ideological space that is consistent with what is known about their leftward leanings. "Most Jesuits," he notes, "would call themselves more liberal and more pastoral than the current hierarchy and the diocesan clergy, especially on the question of sexual morals. Most Jesuits would be slower to identify themselves as more liberal than most of the American Catholic laity, though this is probably as true."

Trying to situate himself and his fellow Jesuits relative to the recent evolution of the church, he reaches an unresolved tension between admiration for the leadership of the papacy and worry about the erosion of the cutting-edge position of Jesuits. The ideals of the church are admirable; the stopgap absorption of once adventurous religious orders like the Jesuits into what some view as comparatively pedestrian pastoral chores is alarming:

> I agree with several trends out of Rome. I appreciate the steps that John
> Paul II has taken to increase the sense of the church being a world church
> by his travels and his tackling of broad social and cultural issues. I ap-
> preciate the full frontal attack on Western capitalistic materialism. I
> think the statements of General Congregation 34 on culture and mission
> dovetail with many of these Roman directions. As a young Jesuit eager
> to "think with the church," I take this very seriously.

So far, so good. The young Jesuit applauds the critical stance adopted by the pope, along with the sympathetic yet cautious approach to the cultures of advanced industrial societies formulated by the leadership of the Society. Trouble sets in, he argues, with attempts to bring such resolutions down to earth through the overworked mediocrities who actually run the church:

> I am worried, however, by the less pastoral tone taken by bishops and
> much of the diocesan clergy in the United States. In good humanistic
> tradition, I think our criticisms of the society around us have to be ulti-
> mately directed at uncovering the good in the basic expression of our
> humanity; I fear that a poorly and dogmatically trained local clergy and
> an excessively aggressive hierarchy threaten to throw out the baby with
> the bath water in their attacks on the Western world. In reaction, many

Jesuits are drawn to filling in the pastoral lacunae this leaves. As an attitude, I am comfortable with this; as it draws us into more and more parish work, I disagree.

In some instances, suspicions about the character and personal habits of reformers go hand in hand with a strong dose of conservatism about the posture of the Society regarding the rest of the institutional church. A sixty-three-year-old professor of English literature, five years short of marking his golden anniversary as a Jesuit, comments on the possible demise of the order if it follows what he views as a politicized course. He reflects on the prospect of organizational extinction with seeming impartiality while suggesting that blame for collapse can be laid on Jesuits themselves:

> If the stance of the Society is widely perceived as anti-institutional hierarchy, anti-Vatican, anti-pope, and if political and politically correct norms are used to select candidates for the Society, most of those who wish to serve Christ's church will go elsewhere. Many groups of religious men and women have vanished; witness Belgian sisterhoods even prior to Vatican II. A safe prophecy would be that several congregations of men and women are currently on the road to extinction. Whether or not the Society survived was a matter of "indifference" to St. Ignatius and should be to every Jesuit. Faith in the survival of the church, not of the Society, is a mark of the Jesuit.

What accounts for the apparently suicidal penchant for opposition to the church? The answer, according to this Jesuit, is permissiveness. Modern norms of sexual behavior have infected the Society. Ascetical methods of character formation have receded, and laxity, including personal indiscipline and institutional dissent, has set in. The breakdown of authority follows on self-indulgence: [8]

> Our post-Freud etcetera understanding of the person has us less convinced that knowledge and will power can control life. However, the effort to achieve rational coherence is still a mark of intelligent life, and self-discipline is still important in the tests of character. Sexual behavior has always been an important social and religious test of our views on the roles of rational coherence and self-discipline and our willingness to accept the consequences of our acts. Society has always been divided between those who say they cannot help themselves and those who believe in the training and exercise of free will.

Apart from the safety valve of leaving the order, then, there are several ways in which concern over the troubles of the Society is diverted from building toward intolerable levels. Many Jesuits get on with their jobs, finding personal satisfaction and meaning in the daily grind, ignoring the infighting that goes on above their heads. This is the one-day-at-a-time solution. A few are cynical, but many appear to be simply dedicated rather than flamboyantly heroic. They acquiesce in what they consider to be irrelevant directions for the sake of getting the job done.

A second, smaller group is composed of men who look on themselves as keepers of the flame, holding to the Jesuit tradition of obedience to Rome, resisting faddish reforms and put off by dissent. They claim to be interested in "quality"—in the devotion and zeal of the Society—and to be relatively unfazed by the decline in numbers.[9]

A third group is torn between the Society and the institutional church, which they see in considerable tension. These men, many of them younger Jesuits, tend to be unimpressed by the emancipatory exaltation of the 1960s and 1970s, a little bored by the war stories about them, and suspicious of those whose discourse is framed by these battles. Yet they are also repelled by the bunker, the die-hard reactionaries craving the purity of absolutes, and they are uninspired by those whom they take to be conservatives by force of habit.

5

All the patterns just described—the low profile, the conservative, the ambivalent—are coping mechanisms, enabling Jesuits to get on with their lives with a sense of fulfillment even if they are hobbled by doubt or resentment. Their work is fulfilling enough that organizational hassles and goings-on in high places are treated, like the whims of the gods, as tolerable inconveniences. They are items of gossip, not incentives to opposition.

Other Jesuits contemplate their circumstances from this side and that, turning the situation over and over, even if no solutions are in sight. Notice how this fifty-nine-year-old professor of theology scans the tiers of the Society's world, from falling numbers to the logistics of staffing to the intellectual impact of a less Eurocentric and male-dominated Catholicism. He begins with a commonplace set of observations about the numbers problem. "An enormous [challenge] in the U.S.," he notes, "is our being able to face up to loss—to do this in a way that energizes us to reimagine ourselves working with laypeople having much more of a say in the power and our being ancillary to them." Then he hops to the international scene:

> India and Africa will have the numbers yet those are different cultures. Why the loss? For the very reason that in India and Africa it's going up. . . . There was an intact Catholic culture that supported the ideal [of vocations], and when that started splitting up you didn't have the plausibility structure. The motivation, the social reinforcement isn't there. Clergy don't have the same pipeline of moving into an acknowledged role. . . . The idea of a lifetime commitment is not there. People don't think in terms of religious life as a holier mode.

Next the theologian looks at how the protracted shortfall in numbers affects options for ministry. He examines how efforts at reform not only run up against the scarcity of manpower but are compounded by localism and market pressures. The drive for survival, multiplied by the demands of local ministries, places a low ceiling on incentives for cooperation across institutions:

> I think one of the in-house things is how to organize ourselves in the U.S. in a way that doesn't tie up too many people in administration. A couple of years ago, we explored trying to realign the provinces, not just regrouping, according to where conflicts are. (A lot of people would be in the South, if that were to happen.) Dividing up the whole thing, not keeping the present lines and merging. [The trouble is that] some provinces have big bucks, small bucks in others. Also, people have done more identifying with the provinces. . . . You give yourself to the Society, not to a province. But people really identify with the province.
>   I'm on the ———— University board. It's hard to get a plan, with each place competing to get the young Jesuits at their school.

From an examination of administrative nitty-gritty and the clutter of obstacles to intra-Jesuit coordination, the Jesuit turns to consider the theological repercussions of the internationalization of the Society and other structural changes, like the women's movement:

> The enormous thing for me is the encounter with world religions and how to deal with multiple salvations. They can't be put together into one ultimate goal that all these lead to because that means you're going to say what the goal is from your tradition. It's much more pluralistic than anyone wants to put it. This is a mind-bending topic: how to make sense of our Jesus Christ in relation to these other religions. Even the ways we pose the problems are shaped by the issue of uniqueness, which

may not be an Eastern view. I don't know what the answers are going
to be on that. We need incredible patience. The whole feminist critique
is a very serious one. . . . Can Jesus Christ do justice to women and their
concerns? My resurrection hope is that he will and that he can.

Ruminations like these wander all over the lot. It is hard to find a center point, except for a sensitivity to how developments in various areas
of religious life—the demographic and the doctrinal, for example—
spill over into one another. Catholicism is cast as an intricate ecosystem
whose elements connect and resonate in curious ways. Conservatives
get the impression of a wayward, dizzying relativism. Other Jesuits look
at such probing as an exercise in open-ended pluralism, a clamor of
strange, attractive voices. The questions that come up—about ministry,
about the ordination of women and married men, about the mystery of
Christ, and so on—wait for such Jesuits around bends in a road they
have set out on without quite choosing it, unable to turn back and not
in sight of journey's end. They may lack a coherent cause, but they have
glimpses of adventure.

Persisting in the search has two drawbacks: the danger of run-ins
with guardians of orthodoxy and the risk that the exploration itself is
too much of a hermetic puzzle to be of interest except to a small circle
of theological adepts. However, the telltale sign of crisis—the fall in religious vocations—is genuine. Whether out of incorrigible curiosity or
obstinate conscience, the polemic over these issues simmers on despite
the risk of suppression and the elusiveness of unequivocal answers.

The sense of urgency is heightened by a perception that, like a train
wreck in slow motion, long-term social and demographic forces are
smashing up against the creaky machinery of the church and religious
life. The feature that distinguishes this view from the cyclical, *plus ça
change* . . . diagnosis of the troubles of the Society is the weight given to
a developmental, contingent reading of church history. Images of turning points, crossroads, and strategic choices replace the go-around of a
vast pageant circling back on itself. The tired wisdom of having seen it
all before, the conviction that this too will pass, does not fit the present
crisis. Ecclesiastical time may flow slowly, but it doesn't run in reverse.

6

What bothers this sixty-eight-year-old Jesuit? "Celibacy, that sort of
issue," he notes, then quickly indicates that the controversy itself is

inseparable from the dissonance of traditional authority smashing up against cultural change:

> I feel very controlled; that control is what it's all about. I also think it touches us closely here [at a theologate]: training for ministry, who are ministers? There's almost a paranoia about what you can say about certain issues. It's very detrimental to the church. For example, the women's ordination issue. Why is that forbidden to even be talked about? Everybody's talking about it. I have no problem [with the ordination of women], but there are sociological issues with this. This is not just the First World where the discussion is more advanced and the whole situation of women is so different. The church has so many different cultures. To try to impose sixteenth-century methods of repression is ridiculous.[10]

The sticking point is not only the set of controversies surrounding pelvic theology but a style of governance that tries to stifle conversation about these and a range of similar matters. The result, the Jesuit feels, is a false order imposed without consent or legitimate debate. Grandeur on the outside distracts from repression on the inside:

> I think the pope is, in many ways, a magnificent world leader. He stands for certain things; he's clear about them; he has a certain magnetic personality, and he's a very genuine, upright person. People on the outside might disagree with this or that policy, but he stands for peace; he stands for justice and so forth.

John Paul II turned out to be even more of an autocrat than his predecessors, heroic in his virtues but with one disastrous flaw:

> Inside the church, though, he's a disaster. The key issue is the appointment of bishops. How can an institution simply not take the best and the top people for these key positions, but ciphers? People have said to me, "How would you rate him as a church scholar?" and I've said, "Probably the worst pope of all times." Qua pope—not qua human being, not qua world leader, but qua pope. That is to say, what is a pope to do? He is a symbol and force for unity, for consensus, the ultimate judge, but not prosecuting attorney, not warden. With the state of the episcopacy in the past, because of the different ways bishops got into office in the past, there was always room for some kind of regeneration— but the Holy Spirit's really going to have to go to town with this one!
>
> He's not one of the worst popes; he's *the* worst; don't misquote me. There's a cutting off of dialogue, a listening to one side, at least that's the impression he gives. Control, not listening.[11]

For all his severity in condemning one pope, the Jesuit refrains from extending his criticism to the structure of the papal office, leaving the door open to better times with the accession of fresh leadership. Nevertheless, he is chagrined by the disjuncture between an outmoded authoritarianism and the mounting pressure of systemic shifts represented by the spread of the women's movement and similar transformations. It is not as if a beneficent changing of the guard will put the church back on course by itself, for that new course remains to be plotted.[12]

A complex of structural changes has shattered the social and cultural terrain of Catholicism and has undermined the feasibility of a restorationist revival, except in the short run. Jesuits can't go home again. The march of long-term historical forces, this interpretation suggests, promotes the dissolution of old hierarchies.[13] Even if the outlines of a new institutional architecture are barely discernible, the momentum is cause for optimism among some progressives. "I am concerned about the interface of the Society and the hierarchical Catholic church," a fifty-four-year-old formation director admits. But he is hopeful that the Jesuits will be vindicated, in part because he believes that history is on their side:

> I have no doubts about the path the Society has found itself called to over the last four congregations and two generals. That is the Society I belong to and am called to develop. John Paul II's intervention in the Society's government in the early '80s was for me a kind of humiliation that Ignatius envisioned for the Society and experienced himself more than once. It was, to say the least, painful for us: We seemed to be doubted by the very man we were trying most to serve. It was Ignatius himself that taught us the crucial grace of such humiliation.

Other Jesuits also feel that the Society is at a tipping point. A sharp departure has taken place from what has gone before, signaled by the free fall in recruitment. However, these men are not so sanguine about the prospects of getting back on track. Their hopes for the Society are guarded in the face of unresolved turmoil on the inside and the self-fulfilling prophecy of a downward spiral. "One of the big challenges is that for the first time in its history the Society has been in a declining numbers situation," a fifty-seven-year-old university professor and rector of his community says, acknowledging the novelty of the challenge confronting Jesuits. The problem is not just the slumping demographics but the divisions these pressures set up between Jesuits and the Vatican and among Jesuits themselves:

There's a kind of a wonderment, a discouragement, an "are we dying?" I think that's something that we need to be able to face head on, to be hopeful and renew our trust in God. God began the Society, and if God wants it to continue, there's no reason that it can't. It may be smaller. That's a real challenge.

There's a great diversity of views about things in the Society, about what the church is, where the church is going, what it ought to be, and our relationship to the papacy, and some of that can be very divisive. It can immobilize us and make us unsure of ourselves and unsure about the future. I think one of the ways it comes out is in attracting young men who might have a vocation to the Society. If people feel the Society is basically over, then that enthusiasm isn't there. So, the divisions that exist in the Society are a real challenge for us.

7

The step from inching up to the abyss to peering into it is short. Some Jesuits have resigned themselves to the prospect of the extinction of the Society. The question is no longer survival but how long the death will take. Anger flares up not at the Society but at a church that thwarts the new ideal of resignation and honorable withdrawal: the handover of once-clerical roles to the laity. This is the perspective of a fifty-nine-year-old spiritual director:

> The major problem the Society faces is that we are part of an increasingly dysfunctional church. Much of our treatment officially of women, of married peoples' experience, of the appointment of bishops and consequently of diocesan and parish governance is simply terrible. The priest pool is nonexistent, and we are in danger of simply plugging the gaps, to our own demise and contributing to the slow death of what needs to die rapidly. . . .
>
> The Society [should] simply refuse to put collective fingers in the dike. If tomorrow we said we would only help out in parishes that had competent lay leadership in administrative positions, we could force the change that needs to happen, or at least a collective reflection on the problems of who we ordain. The single most difficult thing about being a Jesuit today for myself, and for many whom I know best, is that we are instantly and unavoidably perceived to be representatives of the institutional church, which is a constantly compromising position to be in.

There is regret at lives dedicated to a losing cause. There is also a desire to pass on the torch. There is a compulsion to set things right, to salvage dignity and meaning from loss by facilitating the transition to a lay-centered church. The urge toward reconciliation in the transfer of authority to those who have been excluded overtakes the old militancy, and a new composure sets in, as happens with this sixty-five-year-old retreat master, whose anguish has abated:

> Some major problems facing the Society today: facilitating the death and dying process in the Society and church; attracting new Jesuits; handing over half of our ministries to laity that we've prepared well; challenging the hierarchy to move into the twenty-first century; establishing a good dialogue with the boomers and generation X; working for the reconciliation of women and men.
>
> The church as we have known it is dying, at least in the West. . . . Its growing poverty will make possible many changes: the ordination of women and married men; the ascension of laity to administrative and magisterial positions of leadership; the growth of local churches; the dismantling of the Vatican and its bureaucracies; the movement to a servant leadership. . . . I hope and pray that the Society will help to facilitate this death and resurrection. I'm hopeful that there's a freedom, courage, vision in the Society to enter into this paschal mystery.

Here the chords of mourning and release from sorrow are intermingled. A bare-bones coherence arises from despair. The Jesuit's voice relaxes into the rhythmic eloquence of hope and acceptance. He expects the Society to die, but he trusts that a transfigured Society will attract "new Jesuits." How this resurrection will transpire and what shape it will assume are left vague, but the feeling that it will occur is strong.

Composure of this sort comes and goes, flickering in the face of decline. Sometimes the emergence of a new institutional order is hinted at, and even if what is foreshadowed lacks definition, the vision looks like something worth pursuing in contrast to the present straits. "The lessening of our numbers and of vocations" is the main problem for a fifty-five-year-old university administrator, as it is for most of his colleagues. In this decline, however, he discerns the makings of a qualitative transformation:

> I suspect that this is not just a temporary aberration that will soon be corrected but that we are moving into an age of the laity where religious life will constitute a far less significant part of the church's life than previously. We are challenged to begin thinking not in terms of how we can do the same kind of work with fewer people, but what kind of church

we are living in, and what kinds of work we are being called to today in that church. That will probably involve letting go of institutions (physical plants and frames of mind) that we have become used to and comfortable in.

While there is no blueprint for how the transition is to occur, the basic idea is not to stand in the way of a historical evolution. The Jesuit calls for "openness to the spirit, willingness to change and let go, less privatism in our apostolates and more openness to the church and the movement of society as a whole." The hidebound conservatism that needs to be abandoned is more clearly focused than the alternatives to it:

> I am appalled by the direction of the present papacy toward absolute central control of the church, the appointment of inferior quality bishops whose principal value seems to be conformity with Rome, creeping infallibilism that regards any statement from Rome as virtually irreformable, the attempts by Rome and the episcopacy to control the university and the intellectual life of the church, substituting catechism for theology, obedience for intellect. I am scandalized by Rome's intransigent refusal to reexamine its doctrines regarding gender and sex (birth control, ordination of women, married clergy, homosexuality, divorce and remarriage). . . . I am scandalized by the attempts to quash dissent and any challenge to papal power which in their tyranny have the counterproductive result of undermining the power they are trying to uphold. Frankly I think the church is being governed by thugs.

The gist of such interpretations is the dual nature of the crisis facing the Society: a steady decline in membership and the damage wreaked by a reactionary Vatican and a pliant episcopate. It is the combination of the two that drives many Jesuits not just to an awareness of dysfunction but to a suspicion that the enterprise may have lost meaning. A thirty-five-year-old student of theology summarizes both the inexorable demographic trends and the policies that, he feels, have the effect of alienating the few who hang on. "I think the leadership [of the Society] is in denial about the future," he remarks:

> My province has seventeen people [who] left before ordination, this for a province that runs five high schools, two universities, and a few parishes and retreat centers. Further, community life for many of the young does not provide enough affective support to sustain vocations for long. My novice master left to marry, my formation director left for a rela-

tionship with another man, etcetera. One cannot help but get the sense that we of this generation of Jesuits may be the "last of the Shakers."

The problem is not just that Jesuits contribute less and less to the functioning of institutional ministries. Jesuits are also put off by an understanding of faith and a system of church governance that prizes obeisance over reasoned commitment. The normative bands tying religious devotion to intelligent conviction are stretched very thin. The implicit contract of Jesuit life comes close to snapping:

> I believe the church teachings . . . have much to offer; the problem is that they are taught in a way that forbids conversation and discussion. Implicitly, intelligence is understood in a limited way: the capacity to adopt what authorities mandate.
>
> The church's directions today are backwards. Morale is terrible for many priests, not just Jesuits. There's a sense that the crazies in the church have been in power for a while now, and anything that was progressive and hopeful has been squashed. The Society suffers because it has to be "careful" rather than prophetic. This raises the question for many: What's the point of giving my life to an institution that isn't doing much?

"I find myself much more cynical than when I first entered," the Jesuit concludes. "I believe Christ saves in spite of the church, seldom because of her. I've become much more enlivened by the gospel portraits of Jesus and less trusting of religious institutions."

The swipe at "institutions" could be dismissed as an assortment of countercultural clichés left over from the 1960s, exalting spirituality over religion, except for the connection between disdain for church officialdom and doubts about the utility of clerical ministry.[14] The dysfunctions of the church are graver than the mildly scandalous screw-ups of any large organization. Worry about disorder and control reflects not only a distrust of the laity but also deep anxiety about the fading distinctiveness of the priesthood. "The order is dying," a Jesuit high school president declares:

> Here's a radical idea that would be fun to deal with and argue about and say, "What are we really trying to achieve? What is the apostolic orientation of the order, and has it been incidental that it has been celibate men in it?" If the apostolate is the issue—not the doers are the issue—well, the doers can be of a bunch of different kinds. They could be celibate priests, and they could be married ladies, and they could be who knows what.

Speculation along these lines is ruthlessly pragmatic. If the celibate male priesthood has become peripheral as a means for enhancing ministerial service, what is left of sacerdotal identity or of the functions of activist religious orders like the Jesuits?

8

Jesuits, then, are divided about the corporate direction of the order and doubtful about the rationale of ordained ministry. There is a growing disconnect between the functions performed by institutions with which Jesuits are affiliated and the symbolic status of the priesthood. The difficulty is less old-fashioned anticlericalism, in which the sacred and profane were squarely antithetical, than a fifth-wheel syndrome. Jesuits come close to being present as iconic decor, part of the atmosphere, for operations largely staffed and run by laypeople.

The separation between the functions of Jesuits and the symbolism of the priesthood entails a lack of fit between the raison d'être of religious life and ministerial reality. Ordination no longer seems a necessary, much less a sufficient, condition for ministry. The same goes for the connection between celibacy and the priesthood. There appears to be no way to come up with a solution for a shrinking clerisy that does not require the revision of long-standing norms about the celibate male priesthood. Progressive measures, like a married clergy, would almost certainly speed up the decline in the number of candidates for holy orders in celibate groups. And though they may slow the decline, conservative policies—that is, cleaving to the status quo—show little promise of actually reversing it. With no solution in sight under the conventional framework, examination of options gets short-circuited.

A related inhibition against exploring alternatives to traditional understandings of ordained ministry is the fear that debate, once started, has no fail-safe mechanism. This is a variation on the slippery-slope problem: the dread of losing control utterly if control relaxes a bit. The fear is not unfounded. Questions surrounding the celibate priesthood are bundled with sensitive issues surrounding sexuality and the role of women. Contemplating modifications in the requirements for priesthood opens up divisions concerning the structure of authority and eventual changes in the substance of the magisterium.

The logic of the impasse resembles the dilemma created by attachment to the archaic paradigm of a tight partnership between church and state that John Courtney Murray challenged in trying to develop a workable model for Catholicism in a pluralistic context. By the second half of the twentieth century, Murray came to realize, not only had traditional guidelines for church-state relations threatened to become counterproductive. In an increasingly democratic world, the old rules behind this symbiosis were also losing legitimacy. Dysfunction fueled the disintegration of meaning. Murray argued for prudential acceptance of a religious tolerance that the church had virtually no choice but to concede anyway, after the triumph of the democracies in World War II. This reluctant wisdom turned into a more fulsome endorsement of democratic values as a guide to church-state relations in the wake of Vatican II.[15]

The loosened nexus between the practice of ministry and the traditional ideal of priesthood poses a similar incongruity. The problem is not with church policy *ad extra,* however, but with a serious misfit in the internal workings of the institution.

Under the current dispensation, the advance of pluralism within the church remains shadowy and illegitimate even if the phenomenon is widespread in the form of apostolic decentralization, surreptitious dissent, and clandestine miscreance.[16] Jesuits have long experience in accommodating to the hierarchical culture of Catholicism while managing to get their own way now and again. The present crisis is distinctive, however, because piecemeal maneuvers—the therapeutic remedies, the occasional inventiveness in ministry—that have guaranteed survival may impede or draw energy away from institutional creativity and original thought on a larger scale. The issues are ideological and strategic, and they may require more than ad hoc solutions. In the words of a fifty-nine-year-old theologian,

> Such things as morals and questions of ordained ministry, the image and role of the priest, how it fits with Jesuit works and so on, and still more generally questions of doctrine today: I long for a clear field to discuss these issues. I do not see them as intractable questions; there are solutions; there are ways of viewing priesthood today that make complete sense. But the issues cannot be discussed freely, old formulas cannot be challenged. And Jesuits today have been ordered by the general (in the 1980s, not recently) not to criticize the papacy or its positions overtly. Many of the forms in which the church, the faith are being presented today are archaic and counterproductive. But they cannot be replaced without extensive responsible discussion. But this is in effect forbidden to Jesuits today, except by tiny increment and indirection. I lay the blame on much of the problems of the church . . . in Western societies to the poor leadership in the church today.

9

Even though such transformations exert pressure for change, political regimes rarely collapse straight out as a result of incongruities between shifts in underlying social and cultural conditions and outmoded organizational practices. The systemic precursors of such upheavals tell us little about the specific maneuvers that go into these transitions or about the direction they are likely to take.[17] The incongruity argument—death by obsolescence—is even more specious for religious institutions like the Catholic church. Because assimilation risks the loss of identity, adaptation may have less to recommend it as a strategy of survival for the Society than resistance to change. A countercultural slant of some sort appears to be a necessary condition for religious durability.[18] Like the bumblebee, the ancien régime looks aerodynamically improbable, but still it flies.

Yet the intuitive sense that institutional habits cannot be persistently out of sync with underlying social conditions has real bearing on the plight of the Jesuits. The numerous apostolic commitments of the Society of Jesus and activist orders fashioned in its mold require adaptation to practical exigencies in husbanding resources and a modicum of fairness in dealing with their clientele. They cannot simply circle the wagons and wait things out. The tension between adaptive pulls and contrarian pushes accounts for much of the characteristic instability in Jesuit affairs.

The supposition that a democratizing DNA is built into long-term structural modernization, sweeping churches as well as political institutions before it, also suggests that democratization, when it occurs, is propelled upward from the grassroots. But democratization from the top down, arranged between elites and contenders for power, appears in fact to be more frequent.[19] However this may be, changes that have occurred from the ground up in the Society of Jesus have been more individual than collective, without direct political repercussions for the authority of the clerical establishment. A therapeutic strategy, geared to the case-by-case remediation of personal problems, and absorption in the day-to-day tasks of middle-level ministry promote short-term flexibility.

Another mechanism that blunts the push for democratization is the exit option. The supposition that marginalized strata want nothing so much as to be included in a new, expanded system is commonplace.[20] But the costs of leaving the church, and of leaving the priesthood, have dropped relative to the costs of reforming the hierarchy from within. As a result, those who remain to struggle for change are frequently met with theoretical sympathy but operative indifference from potential constituencies who are free to shop around for their spiritual niche. The Society of Jesus is a voluntary organization, and it is often easier for Jesuits to head toward the exit, if push and pull factors work in concert, than to stand and fight.[21]

The exit option can be understood as the limiting case along a spectrum of alternatives that release tensions but that stop short of rebellion. Some Jesuits, and even more former Jesuits, look on the ecclesiastical setup as a bachelors' club forbidding clerical entitlements to "ex-priests," women, and married persons. They favor a more inclusionary arrangement. Yet many others, particularly Jesuits themselves, are driven less by a demand for inclusion and participation (though they do not strenuously oppose the idea) than by the urge toward self-determination. This translates into carving out a niche within the hierarchy that allows for a customized spiritual and sexual settlement and for a decent amount of leeway on the job.

In the eyes of church officials, the impulse toward self-determination may smack of individualism, "pride," and a host of other age-old and modern vices. But the relentlessly practical nature of this maneuvering shies away from collective confrontation since the sought-for rewards can usually be had without the costs of coordinated action. In addition, the drop in the number of Jesuits means that those who remain, because they are in scarce supply, have considerable leverage with their superiors when they come to work out assignments through mutual consultation.

Still another mechanism for containing change is the set of procedures for leadership succession at the highest levels of both the Society of Jesus and the church itself. These electoral rites mitigate the scramble for power that plagues authoritarian systems without such rules in place. Also, the transformation of the papacy into a variant of autocratic populism circumvents democratic reforms.[22]

The recitation of factors that contribute to averting or subduing change—the therapeutic, largely individualistic nature of reform in the Society of Jesus; the concentration on midrange apostolic opportunities; the easy availability of the exit option; the priority of self-determination over systemwide inclusion; the presence of procedures for replacing leadership at the very top; and the appeal of strongman showmanship— serves as a reminder that the transformation of the Jesuits does not follow spontaneously from ineluctable trends and that this transformation need not add up to democracy. Forecasts that rely on the convergence of the serial Ds—dissent, dysfunction, and demographic decline—give the impression that not only change but its direction are preordained conclusions. The conviction of being on the side of an irresistible juggernaut instills hope and has a certain prophetic flair, but it can also encourage a disregard for the concrete circumstances of tactical action. This inclination to overlook or dismiss the organizational details seems to be widespread among Catholics for whom politics has become what sex was once supposed to be: dirty, unseemly, and not much fun.[23] The age of the laity is not just ushered in.

This said, long-term shifts have in fact altered the field on which the future of the Society of Jesus will be played out. Even for most conservatives, the ideal is no longer sempiternal stasis. That rhetoric is no more acceptable in postconciliar times than are blatant appeals to authoritarianism in contemporary politics.[24] Instead, conservatives and progressives fight over defining the "true spirit" of Vatican II.[25]

This leaves room for maneuver. The battle in which Jesuits are involved is not between change and no change but over who will control it, or have the appearance of legitimacy in managing it, and, second, over the areas in which change will occur.[26]

The first question touches on the balance of authority and representation between clergy and laity. The issue is not the circulation of elites—that is, its transfer from one cleric to another—but reconfiguring the structure of leadership along lay as compared to clerical lines.[27]

The ongoing laicization of the ministerial operations connected with the Society of Jesus gives the issue a practical edge. This trend raises questions about the balance between centralized authority and home rule in the apostolic infrastructure of the church: the schools, hospitals, and other services.

Substantial decentralization has already occurred. A key question is where this de facto laicization leaves not only traditionally activist orders like the Jesuits but also the ecclesiastical hierarchy and the priesthood itself. "That crowd," in the argot of a dyspeptic laity, may become increasingly ornamental. But a purely instrumental reallocation of power will not suffice. In an operation that relies as heavily on symbolism as on performance, whatever new leadership emerges will need its share of legitimate authority, besides certification on grounds of merit.

Changes in the magisterium, especially in the substance of doctrine about divorce, women's ordination, and the like, make up another contested domain: the policy controversies over sexual roles that are closely linked to questions of ecclesiastical authority. These are the supremely symbolic issues on which a middle ground is hard to find; they have tremendous mythic charge. They bear on most of the core truths of Catholicism, plus a few traditional "disciplines" such as the celibacy requirement for ordained ministry, that have been shrouded in an aura of inalterability. The great difficulty in institutional Catholicism is that, in addition to controversy over one or another matter of policy, the lines of authority themselves are in dispute.[28]

As control over the direction of institutional ministries slips out of clerical hands, the temptation for the ecclesiastical establishment to draw the line on challenges to honorific and sexual codes probably increases. The fear is that alterations in the structure of authority will result in the alteration of doctrine at the symbolic crux of Catholicism.[29] As laypeople continue their long march through the apostolic institutions, a fall-back strategy is to roll up the drawbridge to the magical castle of sexual morality and clerical purity.

Resistance to change in Catholicism involves the defense of symbolic capital, accretions of images and forms as well as "the deposit of faith" that, in the eyes of traditionalists, have an organic harmony. The power of symbolic capital comes from its fusion of a certain intellectual sophistication that can be articulated and a precognitive, irrational core that eludes dispassionate analysis. This is the church of absolute truth and the God of infinite compassion. In the eyes of the keepers of the museum, it makes about as much sense to tinker with this patrimony as it would to improve on a Raphael or a Michelangelo. The guardians of doctrinal correctness and religious identity are like an elderly couple with a huge stock of invaluable antiques on the walls and in the corners of their home. They are proud to have the treasures on display but are terrified of letting the children and grandchildren, some of them ignorant and careless and lacking in manners, visit and risk damaging what cannot be replaced. The Latin mix of wonderful art and wretched politics fits this simile.

EPILOGUE: EVENING'S EMPIRE

I

The most remarkable pattern to emerge from the historical panorama presented at the beginning of this book is the odd combination of longevity and volatility that distinguishes the Society of Jesus. Nearly 500 years of existence make for tradition as mundane institutions go, yet the tradition itself appears to be curiously unstable. The order has been expelled from various countries about thirty-five times, from some of them more than once, not counting the cases in which it came within a hair's breadth of having its operations shut down. Misadventure is not new to the Jesuits.[1]

The difficulties facing the Society of Jesus today, however, are of a different kind and magnitude from the problems it has weathered before. After Vatican II, a seismic upheaval took place in the moral culture of Catholicism. The traditional sexual code lost credibility, and because these core beliefs are tied in with deference to religious authority, the hierarchical structure of the church was shaken.[2]

Second, laypeople are far more numerous and influential in operations affiliated with the Society of Jesus than they once were. Professionalization of the works has driven an organizational change accelerated by the drop in clerical numbers. Quite apart from the first, cultural transformation, a panoply of church-related ministries has grown up in which the role of the clergy generally, and apostolic orders like the Jesuits in particular, is less clear than it used to be. Jesuits have opened the direction of their ministries to lay professionals, but the top tiers of the church remain confined almost exclusively to the clergy. A hierarchy that once took deference for granted has become, like an old-time party machine, rather sclerotic. Decentralized operations staffed and run mostly by laypeople exist alongside a governance structure dominated by septuagenarian celibates.[3]

Aside from vocal disaffection on the Catholic left, the chief consequence of the growing imbalance between lay responsibility for ministerial operations and priestly dominance of potentially representative institutions appears to be puzzlement about the role of Jesuits rather than strident anticlericalism. Such ambivalence, common enough among lay coworkers, is not entirely absent among Jesuits themselves. In their quiet way, internal doubts such as these may be as subversive as direct attacks on the ecclesiastical order.

A third difficulty facing the Society springs from the cultural break with the past and the demographic and institutional realignment just described. The coming of age of American Catholicism posed a dilemma of mission and identity for the priesthood. What is the purpose and distinctiveness of the traditional forms of religious life represented by the Jesuits, now that the moral order on which they rested has splintered and the tasks they set for themselves are increasingly carried out by ordinary Catholics and indeed by secular agencies? The priesthood was once an anomaly to those on the outside of Catholicism, standing as a sign of subcultural solidarity against the ways of the world. Priests were supposed to be leaders. Now, with Catholic assimilation, the clergy has started to appear aberrational *inside* the church.

The cumulative nature of this set of transformations—the tectonic shift in moral thinking, the ascent of the laity in ministerial operations once manned by clerics, and deep ambivalence about a rendezvous with modernity that threatens religious identity—has pushed the priesthood and the leadership of the church into a quandary. No such combination of changes had assaulted the Jesuits before.

The severity of the crisis can be appreciated by stepping back and locating it toward the end of a developmental arc originating at least a millennium ago. By the twelfth century, the custom of requiring celibacy as a condition for holy orders had been formally enshrined in church policy. The founding of the Society of Jesus in the sixteenth century, which solidified the passage from a monastic to an activist model of religious life, represented another breakthrough in the organizational evolution of Catholicism.

Developments like these were incorporated into an even more ambitious design promoting the supremacy of the institutional church in the political realm. Though the project gained little traction in the United States (and hence generated much less anticlericalism than in continental Europe and parts of Latin America), it was not until Vatican II that the "caesaro-papist" ideal—the norm that church and state should be joined and that "error has no rights"—was officially cast aside. Despite setbacks, ecumenism nowadays clings to respectability.[4]

This strategic concession to a historical struggle in which the democratic powers had emerged victorious was followed by an unintended meltdown at the interior of Catholicism. It is this collapse and its ramifications for the Society of Jesus, more than changes in the church's stance toward the world outside, that have concerned us here. The unanticipated consequence of Vatican II—the drop in vocations to the consecrated life—was at least as important as the deliberate retreat from an ideal of moral hegemony and the acceptance of pluralism in a multi-denominational world. As manpower shrank, clerical control of operations within the church receded. This was not supposed to happen. After surrendering its pretensions to political dominance on the outside, the church was caught off guard by disarray on the inside.

The gradual curtailment of sacerdotal functions—especially of those, such as education, associated with activist orders like the Jesuits—has thrown the priesthood into disarray. Together with mounting skepticism about the sexual magisterium, the shrinking of clerical tasks has stretched the link between ministerial effectiveness and celibacy. As the functional roles of the priesthood have shrunk and as the restriction of sacerdotal status to celibate males has become less defensible, the ceremonial and symbolic aura of traditional priesthood has faded as well.[5] The shriveling of activities that once "belonged to" the priesthood has produced a crisis of credibility and clerical identity.

Boiled down, two developments have radically altered the world of the Society of Jesus and have produced demoralization and conflict within its ranks. One is institutional and the other ideational, and both have shaken traditional beliefs about the consecrated life.

The first is the long-term decomposition of incentives for religious vocations—in particular, the diminishing functions of and ambivalence about the priesthood. This change is clearest in the decentralization of the works and the laicization of ministry. Demographically and organizationally, the fulcrum has pitched away from the clergy.

The other big shift is the loss of confidence in absolute truth claims, crystallized by but not confined to the shake-up in moral theology and beliefs in sexual ethics, in addition to liberalizing undercurrents in

Christology.[6] Dissent from the magisterium is a fact of life in the Society of Jesus.

In neither case has the loss of control and conviction been total. What has come close to disappearing is the *distinctiveness* of the priestly role as conceived by Jesuits and, to a lesser extent, of the moral sanctum of Catholicism.[7] Much of what Jesuits do remains valuable. Much of what they believe in and stand for is appreciated and shared by adherents of neighboring religions and ethical traditions. But there seems to be less and less that sets the Society of Jesus apart, at least with respect to an edge on the truth or expertise in pedagogy, social action, and pastoral practice. Obliteration by assimilation has become a real threat. Jesuits have begun to look as flawed and intermittently heroic as the rest of us.

2

It would be a mistake to treat this account of the decline of the Jesuits as a monotonic forecast. While the downward trajectory it depicts may be more interesting than the swing-of-the-pendulum wisdom to the effect that there is nothing wrong with institutional Catholicism and the Jesuits that a new pope will not cure, the supposition that decline is inexorable or that it is headed in a single direction amounts to triumphalism in reverse.[8] It is evening but not quite an end time.

Two major developments slow down the disintegration of the Society of Jesus and suggest that it is mutating along multiple pathways. The first condition impedes collapse by according the Jesuits wiggle room at lower and middle levels of the clerical system. The second condition allows for a diversity of habitats for various identities and interests within the order. This mélange of countercultures not only extends the system's life span but also, by virtue of its complexity, keeps the course of the Jesuits beyond the range of confident prediction. The Society is going in several directions at once.

Jesuits are embedded in a three-tiered hierarchy that stretches from the spiritual and psychosexual concerns of individuals to their workaday lives, frequently in concert with others, toward the upper reaches of the church from which strategic guidelines emanate. This stratified arrangement reinforces power at the top and allows autonomy toward the bottom.

Spiritually, Jesuits have reinvented themselves. They have undergone therapeutic rehabilitation, and they exercise substantial discretion in their personal affairs. This transformation has not only entailed a revival of the one-on-one manner of handling the *Spiritual Exercises*. It has also been accompanied by a rethinking of moral theology, the norms surrounding sexual behavior, and the role of women. Designated as desirable, change at the individual level has progressed because it has been possible. Spiritual direction is a field in which Jesuits excel. Ordinarily, such undertakings are neither organizationally complex nor politically controversial.[9]

The middle, ministerial tier is where Jesuits come increasingly in contact with the laity and where organizational imperatives count at least as much as the pursuit of individual fulfillment. There is some Jesuit-versus-non-Jesuit friction in this zone, but it doesn't differ much from the style of conflict and human relations management over agenda setting prevalent in many secular institutions. Battles are mostly about establishing programmatic and budgetary priorities, not principles of hierarchy.

The performance of Jesuits at this intermediate level defies generalization. Whatever their difficulties in coordinating their activities to enhance corporate impact, and whatever their psychosexual problems, Jesuits tend to be a bit more content with what they are doing than their former colleagues who have left the order.[10]

As for Jesuit community life, its hallmark is how wildly the experience of it varies from good to bad and how residual it has become, relative to the cultivation of friendships outside the Society. Increasingly, expectations about fraternal solidarity get transferred away from separate communities to the far-flung network of the Society and toward the transcendent brotherhood-in-motion of the international order. Jesuit community is at least as virtual and notional as it is physical and tied to place.

As for the transition to Jesuit-lay collaboration, this is an accomplished fact or close to it. The sticky questions have to do less with the transfer of power than with preserving the Ignatian outlook of the institutions and finding meaningful roles for Jesuits themselves.

Finally, at the peak of the hierarchy, where the dealings of the Society with the Vatican are played out, clericalism prevails. There, Jesuits, other religious congregations, and episcopal conferences have practically no power at all.[11] The prevalent style is a variation on the autocratic populism familiar to observers of Latin American politics.[12] Adept utilization of the mass media, in conjunction with supine institutions, help keep the spotlight on the charismatic center.[13]

The arrangement permits consultation among Jesuits themselves and between Jesuits and their lay partners; it also allows Jesuits substantial self-determination. Such de facto flexibility brakes the slide of religious life. Whether it can reverse the decline is doubtful. The reliance on costly practices such as celibacy combines with exclusionary customs, like forbidding the priesthood to women, to exacerbate divisiveness and drain meaning from the enterprise. Like goulash communism, the system is moderately workable but only partially legitimate.[14]

The other mechanism of survival for Jesuits involves a variety of normative and lifestyle responses to the erosion of priestly identity. Compared to the flexible hierarchy itself, which is a fairly traditional arrangement in Catholicism, these responses are new or have gained prominence in recent years.

Jesuits have sought surrogates for the battered moral code of tradition and the toppled landmarks of certainty and belonging—notably, the parochial neighborhoods and subcultures that characterized American Catholicism through the 1950s—in countercultures constructed out of ideological, sexual, or relatively esoteric spiritual identities. These networks are fluid communities that provide a sense of attachment and of taking part in a venture larger than the cultivation of the self but that stop short of absorption in a homogeneous mainstream.[15]

Countercultures within the Society act as partial replacements for the sense of collective identity once provided by the old Catholic subculture and especially by celibacy. The cliques also strive to make up for the emptiness of the individualistic free-for-all released by the 1960s. As these mores have been eclipsed or have fallen into disrepute, new signs of group attachment—including but hardly confined to the gay network—have arisen to take their place in establishing recognizable yet ambivalent insider/outsider boundaries. Homosexual orientation has gained prominence as a social identity within the clergy at the same time that celibacy as a collective discipline, setting the priesthood apart, has gone into decline.

Reduced to collective remedies for personal insecurity, that is, to support groups, the networks would seem to amount to little more than centrifugal fragments. They do compensate for anxiety over the loss of identity, and they do have an in-group/out-group edge to them, tending toward the touchy and intolerant. But some of these spin-offs—the faith-and-justice movement is a good example, the neoconservative upsurge is another—also have a body of ideas behind them, and they can appeal to various strands in the Catholic tradition to ratify their agendas.[16] A similar claim might be made for those who have been exploring non-Western spiritualities inasmuch as they follow in the footsteps of Jesuit missionaries who long ago ran into trouble with Rome for going native.[17]

Anxiety brought on by the dissolution of sheltering traditions is not the only reason for the popularity of countercultural factions in the Society of Jesus. Frequently, they represent tangible interests and, by preventing burnout, help get things done. The point is that insecurity contributes to the attraction of causes that, by setting many Jesuits apart, help shore up their battered identity. The countercultures are human-scale solutions to psychological and sometimes to ministerial needs.

The networks are ideologically diverse. At least at first glance, they seem to have practically nothing in common except their rejection of the American mainstream. In one way or another, the principal counter-cultures within the Society—those marked by a social justice commitment, by homosexual orientation, by a neoconservative restorationist agenda, and by attachment to a variety of spiritual paths following the Eastern turn—all reject the status quo of advanced industrial society. Adherents tend to look on themselves as members of victimized minorities. They identify with marginal groups and long-shot causes in part because they feel marginal themselves.[18]

Whether or not Jesuits in educational apostolates participate in this countercultural setup is a nice question. The quandary points to a possible shortcoming in the argument about midrange factions as forms of compensatory attachment and social identity. The suggestion is that the high schools and, even more, the colleges and the universities are out of the countercultural loop, so much a part of traditional Jesuit ministry and so compromised by mainstream values that their apostolic rationale is largely conventional.

Two points are worth considering here. There happens to be a good deal of antiestablishment talk in Jesuit higher education, especially among those who complain about the secularizing bias against the discussion of religion in academic fora.[19] Second, while the countercultures are ideologically diverse, they are not channeled into hermetically separate apostolic sectors. Sexual orientation, for example, does not determine ministerial choice. And within education a number of subcultures coexist. Nothing prevents Jesuits from belonging to more than one of these groups.

Some of the countercultures address both functional and symbolic needs, while others look more like pure identity movements. The faith-that-does-justice school gives priority to the collective, apostolic work of Jesuits, paying less attention to therapeutic concerns. Without a comparable ministerial program, the gay counterculture offers an identity to hold on to—a lifestyle, a shared sensibility—but not as elaborate an agenda for action.[20]

The countercultures differ as well in their attitudes toward joint endeavors. Neoconservative Jesuits seem more committed to the institutional ministries of the Society. Jesuits who have taken a serious interest in Eastern religions, ecological spirituality, and the like appear to be relatively indifferent to the established operations of the order, and they are probably less attuned to collective action than to the pursuit of interior equilibrium.

Despite these differences, the countercultures that have grown up in the Society all add a normative and affective ethos to the pragmatic construction of niches that goes on toward the lower levels of the hierarchy. They reflect a nesting instinct in the midst of the ideal of Jesuit mobility and in the face of frantic schedules. They restore a sense of embattled brotherhood and collective endeavor that comes across only sporadically in the everyday adjustment of individual Jesuits, and they supplement the shared experience of Ignatian spirituality.[21] The pleasures of heterodoxy—of firming up identity by being different—stand midway between the notion that virtue is its own reward and the gratifications of outright success.

Together with the flexibility built into the multiple levels of hierarchical Catholicism, the countercultures have profoundly ambiguous consequences for the Society of Jesus. They allow for an operative pluralism in a system where open pluralism is moot. Diversity of this sort prevents the Society from turning into a brittle sect. The order stays afloat. Whether it stays on course is another matter. The rise of the laity and the rupture in Catholic moral thought, mentioned earlier, rule out any finely meshed integration. No single dynamic propels the overall machinery one way or another. The result is remarkable longevity and low predictability.[22]

3

The Society of Jesus has always been an unstable compound. Now the situation of the order within the church verges on an impasse. Stripped to its essentials, this is the "love it or leave it" status quo. So far as the Vatican is concerned, only docile submission to Rome is acceptable. The alternative to obedience is to get out. Declining applicants to and frequent departures from the celibate priesthood are a lamentable but acceptable cost, a lesser evil, compared to straying from tradition itself. The enemy is pluralism, and the archenemy is permissiveness.

All this polarization, however, is touched with insubstantiality, long on polemics but short on control.[23] Jesuits can in fact choose to drop out rather than confront ecclesiastical power. Secession is individual, man by man, and most go quietly, some nursing their wounds. For their part, church authorities often find it easier to expel the more boisterous dissidents or let them leave than to exact strict conformity from those who stay. There is little mobilization against authoritarian measures. The safety valves of defection and local adaptation, as well as ordinary prudence, discourage this. Church authorities complain about individual laxity. At the same time, the costs of supervision in a ramshackle hierarchy encourage such behavior. The occasional private vice is more common but less threatening than collective opposition. Then, too, it is not just the scourge of individualism but the costs of organized resistance that account for some of the privatization and furtive escapism in clerical life.

The love-it-or-leave-it syndrome prevails almost wholly in the relations between the Vatican and the Jesuits. Elsewhere, lower down the hierarchy, among those who remain in or stay on the fringes of the Society, the plebes know better. Options are more numerous and less stark. Even at the top, antagonisms do not burn at white heat. Peter-Hans Kolvenbach, the Dutch general of the Society since 1983, with long experience in the Middle East before coming to Rome, is known for his skill at massaging the grandees of the papal court.

As a description of church politics on a daily basis, then, the either-or scenario squashes the decisions of clerical life into one dimension with two outcomes only: the ins versus the outs. We need to come up with a construct that respects the complexity of the Jesuits' world without getting overwhelmed in detail.

The starting point is simple. The central idea of the following paragraphs is that there are various types as well as degrees of Catholicism. This notion, picked up from our analysis of spirituality, allows us to make a more rounded assessment of the options facing the Jesuits than one that treats these alternatives as points along a single continuum of fidelity and disloyalty.[24]

Imagine first a division between "hierarchy" and "democracy." The split is a matter of some definitional intricacy, but forget these nuances

Institutional form

Behavioral style	Hierarchical	Democratic
Militant	Militant hierarchy	Competitive democracy
Irenic	Pastoral hierarchy	Irenic democracy

Figure 4. Types of Catholicism

for now. The second division—between the "militant" (or agonistic) and the "irenic" (or conciliatory)—is between styles rather than forms of church governance. Crossing one dimension with the other, we come up with four categories expressing pure and mixed types of Catholicism (see figure 4).[25]

Militant hierarchy is the ecclesiastical model characteristic of preconciliar times and, with a few twists, the restorationist ideal sponsored by the papacy of John Paul II. Diametrically opposite is *irenic democracy,* a condition inspired by images of the communal love-ins buoyed by the euphoria of the late 1960s and early 1970s. Both are stylized ideal types. They crystallize the pair of reciprocally demonizing alternatives that caught the imagination of conservatives and progressives around the time of Vatican II.

The distance between the church imagined as a militant hierarchy and the church envisioned as an irenic democracy corresponds to the movement from a masculine to a more feminine manner discernible among both Jesuits and former Jesuits. While the institutional framework of the church and the Society of Jesus has remained mostly in place, the ethos of religious practitioners like the Jesuits has shifted from a masculine assertiveness to a feminine emphasis on conciliation and healing or, if that vocabulary sounds stereotypical, from fear of a capricious, vengeful deity to the embrace of a loving God.

We need to consider two messier combinations as well. One of these, *pastoral hierarchy,* covers the off-the-books modus operandi among Jesuits and the larger church documented throughout this study. On-the-spot pragmatism and compassion are the touchstones. While external reverence for the powers that be is kept up, the gravitational pull of concrete service proves irresistible.

This compromise melds with the long-standing paternalism of the church, shorn of its doctrinaire edge. A tendency to sentimentalize power makes up for whatever faint opposition or cynicism such an approach lets slip by.[26] The hierarchy may not be theologically correct, procedurally impartial, or particularly holy. But it is benign. Backsliding, incidental corruption, and bureaucratic shenanigans are not worth shouting about. Success in this political culture depends on silence and respect for backroom deals.

In more assertive form, the style shows up as a variant on the faith-and-justice agenda that gives priority to righting social wrongs ahead of respect for juridical niceties or intellectual debate. The clientele includes the marginalized and the poverty-stricken outside as well as inside the church but not (or mainly as an afterthought) in-house dissenters. Remember the Jesuit who, given the choice, would side with the advocates of social equality rather than with the defenders of civil liberties and other bourgeois decencies. Quarrels about doctrinal issues begin to look peevish in balance with action on behalf of social justice.

The fourth option—variations on in-your-face, *combative democracy*—is far less legitimate within the Society of Jesus than pastoral hierarchy. It does not have much of a foothold in the order, except among a few of the social action types and a scattering of theologians. But the freewheeling style cannot be dismissed as the sport of a trifling minority. Just as pastoral hierarchy sums up the approach that Jesuits often resort to within the church, toe-to-toe democracy expresses the norms of the world in which many Jesuits live as they deal with "externs." It is the air they breathe when they mix it up on the outside. Though they may talk a different game, couched in the language of irenic democracy, many Jesuits lead a dual life between the demands of competitive professionalism and the pull of pastoral hierarchy.[27] Because the liberal tradition is part of their political culture, the American Jesuits feel this pressure acutely.

4

There is a final puzzle that needs to be addressed as a preface to scanning the practicalities of reform. Why have the stewards of the church proved to be so adamant about *any* sort of organizational reform in the Society of Jesus?

Think of concentric circles set up in a series of defensive perimeters. The outside ring is the most expendable. For the church, and arguably for the Society of Jesus, this front line is the external political environment. After decades of hostility and suspicion, Catholicism conceded the acceptability and eventually the goodness of democracy as a secular development. Pluralism was accorded legitimacy on the outside, provided that it did not intrude on the hierarchy of the church. Though it traditionally preferred dealing with autocratic regimes and though, indeed, it remains one itself, the church has few qualms about pressing its claims under democratic ground rules.

A second, more sensitive layer is composed of "the works." This ministerial realm has become more and more laicized. As the Society's control over such operations has waned, Rome has intervened, for example, to salvage the Catholic identity of the order's colleges and universities.

Why this sensitivity about the apostolates as compared to the knack for accommodating political institutions? Aside from the fact that they are at least nominally Catholic, the ministerial operations incorporate social mores and transmit values that, Rome supposes, are less superficial than most changes in government or public policy. The schools in particular are viewed as ethical transmitters as well as intellectual agencies or service operations pure and simple. They are supposed to socialize upcoming generations in time-honored values. If they lose that quality, they stop being Catholic.

At a third circle, closer to the core, we come to a realm—the sexual code—that is more cultural than institutional, and it is touchier still. The psychosexual and demographic revolution of the 1960s, signaled by the pill and the entrance of women into the workforce, upset the moral theology of the church, gender hierarchies, and the clerical authority structure. In the eyes of many conservatives, this zone is just about non-negotiable.[28] Lay incursions into ministry threaten clerical control over what the church does. Upheavals in the sexual code jeopardize what the institutional church is.

The sexual revolution reverberated in many areas and in one especially for Jesuits: the leadership of the celibate priesthood. Laicization of the works brings into question the privileged link between ordination and qualification for ministry. Doubts about the sexual magisterium spill over into doubts about celibacy as a precondition for priesthood.

Lastly, we come to the matter of Christology. Is the risen Jesus figurative, or divine, or what? Do other religions have comparable saviors? In what sense is the priest a figure of Christ? For many traditionalists, the questions themselves border on the blasphemous. For some Jesuits, and of course former Jesuits, the answers are unsure.[29]

You can go along with this portrayal of the rising flammability of controversies, from the political and mainly institutional toward issues that touch on personal behavior and core beliefs, and at the same time suspect it of naïveté. If Catholic reality were this linear, the church should make a greater fuss over transgressions involving the internal workings of religious life than it does about excluding women from priestly ordination. However, the concerns of ecclesiastical authorities may actually be the reverse.

Why? Opening up holy orders to women requires visible change, while the zone of in-house infractions and beliefs is less conspicuous. The difference between rigidity at the top and flexibility at the bottom of the hierarchy follows a gradient running from the public offense to private deviance. Deference and the appearance of obedience matter a lot in Catholicism since those in authority have few material resources and even less coercive power to exact compliance.

Now we are in a position to speculate about what might be changeable and what cannot be bargained away in the Society of Jesus.

5

The Society of Jesus is a hybrid organization, imperfectly comparable to political systems. There is no military waiting to intervene, no economy on whose performance the stability of government depends, and it is hard to say whether we are talking about "citizens" or "disciples" or both.[30] No new dominant model of the institutional church has emerged, nor has the old regime disintegrated. Instead, what has occurred is a multiplication of countercultures within the Society (and the church) vying for recognition. Little consensus exists among the major players— Jesuits themselves and other religious and clerics, not to mention members of the laity—about the direction in which the church or the Society should move.[31]

Uncertainty about the direction of the clerical enterprise is probably as much an incitement to polarization as the head-on clash of antithetical beliefs. *Any* decisive resolution, a firm stand for *something,* seems appealing. Nevertheless, identifying specific but still significant areas that might be susceptible to negotiation may be more productive than either refusing to budge at all or embracing wholesale reform. In Catholicism, such an approach means focusing on institutional reconstruction.[32] This tactic reverses the sequence that prevailed at Vatican II, which relied on exhortations for a change in hearts and minds and only secondarily on organizational restructuring.

A pair of related institutional issues comes up right away. One is the "who participates?" question—that is, who has the opportunity to exercise sacerdotal ministry? The question of *inclusion* bears on the ordination of women and married persons.

The second issue revolves around the "Who is consulted?" question—whose views are heard and who takes part in strategic decision making within the church? The agenda of reform posed by the question of *consultation* directly affects the status of synods and bishops' conferences and, somewhat less directly, the position of religious congregations like the Society of Jesus.

The first issue has to do with how clerical elites treat Catholics on the fringes of the structure of authority. It raises the possibility of reconfiguring the Society of Jesus and expanding the composition of the priesthood generally. The second has to do with how organized interests in Catholicism treat one another, once they're on the inside. It is directed at the division of power between the Society of Jesus, for example, or this or that bishops' conference, and the commissions of the Vatican curia.[33]

The questions have one thing in common. Both concern matters of traditional discipline and long-standing mores rather than fixed principle or revealed truth. The controversies they arouse revolve around rival views of ecclesiological design, not "faith and morals." In this respect, they pass the minimal test of negotiability.

For all this, organizational questions remain extremely sensitive. Either celibacy is a requirement for the priesthood or it is not; there are no two ways about it. The same goes for the ordination of women. Even if such questions are construed as issues of form rather than substance, any change in the institutional architecture of the Society and the church would by definition be highly visible. Controversies like these are "special" because they put change out in the open. In one way or another, raising such issues implies an attack on clerical prerogatives—a constitutive part of the Roman Catholic order of things for so long that it has passed from being merely an organizational property to a tradition that is part of a culture and a way of life.[34]

Yet it is not as if the agenda of institutional reform lacks precedent. The conciliar tradition furnishes a historically respectable alternative to the legacy of papal supremacy with which the Jesuits have been identified since their founding.[35] Similarly, the principle of subsidiarity—of maximum feasible decentralization—can be urged on the management of the internal affairs of the church, as it has been for relations between church and state.[36]

Organizational crafting by way of legislative design reshapes the rules of the game without attempting to get directly at beliefs and values.[37] But constitutional reform does change the odds for or against the passage of specific policies (in the church, changes in doctrinal prescriptions and ordinances) by altering the rights of contending interests.

The larger lesson is that doctrinal development in core domains like sexuality and Christology may go in unexpected directions under less stringently hierarchical arrangements. This is not only because institutional reform would alter the balance of participation and decision making and enhance the probability of change. Alongside whatever organizational reconfiguration takes place is the ongoing internationalization of the church.

Developments in Christology, for example, might play out along latitudinarian lines, responding to the sensitivities of cultures with diverse understandings of redemptive icons and divinity. But thinking about the sexual code might follow a program less to the liking of American liberals, if traditional views about the status of women and prescribed social hierarchies in non-Western cultures are taken into account.[38] "When it comes to sex," one Jesuit noted, referring to the image of libidinous mayhem projected by American popular culture, "we have no credibility."

So, as the internationalization of the Society and the church unfolds, and if the ground rules for ministry and intramural consultation are revised, the number of variables affecting the fate of the Jesuits rapidly thickens. Institutional reforms and the pressure of demographic change would open up and clarify the game, but they also render it more complex.

When Jesuits and former Jesuits talk about reform in the church, then, they invariably speak of altering the norms of *inclusion* (for example, ordaining women and married people) and *consultation* (preventing the "emasculation" of episcopal conferences or, conversely, curbing the primacy of the papacy).[39] These are classically American demands, with a strong democratizing slant. All this occurs within the widening context of the *internationalization* of Catholicism. The prospect of institutional reforms that encourage inclusion and consultation—in effect, "participation" and "representation"—heightens the sense of risk among conservatives. Uncertainty about the consequences of reform increases for progressives and conservatives alike as the internationalization of the church gathers speed.[40]

Aside from the drop in clerical numbers, the internationalization of

Catholicism stands as the most striking demographic and institutional effect of Vatican II. The process of globalization has gone further than the impulse behind inclusion and consultation. Its impact on this latter pair of movements is unclear. Our received ideas about democratization are almost entirely confined to the dynamics of national politics. What this means for the reform of an organization of global scale remains to be thought through.[41]

6

In order for intransigence to give way to change in the ecclesiastical politics surrounding the Society of Jesus, a pair of conditions has to fall into place. The first and more important pertains to the guardians of orthodoxy, the second to the advocates of reform.

Sooner or later, the costs of maintaining the status quo have to be perceived as greater than the risks of change. The principal cost is the steady drain on personnel and the cumulative reduction in the capacity to provide spiritual services. The major risk is that of hastening this seepage to the point where the clerical establishment disintegrates altogether. Immobilism stems from anxiety that tampering with a bad situation will make matters worse. Far from looking like an improvement, the alternative to paralysis is seen as tantamount to suicide.

Nevertheless, there is some indication that change in one area may not act as a trip wire setting off change all the way down the line.[42] The tightly knit system of beliefs linking sexuality and authority in Catholicism is at least as much a human construction—a combination of revocable "disciplines" with core tenets—as it is an impermeable trove of universal truths[43] Once this frame of mind is recognized as an artifact, either-or thinking may lose its spell.[44]

The second condition that would have to obtain for reform to get rolling also involves a cost-benefit calculation, this time on the part of proponents of change within the clergy. What are the inducements and payoffs for investing in systemwide changes, compared to the personal rewards that can be had from making do within the system or simply leaving it?

Advocates of change in the Society of Jesus have to deal with a collective action problem. The therapeutic mode of resolving difficulties in Jesuit life coexists with a penchant for seeking validation and security within small-scale countercultures and modest support groups. Concerted action in the name of opposition is not the strong point of disaffected Jesuits, in part because of the penalties that can be imposed by clerical superiors, in part because meaningful compensations are at hand, and in part because they can drop out.[45] In addition to the daunting effort required to overcome such obstacles, there is the real problem of estimating the effects of change, given the multilevel complexity of the Society and the hazy or abstruse nature of some of the theological issues regarding Christology, for example. The difficulty of thinking strategically in such matters is not simply the result of therapeutic myopia.

Partisans of reform, while they may be in the majority, probably face an organizational deficit vis-à-vis their conservative peers in the church at large. The latter seem to be more adept than the divided and individualistic progressives at the "grown-up" politics of working the institutional hierarchy to their advantage.[46]

If there is a bright side to this limbo of idealism and discretion, it is that the ensemble of attitudes does not vigorously oppose change. On the contrary, most Jesuits favor some sort of institutional reform. The legitimacy of the clerical status quo is patchy, and a yearning for some sort of change is evident. A sympathetic distribution of opinion, however, is not a set of demands, much less collective action or a political movement. The organizational incentives for reform among Jesuits are weaker than the preferences favoring it in principle. Most dissent remains latent. The impetus for change will likely come from the leadership of the church, as it did at Vatican II.[47]

7

The outward maintenance of order has failed to generate inner conformity in the Society of Jesus. Underlying the gradient of control from public appearance to private reality is a continuum from institutional stasis through flexibility in behavior to dissent in belief.

There is a hopeful irony in this disjuncture. If institutional rigidity in Catholicism has been unable to bring actual behavior and beliefs in line with orthodoxy, it is improbable that institutional reforms of the sort discussed here—relaxing the exclusionary rules for ordination, promoting consultation, and the like—would threaten the "deposit of faith" as much as conservatives suppose. "Democratization" is not self-evidently destabilizing. We know more about how cultural drives, including religion-inspired movements, can overthrow or reform existing institutions than about the reverse—how organizational change may transform cultural beliefs.[48]

In the end, we have to recognize that the links between institutional transformation and changes in spiritual norms and religious practices might be very loose indeed.[49] A hallmark of democratization is the indeterminacy of political outcomes because of the built-in freedom of choice. The effects of organizational reform in the case of "outputs" like religiously defined virtue may be especially mysterious. When it comes to the transformation of cultural institutions such as the Society of Jesus, the slack between organizational change and change in beliefs is very hard to estimate.[50] The effects of institutional reform on the symbolic capital of Catholicism—on spirituality, devotional habits, and codified beliefs—are elusive. As with the transition from sacred to secular art, or from the gold standard to floating exchange rates, the consequences of such change in Catholicism need not entail catastrophe, even if the process is unstable.

8

A couple of structural constraints hem in speculation about the reform of religious life in Catholicism. One derives from the paradox of individualism. The drift of opinion inside the Society of Jesus, and among American Catholics generally, favors change in such areas as women's ordination and the ordination of married people.[51] But the incentives to press for these reforms in organized ways are modest. The demand expressed in the profile of opinion is inchoate and diffuse. Gratification obtained from customized versions of spirituality and from attending to tactical, ministerial tasks undermines confrontational strategies; so does the opportunity to leave. When push comes to shove, ecclesiastical power is usually circumvented and mollified, not challenged. Deference rules.

The paradox resides not only in the imbalance between opinion favoring change and the weak incentives to collective action. Inadvertently or otherwise, intellectual censorship and restrictions on institutional innovation imposed by a traditional hierarchy encourage therapeutic venting and apostolic making do instead of concerted mobilization. Forces on the demand side of change are not as strong as a simple toting up of attitudes might suggest.[52] Most Jesuits keep a commonsensical eye on what matters for ministry and on their spiritual lives, without fretting about a repressive situation they feel they cannot alter. Because "the life" is not as attractive as it used to be, it doesn't attract many candidates. But it has its compensations.

A second factor complicates thinking about the consequences of change. This is the internationalization of the Society of Jesus and of the church itself. Reforms that are acceptable in advanced industrial societies are probably less welcome elsewhere. Once the heterogeneity of the constituencies of Catholicism is taken into account, the likelihood that reforms and the reactions to them will head down a straightforward liberal path seems pretty small.

Considering the internal and international dimensions of reform at once can put a damper on rethinking traditional religious life as epitomized in the Society of Jesus, if for no other reason than it is easy to label almost any proposal as "simplistic." But sticking with the status quo, fixed on the precept that toughing it out is a tried-and-true strategy of institutional survival in Catholicism, is itself dubious. The costs of changing nothing are not negligible.

If we confine discussion to the organizational features of the Society of Jesus, three major options present themselves. One amounts to following the present course. The default option is premised on the permanence of celibacy as a requirement for the priesthood. Under these conditions, a much reduced Society of Jesus may survive in the United States as a congeries of countercultures, making efforts to pass the Ignatian torch on to the laity. This scenario envisions traditional religious life as an institutional trace element or a vestigial network more than as a model of apostolic organization. Institutional identity is preserved but (because of the drop in recruits) at considerable cost in ministerial vitality and direction.

A second option also retains celibacy as a condition for the priesthood but reconfigures the Society of Jesus, opening up membership to laypersons. Historically, experiments along these lines have crystallized into hybrid organizations like Opus Dei or "third orders," with the clerical arm plainly dominant.

The Society has a few pilot projects of this general type—the Ignatian Associates in Wisconsin, for example, and the Ignatian Lay Volunteers in Maryland—all of which steer clear of extending the Jesuit franchise to nonclerical members. The hope is that such movements will expand resources for ministry; they may even evolve into novel forms of religious life. The problem with them is the reverse of the trade-off affecting the default option. While they may attract ministerial talent, groups that contemplate incorporating laypersons as full-blown Jesuits threaten the institutional identity inherited by the Society.[53] The change would involve rewriting the sixteenth-century constitutions of the order. Whatever the juridical obstacles may be, many Jesuits remain skeptical about the magnitude of the demand for such mixed arrangements among the laity. One Jesuit, a sociologist in his sixties, draws a contrast between the Wisconsin experiment, which incorporates laypeople into the Society, though without the status of vowed Jesuits, and the more common ventures in Jesuit-lay collaboration, such as those pioneered in the Oregon province and other locales. "It seems to me," the Jesuit observes, "that most laypeople are not looking for a quasi-religious life. They're looking for meaningful work and collaboration to the point of having a say in that work."

A third option entails opening the priesthood to married men and women. At a time when vows of celibacy have little public support, the immediate consequence would almost certainly be an increase in the diocesan clergy, together with a further shrinkage in religious orders, like the Jesuits, whose members live in community. Such a transformation might also give greater impetus to experiments along the lines of the second option outlined previously, separating the term "Jesuit" from exclusive association with the clergy. In addition, reform on this scale might stimulate the formation of new congregations, somehow composed of a married clergy, perhaps drawing on the *Spiritual Exercises* and modeled after Ignatian ministerial outreach.

Weighing the benefits and disadvantages of these scenarios in public is politically charged. "The most perilous moment for a bad government," Tocqueville noted, "is when it seeks to mend its ways."[54] Yet silence only puts off the day of reckoning. It is not as if "the people of God" have rejected en masse the institutional church. It is true, however, that a fissure has opened between the governing class of Catholicism, made up of the Vatican and much of the episcopal empire, and its managerial class, represented not just by religious orders like the Jesuits but also by laypeople without authority commensurate with their increasing responsibility. Institutional mechanisms for adjudicating conflicts arising from this gap have yet to be put in place, and associational formats for channeling new spiritual impulses still have to be worked out. The absence of such outlets perpetuates an intransigence that mistakes not listening to the opinions of others for adherence to principle.

Membership in the Society of Jesus in the United States peaked in 1965, at 8,393 men. By 2000 it had been cut by more than half, falling to 3,635. The Jesuit Conference in Washington estimates that by 2010 the number of American Jesuits may level off at around 2,000. What is certain is that at about that time the remaining Jesuits will be younger since old age will have taken its toll on a membership currently skewed toward the elderly.

Figure 5 documents two trends, starting in 1960, just before Vatican II, and ending in 2000. One is the high point in membership in the mid-1960s, shown in the hump toward the upper left of the graph, and the decline in membership since that time. The other is the cumulative number of departures (excluding deaths) from the Society in the United States over the same period. The accelerated rate of departures can be seen from the late 1960s through the late 1970s. After this time, the curve, though still ascending, becomes less steep.

The gist of the graph is that more men (5,892) have left the Society of Jesus in the United States since 1960 than are currently members of it (3,635). The presentation can be deceptive because the initial point (1960) is arbitrary. Had we started the series later (1970, 1980), the total number of departures would of course be smaller. In addition, not all the men who left are presently alive. Nevertheless, the baseline of 1960—the eve of Vatican II—enables us to capture the volume of those choosing the exit option from just before the dawn of the new dispensation onward.

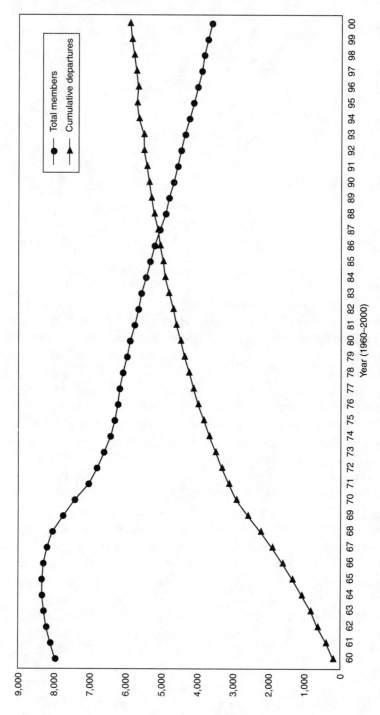

Figure 5. Total membership in United States of the Society of Jesus and cumulative number of departures, 1960–2000

SAMPLING

Fieldwork was conducted in two waves. The first data collection was carried out between November 1994 and April 1998. The bulk of the material consists of personal interviews (100) and "essays" (330) provided by Jesuits and former Jesuits ranging in age from twenty-eight to eighty-five. A smaller, follow-up survey was conducted from November 1998 through February 1999.

Slightly different versions of same set of questions were used for the interviews and the essays; the first was lengthier, the second a bit compressed.

The sample covers men from all the ten provinces of the United States "Assistancy" of the Society of Jesus.[1] Table 1 lays out our samples of Jesuits (224) and former Jesuits (206) by the ten provinces in the United States Assistancy from left to right in descending order of the number of respondents. There is a close match between the population of Jesuits and the sample of Jesuits and former Jesuits according to province size. The top five provinces in the population are the top five in the samples, but toward the lower end the correspondence between population and samples strays a bit. For example, though it comes out second smallest in our sample, Detroit is in fact the "littlest" province in the United States.

Sampling procedures depart from scrupulously scientific method in other respects. We relied as much on personal contacts and recommendations as on random drawings. In cases where we resorted to the equivalent of cold calling from province lists, the response rate averaged close to 30 percent. In the end, more than half the responses were obtained through nonrandom methods. Snowball sampling was a favored technique. Once a few responses came in, we asked these men to nominate others who might be interested in taking part in the study and so on through several iterations.

An obvious difficulty with snowball sampling is the potential for ideological bias, assuming a tendency for the men to nominate like-minded acquaintances. We reduced this problem by stating that we were "not particularly interested in talking with people who agree with you, or us."

If there is a serious problem with using this method among Jesuits and former Jesuits, it may be less a matter of ideological bias than a reflection of the tendency for contacts to be concentrated within age cohorts and the tendency to overlook the generally less articulate and less visible Jesuits in parish work, compared to those in education.

Young former Jesuits are especially hard to find not only because they

TABLE I
DISTRIBUTION (%) OF FORMER JESUIT (FSJ) AND
JESUIT (SJ) SAMPLES BY PROVINCE (N IN PARENTHESES)

	CA	NY	MD	WI	NE	MO	OR	CHI	DT	NO	Totals
FSJ	51	47	34	50	52	64	36	44	56	41	47.9
	(37)	(23)	(16)	(23)	(22)	(25)	(13)	(16)	(19)	(12)	(206)
SJ	49	53	66	50	48	36	66	56	44	59	52.1
	(35)	(26)	(31)	(23)	(20)	(14)	(23)	(20)	(15)	(17)	(224)
Totals	16.7	11.4	10.9	10.7	9.8	9.1	8.4	8.4	7.9	6.7	100
	(72)	(49)	(47)	(46)	(42)	(37)	(36)	(36)	(34)	(29)	(430)

NOTE: The provinces are listed from left to right in descending order of size: California, New York, Maryland, Wisconsin, New England, Missouri, Oregon, Chicago, Detroit, and New Orleans.

are thin on the ground (fewer have been entering, so the absolute number of departures is down) but also because the bulk of former Jesuits and Jesuits are middle-aged and older and have spotty contact with the younger men. The rarity of younger former Jesuits is compounded by their remoteness from older Jesuits and former Jesuits. As we noticed the small number of returns from younger former Jesuits, we redoubled our efforts to reach them. Similarly, the scattered locations and low profiles of Jesuits in pastoral work render them less likely to be sampled on the basis of nominations, so we redoubled our efforts in this area too.[2]

Since essentially nothing systematic is known about the demographic characteristics of former Jesuits, the accuracy of that part of the sample is virtually impossible to gauge. Some province offices maintain lists of the names and addresses of former Jesuits, but few of them are up to date.

As for Jesuits themselves, our sample underrepresents the very old (over seventy-five). The average age of Jesuits in the United States has reached the low sixties, and the infirm elderly make up a large portion of the total number. While we have a few respondents from among the oldest cohorts, we sampled lightly in this age-group because of the difficulty many of them had in responding.

Table 2 gives the breakdown of former Jesuits and Jesuits by age cohorts. An indication that the sample of former Jesuits is not far off is that the largest numbers are in the sixty-to-sixty-nine (37.3 percent) and fifty-to-fifty-nine (35.8 percent) cohorts. Most of these men left the Society in the late 1960s and during the 1970s, when departures were at their peak, and they constitute the most numerous cohorts of former Jesuits.

TABLE 2
DISTRIBUTION (%) OF FORMER JESUIT AND
JESUIT SAMPLES BY AGE COHORT (N IN PARENTHESES)

Age	Former Jesuits	Jesuits	Totals
28–39	7	18	12.6 (54)
40–49	12	14	13.3 (57)
50–59	37	25	30.5 (131)
60–69	37	26	31.0 (133)
70+	8	17	12.6 (54)
Totals	47.8	52.2	100.0 (429)

TABLE 3
OCCUPATIONAL DISTRIBUTIONS (%) OF FORMER JESUITS
AND JESUITS, IN DESCENDING ORDER OF FREQUENCY

Occupation	Former Jesuits	Jesuits	Totals	N
Higher education	30	26	27.9	(118)
Pastoral work	7	31	19.1	(81)
Law/business	19	1	9.2	(39)
Secondary education	6	10	8.0	(34)
In studies	2	12	7.1	(30)
Province staff	—	11	5.9	(25)
Writing/editing	8	4	5.9	(25)
Therapy, counseling work	11	1	5.7	(24)
Social work	8	3	5.7	(24)
Miscellaneous white-collar work	11	0.4	5.4	(23)
Totals	100	100	100	
	(200)	(223)		(423)

MANPOWER

One indication that the sample of Jesuits may be similar to the population of Jesuits is that their job profile corresponds closely to the distribution of ministerial activities that can be estimated from province catalogs. Table 3 gives the occupational breakdowns of Jesuits and of former
Jesuits.

    Among Jesuits, a slightly greater proportion (31 percent) are in pas-
toral activities than in higher education (26 percent). This difference
reflects the trend toward parish work, spiritual direction, and the like
that we picked up from an analysis of information culled from province
catalogs on a decennial basis (1966, 1976, 1986, and 1996). We had resources to trace manpower distributions for these four years in three

TABLE 4
JESUIT MANPOWER DISTRIBUTION, THREE PROVINCES,
1966, IN PERCENTAGES (N IN PARENTHESES)

Apostolate	CA	MD	NE
Staff (provincial office, etc.)	3.8	3.3	6.7
	(34)	(28)	(74)
Formation staff	0.6	0.4	0.3
	(5)	(3)	(3)
Seminary professor	3.7	3.1	3.8
	(33)	(26)	(42)
Novice, scholastic	28.9	26.3	18.7
	(256)	(220)	(207)
Theologian or tertian	10.2	11.2	10.5
	(90)	(94)	(116)
Graduate student	3.4	4.2	4.2
	(30)	(35)	(47)
Brother	9.1	6.9	4.7
	(81)	(58)	(52)
Sabbatical	—	0.4	—
		(4)	
Retired	1.2	1.3	1.2
	(11)	(11)	(13)
Higher education	16.7	20.2	21.8
	(148)	(169)	(242)
Secondary education	11.1	11.8	15.3
	(98)	(99)	(170)
Editor, media, social action	2.0	2.2	2.5
	(18)	(18)	(28)
Pastoral (parish)	5.3	5.3	4.7
	(47)	(44)	(52)
Pastoral (without parish)	1.6	—	1.5
	(14)		(17)
Retreats, chaplaincies, campus ministries	2.4	3.3	4.2
	(21)	(28)	(46)
Totals	100.0	99.9	100.1
	(886)	(837)	(1,109)

NOTE: CA = California; MD = Maryland; NE = New England.

large provinces—California, Maryland, and New England—and for the 1996 cross section we were able to cover three more: Chicago, Detroit, and Missouri.

The data presented in tables 4, 5, and 6 break this information down in detail. The gist of the numerical blizzard is the slow, steady movement out of education and into pastoral ministries.

It is of some interest to compare the figures on manpower distribution in the United States with equivalent data from India, now the larg-

TABLE 5
JESUIT MANPOWER DISTRIBUTION, THREE PROVINCES,
1976 AND 1986, IN PERCENTAGES (N IN PARENTHESES)

Apostolate	1976			1986		
	CA	MD	NE	CA	MD	NE
Staff (provincial office, etc.)	4.5	5.7	8.1	6.1	5.8	7.0
	(31)	(37)	(70)	(40)	(33)	(49)
Formation staff	0.4	0.6	0.6	0.6	0.9	0.4
	(3)	(4)	(5)	(4)	(5)	(3)
Seminary professor	2.3	0.5	2.5	2.0	1.1	2.1
	(16)	(3)	(22)	(13)	(6)	(15)
Novice, scholastic	15.0	10.8	7.3	14.4	8.6	6.0
	(104)	(70)	(63)	(94)	(49)	(42)
Theologian or tertian	7.1	5.4	5.0	4.0	6.2	3.4
	(49)	(35)	(43)	(26)	(35)	(24)
Graduate student	3.0	4.8	2.7	4.6	3.5	4.3
	(21)	(31)	(23)	(30)	(20)	(30)
Brother	7.8	7.1	4.3	6.9	6.5	4.3
	(54)	(46)	(37)	(45)	(37)	(30)
Sabbatical	1.0	0.9	2.1	0.9	2.5	1.5
	(7)	(6)	(18)	(6)	(14)	(6)
Retired	1.7	2.2	4.8	2.0	2.8	6.3
	(12)	(14)	(42)	(13)	(16)	(44)
Higher education	20.4	23.4	24.9	18.5	21.6	22.0
	(142)	(152)	(207)	(121)	(123)	(154)
Secondary education	14.1	12.8	13.6	12.3	9.2	10.6
	(98)	(83)	(118)	(80)	(52)	(74)
Editor, media, social action	4.0	4.8	3.5	5.1	6.5	5.0
	(28)	(31)	(30)	(33)	(37)	(35)
Pastoral (parish)	8.6	9.5	10.3	9.0	12.0	8.9
	(60)	(62)	(89)	(59)	(68)	(62)
Pastoral (without parish)	4.0	3.5	5.2	7.0	4.6	8.9
	(28)	(23)	(45)	(46)	(26)	(62)
Retreats, chaplaincies, campus ministries	6.0	8.2	6.3	6.6	8.1	9.9
	(42)	(53)	(55)	(43)	(46)	(69)
Totals	99.9	100.2	100.2	100.0	99.9	100.6
	(695)	(650)	(867)	(653)	(567)	(699)

NOTE: CA = California; MD = Maryland; NE = New England.

est of the Jesuit "assistancies." Table 7 highlights the major differences. For example, the proportion of retired Jesuits in India is smaller because Jesuits there are younger. Some of the other differences reflect different ministerial traditions, priorities, and social settings. Even though it has fallen in recent years, the proportion of American Jesuits in higher education is still greater than in India, where the proportion working in social ministries is larger.

TABLE 6
JESUIT MANPOWER DISTRIBUTION, SIX PROVINCES,
1996, IN PERCENTAGES (N IN PARENTHESES)

Apostolate	CA	CHI	DT	MD	MO	NE
Staff (provincial office, etc.)	3.0	6.9	2.8	3.9	2.9	3.4
	(15)	(19)	(6)	(17)	(9)	(16)
Formation staff	1.0	2.9	2.8	1.6	1.9	2.3
	(5)	(8)	(6)	(7)	(6)	(11)
Seminar professor	0.6	1.8	2.3	2.3	1.3	3.6
	(3)	(5)	(5)	(10)	(4)	(17)
Novice, scholastic	9.1	5.1	2.3	1.1	3.2	3.0
	(46)	(14)	(5)	(5)	(10)	(14)
Theologian or tertian	2.8	2.9	4.7	5.5	1.9	2.3
	(14)	(8)	(10)	(24)	(6)	(11)
Graduate student (religion)	1.6	1.1	1.4	1.6	1.6	0.6
	(8)	(3)	(3)	(7)	(5)	(3)
Graduate student	1.0	3.2	0.9	2.1	3.5	2.1
	(5)	(9)	(2)	(9)	(11)	(10)
Brother	7.8	6.1	8.0	5.5	6.1	6.1
	(39)	(17)	(17)	(24)	(19)	(29)
Sabbatical	1.8	1.4	2.3	2.3	1.9	1.3
	(9)	(4)	(5)	(10)	(6)	(6)
Retired	10.9	13.4	12.7	9.8	11.8	19.5
	(55)	(37)	(27)	(43)	(37)	(92)
Higher education	18.5	14.1	17.9	19.2	18.2	18.0
	(93)	(39)	(38)	(84)	(57)	(85)
Secondary education	14.3	7.9	15.9	9.3	10.5	6.3
	(72)	(22)	(34)	(41)	(33)	(30)
Editor, media, etc.	1.0	2.2	0.5	0.4	1.2	0.8
	(5)	(6)	(1)	(2)	(4)	(4)
Pastoral (parish)	14.7	8.3	5.2	14.4	16.9	12.3
	(74)	(23)	(11)	(63)	(53)	(58)
Retreats, chaplaincies, campus ministries	10.0	18.4	14.6	15.4	13.2	14.6
	(50)	(48)	(28)	(67)	(41)	(69)
Social, other	2.0	4.3	5.7	5.5	4.0	3.5
	(10)	(12)	(12)	(24)	(13)	(17)
Totals	100.1	100.0	100.0	99.9	100.1	99.7
	(503)	(277)	(213)	(437)	(314)	(472)

NOTE: CA = California; CHI = Chicago; DT = Detroit; MD = Maryland; MO = Missouri;
NE = New England.

ACCURACY AND LIMITATIONS OF THE SAMPLES

Because the samples are purposeful rather than random, estimates of
response rates are practically meaningless. Still, it is natural to inquire
about the reasons for nonresponse. A serious concern is self-selection
bias. With regard to former Jesuits, a case can be made that we under-

TABLE 7
JESUIT MANPOWER DISTRIBUTION, SOUTH ASIAN
ASSISTANCY (INDIA), 1996, IN PERCENTAGES
(N IN PARENTHESES)

Ministry	Totals
Administrative staff (provincial office, rector only, etc.)	6.2 (220)
Formation personnel	3.0 (108)
Seminary instructors	4.3 (153)
Novices, juniors, collegians, philosophers, brothers in early formation	22.4 (798)
Scholastics/brothers in regency	4.9 (175)
Scholastic/brothers in special studies, theologians, tertians	9.3 (333)
Sabbatical, awaiting assignment	2.2 (77)
Retired	3.3 (116)
Higher education	7.2 (258)
Primary and secondary education	12.1 (436)
Communications ministry: editor, writer, media, etc.	2.2 (80)
Pastoral (parish)	11.0 (392)
Pastoral (no clear parish assignment)	2.9 (105)
Renewal ministry: retreats, chaplaincies, spiritual direction	3.3 (119)
Social ministry, community organization	5.4 (193)
Total	99.7 (3,563)[a]

[a] One Indian province, with a total of 160 Jesuits, did not respond to the questionnaire on which these data are based. Information was collected under the direction of Robert Schmidt, S.J., socius to the provincial of India. We are grateful to Fr. Varkey Perekkatt, S.J., the provincial of India, and to Fr. Schmidt for providing these materials.

represent those who have walked away from it all and just don't care to respond. These are generally not the more involved or nostalgic types who show up at reunions of former Jesuits. On the other hand, some men who are conflicted by their experience may not be able to bring themselves to talk about it. Their problem is not indifference but fear of working through intensely painful memories. The net result may be a wash as far as the disposition to take part in a study like ours goes.

Another source of bias may be ideological in the sense mentioned earlier. A few Jesuits (no more than half a dozen) expressly declined to take part in the study because they were convinced it was rigged to show the Society in a bad light. Refusals of this nature did not occur among former Jesuits. Almost certainly, the actual number of Jesuits who turned down requests to respond because of concern about the grinding of axes is larger than the number who declined and made clear their reason for doing so. Our presumption is that most of these Jesuits tend to be somewhat more conservative than those who chose to respond, although this cannot be uniformly the case. For example, some social activists in the Society, who style themselves as progressives, are apt to be impatient with "that academic stuff." The match between worry about criticism of the Society and a conservative clericalism is only approximate.

In the end, however, it is likely that we got the central tendencies right. If we suppose that refusals among Jesuits lean uniformly toward the conservative side, we would expect there to be no significant differences between Jesuits who do respond and largely liberal former Jesuits. In other words, this sampling lacuna would cause us grossly to underestimate the "true conservatism" of Jesuits, for we would be talking only to liberal Jesuits. But this does not happen. Jesuits turn out regularly to be *more* conservative—sometimes only by a bit, sometimes by a lot— than former Jesuits. It may be that we underestimate the absolute level of conservatism among Jesuits, but in relative terms, compared to tendencies among former Jesuits, our estimates are serviceable.

Another sign that the samples are reasonably accurate comes from the analysis presented in chapter 2, where we examine the social origins of Jesuits and former Jesuits. For example, the demonstration that Jesuits and former Jesuits who entered in the 1930s and 1940s typically come from more modest economic circumstances than their younger peers approaches a banal confirmation of the expected—namely, that the immigrant and postimmigrant Catholicism of decades ago in the United States had more of a working-class profile than it does now. All the same, if anything else emerged from the analysis, we would have reason to doubt the validity of the data.

A final point about the sampling design. The sampling units are *individuals* within the ten provinces of the Society of Jesus in the United States. An alternative might have designated *institutions*—for example, high schools, retreat houses, colleges, and universities—as the units within which individuals were to be sampled. Had we followed this course, the study would have accentuated the ministerial operations of the Society more than it does, and the book would have a lot more case study material.[3] We would have acted more like anthropologists dealing with "informants" than surveyors dealing with "respondents." Primarily because of the Jesuit/former Jesuit contrast, we decided to go with the individual design.

OPINIONS

The interviews and written statements were structured along mostly open-ended lines. The men responded to a series of "essay questions" at whatever length they saw fit. We wanted to explore the thinking of Jesuits and former Jesuits in depth, hence the reliance on qualitative evidence. The questions designed to elicit these open-ended responses came in two forms. One version was used in semi-structured, face-to-face interviews that we tape-recorded with 100 men. We couldn't do this with the entire sample because the men were spread throughout the United States and the expense of conducting personal interviews with each of them was prohibitive. A set of essay questions was included, along with the slightly more discursive text of the personal interview guide, in mailings sent to Jesuits and former Jesuits, 330 of whom responded in writing at a distance. These men answered whichever set of questions they pleased. Here are the two drafts of the questions that got the men talking and writing.

CORE THEMES: INTERVIEW GUIDE

1. *Childhood and Youth*
   What kind of world did you grow up in?
   Influence of parents, home environment
   Influence of school, parish
   Circumstances that may have encouraged Jesuit vocation
   Factors that may have discouraged Jesuit vocation
2. *Motivations for Entering the Society*
   Expectations and aspirations regarding religious life. What benefits did you foresee, what ideals did you aspire to?
   Influence from books?

Role of individuals?
School and school companions?
What was the Society you found on entering?

3. *Formation*
Positive features of formation
Possible negative features of formation

4. *Staying/Leaving*
Circumstances and reasons for remaining in the Society
Motivations for leaving
Perceptions of reasons for staying/leaving of others? How "representative" has one's own experience seemed?

5. *Work/Ministry*
Challenges in work within the Society
Possible changes in work, jobs, career lines
Satisfying aspects of work. Frustrations. (For former Jesuits, both past and present work)
Connections/separation between work and apostolic/Jesuit mission
How did/do you deal with obedience?
Describe "typical" workday.

6. *Friendships*
Quality of community life in the Society. Specific instances.
Apostolic teams? More or less isolated work?
Friends inside the Society, friends outside
Women friends
For former Jesuits, how much contact with Jesuits and former Jesuits?

7. *Spirituality I*
Growth in intimacy with Christ
Sense of distance from, union with the divine
Satisfaction/difficulty with prayer and sacramental life
What has been your experience of Ignatian prayer in sacramental life?
Possible crises, turning points, conversion experiences?

8. *Sexuality*
How have you dealt with sexuality?
Advantages/drawbacks of celibacy. What has your experience of celibacy entailed? what values? what drawbacks?
Questions of sexual preference among Jesuits and former Jesuits.
How have relations with women changed?

9. *Spirituality II*
   What are the most meaningful aspects of Ignatian spirituality?
   What might have become less meaningful? more meaningful?
   What impact has Ignatian spirituality had on daily life?
   What seems distinctively Catholic about your experience of
   spirituality?
   Possible influences from other religious traditions, spiritual
   sources?

10. *Challenges*
    What do you see as the major challenges facing the Society
    today?
    Do you see any particular avenues for meeting these
    challenges?
    What do you think about the current directions of the Catholic
    church (the institution, hierarchy, Vatican)? How do these direc-
    tions affect the Society?

11. *Some Issues*
    Has your thinking changed (and if so how) regarding the church's
    teaching on (a) moral and sexual issues, and (b) economic and
    social justice issues?

ESSAY QUESTIONS

1. What were some of the most important family and/or
   community-educational influences that brought you into
   the Society?

2. What were your motivations for entering the order?

3. What were some of the high points and the low points of your
   years of formation in the Society? What motivations kept you in
   the order?

4. Why do you think men leave the order, and why do you think
   others stay?

5. How has your spirituality changed over time? Perhaps you could
   compare your present spiritual life to earlier phases.

6. (For all) How do you integrate sexuality into your life? (For
   former Jesuits) Please compare this to your experiences as a
   Jesuit. What have you learned in this area in your post-Jesuit
   years?

7. How would you assess the quality of community life in the Society? Friendships in and outside the Society?

8. Please describe a typical work day. After you've made this description, how would you interpret the connections between your work and any sense of ministry?

9. What do you see as the major problems facing the Society today, as it moves into the new century? Do you see any particular avenues for solving these problems?

10. What do you think about the directions of the Catholic church (the institution, hierarchy, Vatican) today? How do you think these directions affect the Society?

11. Has your thinking changed (and if so how) regarding the church's teaching on (a) moral and sexual issues, and (b) economic and social justice issues?

12. What have we left out of these questions that you would like to talk about? Please do so.

The quantity of such evidence—over 400 transcripts and typed or handwritten reflections—creates problems of its own. It will not do to treat this geyser of ideas and anecdotes as a torrent of oral history, as raw material simply to be downloaded.

In addition to the standard information on age, years in the Society, and other background demarcators, the men supplied information about where they stood on a variety of numerical scales—their positions on moral-sexual issues, their evaluations of the performance of the Society and of the directions of the institutional church, and the like.

We used these measures gingerly in order to avoid the impression of psychometric testing and to maintain rapport through a humanistic approach with which almost all men experienced in the ways of the Society are comfortable. Our primary interest from the outset was in the discursive thoughts of Jesuits and former Jesuits about their experiences in the Society. The scores are valuable as anchors for the qualitative interpretation. But the sifting of the discursive information was done the old-fashioned way, by hand, reading the responses over and over again, highlighting and collating passages with colored markers. The process is more like editing piles of photographic slides than most social scientists care to admit.

At the heart of our study is an exploration of how Jesuits and former Jesuits have changed along several dimensions. Two key dimensions concern "sexual-moral" and "social-political" issues. Presented with a

TABLE 8
AVERAGE SCORES ON SEXUAL-MORAL AND SOCIAL-
POLITICAL ISSUES, WHEN ENTERING SOCIETY
AND TODAY, BY FORMER JESUITS AND JESUITS
(I = LIBERAL, IO = CONSERVATIVE; N IN PARENTHESES)

	Former Jesuits	Jesuits
Sexual-moral then	7.1 (138)	7.0 (165)
Sexual-moral now	3.8 (139)	4.5 (166)*
Social-political then	4.9 (138)	5.6 (160)*
Social-political now	3.5 (139)	3.8 (165)

* Difference between Jesuits and former Jesuits significant at $p < .01$.

ten-point scale going from "liberal" (I) to "conservative" (IO), the men
were asked the following:

· With regard to *sexual and moral* issues, how would you characterize yourself *at the time you entered* the Society?

· With regard to *sexual and moral* issues, how would you characterize yourself *nowadays?*

· With regard to *social and political* issues, how would you characterize
  yourself *at the time you entered* the Society?

· And *nowadays*, with regard to *social and political issues*, how would you
  characterize yourself?

Table 8 gives the average scores on these indicators, divided between former Jesuits and Jesuits.

Changes reported from "then" to "now" are much larger than the differences between Jesuits and former Jesuits, even though on the average
Jesuits are slightly more conservative than former Jesuits. Even more important, the amount of change reported on sexual-moral issues is greater
than the change on social-political issues. Most of the men characterize
themselves as having been moderate liberals in the social-political
domain to begin with, when they entered the Society, while on moral-
sexual questions they remember themselves as being conservative at the
time. The cultural revolution of the 1960s cut deeper into their sexual
than their social beliefs.[4]

In the follow-up survey, several questions eliciting perceptions of the
Society of Jesus and the institutional church were posed. The crucial
items include the following:

· Overall, how satisfied or dissatisfied are you with the direction that the institutional church has taken over the past few years?

TABLE 9
AVERAGE EVALUATIONS OF THE CHURCH, OF THE
DIRECTION OF THE SOCIETY, AND OF JESUIT
MINISTRIES, BY JESUITS AND FORMER JESUITS
(1 = DISSATISFIED, 10 = SATISFIED)

Satisfaction with . . .	Former Jesuits	Jesuits
Institutional church	3.9	5.7 *
Society of Jesus	6.9	8.3 *
Jesuit ministries	7.1	8.2 *

* Difference significant at $p < .01$.

· And how satisfied or dissatisfied are you, in general, with the direction that the Society of Jesus has taken over the past few years?
· More specifically, what's your impression of Jesuit ministries today? How well or poorly do you think they're performing?

The ten-point scales for the first two questions run from "dissatisfied" to "satisfied"; for the third item, the ten-point scale runs from "poorly" to "well."

The results for the first two items are discussed in chapter 10 (figure 3). Here, table 9 shows the average scores for responses to all three questions.

Jesuits tend to be more satisfied than former Jesuits with the institutional church, the direction of the Society, and the performance of Jesuit ministries. The big difference occurs not between Jesuits and former Jesuits, however, but in the generally positive evaluations of the direction and the apostolic performance of the Society, compared to the less enthusiastic endorsement of the institutional church on the part of both Jesuits and former Jesuits.

Figure 6 breaks down these overall results across age cohorts of Jesuits. The big dip in evaluations of the institutional church occurs among the fifty- to fifty-nine-year-olds, the "bridging generation." It is these men who experienced most sharply the promise of Vatican II and the letdown of its aftermath.

Much of the analysis in chapter 10 concerns the connections between preferences on social-political and sexual-moral issues on the one hand and how Jesuits and former Jesuits perceive the Society and the church on the other. The basic question has to do with the extent to which the opinions of the men regarding crucial policy areas and norms color their views of institutional operations. Table 10 arrays the corre-

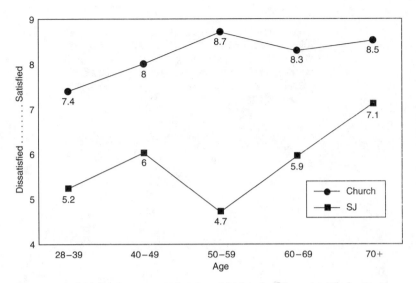

Figure 6.   Satisfaction among Jesuits with the church and with the Society of Jesus by age cohorts

lations between the indicators of opinion on moral-sexual and social-political issues (listed in table 8) with the evaluations of the Society and the institutional church (listed in table 9) for former Jesuits and then for Jesuits.

Before we touch on the highlights, it is worth noting that we added an extra indicator derived from the question "All in all, how satisfied or dissatisfied are you with your work?" and correlated responses to this question with judgments of the Society and the church. This lets us check whether day-to-day experience, apart from ideological orienta-tion, affects the way Jesuits and former Jesuits see the Society and the church. Among Jesuits, satisfaction with work turns out to be modestly associated with approval of the path of the institutional church; the cor-relation between the two is small (.20) but statistically significant.

Several other important connections come to light. First, among Je-suits and former Jesuits alike, there are substantial positive correlations between satisfaction with the institutional church and conservative po-sitions on sexual-moral *and* social-political issues. So, for example, among Jesuits, the correlation between satisfaction with the institutional church and conservatism on sexual-moral issues is a hefty .41 and among former Jesuits .34—no surprise here. It is the positive correla-

TABLE 10

CORRELATIONS BETWEEN OPINIONS ON SEXUAL-MORAL
AND SOCIAL-POLITICAL ISSUES (AND SATISFACTION
WITH WORK) AND PERCEPTIONS OF THE CHURCH,
THE DIRECTION OF THE SOCIETY OF JESUS,
AND THE PERFORMANCE OF JESUIT MINISTRIES
AMONG FORMER JESUITS AND JESUITS

	Former Jesuits				
	Moral Then	Moral Now	Social Then	Social Now	Work Satisfaction
Institutional church	.03	.34*	.08	.33*	.00
SJ direction	.03	−.18	.06	.08	−.01
SJ performance	.07	.18	.14	.04	−.01

	Jesuits				
	Moral Then	Moral Now	Social Then	Social Now	Work Satisfaction
Institutional church	.11	.41*	.04	.30*	.20*
SJ direction	−.02	−.18	−.05	−.39*	.09
SJ performance	−.02	−.23*	−.05	−.35*	.09

* Correlation significant at $p < .01$.

tion between satisfaction with the institutional church and conservatism on *social-political* issues—.30 among Jesuits, .33 among former Jesuits—that comes as a surprise. One might have thought that, in light of
the social magisterium, the association should be the other way around,
that is, the more *progressive* on social-political matters, the more supportive of the institutional church.

Second, some connections obtain only for Jesuits themselves, evidently because they are more involved in the day-to-day operations of
the Society. The more to the social and political left Jesuits claim to be,
the more satisfied they are with the directions of the Society (−.39)
and the performance of Jesuit apostolates (−.35). The faith-and-justice
tenor of declarations from recent general congregations has resonated
positively among Jesuits who call themselves progressives. This sets them
apart from former Jesuits, who essentially make no association between
their stands on these issues and their views of the Society.

Results like these raise an important question. What is the connection
between satisfaction with the institutional church and satisfaction with
the Society of Jesus? Again, a telltale difference emerges between Jesuits

and former Jesuits. Among former Jesuits, the connection is positive. Those who are satisfied with the institutional church are also likely to be satisfied with the direction of the Society (.31) and to applaud the performance of Jesuit ministries; conversely, those dissatisfied with the church are also inclined to be dissatisfied with the Society.

However, among Jesuits themselves, there is essentially *no* association between the pertinent measures. Though they are in the right direction (positive), the correlations are statistically insignificant: .08 and .05. In this area, Jesuits tend to compartmentalize their opinions. There is a disconnect between how they view the Society and the way they look at the church. While the two dimensions are not locked in a zero-sum relationship, going in opposite directions, neither are they in harmony.

ODDS AND ENDS

"There can be no innocent narrative of the Famine," a historian of the Irish catastrophe of the nineteenth century acknowledged.[5] Much the same goes for studies of the Jesuits. Over the years, many authors have treated the Society of Jesus as the occasion for exotic tales of skullduggery and the sharpening of polemical axes. Clinical dispassion is not their strong point. The imagery of Jesuitica resembles the accounts of lurid practices in overheated lands that once issued from Orientalists.[6] "These men are so learned and mysterious," the wife of a former Jesuit remarked, tongue in cheek, "they talk with each other over the phone in Latin."

Here are a few observations that may help put whatever biases and omissions afflict *Passionate Uncertainty* in perspective. First, some capsule background.

Eugene Bianchi was a member of the Society of Jesus, from the California province, for twenty years. He left the order in 1968. He is a founding member of what became CORPUS, an advocacy association of ex-priests, and a contributor to the *National Catholic Reporter,* a publication of the Catholic left.[7]

Peter McDonough, never a Jesuit, spent nine years in Jesuit schools. Most of his work as a political scientist has involved the study of authoritarian regimes and transitions to democracy in Brazil and Spain.

Aside from the prejudices that might flow from personal experience and professional specialization, a number of practical and editorial questions need to be addressed. Writing about living Jesuits and former

Jesuits presents an evident difficulty. It is one thing to cultivate the genre of the picaresque Jesuits of yore, the buccaneers of Counter-Reformation Catholicism. The closer you get to the present, however, the more likely you are to trample on sensitive toes.

The guarantee of confidentiality takes care of part of this problem. The technique implies one big trade-off, however. The downside of presenting so many nameless excerpts is the talking-heads effect. We decided not to attribute fictional names to the respondents, mainly because this sounded sappy ("'Celibacy,' Fr. Bob avers . . ."). We also decided to go with a broad selection from across the 430-man sample, for reasons of representativeness, rather than discuss a handful of cases in depth. We furnish only the skimpiest of personal description (usually, age and profession) as insurance to preserve anonymity. We considered but discarded the idea of creating a few composite characters out of bits and pieces of real individuals in order to safeguard the documentary integrity of the evidence.

A reviewer of an earlier draft claimed that the stream of confidential talk was a relief from the great-man methodology that used to dominate histories of the church and the Society. If it is, we welcome the fact, even if that was not our intention.

But individual confidentiality does not resolve issues bearing on the reputation of the Society of Jesus as a corporate body and the harm that personal revelations, however anonymous, may wreak on support for its ministries. There is no optimal solution to this dilemma. A let-the-chips-fall-where-they-may approach is risk free for tenured academics, but it may not be in the interests of the subjects of research. Still, restraint in these matters flirts with a self-censorship that violates scholarly standards. Perhaps the best that can be said here is that holding back perpetuates the assumption that readers cannot handle departures from airbrushed renditions of religious life.[8]

Another question for which there is a slightly better but still no fully satisfactory answer concerns the norm of evenhandedness in research. Our samples of Jesuits and former Jesuits are reasonably accurate, and this buttresses the validity of the data. But it does not guarantee analytical objectivity. After all, we are trafficking mostly in memories, perceptions, and evaluations, and we have our own biases besides.

What to do? Social science is replete with epistemological disquisitions, almost all of them unreadable, on the topic. We have followed two rules.

The first is to give the bad guys some of the good lines. A distressing

number of people who write about religion, and the Jesuits in particular, seem to believe that they are in the business of preparing a legal
brief, hammering away at one side of the argument, as if to make up for
the elusiveness at the core of the subject. Or the going gets catechetical.
Each story has a moral, and each moral is supposed to be consistent
with an uplifting message. Or the tone turns exquisite, as if spiritual experience were one of the more rarefied branches of fly-fishing.

"Giving the bad guys some of the good lines" boils down to abjuring
the politically correct. At a subtler level, it means avoiding the esthetic
fallacy of equating important themes with pretty pictures.

The second rule is that an undertaking like *Passionate Uncertainty*
should come close to ensemble art. Frequently this entails nothing more
than the scholarly practice of circulating drafts among Jesuits and former Jesuits, in addition to academic colleagues, for their comments and
correcting the analysis in light of such feedback. Sometimes the process
gets fairly intense. The back-and-forth on selected passages quickens,
and rival interpretations come fast and furious. Once in a while a friend
is lost. The gains in accuracy and insight probably outweigh the disadvantages. In the end, after so much interaction, it is often hard to tell
where specific ideas have come from. The final product differs from
what it would have been had we been dealing with inert texts.[9]

The outgoing Jesuits are not unlike migrant groups who are proud of
their adaptability yet jealous of the recesses of their identity. Many Jesuits and former Jesuits judge anything written about the Society by
several criteria. What are the key conclusions, the bullet points? In particular, is the message thumbs up or thumbs down? A second type of
question is the converse of this: Is the texture of Jesuit life rendered sen-
sitively? Are the fugitive nuances and stray details there? Third, what is
the agenda of the authors? What are they up to? And lastly, what is the
practical use of any of this?

We have offered a few provisional answers to these concerns. In practice, we have followed a piece of advice that William Klein gave somewhere to his fellow street photographers: try and get as close to the action as you think you can and when you've done this, take another step
or two closer, and get to work. The task then is to conjure up a plausible vision from multiple perspectives. The challenge is to recompose
the smithereens and odd angles without forcing them into a harmony
they cannot support. If nothing else, we may be left with the poetry of
our common solitude. In his introduction to a collection of contemporary short stories, Tobias Wolff noted that

many of the stories in this book confront difficult material: violence, sickness, alcoholism, sexual exploitation, marital breakup. Well, so do we. I have never been able to understand the complaint that a story is "depressing" because of its subject matter. What depresses me are stories that don't seem to know these things go on or that hide them in resolute chipperness; "witty" stories, in which every problem is an occasion for a joke, "upbeat" stories that flog you with transcendence. Please. We're grown-ups now; we get to stay in the kitchen when the other grown-ups talk.[10]

PROLOGUE

1. Giles of Viterbo at the opening session of the Fifth Lateran Council, 1512, quoted by John W. O'Malley, S.J., *Giles of Viterbo on Church and Reform* (Leiden: Brill, 1968), 179–91.

2. *Collected Poetry and Prose* (New York: Library of America, 1997), 835.

3. A. Lynn Martin, *The Jesuit Mind: The Mentality of an Elite in Early Modern France* (Ithaca, N.Y.: Cornell University Press, 1988).

4. See Klaus Schatz, S.J., *Papal Primacy: From Its Origins to the Present* (Collegeville, Minn.: Liturgical Press, 1996).

5. See Martin Conway, *Catholic Politics in Europe, 1918–1945* (London: Routledge, 1997).

6. See Joseph A. Komonchak, "Catholic Principle and the American Experiment: The Silencing of John Courtney Murray," *U.S. Catholic Historian* 17 (1999): 28–44.

7. See J. Leon Hooper, S.J., and Todd David Whitmore, eds., *John Courtney Murray and the Growth of Tradition* (Kansas City, Mo.: Sheed & Ward, 1996).

8. For a critical perspective, see the two volumes by Joseph M. Becker, S.J., *The Re-Formed Jesuits: A History of Changes in Jesuit Formation during the Decade 1965–1975* (San Francisco: Ignatius Press, 1992), and *The Re-Formed Jesuits: Changes in Religious Lifestyle, Dress and Demographics* (San Francisco: Ignatius Press, 1997). Compare William A. Barry, S.J., "Jesuit Formation Today: An Invitation to Dialogue and Involvement," *Studies in the Spirituality of Jesuits* 20 (November 1988), and Katarina Schuth, O.S.F., "Preparing Priests for Parish Ministry," *America,* March 20, 1999, 6–10.

9. See Martin R. Tripole, S.J., ed., *Promise Renewed: Jesuit Higher Education for a New Millennium* (Chicago: Loyola University Press, 1999).

10. See Lawrence James, *Raj: The Making and Unmaking of British India* (London: Little, Brown, 1997), and Thomas R. Metcalf, *Ideologies of the Raj* (Cambridge: Cambridge University Press, 1995).

11. See George Weigel, *Witness to Hope: The Biography of Pope John Paul II* (New York: HarperCollins, 1999).

12. The pontifical delegate, Paolo Dezza, S.J., died a cardinal at the age of ninety-eight a week before Christmas 1999.

13. Teresa Whitfield, *Paying the Price: Ignacio Ellacuría and the Murdered Jesuits of El Salvador* (Philadelphia: Temple University Press, 1994).

14. See Murray Polner and Jim O'Grady, *Disarmed and Dangerous: The Radical Life and Times of Daniel and Philip Berrigan* (New York: Basic Books, 1997).

15. See Teotónio R. De Souza and Charles J. Borges, S.J., eds., *Jesuits in India in Historical Perspective* (Macau: Instituto Cultural de Macau/Xavier Center of Historical Research, 1992).

16. See John Fulton, "Modernity and Religious Change in Roman Catholicism: Two Contrasting Paradigms," *Social Compass* 44 (1997): 115–29. There is a tendency to conflate the emergence of an operative pluralism in theological circles with the consolidation of a legitimate, more or less consensual paradigm on the ecclesial side, that is, within the institutional church. See Chester Gillis, *Pluralism: A New Paradigm for Theology* (Louvain: Peeters Press/W. B. Eerdmans, 1993).

17. Compare William A. Barry, S.J., "U.S. Culture and Contemporary Spirituality," *Review for Religious* 53 (1995): 6–21; Jennifer Egan, "Why a Priest: The Last Counterculture," *New York Times Magazine*, April 4, 1999, 28–59, and Eugene McCarraher, *Christian Critics: Religion and the Impasse of Modern American Social Thought* (Ithaca, N.Y.: Cornell University Press, 2000).

18. The countercultural turn is hardly unique to the Jesuits, nor does it invalidate the positions themselves. See Kai T. Erikson, *Wayward Puritans: A Study in the Sociology of Deviance* (New York: John Wiley & Sons, 1966); Donald E. Miller, *Reinventing American Protestantism: Christianity in the New Millennium* (Berkeley and Los Angeles: University of California Press, 1997); and R. Laurence Moore, *Religious Outsiders and the Making of Americans* (New York: Oxford University Press, 1986).

19. The claim made here resembles the description of the limited triumphs of the Capuchins and the Jesuits in the early days of the Counter-Reformation. R. Po-chia Hsia argues that "their success lay in transforming the emotions of a Catholic society of orders while leaving essentially intact its structures of power" (*The World of Catholic Renewal, 1540–1770* [Cambridge: Cambridge University Press, 1998], 30). See also Louis Châtellier, *The Religion of the Poor: Rural Missions in Europe and the Formation of Modern Catholicism, c. 1500–c. 1800* (Cambridge: Cambridge University Press, 1997).

20. See Michael Coyne, *Second Spring: The Regeneration of the Jesuits* (Richmond, Australia: Aurora Books, 1998).

21. See James H. Provost, "Safeguarding the Faith," *America*, August 1, 1998, 8–12.

22. The style is common in Mediterranean and Latin American politics. See David G. Schultenover, S.J., "The Church as a Mediterranean Family," *America*, October 8, 1994, 9–13, and Kurt Weyland, "Neoliberal Populism in Latin America and Eastern Europe," *Comparative Politics* 31 (1999), 379–401.

23. See Philip Rieff, *The Triumph of the Therapeutic: The Uses of Faith after Freud* (New York: Harper & Row, 1966), and James Tucker, *The Therapeutic Corporation* (New York: Oxford University Press, 1999).

24. Compare Benedict Anderson, *Imagined Communities: Reflections on the Origin and Spread of Nationalism*, rev. ed. (London: Verso, 1991). As an anonymous reviewer of an earlier draft put it, "General Congregations of the Society that have been held in Rome in recent decades have generated considerable documents with ideals and guidelines from Jesuit life and practice. With the absence now of common practices that define identity, texts figure prominently in carrying identity for Jesuits."

25. See Avery Dulles, S.J., "The Ignatian Charism and Contemporary Theology," *America*, April 26, 1997, 14–22.

26. The division runs deeper than the split between conservatives and progressives. There are at least a few Jesuits and former Jesuits on the left who are as rigid in their penchant for prophetic action as zealous reactionaries. Compare S. N. Eisenstadt, *Fundamentalism, Sectarianism, and Revolution: The Jacobin Dimension of Modernity* (Cambridge: Cambridge University Press, 1999), and Milton Rokeach, *The Open and Closed Mind: Investigations into the Nature of Belief Systems* (New York: Basic Books, 1960).

27. Some years after ordination, most Jesuit priests take a fourth vow of obedience to the pope, in addition to the vows of poverty, chastity, and obedience (to superiors) that are standard for religious orders. Only these "professed fathers" can assume positions of leadership in the Society. The vow seriously restricts protest and dissent, though it is open (like many constitutional provisions) to stricter or looser interpretation. See John W. O'Malley, S.J., "The Fourth Vow in Its Ignation Context: A Historical Study," *Studies in the Spirituality of Jesuits* 15 (January 1983).

28. The phrase is Perry Anderson's, used to describe the state of Italian higher education in "On Sebastiano Timpanaro," *London Review of Books*, May 10, 2001, 8–12. In Jesuit circles, "creative fidelity" and "interior freedom" are translations of "critical support."

29. See Richard Falk and Andrew Strauss, "Toward Global Parliament," *Foreign Affairs* 80 (2001): 212–20, and John Keane, "Who's in Charge Here? The Need for a Rule of Law to Regulate the Emerging Global Society," *Times Literary Supplement*, May 18, 2001, 13–15.

30. One of the most valuable is the series *Studies in the Spirituality of Jesuits*, issued by the Institute of Jesuit Sources in St. Louis, Missouri.

31. Of the 430 responses, 100 are in the form of personal interviews, and the rest are written statements mailed to us.

32. This is the personal level to which William James deliberately restricted his analysis of *The Varieties of Religious Experience*. Our approach, which attempts to sketch in some of the connections between the individual and collective dimensions of Jesuit life, is more in the spirit recommended by Clifford Geertz, "'The Pinch of Destiny': Religion as Experience, Meaning, Identity, Power," *Raritan* 18 (1999): 1–19. "It is not in solitude," Geertz argues on page 18, "that faith is made."

33. For a useful discussion of the challenges involved in extrapolating from

micro-analysis to macro-inferences, see Gosta Esping-Andersen, "Two Societies, One Sociology, and No Theory," *British Journal of Sociology* 51 (2000): 59–77.

34. See Patrick M. Arnold, S.J., *Wildmen, Warriors, and Kings: Masculine Spirituality and the Bible* (New York: Crossroad, 1992); Donald Capps, *Men, Religion, and Melancholia: James, Otto, Jung, and Erikson* (New Haven, Conn.: Yale University Press, 1997); Mary Chapman and Glenn Hendler, eds., *Sentimental Men: Masculinity and the Politics of Affect in American Culture* (Berkeley and Los Angeles: University of California Press, 1999); Bill Desowitz, "Finding Spiritual Rebirth in a Valley of Male Ennui," *New York Times,* December 12, 1999; Susan Faludi, *Stiffed: The Betrayal of the American Man* (New York: Morrow, 1999); Adam Gopnik, "America's Coach," *The New Yorker,* September 20, 1999, 124–33; Richard Sennett, *The Corrosion of Character: The Personal Consequences of Work in the New Capitalism* (New York: W. W. Norton, 1998); Kim Townsend, *Manhood at Harvard: William James and Others* (New York: W. W. Norton, 1996); and Heather A. Warren, "The Shift from Character to Personality in Mainline Protestant Thought, 1935–1945," *Church History* 67 (1998): 537–55.

35. See, for example, Gerald M. Fagin, S.J., "Fidelity to the Church—Then and Now," *Studies in the Spirituality of Jesuits* 31 (May 1999).

36. Zack Taylor, a classmate of the Jesuit, now deceased, who coined this cry from the heart, passed it on to us.

37. Tim Page, ed., *The Diaries of Dawn Powell, 1931–1965* (South Royalton, Vt.: Steerforth Press, 1995), 118–19. The journalist and novelist Pete Hamill makes much the same point: "The trick is to see the world as a skeptic, not a cynic, while allowing for the wan possibility of human decency" (*Piecework* [Boston: Little, Brown, 1996], 6).

38. Toward the end of the *Spiritual Exercises,* Ignatius spells out eighteen "rules for a true attitude of mind within the church militant," beginning with "Laying aside all our own judgments, we ought to keep our minds open and ready to obey in everything the true bride of Christ Our Lord, our holy mother, the hierarchical church" (Joseph A. Munitz, S.J., and Philip Endean, S.J., eds., *Saint Ignatius of Loyola: Personal Writings* [London: Penguin, 1996], 356).

CHAPTER 1

1. Compare Raymond Hedin, *Married to the Church* (Bloomington: Indiana University Press, 1995).

2. See Dennis J. Billy, C.S.S.R., "Called to Community," *Review for Religious* 54 (1996): 371–82.

3. Compare Alan Page Fiske and Philip Tetlock, "Taboo Trade-Offs: Reactions to Transactions That Transgress the Spheres of Justice," *Political Psychology* 18 (1997): 255–97.

4. Compare Helen Rose Ebaugh, "Patriarchal Bargains and Latent Avenues of Social Mobility: Nuns in the Roman Catholic Church," *Gender and Society* 7 (1993): 400–14.

5. See the magisterial treatment by J. B. Schneewind, *The Invention of Au-*

tonomy: A History of Modern Moral Philosophy (Cambridge: Cambridge University Press, 1998); compare Thomas C. Heller, Morton Sosna, and David E. Wellbery, Reconstructing Individualism, Autonomy, Individuality, and the Self in Western Thought (Stanford, Calif.: Stanford University Press, 1986).

6. See John P. Langan, S.J., "The Good of Obedience in a Culture of Autonomy," Studies in the Spirituality of Jesuits 32 (January 2000). Compare Robert N. Bellah et al., The Good Society (New York: Alfred A. Knopf, 1991); Paul Heelas, The New Age Movement (Oxford: Blackwell, 1997); Ronald Inglehart, Modernization and Postmodernization (Princeton, N.J.: Princeton University Press, 1997); and Ronald Schleifer, Modernism and Time: The Logic of Abundance in Literature, Science, and Culture, 1880–1930 (Cambridge: Cambridge University Press, 2000).

7. See Donna J. Markham, O.P., and Fran A. Repka, R.S.M., "Personal Development and Boundaries Shape Ministry," Human Development 18 (1997): 33–45.

8. This change is analogous, of course, to transformations in the larger society regarding companionate marriage, the sexual expectations of women, and the like. See Lawrence Birken, Consuming Desire: Sexual Science and the Emergence of a Culture of Abundance, 1871–1914 (Ithaca, N.Y.: Cornell University Press, 1988); Francesa M. Cancian, Love in America: Gender and Self-Development (Cambridge: Cambridge University Press, 1987); John Demos, "The Changing Faces of Fatherhood," in Past, Present, and Personal: The Family and the Life Course in American History (New York: Oxford University Press, 1986); and Paul Robinson, The Modernization of Sex: Havelock Ellis, Alfred Kinsey, Williams Masters and Virginia Johnson (Ithaca, N.Y.: Cornell University Press, 1992).

9. The difference is the same as the statistical one between multiplicative and additive probabilities.

10. Compare Helen Rose Ebaugh, "The Growth and Decline of Catholic Religious Orders of Women Worldwide: The Impact of Women's Opportunity Structures," Journal for the Scientific Study of Religion 32 (1993): 68–75.

11. See Stephen Kern, The Culture of Love: Victorians to Moderns (Cambridge: Cambridge University Press, 1992); Steven Seidman, Embattled Eros: Sexual Politics and Ethics in Contemporary Society (Boston: Routledge, 1992); and Arlene Skolnick, Embattled Paradise: The American Family in an Age of Uncertainty (New York: Basic Books, 1991).

12. Compare Duane F. Alwin, "Religion and Parental Child-Rearing Orientations: Evidence of a Catholic-Protestant Convergence," American Journal of Sociology 92 (1986): 412–40; Allen E. Bergin, "Psychotherapy and Religious Values," Journal of Consulting and Clinical Psychology 48 (1980): 95–105; and Owen Flanagan, Varieties of Moral Personality: Ethics and Psychological Realism (Cambridge, Mass.: Harvard University Press, 1991).

13. See G. W. Bowersock, Martyrdom and Rome (Cambridge: Cambridge University Press, 1995), and Lacey Baldwin Smith, Fools, Martyrs, Traitors: The Story of Martyrdom in the Western World (New York: Alfred A. Knopf, 1997).

14. See Peter Occhiogrosso, Through the Labyrinth: Stories of the Search for Spiritual Transformation in Everyday Life (New York: Viking, 1991).

15. Compare Helen Rose Ebaugh, Jon Lorence, and Janet Saltzman Chafetz, "The Growth and Decline of the Population of Catholic Nuns Cross-Nationally, 1960–1990: A Case of Secularization as Social Structural Change," *Journal for the Scientific Study of Religion* 35 (1996): 171–83.

16. Compare Roy F. Baumeister, *Escaping the Self: Alcoholism, Spirituality, Masochism, and Other Flights from the Burden of Selfhood* (New York: Basic Books, 1991), and Richard M. Gale, *The Divided Self of William James* (Cambridge: Cambridge University Press, 1999).

17. See Lawrence Boadt, C.S.P., and Michael J. Hunt, C.S.P., eds., *Why I Am a Priest: Thirty Success Stories* (Mahwah, N.J.: Paulist Press, 2000).

18. See Hugh Kenner's introduction to Henry James, *The Figure in the Carpet and Other Stories* (London: Penguin, 1986).

19. The following passage is diagnostic: "In past ages . . . things were so bad that 'a reason to believe, a way to take the world by the throat' was hard to get except by looking to a power not ourselves. In those days, there was little choice but to sacrifice the intellect in order to grasp hold of the premises of practical syllogisms—premises concerning the after-death consequences of baptism, pilgrimage, or participation in holy wars. To be imaginative and to be religious, in those dark times, came to almost the same thing—for this world was too wretched to lift up the heart. But things are different now, because of human beings' gradual success in making their lives, and their world, less wretched. Nonreligious forms of romance have flourished—if only in those lucky parts of the world where wealth, leisure, literacy, and democracy have worked together to prolong our lives and fill our libraries. Now the things of this world are, for some lucky people, so welcome that they do not have to look beyond nature to the supernatural and beyond life to an afterlife, but only beyond the human past to the human future" (Richard Rorty, "Religious Faith, Intellectual Responsibility, and Romance," in Ruth Anna Putnam, ed., *The Cambridge Companion to William James* [Cambridge: Cambridge University Press, 1998], 97). See also Rorty, *Philosophy and Social Hope* (London: Penguin, 1999).

20. Compare this with the statement by a former Jesuit in his sixties: "All I wanted [in] my life was to be a Jesuit priest. But it did not work! In a sense it's that simple. It did not work, like a marriage that does not work no matter [what] the desire."

21. See John W. O'Malley, S.J., John W. Padberg, S.J., and Vincent T. O'Keefe, S.J., *Jesuit Spirituality: A Now and Future Resource* (Chicago: Loyola University Press, 1990).

22. See Liam Hudson and Bernadine Jacot, *Intimate Relations: The Natural History of Desire* (New Haven, Conn.: Yale University Press, 1995).

23. See Joseph M. Becker, S.J., "Changes in U.S. Jesuit Membership, 1958–1975," *Studies in the Spirituality of Jesuits* 9 (January–March 1977), and the comments in the same issue by Ladislas Orsy, S.J., et al.

24. The experience of prayer should not be confused with tranquility, as this statement by an eighty-year-old Jesuit indicates: "One cannot persevere in the Society without prayer. . . . A certain amount of pain and suffering, the consequence of original sin, is the lot of everyone. But trials, if overcome, can have

a positive effect on one, which even the pagan Greeks could understand on a merely natural level, as may be perceived in their conviction: *páthos, máthos* (to suffer is to learn). God tries souls as in a furnace."

25. See Liam Hudson and Bernadine Jacot, *The Way Men Think: Intellect, Intimacy and the Erotic Imagination* (New Haven, Conn.: Yale University Press, 1991).

26. See Philip Jenkins, *Pedophiles and Priests: Anatomy of a Contemporary Crisis* (New York: Oxford University Press, 1996).

27. See Joseph A. Tetlow, S.J., *Ignatius Loyola: Spiritual Exercises* (New York: Crossroad, 1992).

28. Gerald A. Arbuckle, S.M., *From Chaos to Mission: Refounding Religious Life Formation* (London: Geoffrey Chapman, 1996).

29. See Tim Carrigan, Bob Connell, and John Lee, "Toward a New Sociology of Masculinity," *Theory and Society* 14 (1985): 551–604; Abraham H. Maslow, *The Further Reaches of Human Nature* (New York: Viking, 1981); and John O'Neill, "The Disciplinary Society: From Weber to Foucault," *British Journal of Sociology* 37 (1980): 42–60. Compare Louis Dumont, *Essays on Individualism: Modern Ideology in Anthropological Perspective* (Chicago: University of Chicago Press, 1986).

30. Some of the attraction of Eastern religions, in particular various types of Buddhism, is linked to exasperation with the agonistic style of traditional Jesuit spirituality. See Elizabeth Hillis, O.C.D., "Encountering Hinduism: Being Stretched by God," *Review for Religious,* July–August 1998, 342–53; Charles S. Prebish, *Luminous Passage: The Practice and Study of Buddhism in America* (Berkeley and Los Angeles: University of California Press, 1999); and Charles S. Prebish and Kenneth T. Tanaka, eds., *The Faces of Buddhism in America* (Berkeley and Los Angeles: University of California Press, 1998). The rejection of this spirituality seems particularly strong among older former Jesuits whose memories of the Society fasten on the repressiveness and militancy of the preconciliar order. Many of them came up for air, as it were, during the late 1960s and early 1970s when Eastern spiritualities were gaining a larger audience. The flavor of this orientation is captured in the reflections of another Catholic, writing in the 1950s: "Catholic dualism is behind the error of Western Civilization with its war of machines, each machine claiming the 'Good.' . . . Augustine and Aquinas say that Being is good, Non-Being is evil. Buddha says that Being is a manifestation from Mind, which is emptiness, and non-being is emptiness, and so being and non-being are the same, arbitrary conceptions, mere dualisms, mere figures of speech, undifferentiated in emptiness. . . . Dynamism and Dualism are the same thing, and both hasten to decay. . . . Aquinas is as irrelevant and as ignorant as a pretentious child" (Jack Kerouac, *Some of the Dharma* [New York: Viking, 1997], 66–67).

31. Compare Lawrence A. Scaff, *Fleeing the Iron Cage: Culture, Politics, and Modernity in the Thought of Max Weber* (Berkeley and Los Angeles: University of California Press, 1989).

32. See Steven M. Avella, *The Confident Church: Catholic Leadership and Life in Chicago* (Notre Dame, Ind.: University of Notre Dame Press, 1993),

and Clyde F. Crews, "American Catholic Authoritarianism: The Episcopacy of William George McCloskey, 1868–1909," *Catholic Historical Review* 70 (1984): 560–80.

33. Setting aside the upward spike in departures in the late 1960s through the mid-1970s, some Jesuits argue that current attrition rates may not be much higher than they were in the old days. Departures before Vatican II were hidden because of the shame attached to them. Jesuits frequently make the point, which would take some archival digging to verify, that contemporary attrition is not out of line with what went on in "the good old days." *Company* magazine, a periodical that began publication in 1983 to showcase the activities of American Jesuits and their colleagues, publishes annual biographical information on men entering the Society; 1983 was the last year in which over 100 (111) men entered, the last year for 70 was 1987, and the last year for more than 50 (56) was 1993. The attrition rate for the oldest classes (those who entered between 1983 and 1986) varies between 62 and 72 percent. On this basis, the Society is likely to lose about two-thirds of its recruits. This retention rate is probably lower than it was in the old days.

CHAPTER 2

1. See Susan Kwilecki and Loretta S. Wilson, "Was Mother Theresa Maximizing Her Utility? An Idiographic Application of Rational Choice Theory," *Journal for the Scientific Study of Religion* 37 (1998): 205–21; compare Rodney Stark and Roger Finke, *Acts of Faith: Explaining the Human Side of Religion* (Berkeley and Los Angeles: University of California Press, 2000), and Lawrence A. Young, ed., *Rational Choice Theory and Religion: Summary and Assessment* (New York: Routledge, 1997).

2. See table 3 for the occupational breakdown among Jesuits and former Jesuits.

3. See Barbara Zajac, "Becoming a Nun: A General Model of Entering Religious Life," *Review for Religious* 58 (1999): 403–23.

4. George Moorhouse, *Against All Reason: The Religious Life in the Modern World* (London: Weidenfield & Nicholson, 1969).

5. See Thomas R. Rochon, *Culture Moves: Ideas, Activism, and Changing Values* (Princeton, N.J.: Princeton University Press, 1998), and Henri Tajfel, *Human Groups and Social Categories* (Cambridge: Cambridge University Press, 1982).

6. See James Terence Fisher, *The Catholic Counterculture in America, 1933–1962* (Chapel Hill: University of North Carolina Press, 1989).

7. See Jonathan Luxmoore and Jolanta Babiuch, "The Catholic Church and Communism, 1789–1989," *Religion, State and Society* 27 (1999): 301–14.

8. Brian Paulson, S.J., "Good News," *Company: A Magazine of the American Jesuits*, winter 1998–99, 7.

9. See Jean Lacoutre, *Jesuits: A Multibiography* (Washington, D.C.: Counterpoint, 1995), and Constance Jones Mathers, "Early Spanish Qualms about Loyola and the Society of Jesus," *Historian* 53 (1991): 679–90.

10. See Peter Brown, *The Cult of the Saints: Its Rise and Function in Latin Christianity* (Chicago: University of Chicago Press, 1981), and Kenneth L. Woodward, *Making Saints: How the Catholic Church Determines Who Becomes a Saint, Who Doesn't, and Why* (New York: Simon & Schuster, 1991).

11. See Raymond T. Gawronski, S.J., "Why They Hate John Paul II," *New Oxford Review*, June 1997, 8–14.

12. Compare Catherine L. Albanese, "The Aura of Wellness: Subtle-Energy Healing and New Age Religion," *Religion and American Culture* 10 (2000): 29–55, and David Toolan, S.J., *Facing West from California's Shores: A Jesuit's Journey into New Age Consciousness* (New York: Crossroad, 1987).

13. See Tim Unsworth, *The Last Priests in America: Conversations with Remarkable Men* (New York: Crossroad, 1991).

14. Not only are these countercultural rationales ideologically diverse; some are more clearly action oriented than others. The faith-and-justice movement promotes a fairly clear set of policy prescriptions and behavioral demands, while the counterculture based on homosexual orientation more closely resembles an identity or lifestyle movement, without so prominent a policy agenda.

15. Dolores Liptak, R.S.M., *Immigrants and Their Church* (New York: Macmillan, 1989), and Eugene McCarraher, "Smile, When You Say 'Laity': The Hidden Triumph of the Consumer Ethos," *Commonweal*, September 12, 1997, 21–25.

16. See Andrew M. Greeley, *The Catholic Myth: The Behavior and Beliefs of American Catholics* (New York: Charles Scribner's Sons, 1990).

17. See Jay P. Dolan, "Religion and Social Change in the American Catholic Community," in David W. Lotz, ed., *Altered Landscapes: Christianity in America, 1935–1985* (Grand Rapids, Mich.: William B. Eerdmans, 1989).

18. There are also signs that families of newly arrived ethnic groups, especially those from Southeast Asia, supply above-average numbers of candidates to the priesthood, notably in California.

19. Compare Alan E. Bernstein, *The Formation of Hell: Death and Retribution in the Ancient and Early Christian World* (Ithaca, N.Y.: Cornell University Press, 1993).

20. Compare Thomas J. Curran, *The Irish Family in Nineteenth-Century America* (Notre Dame, Ind.: University of Notre Dame Press, 1980).

21. See Carol K. Coburn and Martha Smith, *Spirited Lives: How Nuns Shaped Catholic Culture and American Life, 1836–1920* (Chapel Hill: University of North Carolina Press, 1999).

22. Compare Doris Kearns Goodwin, *Wait till Next Year: A Memoir* (New York: Touchstone/Simon & Schuster, 1998); Elliott Willensky, *When Brooklyn Was the World, 1920–1957* (New York: Harmony, 1986); and James Q. Wilson, "A Guide to Reagan Country," in Theodore Solotaroff, ed., *Writers and Issues* (New York: New American Library, 1969).

23. Michael Lesy, *Wisconsin Death Trip* (New York: Pantheon, 1973), and Jacob A. Riis, *How the Other Half Lives: Studies among the Tenements of New York* (1890; reprint, London: Penguin, 1997).

24. See Paul Boyer, *Urban Masses and the Moral Order in America, 1820–1920* (Cambridge, Mass.: Harvard University Press, 1978); Andrei Codrecu and

Terence Pitts, eds., *Reframing America* (Tucson, Ariz.: Center for Creative Photography, 1995); Harvey Green, *The Uncertainty of Everyday Life, 1915–1945* (New York: HarperCollins, 1992); Michael Lesy, *Bearing Witness: A Photographic Chronicle of American Life, 1860–1945* (New York: Pantheon, 1982); and Arthur Rothstein, *The Depression Years* (New York: Dover, 1978).

25. Compare Daniel J. O'Neil, "The Cult of Self-Sacrifice: The Irish Experience" (paper presented at the annual meeting of the American Political Science Association, Chicago, September 3–6, 1987).

26. See William Leach, *The Land of Desire: Merchants, Power, and the Rise of a New American Culture* (New York: Pantheon, 1993), and W. T. Lhamon, Jr., *Deliberate Speed: The Origins of Cultural Style in the American 1950s* (New York: Smithsonian Institution Press, 1990).

27. In at least one case, the exception to this rule, involving "the son of a Jesuit," is striking. Here are the words of a thirty-one-year-old Jesuit: "Undoubtedly, the most important family/community/educational influence which brought me into the Society was being in a family which had been educated by the Jesuits for the last seventy-five years and feeling very much at home with the vision and mission of the Society. Both my father and my uncle (mother's brother) had been in the Society for twelve years each. Although I never thought of myself as being influenced by that directly, I did grow up in an environment where the Society was a very familiar group of people. I have often thought that I'm pretty lucky to have a family which has a relatively good sense of what the Jesuits are about. I cannot underestimate that influence."

28. Compare Judith Stacey, *Brave New Families: Stories of Domestic Upheaval in Late Twentieth Century America* (New York: Basic Books, 1991), and Jessica Weiss, *To Have and to Hold: Marriage, the Baby Boom, and Social Change* (Chicago: University of Chicago Press, 2000).

29. The men were presented with ten-point scales, with 1 standing for "close" and 10 for "distant," and asked, "With regard to your parents, how close or distant would you say your relations with your father were when you were growing up? And your mother?" The average "mother" score for former Jesuits is 3.0, for Jesuits 2.7. The average "father" scores are 5.1 and 4.3, respectively. As expected, both Jesuits and former Jesuits felt, on the average, closer to their mothers than their fathers. The differences between Jesuits and former Jesuits, though small, are statistically significant.

30. See Neera Kapur Badhwar, "Altruism versus Self-Interest: Sometimes a False Dichotomy," *Social Philosophy and Policy* 10 (1993): 90–117, and "Self-Interest and Virtue," *Social Philosophy and Policy* 14 (1997): 226–63.

31. See Joseph P. Chinnici, O.F.M., *Living Stones: The History and Structure of Catholic Spiritual Life in the United States,* 2d ed. (Maryknoll, N.Y.: Orbis Books, 1996).

32. In the vocabulary of economic rationality, their time horizons were infinite.

33. See the interesting series of articles by Andrew Abbott that questions standard causal explanations in these and other matters, for example, "The Causal Devolution," *Sociological Methods and Research* 27 (1998): 148–81, and "Seven Types of Ambiguity," *Theory and Society* 26 (1997): 357–91.

34. Compare Andrew Abbott, *The System of Professions* (Chicago: University of Chicago Press, 1988).

35. See Peter Steinfels, "Beliefs," *New York Times*, September 19, 1998.

36. See, for example, Steve Bruce, *Religion in the Modern World: From Cathedrals to Cults* (New York: Oxford University Press, 1996); Thomas Kunkel, *Enormous Prayers: A Journey into the Priesthood* (Boulder, Colo.: Westview Press, 1998); Charles R. Morris, *American Catholic: The Saints and Sinners Who Built America's Most Powerful Church* (New York: Times Books, 1997); and Thomas P. Rausch, S.J., *Catholicism at the Dawn of the Third Millennium* (Collegeville, Minn.: Liturgical Press, 1996).

37. Compare Christian Smith, *American Evangelicalism: Embattled and Thriving* (Chicago: University of Chicago Press, 1998).

38. See David L. Fleming, S.J., "Discerning Our Celibate Way in Our Culture," *Review for Religious* 59 (2000): 139–47.

39. See Richard Cimino and Don Lattin, *Shopping for Faith: American Religion in the New Millennium* (San Francisco: Jossey-Bass, 1998), and Wade Clark Roof, *Spiritual Marketplace: Baby Boomers and the Remaking of American Religion* (Princeton, N.J.: Princeton University Press, 1999).

CHAPTER 3

1. Compare Charles E. Curran, "Two Traditions: Historical Consciousness Meets the Immutable," *Commonweal*, October 11, 1996, 11–13, and John S. Grabowski and Michael J. Naughton, "Doctrinal Development: Does It Apply to Family and Sex?" *Commonweal*, June 6, 1997, 18–20.

2. Compare Richard M. Hogan and John M. LeVoir, *Covenant of Love: Pope John Paul II on Sexuality, Marriage, and Family in the Modern World* (New York: Doubleday, 1985); Richard A. McCormick, S.J., *The Critical Calling: Reflections on Moral Dilemmas since Vatican II* (Washington, D.C.: Georgetown University Press, 1989); and R. F. Trevett, *The Church and Sex* (New York: Hawthorn Books, 1960). At the highest level of the church, a kind of aesthetic theologizing has developed parallel to the sexual code strictly construed. See, for example, Michael Novak, "Body and Soul," *The Tablet*, February 10, 2001, who claims (p. 183) that "Wojtyla's views on sex reflect the riches of the Catholic tradition—erotic, poetic, profound." Compare James F. Keenan, S.J., "Moral Theology and History," *Theological Studies* 62 (2001): 86–104.

3. The social magisterium has been relatively progressive since the last decade of the nineteenth century; see George W. Forell, *Christian Social Teaching* (Garden City, N.Y.: Doubleday, 1966); Ann Fremantle, *The Social Teachings of the Church* (New York: American Library, 1963); and David O'Brien and Thomas A. Shannon, eds., *Renewing the Earth: Catholic Documents on Peace, Justice, and Liberation* (Garden City, N.Y.: Doubleday, 1977).

4. See David Allyn, *Make Love Not War: The Sexual Revolution, an Unfettered History* (New York: Little, Brown, 2000), especially pp. 108 ff., and Peter N. Stearns, *Battleground of Desire: The Struggle for Self-Control in Modern America* (New York: New York University Press, 1999).

5. Compare Brian Fallon, *An Age of Innocence: Irish Culture 1930–1960* (Dublin: Gill & Macmillan, 1998).

6. Compare Stanley Feldman and John Zaller, "The Political Culture of Ambivalence," *American Journal of Political Science* 36 (1992): 268–307.

7. See "Ratzinger *Contra Mundum*," *Inside the Vatican*, March 1999, 20–21; see also Francis X. Clooney, S.J., "Relativism in Perspective," *Commonweal*, January 31, 1997, 9–10; David L. Schindler, "'The Religious Sense' and American Culture," *Communio* 25 (1998): 679–99; and Mary Jo Weaver and R. Scott Appleby, eds., *Being Right: Conservative Catholics in America* (Bloomington: Indiana University Press, 1995).

8. See Albert J. Jonsen and Stephen Toulmin, *The Abuse of Casuistry: A History of Moral Reasoning* (Berkeley and Los Angeles: University of California Press, 1988).

9. The statistical evidence for these associations is presented in chapter 10 and the methodological notes.

10. Compare Michael Levenson, *Modernism and the Fate of Individuality* (Cambridge: Cambridge University Press, 1991).

11. See Robert H. Vasoli, *What God Has Joined Together: The Annulment Crisis in American Catholicism* (New York: Oxford University Press, 1998).

12. For a vigorous defense of the traditional position, see John Finnis, *Moral Absolutes: Tradition, Revision and Truth* (Washington, D.C.: Catholic University of America Press, 1991), and *Moral, Political, and Legal Theory* (New York: Oxford University Press, 1998). See also Dennis J. M. Bradley, "John Finnis on Aquinas 'the Philosopher,'" *Heythrop Journal* 41 (2000): 1–24, and Jean Porter, "Reason, Nature, and the End of Human Life: A Consideration of John Finnis's *Aquinas*," *Journal of Religion* 80 (2000): 476–84.

13. James R. Kelly, "Catholic Sexual Ethics since Vatican II," in Helen Rose Ebaugh, ed., *Vatican II and U.S. Catholicism* (Greenwich, Conn.: JAI Press, 1991), 152.

14. This is the world explored by Graham Greene. See Karl Miller, "Dirty Business," *Times Literary Supplement*, September 30, 1994, 3–4.

15. Compare Anthony Giddens, *The Transformation of Intimacy: Sexuality, Love and Eroticism in Modern Societies* (Cambridge: Polity Press, 1992).

16. This connection is treated at length in chapter 10.

CHAPTER 4

1. Compare Joseph Allen Boone, *Libidinal Currents: Sexuality and the Shaping of Modernism* (Chicago: University of Chicago Press, 1997), and Richard A. McCormick, S.J., "Pluralism in Moral Theology," chapter 7 in McCormick, *The Critical Calling: Reflections on Moral Dilemmas since Vatican II* (Washington, D.C.: Georgetown University Press, 1989).

2. See Stephen J. Rossetti, "Statistical Reflections on Priestly Celibacy," *America*, June 18–25, 1994, and A. W. Richard Sipe, *Sex, Priests, and Power: Anatomy of a Crisis* (New York: Brunner/Mazel, 1995), 131–57.

3. A telling sign that homosexuality is widespread among Catholic priests is the high reported incidence of priests dying from AIDS; the rate is estimated to be at least four times that of the general population. See Judy L. Thomas, "Catholic Priests Are Dying of AIDS, Often in Silence," *Kansas City Star,* January 29, 2000. See also Judy L. Thomas, "Seminary Taught Spirituality, Liturgy and Latin; Sexuality Was Taboo," *Kansas City Star,* January 30, 2000; "Vibrant Leaders Kept AIDS Secret," *Kansas City Star,* January 31, 2000; and "How the Survey Was Done" (available at http://www.kcstar.com/projects/priests). The study was attacked on the grounds of sampling deficiencies; for a judicious assessment, see James J. Gill, S.J., "Too Many Sexual Casualties," *Human Development* 21 (2000): 3–4.

4. "In studying people of different cultures," Hortense Powdermaker remarked in her classic research on the habits of a distinctive American enclave, "the social anthropologist is usually more concerned with attitudes toward sex than with a statistical enumeration of the frequency of the biological act" (*Hollywood: The Dream Factory* [Boston: Little, Brown, 1950], 23). Our position is the same.

5. Joseph Fichter, the late Jesuit sociologist who long advocated optional celibacy for the diocesan clergy, resigned from the board of the *National Catholic Reporter* in disagreement with what he took to be the paper's "preoccupation with sexuality." See Joseph H. Fichter, S.J., *The Sociology of Good Works: Research in Catholic America* (Chicago: Loyola University Press, 1993), 155 ff.

6. See E. Boyd Barrett, *The Jesuit Enigma* (New York: Boni & Liveright, 1927), and Count Paul Von Hoensbroech, *Fourteen Years a Jesuit: A Record of Personal Experience and a Criticism,* trans. Alice Zimmern (London: Cassell, 1911).

7. See, for example, Lisa Sowle Cahill, *Sex, Gender and Christian Ethics* (Cambridge: Cambridge University Press, 1996), and Charles E. Curran, Margaret A. Farley, and Richard A. McCormick, S.J., eds., *Feminist Ethics and the Catholic Moral Tradition* (New York: Paulist Press, 1996).

8. Sheila Murphy, *A Delicate Dance: Sexuality, Celibacy, and Relationships among Catholic Clergy and Religious* (New York: Crossroad, 1992). For an attack on this direction, aimed at mainstream Protestant denominations, see Thomas C. Reeves, *The Empty Church: The Suicide of Liberal Christianity* (New York: The Free Press, 1996).

9. At the annual meeting of the American Political Science Association in Atlanta in September 1999, Francis George, cardinal of Chicago, spoke in defense of celibate priesthood in the midst of a "protestantized America." His central point was that the symbolism of the Catholic priesthood was lost in a utilitarian culture. The occasion was a panel devoted to the thought of Pope John Paul II.

10. See John B. Foley, S.J., "Stepping into the River: Reflections on the Vows," *Studies in the Spirituality of Jesuits* 26 (September 1994).

11. See Philip Sheldrake, S.J., "Celibacy and Clerical Culture," *The Way Supplement* 77 (1993): 26–36.

12. Awareness of gradations and the complexity of circumstances can scarcely be thought of as new with Jesuits, as anyone familiar with the tradition

of casuistry will recognize. However, the treatment of sexuality in these terms almost certainly differs from the past, with the watershed being Vatican II. See James F. Keenan, S.J., and Thomas A. Shannon, eds., *The Context of Casuistry* (Washington, D.C.: Georgetown University Press, 1995). For a recent clarification of Jesuit policy on chastity, see the section (2.3) titled "Chastity in the Society of Jesus" in "Interim Documents of General Congregation 34 of the Society of Jesus," supplement to *National Jesuit News,* April 1995.

13. Compare Oded Heilbronner, "From Ghetto to Ghetto: The Place of German Catholic Society in Recent Historiography," *Journal of Modern History* 72 (2000): 453–95.

14. See David A. Hollinger, *Postethnic America: Beyond Multiculturalism* (New York: Basic Books, 1995).

15. Compare Robert E. Lane, *The Loss of Happiness in Market Democracies* (New Haven, Conn.: Yale University Press, 2000).

16. Remember from chapter 2 that there is no significant difference in the closeness/distance of community ties reported by younger and older Jesuits and former Jesuits. For some, what seems to have occurred is a fraying in the importance of and the attention paid to such ties, with the result that alternative bonds are sought out. For others, especially older Jesuits, the drive was to escape the parochialism associated with traditional immigrant enclaves without forsaking the prestige they accorded the priesthood. By contrast, younger men have joined the Society during a period when the communities surround the priesthood with much less glamour, so they have less reason to cloak their sacerdotal identity in community norms. In both cases, the key factor is the declining salience of community as a point of reference, not the decline of community itself.

17. See Peter McDonough, *Men Astutely Trained: A History of the Jesuits in the American Century* (New York: The Free Press, 1992).

18. See Jay P. Dolan, *The American Catholic Experience* (Garden City, N.Y.: Doubleday, 1985).

19. See James B. Twitchell, *For Shame: The Loss of Common Decency in American Culture* (New York: St. Martin's Press, 1997), 146 ff.

20. Compare Michael Bronski, *The Pleasure Principle: Sex, Backlash, and the Struggle for Gay Freedom* (New York: St. Martin's Press, 1998).

21. For a reasoned discussion of the appeal and weakness of identity movements, see Rogers Brubaker and Frederick Cooper, "'Beyond Identity,'" *Theory and Society* 29 (2000): 1–47.

22. Paul Berman, *A Tale of Two Utopias: The Political Journey of the Generation of 1968* (New York: W. W. Norton, 1996), situates changes in Catholicism alongside several other upheavals of the time.

23. An early statement is by Robert N. Bellah et al., *Habits of the Heart: Individualism and Commitment in American Life* (Berkeley and Los Angeles: University of California Press, 1985). See also James R. Kelly, "Culture: Whose Standards Will Prevail?" *Church,* summer 1994, 50–55; David G. Meyers, *The American Paradox: Spiritual Hunger in an Age of Plenty* (New Haven, Conn.: Yale University Press, 2000); and Robert D. Putnam, *Bowling Alone* (New York: Simon & Schuster, 2000).

24. Compare John J. McNeill, *The Church and the Homosexual* (New York: Pocket Books, 1978), and James Martin, S.J., "The Church and the Homosexual Priest," *America*, November 4, 2000, 11–15.

25. The widespread belief that some homosexuals may be drawn to the Society because of an extraordinary passion for service and nurture that surpasses, on the average, the quotient of empathy and altruism to be found among heterosexuals resembles the idea of gender differences in sensibility, fostered by Carol Gilligan and others. But evidence for this is elusive, even if the perception of such traits, as of a flair for style and aesthetic sensitivity, is strong. See Michael Slote, "The Justice of Caring," *Social Philosophy and Policy* 15 (1998): 171–95.

26. The organization is controversial, barely recognized if at all in most parishes. For a map of the backcountry of this and similar groups in Catholicism, see Shawn Zeller, "Dignity's Challenge: Can Homosexuals Feel at Home in Catholicism?" *Commonweal*, July 14, 2000, 17–19.

27. See Charles M. Shelton, S.J., "Friendship in Jesuit Life: The Joys, the Strengths, and the Possibilities," *Studies in the Spirituality of Jesuits* 27 (November 1995).

28. This is the assumption made by Richard P. McBrien, "Homosexuality and the Priesthood: Questions We Can't Keep in the Closet," *Commonweal*, June 19, 1987, 380–83.

29. Philip Lyndon Reynolds, "Scholastic Theology and the Case against Women's Ordination," *Heythrop Journal* 36 (1995): 249–85.

CHAPTER 5

1. Quoted by John Klause, "Hope's Gambit: The Jesuitical, Protestant, Skeptical Origins of Donne's Heroic Ideal," *Studies in Philology* 91 (1994): 181–215.

2. See John O'Malley, S.J., *Trent and All That: Roman Catholicism in the Early Modern Era* (Cambridge, Mass.: Harvard University Press, 2000).

3. See Bernard McGinn and John Meyendorff, eds., *Christian Spirituality: Origins to the Twelfth Century* (New York: Crossroad, 1997), and Jill Raitt, ed., *Christian Spirituality: High Middle Ages and Reformation* (New York: Crossroad, 1996).

4. See the preface and introductory notes by Joseph A. Munitiz, S.J., and Philip Endean, S.J., to Saint Ignatius of Loyola, *Personal Writings* (London: Penguin, 1996).

5. See Euan Cameron, "The Power of the Word: Renaissance and Reformation," in *Early Modern Europe* (New York: Oxford University Press, 1999), and Deborah Kuller Shuger, *The Renaissance Bible: Scholarship, Sacrifice, and Subjectivity* (Berkeley and Los Angeles: University of California Press, 1994).

6. John W. O'Malley, S.J., *The First Jesuits* (Cambridge, Mass.: Harvard University Press, 1993).

7. See Wade Clark Roof, "God Is in the Details: Reflections on Religion's Public Presence in the United States in the Mid-1990s," *Sociology of Religion*

57 (1996): 149–62, and Robert Wuthnow, "Restructuring of American Religion: Further Evidence," *Sociological Inquiry* 66 (1996): 303–29.

8. Berry's religious environmentalism, and allied theologies such as that of Matthew Fox, are described by John A. Hannigan, "New Social Movement Theory and the Sociology of Religion," in William H. Swatos, Jr., ed., *A Future for Religion?* (Newbury Park, Calif.: Sage, 1993).

9. See Jack Miles, *God: A Biography* (New York: Alfred A. Knopf, 1995).

10. See Andrew Greeley, *The Catholic Imagination* (Berkeley and Los Angeles: University of California Press, 2000).

11. The *Spiritual Exercises* are divided into four "weeks," which in the full version extend over that period in real time. The First Week concentrates on the retreatant as a penitent, sinful before God; the Second Week moves the exercitant toward an understanding of God's forgiveness.

12. Compare John P. Galvin, "From the Humanity of Christ to the Jesus of History: A Paradigm Shift in Catholic Christology," *Theological Studies* 55 (1994): 252–73, and Donald Gelpi, S.J., "Emerson's Sense of Ultimate Meaning and Reality," *Assen* 15 (1992): 93–111.

13. See Roger Haight, S.J., "The Logic of Christianity from Below" (available at http://bostontheological.org/colloquium/haight.htm).

14. Compare David Lonsdale, S.J., *Listening to the Music of the Spirit* (Notre Dame, Ind.: Ave Maria Press, 1993).

15. See James H. Hayes, S.J., John W. Padberg, S.J., and John M. Staudenmaier, S.J., "Symbols, Devotions and Jesuits," *Studies in the Spirituality of Jesuits* 20 (May 1988).

16. See *The Catechism of Modern Man* (Jamaica Plain, Mass.: St. Paul Editions, 1967).

17. See Leo J. O'Donovan, S.J., ed., *A World of Grace* (Washington, D.C.: Georgetown University Press, 1995).

18. See Stuart B. Schwartz, ed., *Implicit Understandings: Observing, Reporting, and Reflecting on the Encounters between Europeans and Other Peoples in the Early Modern Era* (Cambridge: Cambridge University Press, 1994); Jean-Paul Wiest, "Bringing Christ to the Nations: Shifting Models of Missions among Jesuits in China," *Catholic Historical Review* 83 (1997): 654–81; and Ines G. Zupanov, *Disputed Mission: Jesuits Experiments and Brahmanical Knowledge in Seventeenth-Century India* (New Delhi: Oxford University Press, 1999).

19. See Joseph Tetlow, S.J., "The Most Postmodern Prayer: American Jesuit Identity and the Examen of Conscience, 1920–1990," *Studies in the Spirituality of Jesuits* 26 (January 1994).

20. See, however, Francis X. Clooney, S.J., "In Ten Thousand Places, in Every Blade of Grass: Uneventful but True Confessions about Finding God in India, and Here Too," *Studies in the Spirituality of Jesuits* 28 (May 1996), and David Toolan, S.J., *Facing West from California's Shores: A Jesuit's Journey into New Age Consciousness* (New York: Crossroad, 1987); compare Elizabeth Hillis, O.C.D., "Encountering Hinduism: Being Stretched by God," *Review for Religious* 57 (1998): 342–53.

21. See, for example, Anthony De Mello, S.J., *Sadhana, a Way to God: Christian Exercises in Eastern Form* (St. Louis, Mo.: Institute of Jesuit Sources, 1978); William Johnston, S.J., *The Still Point: Reflections on Zen and Christian Mysticism* (New York: Harper & Row, 1970); and Robert E. Kennedy, S.J., *Zen Spirit, Christian Spirit: The Place of Zen in Christian Life* (New York: Continuum, 1996).

22. The reference is to John Paul II's encyclical *On the Relationship between Faith and Reason* (Washington, D.C.: U.S. Catholic Bishops Conference, 1998).

23. Compare Nick Tosches, *Dino: Living High in the Dirty Business of Dreams* (New York: Doubleday, 1992).

24. See, for example, Gerald Bednar, *Faith as Imagination: The Contribution of William F. Lynch, S.J.* (Kansas City, Mo.: Sheed & Ward, 1996).

25. See Gerald A. Arbuckle, S.M., *Refounding the Church: Dissent for Leadership* (Maryknoll, N.Y.: Orbis Books, 1993), and Patricia Wittberg, S.C., *Pathways to Re-Creating Religious Communities* (New York: Paulist Press, 1996). Compare Helen Rose Fuchs Ebaugh, *Women in the Vanishing Cloister: Organizational Decline in Catholic Religious Orders in the United States* (New Brunswick, N.J.: Rutgers University Press, 1993).

26. Compare Donald E. Pitzer, ed., *America's Communal Utopias* (Chapel Hill: University of North Carolina Press, 1997).

27. Compare Gregg Easterbrook, *Beside Still Water: Searching for Meaning in an Age of Doubt* (New York: William Morrow, 1998).

28. Compare Owen Flanagan, *Self Expressions: Mind, Morals, and the Meaning of Life* (New York: Oxford University Press, 1996); Richard A. Schoenherr, "Power and Authority in Organized Religion: Disaggregating the Phenomenological Core," *Sociological Analysis* 47 (1987): 52–71; and Terrance W. Tilley, "Power, Authority and Life in Catholic Cultures," *Books and Religion* 16 (1989): 26–31.

CHAPTER 6

1. John O'Malley, "Development, Reforms, and Two Great Reformations: Towards a Historical Assessment of Vatican II," *Theological Studies* 44 (1983): 373–406.

2. Ibid., 396.

3. Ibid., 395.

4. See Louis Dupré, *Passage to Modernity: An Essay in the Hermeneutics of Nature and Culture* (New Haven, Conn.: Yale University Press, 1993), and Charles Taylor, *Sources of the Self: The Making of the Modern Identity* (Cambridge, Mass.: Harvard University Press, 1989).

5. Compare John Courtney Murray, S.J., *The Problem of God: Yesterday and Today* (New Haven, Conn.: Yale University Press, 1964).

6. Compare Heather A. Warren, "The Shift from Character to Personality in Mainline Protestant Thought, 1935–1945," *Church History* 67 (1998): 537–55. See also Walter Jackson Bate, *From Classic to Romantic: Premises of Taste*

in Eighteenth Century England (Cambridge, Mass.: Harvard University Press, 1946), and Rhys H. Williams, "Visions of the Good Society and the Religious Roots of American Political Culture," *Sociology of Religion* 60 (1999): 1–34.

7. See Richard Alba, *Ethnic Identity: The Transformation of White America* (New Haven, Conn.: Yale University Press, 1990).

8. Compare Wilfred F. McClay, *The Masterless: Self and Society in Modern America* (Chapel Hill: University of North Carolina Press, 1994).

9. Compare Tom Beaudoin, *Virtual Faith: The Irreverent Spiritual Quest of Generation X* (San Francisco: Jossey-Bass, 1998); Landon Y. Jones, *Great Expectations: America and the Baby Boom Generation* (New York: Ballantine Books, 1980); and Pippa Norris, ed., *Critical Citizens: Global Support for Democratic Governance* (New York: Oxford University Press, 1999).

10. Compare Grace Davie, *Religion in Britain since 1945: Believing without Belonging* (Oxford: Blackwell, 1994).

11. See Mark Buchanan, "We're All Syncretists Now: Not Religious, Just Spiritual," *Books and Culture* 6 (2000) (available at http://www.christianityonline .com/bc), and Nancy Rosenblum, "The Democracy of Everyday Life," in Bernard Yack, ed., *Liberalism without Illusions* (Chicago: University of Chicago Press, 1996).

12. See Fredric Jameson, "Postmodernism, or The Cultural Logic of Late Capitalism," *New Left Review* 146 (1984): 53–92, and Henry F. May, *The Divided Heart: Essays on Protestantism and the Enlightenment in America* (New York: Oxford University Press, 1991).

13. The self-description provided by the university administrator bears some resemblance to the view of California-style churches given by Wade Clark Roof, "Religious Borderlands," *Journal for the Scientific Study of Religion* 37 (1998): 7: "Popular, seeker-style evangelicalism thrives . . . less because of its doctrinal strictures and otherworldliness than because it reframes Christianity in a manner that makes it more palatable. Cultural reframing and emphasis upon personal need and direct religious experience more than anything else explain the appeal of these popular movements."

14. See Gerald A. Arbuckle, F.M., "Suffocating Religious Life: A New Type Emerges," *The Way Supplement: Religious Life in Transition* 65 (1989): 26–39, and Philip Sheldrake, S.J., *Spirituality and History,* rev. ed. (Maryknoll, N.Y.: Orbis Books, 1998).

15. See C. Daniel Batson, *The Altruism Question: Toward a Social Psychological Answer* (Hillsdale, N.J.: Lawrence Erlbaum, 1991).

16. See William McDonough, "Acknowledging the Gift of Gay Priestly Celibacy," *Review for Religious* 55 (1996): 283–96.

17. Avery Dulles, S.J., *Models of the Church* (Garden City, N.Y.: Doubleday Image, 1978).

18. Compare John W. Hazzard, "Marching on the Margins: An Analysis of the Salvation Army in the United States," *Review of Religious Research* 40 (1998): 121–41, and Diane Winston, *Red-Hot and Righteous: The Urban Religion of the Salvation Army* (Cambridge, Mass.: Harvard University Press, 2000).

19. See Fred Kammer, S.J., *Salted with Fire: Spirituality for the Faithjustice*

Journey (New York: Paulist Press, 1995), and Diane Rothbard Margolis, *The Fabric of Self: A Theory of Ethics and Emotions* (New Haven, Conn.: Yale University Press, 1998).

20. Compare William P. Alston, *Perceiving God: The Epistemology of Religious Experience* (Ithaca, N.Y.: Cornell University Press, 1991).

21. See Mario Praz, *The Flaming Heart* (Garden City, N.Y.: Doubleday Anchor, 1958).

22. See John W. Padberg, ed., "Jesuits Praying," *Studies in the Spirituality of Jesuits* 21 (November 1989).

23. The reference is to John F. Haught, *Religion and Self-Acceptance* (New York: Paulist Press, 1976).

24. Compare Catherine L. Albanese, "The Subtle Energies of Spirit: Explorations in Metaphysical and New Age Spirituality," *Journal of the American Academy of Religion* 67 (1999): 305–26, and Daniel J. O'Hanlon, S.J., "Integration of Christian Practices: A Western Christian Looks East," *Studies in the Spirituality of Jesuits* 16 (May 1984).

25. Shrub Oak, constructed in the late 1950s in the lower Hudson River valley, was a large philosophate and theologate mainly for New York province Jesuits.

26. "Woodstock" refers to the Society's theologate located for most of its existence, from the later years of the nineteenth century, in rural Maryland. After Vatican II, at the height of the vogue for "the secular city," the site was sold, and the operation moved to Manhattan, near Union Theological Seminary. This Woodstock is separate from the musical event that took place outside a small town west of the Hudson, in lower New York state, in the summer of 1969.

27. See Ovey N. Mohammed, S.J., "Yoga, Christian Prayer, and Zen," *Review for Religious* 53 (1994): 507–23.

28. See John W. Healey, "When Christianity and Buddhism Meet: A Catholic at the Zendo," *Commonweal*, January 17, 1997, 11–13.

29. See Marcus Borg and N. T. Wright, *The Meaning of Jesus* (San Francisco: HarperCollins, 1999).

30. See J. Leon Hooper, S.J., and Todd David Whitmore, eds., *John Courtney Murray and the Growth of Tradition* (Kansas City, Mo.: Sheed & Ward, 1997), and Francis X. Clooney, S.J., *Hindu God, Christian God: How Reason Helps Faith to Cross the Boundaries between Religions* (New York: Oxford University Press, 2001).

31. See David L. Balch, Everett Ferguson, and Wayne A. Meeks, eds., *Greeks, Romans, and Christians* (Minneapolis: Fortress Press, 1990); R. W. Sharples, *Stoics, Epicureans and Sceptics* (London: Routledge, 1996), 84 ff.; and Harold Bloom, *The American Religion: The Emergence of the Post-Christian Nation* (New York: Simon & Schuster, 1992).

32. See Michael Walzer, *On Toleration* (New Haven, Conn.: Yale University Press, 1997).

33. See Frank E. Reynolds and Jason E. Carbine, eds., *The Life of Buddhism* (Berkeley and Los Angeles: University of California Press, 2000).

34. See Jon Kabat-Zinn, *Wherever You Go There You Are: Mindfulness Meditation in Everyday Life* (New York: Hyperion, 1994).

35. See, for example, the essays collected by Michael J. Himes and Stephen J. Pope, eds., *Finding God in All Things* (New York: Crossroad, 1996), especially Roger Haight, S.J., "Jesus Research and Faith in Jesus Christ," and Paul Crowley, S.J., "The Crisis of Transcendence and the Task of Theology." See also Brian E. Daley, S.J., "'In Ten Thousand Places': Christian Universality and the Jesuit Mission," *Studies in the Spirituality of Jesuits* 17 (March 1985), and John W. Padberg, S.J., "Three Forgotten Founders of the Society of Jesus," *Studies in the Spirituality of Jesuits* 29 (March 1997). Compare John Patrick Donnelly, S.J., and Roland J. Teske, S.J., eds., *Robert Bellarmine: Spiritual Writings* (New York: Paulist Press, 1989).

CHAPTER 7

1. See Anne Klejment, "Rediscovering the Immigrant Catholic Experience," *Journal of American Catholic History* 8 (1988): 56–62.

2. The men were presented with ten-point scales, with 1 representing "negative" and 10 representing "positive," and asked, "On average, how would you characterize your experience with Jesuit community *during your time in formation?* And how would you characterize, on average, your experience with Jesuit community *after formation?*" The average response to the first question was 8.0 and to the second 7.3—a small but significant difference. It is of some interest to break the responses down between Jesuits and former Jesuits. Among Jesuits, the "before" and "after" averages are 8.1 and 7.9, respectively. Among former Jesuits, the corresponding scores are 7.9 and 6.6.

3. Compare Jackson W. Carroll et al., *Being There: Culture and Formation in Two Theological Schools* (New York: Oxford University Press, 1997).

4. Compare Roger Kahn, *The Boys of Summer* (New York: Harper & Row, 1972).

5. See Gregory I. Carlson, S.J., "'A Faith Lived Out of Doors': Ongoing Formation of Jesuits Today," *Studies in the Spirituality of Jesuits* 16 (September 1984).

6. See William A. Barry, S.J., "Jesuit Formation Today: An Invitation to Dialogue and Involvement," *Studies in the Spirituality of Jesuits* 20 (November 1988), and John W. Padberg, S.J., "How We Live Where We Live," *Studies in the Spirituality of Jesuits* 20 (March 1988).

7. The exception for religious orders from the segregated regimen prescribed for the training of diocesan priests is recognized in the revised Code of Canon Law promulgated in 1983.

8. Compare Clement J. Petrik, S.J., "Being Sent: A Personal Reflection on Jesuit Governance in Changing Times," *Studies in the Spirituality of Jesuits* 30 (September 1998).

9. The customary dates were July 30, August 14, and September 7.

10. See the memoir by F. E. Peters, *Ours: The Making and Unmaking of a Jesuit* (New York: Penguin, 1982). Compare Robert E. Burns, *Being Catholic, Being American: The Notre Dame Story, 1842–1934* (Notre Dame, Ind.: Uni-

versity of Notre Dame Press, 1999); David Noel Doyle, "The Irish as Urban Pio-
neers in the United States, 1850–1870," *Journal of American Ethnic History* 10
(1990–91), 36–59; Stephen P. Erie, *Rainbow's End: Irish-Americans and the
Dilemmas of Urban Machine Politics, 1840–1985* (Berkeley and Los Angeles:
University of California Press, 1988); and James M. O'Toole, *Militant and Tri-
umphant: William Henry O'Connell and the Catholic Church in Boston, 1859–
1944* (Notre Dame, Ind.: University of Notre Dame Press, 1992).

11. See Edward W. Schmidt, S.J., "Portraits and Landscapes: Scenes from Our
Common Life," *Studies in the Spirituality of Jesuits* 27 (March 1995), and Ger-
ald L. Stockhausen, S.J., "I'd Love To, But I Don't Have the Time: Jesuits and
Leisure," *Studies in the Spirituality of Jesuits* 27 (May 1995).

12. See Rudolf Otto, *The Idea of the Holy: An Inquiry into the Non-Rational
Factor in the Idea of the Divine and Its Relation to the Rational* (Oxford: Oxford University Press, 1923).

13. Compare Elizabeth McDonough, O.P., "Come Follow Me: Reflections
on Some Current Theories of Religious Life," *Review for Religious* 54 (1995):
166–79, and Sandra M. Schneiders, I.H.M., *New Wineskins: Re-Imagining Religious Life Today* (New York: Paulist Press, 1986).

14. The reference is to the later years of the Jesuit's training, when he was
a student of theology, not a professional theologian.

15. The communities at Georgetown and Santa Clara Universities come close.

16. See Michael Buckley, S.J., *The Catholic University as Promise and Project* (Washington, D.C.: Georgetown University Press, 1998), 17 ff.

17. See Edward J. Ingebretsen, S.J., "'One of the Guys or One of the Gals?'
Gender Confusion and the Problem of Authority in the Roman Clergy," *Theology and Sexuality* 10 (1999): 71–87.

18. See James K. Wellman, Jr., "The Debate over Homosexual Ordination:
Subcultural Identity Theory in American Religious Organizations," *Review of
Religious Research* 41 (1999): 184–206.

19. Compare Charles Shelton, S.J., "Toward Healthy Jesuit Community Living," *Studies in the Spirituality of Jesuits* 24 (September 1992), and Shelton,
"Friendship in Jesuit Life," *Studies in the Spirituality of Jesuits* 27 (November
1995).

20. The phrase "quiche and wine crowd" is used by Fred Kammer, S.J.,
Salted with Fire: Spirituality for the Faithjustice Journey (New York: Paulist
Press, 1995), 91–92. "They were those whose in-groups concealed a kind of ef-
fete narcissism divorced from social reality or personal struggle."

21. On reading this sentence in manuscript, one Jesuit commented, "Was
this historically the case regarding 'particular friendships?' In my understanding,
the prohibition against 'particular friendships' applied only to Jesuits, and after
our early years nobody thought much about it any more." Our point is that
"particular friendships" were discouraged among Jesuits—it was understood
mostly as protection against homosexual liaisons between Jesuits in training—
even if the operative norm relaxed with years of membership in the Society
and that in the old days close relations with "externs" (the word is diagnostic)
were rare. However, Jesuits have a tradition of collaboration with laypersons

that belies caricatures of clerical power. See the chatty compilation by Joseph F. MacDonnell, S.J., *Companions of Jesuits: A Tradition of Collaboration* (Fairfield, Conn.: Humanities Institute, Fairfield University, 1995).

22. Among Jesuits, the correlation between age and responses to the question "How would you characterize, on average, your experience with Jesuit community after formation?" is a modestly positive .21.

23. See John W. O'Malley, S.J., "The Jesuits, St. Ignatius, and the Counter Reformation: Some Recent Studies and Their Implications for Today," *Studies in the Spirituality of Jesuits* 14 (January 1982).

24. See Carlos G. Valles, S.J., *Living Together in a Jesuit Community* (St. Louis, Mo.: Institute of Jesuit Sources, 1988).

25. For a brief but remarkably thorough overview of the problems of religious life in community, see Patricia Wittberg, S.C., "Community and Obedience: Musings on Two Ambiguities," *Review for Religious* 59 (2000): 526–36. See also David L. Fleming, S.J., "Individuals in Community Life," *Human Development* 21 (2000): 5–12.

26. Compare Loren Baritz, *The Good Life: The Meaning of Success for the American Middle Class* (New York: Alfred A. Knopf, 1989); M. P. Baumgartner, *The Moral Order of a Suburb* (New York: Oxford University Press, 1988); and Ray Oldenburg, *The Great Good Place* (New York: Paragon House, 1989).

CHAPTER 8

1. Estimated from reports of the Jesuit Secondary Education Association. See also John W. Padberg, S.J., "Of All Things . . . ," *Studies in the Spirituality of Jesuits* 32 (March 2000): iii–iv.

2. See Catherine M. Harmer, M.M.S., "Religious, the Laity, and the Future of Catholic Institutions," *Review for Religious* 53 (1994): 375–85.

3. Compare George B. Wilson, S.J., "Where Do We Belong? United States Jesuits and Their Memberships," *Studies in the Spirituality of Jesuits* 21 (January 1989). We were able to tally the assignments of Jesuits in three large provinces—California, Maryland, and New England—at ten-year intervals, starting in 1966 and ending in 1996. The results of this exercise are given in tables 4 to 6. It reveals a slow decline in the proportion as well as the number of Jesuits in higher education.

4. For an upbeat reading, see Douglas Letson and Michael Higgins, *The Jesuit Mystique* (Chicago: Loyola Press, 1995).

5. Compare Patricia Wittberg, "Declining Institutional Sponsorship and Religious Orders: A Study in Reverse Impacts," *Sociology of Religion* 61 (2000): 315–24.

6. See Clarke E. Cochran, "Another Identity Crisis: Catholic Hospitals Face Hard Choices," *Commonweal*, February 25, 2000, 12–16, and Charles E. Curran, "The Catholic Identity of Catholic Institutions," *Theological Studies* 58 (1997): 90–108.

7. On a scale running from 1 to 10, where 1 equals "dissatisfied," the average for former Jesuits is 7.9 and for Jesuits 8.4. The difference is statistically

significant. Our results are in line with those reported by Andrew M. Greeley, "A Sea of Paradoxes: Two Surveys of Priests," *America*, July 16, 1994, 6–10.

8. See table 3 for a statistical comparison of the occupational distributions of Jesuits and former Jesuits. We cannot rule out alternative explanations for why men who choose to leave the Society are slightly less satisfied with their work than Jesuits. It could well be, as James T. Fisher noticed in going over an early draft of this book's manuscript, "that a decision to leave a community may be partly grounded in personal characteristics (e.g., a restless, searching nature) less conducive to contentment" (personal communication, August 2000). When we broke levels of satisfaction down by type of work, we found no significant correlation. The data do not permit us to dig much further. Ampler life histories would clarify the causal linkages.

9. See the classic statement by Anthony F. C. Wallace, *The Death and Rebirth of the Seneca* (New York: Alfred A. Knopf, 1970).

10. See Dean Ludwig, "Adapting to a Declining Environment: Lessons from a Religious Order," *Organization Science* 4 1993): 41–56.

11. See Francisco Ivern, S.J., "The Future of Faith and Justice: A Critical Review of Decree Four," *Studies in the Spirituality of Jesuits* 14 (November 1982); John W. Padberg, S.J., *Together as a Companionship: A History of the Thirty-First, Thirty-Second and Thirty-Third General Congregations of the Society of Jesus* (St. Louis, Mo.: Institute of Jesuit Sources, 1994); and John Tagliabue, "Jesuits Redefine Their Role and Ties to the Pope," *New York Times*, March 23, 1995.

12. Compare Joseph F. Conwell, S.J., "The Kamikaze Factor: Choosing Jesuit Ministries," *Studies in the Spirituality of Jesuits* 11 (November 1979).

13. See Simon Peter, S.J., "Alcoholism and Jesuit Life: An Individual and Community Illness," *Studies in the Spirituality of Jesuits* 13 (January 1981).

14. See William H. Cleary, *Hyphenated Priests: Ministry of the Future* (Washington, D.C.: Corpus Books, 1969).

15. See John W. O'Malley, S.J., *The First Jesuits* (Cambridge, Mass.: Harvard University Press, 1993); Gary Remer, *Humanism and the Rhetoric of Toleration* (University Park: Pennsylvania State University Press, 1996); and Erika Rummel, *The Humanist-Scholastic Debate in the Renaissance and the Reformation* (Cambridge, Mass.: Harvard University Press, 1995).

16. See Paul A. Fitzgerald, S.J., *The Governance of Jesuit Colleges in the United States, 1920–1970* (Notre Dame, Ind.: University of Notre Dame Press, 1984).

17. See Geoffrey H. Hartman, *The Fateful Question of Culture* (New York: Columbia University Press, 1997); Alvin Kernan, ed., *What's Happened to the Humanities?* (Princeton, N.J.: Princeton University Press, 1997); and Robert Weisbruch, "Six Proposals to Revive the Humanities," *Chronicle of Higher Education*, March 26, 1999, B4–B5.

18. See Calvin Trillin, *Remembering Denny* (New York: Farrar, Straus & Giroux, 1993).

19. The situation of the humanities across all twenty-eight Jesuit colleges and universities awaits systematic investigation. It is clear that a few colleges and universities, large and small, continue to emphasize the liberal arts, even if the

number of course offerings has fallen off from the peak of the 1950s and 1960s. For example, at St. Joseph's University in Philadelphia, the core curriculum is the same for arts and science and business majors, and it takes up twenty of the forty courses required of undergraduates.

20. See Peter Green, "Homer Lives!" *New York Review of Books,* March 18, 1999, 45–48; James A. Donahue, S.J., "Jesuit Education and the Cultivation of Virtue," *Thought* 67 (1992): 192–206; Paul Nellis, "*Historia Magistra Antiquitatis:* Cicero and Jesuit History Teaching," *Renaissance Studies* 13 (1999): 130–72; and Christopher Stray, *Classics Transformed: Schools, Universities, and Society in England, 1830–1960* (Oxford: Clarendon Press, 1998).

21. Compare George Sher, "Ethics, Character, and Action," *Social Philosophy and Policy* 15 (1998): 1–17. For an account of the movement away from the fusion between academic and moral training in higher education that locates the origins of this change in the later part of the nineteenth century, see John H. Roberts and James Turner, *The Sacred and the Secular University* (Princeton, N.J.: Princeton University Press, 2000).

22. Compare David J. O'Brien, "The Jesuits and Catholic Higher Education," *Studies in the Spirituality of Jesuits* 13 (November 1981); Julie A. Reuben, *The Making of the Modern University: Intellectual Transformation and the Marginalization of Morality* (Chicago: University of Chicago Press, 1996); and Olivier Zunz, *Why the American Century?* (Chicago: University of Chicago Press, 1998).

23. The "nineteenth-annotation retreat" is a variation on the *Spiritual Exercises* designed for people who cannot devote four full weeks to the experience.

24. Compare Alvin Kernan, *In Plato's Cave* (New Haven, Conn.: Yale University Press, 1999); William P. Leahy, S.J., *Adapting to America: Catholics, Jesuits, and Higher Education in the Twentieth Century* (Washington, D.C.: Georgetown University Press, 1991); and Joseph A. Tetlow, S.J., "The Jesuits' Mission in Higher Education: Perspectives and Contexts," *Studies in the Spirituality of Jesuits* 15–16 (November/January 1983–1984).

25. See, however, Arthur F. McGovern, S.J., "Jesuit Education and Jesuit Spirituality," *Studies in the Spirituality of Jesuits* 20 (September 1988).

26. See Michael J. Buckley, S.J., "Jesuit Priesthood: Its Meaning and Commitments," *Studies in the Spirituality of Jesuits* (December 1976), and Avery Dulles, S.J., *The Priestly Office: A Theological Reflection* (New York: Paulist Press, 1997).

27. See Ann Swidler, "Culture in Action: Symbols and Strategies," *American Sociological Review* 51 (1986): 273–86, and Neil J. Smelser, "The Rational and the Ambivalent in the Social Sciences," *American Sociological Review* 63 (1998): 1–16.

28. The theme of Jesuit-lay collaboration had been taken up as early as the mid-1970s during one of Pedro Arrupe's visits to the United States.

29. The Jesuit has in mind scholars like John Dominic Crossan and Elaine Pagels, whose work challenges traditional understandings of the historical Jesus and the origins of Christianity. See John Dominic Crossan, *The Birth of Christianity* (San Francisco: HarperSanFrancisco, 1998); Elaine Pagels, *The Gnostic Gospels* (New York: Random House, 1979); and Richard E. Rubenstein, *When*

Jesus Became God: The Epic Fight over Christ's Divinity in the Last Days of Rome (New York: Harcourt Brace, 1999).

30. Compare David Coghlan, S.J., *Good Instruments: Organization Development for the Renewal of Ministries* (Rome: Center for Ignatian Spirituality, 2000).

31. See Dennis C. Smolarski, S.J., "The *Ratio Studiorum* and New Technology: Opportunities and Challenges," *Explore* 4 (2000): 22–30.

32. Martin R. Tripole, S.J., *Faith Beyond Justice: Widening the Perspective* (St. Louis, Mo.: Institute of Jesuit Sources, 1994), 9, 25.

33. See, for example, David O'Brien, *From the Heart of the American Church: Catholic Higher Education and American Culture* (Maryknoll, N.Y.: Orbis Books, 1994).

34. Compare John A. Coleman, S.J., "A Company of Critics: Jesuits and the Intellectual Life," *Studies in the Spirituality of Jesuits* 22 (November 1990); Lawrence J. Engel, "The Influence of Saul Alinsky on the Campaign for Human Development," *Theological Studies* 59 (1998): 636–61; and Terence McGoldrick, "Episcopal Conferences Worldwide on Catholic Social Teaching," *Theological Studies* 59 (1998): 22–75.

35. Among Jesuits, the correlation between work satisfaction and satisfaction with the institutional church is .20 and between work satisfaction and moral-sexual conservatism .19. The "church question" was phrased as follows, with a dissatisfaction-satisfaction scale running from 1 to 10: "Overall, how satisfied or dissatisfied are you with the direction that the institutional church has taken over the past few years?"

36. The correlation among Jesuits between liberalism on social and economic issues and satisfaction with the performance of Jesuit ministries is .35. The correlation between liberalism on sexual-moral issues and satisfaction with ministries is .23.

37. It should be clear that this line of analysis is based on significant though less-than-robust correlations in the .30 range (reported in note 36). If the coefficients were on the order of .50 or .60, interpretation could be more assertive. The tentativeness of the numeric results almost certainly reflects some of the turbulent story behind the reception of the faith-and-justice line among Jesuits. The justice agenda took off at the Thirty-second General Congregation of the Society (December 1974–March 1975), when Pedro Arrupe was in his prime as superior-general. By the Thirty-fourth General Congregation, twenty years later, a mild reaction ("balance" is the word Jesuits prefer) to this agenda was put in place, in the form, for example, of an insistence on "dialogue with culture."

38. The correlation between work satisfaction and satisfaction with the performance of Jesuit ministries (.09) is in the right direction but too small to reach statistical significance. Likewise, the correlation between work satisfaction and progressivism on social and economic issues is a wholly insignificant .03.

39. See Ralph E. Metts, S.J., and Joseph F. O'Connell, S.J., eds., *Perspectives on Collaboration: A Workbook* (New York: Jesuit Secondary Education Association, 1992).

40. For a step in this direction, see Peter D. Byrne, S.J., "Jesuits and Parish Ministry," *Studies in the Spirituality of Jesuits* 29 (May 1997).

41. See Catherine M. Hammer, "A Vocation to What?," *Human Development* 22 (2001): 9–13.

CHAPTER 9

1. A few (non-Jesuit) Catholic colleges have stayed clear of public support; like their Protestant counterparts, they are very small and theologically conservative. From time to time, one or another Jesuit institution of higher education has forsaken a federal grant out of fear of government monitoring. This happened on at least one occasion at Loyola University, Chicago, under the presidency of Raymond Baumhart, S.J., during the 1980s.

2. Gerald McKevitt, S.J., "Jesuit Higher Education in the United States," *Mid-America* 73 (1991): 209–26.

3. See Alice Gallin, O.S.U., *Independence and a New Partnership in Catholic Higher Education* (Notre Dame, Ind.: University of Notre Dame Press, 1996), and David J. O'Brien, *From the Heart of the American Church: Catholic Higher Education and American Culture* (Maryknoll, N.Y.: Orbis Books, 1994), 57 ff. Martin R. Tripole, S.J., traces this history back even farther, to the late 1940s (despite the subtitle of his article). See Tripole, *"Ex Corde Ecclesiae:* A History from Land O'Lakes to Now," *Review for Religious* 59 (2000): 454–70.

4. See Vincent J. Duminuco, S.J., ed., *The Jesuit Ratio Studiorum: 400th Anniversary Perspectives* (Bronx, N.Y.: Fordham University Press, 2000).

5. The reference is to "Assembly '89," a national convocation of several hundred Jesuits and their colleagues in higher education at Georgetown, ostensibly to celebrate the 200th anniversary of the prep school there. The meeting provided the opportunity for a major stock taking of the mission of Jesuit colleges and universities, and it inspired offshoots such as the "Heartland" get-togethers for representatives of member schools in the Midwest.

6. These operations are jointly sponsored by the Jesuit Conference Board, the Washington-based office composed of the ten superiors of the American provinces, and the board of the AJCU, made up of the presidents of the twenty-eight Jesuit colleges and universities in the United States. A good indicator of the seriousness of the undertaking is that "power Jesuits" have been assigned to it from the outset. The National Seminar bears a strong resemblance to the Seminar on Jesuit Spirituality run out of the Institute of Jesuit Sources in St. Louis, Missouri, under the direction of John Padberg, S.J. Padberg was the first chair of the National Seminar and the founding editor of *Conversations.* Vincent O'Keefe, S.J., who replaced Padberg as chair of the Seminar, was formerly general assistant to Pedro Arrupe and vicar-general of the Society. Jack O'Callaghan, S.J., once general assistant to Peter-Hans Kolvenbach, became chair of the seminar at the end of the 1990s.

7. There is no central source of information on the denominational backgrounds of students (or faculty) in Jesuit secondary and higher education. In part for legal reasons, Jesuit colleges and universities do not systematically collect data on the religious affiliation of their students. Anecdotal evidence suggests that while non-Catholics are more numerous at both levels of Jesuit education

today than before Vatican II, the religious composition of the high schools is on the average more Catholic than that of the colleges and universities.

8. The key documents are compiled in Carl E. Meirose, ed., *Foundations* (Washington, D.C.: Jesuit Secondary Education Association, 1994).

9. Much of the following is paraphrased from a copyrighted document titled "The Legal Status of Jesuit High Schools: Relationships with the Provincial and the Province Corporation," prepared for the Commission on Planning and Development (COPAD), Jesuit Secondary Association, 1975.

10. See Perry Dane, "The Corporation Sole and the Encounter of Law and Church," in N. J. Demerath, III, et al., eds., *Sacred Companies: Organizational Aspects of Religion and Religious Aspects of Organizations* (New York: Oxford University Press, 1998).

11. *Visit of Father General to the American Assistancy, 1971: Talks and Writings* (Washington, D.C.: Jesuit Conference, 1971).

12. See William J. Byron, S.J., *Jesuit Saturdays: Sharing the Ignatian Spirit with Lay Colleagues and Friends* (Chicago: Loyola University Press, 2000).

13. See Thomas F. Troy, "Jesuit Colleges without Jesuits? Ignatian Identity at Risk," *America,* October 25, 1991, 605–8. Christian Life Communities, later-day versions of sodalities and confraternities, have played an important role in socializing lay faculty into the Ignatian ethos.

14. See James A. Donahue, "Jesuit Education and the Cultivation of Virtue," *Thought* 67 (1992): 192–206.

15. See, for example, Joseph F. O'Connell, S.J., *Ignatian Leadership in Jesuit Schools: Resources for Reflection and Evaluation* (Washington, D.C.: Jesuit Secondary Education Association, 1995).

16. Sometimes this repackaging is taken to great lengths, as in the synthesis of modern pedagogical techniques and traditional Jesuit methods by Ralph E. Metts, S.J., *Ignatius Knew* (Washington, D.C.: Jesuit Secondary Education Association, 1995).

17. Michael J. Lacey, "The Conflicted Situation of American Higher Education and the Contribution of Catholics" (talk given at Regis University, Denver, June 1994).

18. See Timothy R. Lannon, S.J., "Why Isn't Anyone Talking about Jesuit Identity?" (unpublished paper, May 1996).

19. The reference is to Paul Reinert, S.J., *To Turn the Tide* (Englewood Cliffs, N.J.: Prentice Hall, 1972). Reinert was president of St. Louis University for twenty-five years, starting in 1949. See also Reinert, *The Urban Catholic University* (Kansas City, Mo.: Sheed & Ward, 1972).

20. Another reason for the arm's-length relations among the colleges and universities may be that unlike the high schools, many of them compete against one another in a national market for research and teaching personnel (including Jesuits). But this factor is probably secondary to the sheer diversity in size and academic ranking.

21. See David Rogers, "Jesuit at Georgetown Ministers to and Lobbies Congress," *Wall Street Journal,* April 29, 1999, A28.

22. Lacey, "The Conflicted Situation of American Higher Education and the Contribution of Catholics."

23. See Scott Appleby, "Ending as It Began: The American Century and the American Dream" (paper presented at the meetings of American Academy of Religion, San Francisco, November 23, 1997).

24. Compare Richard P. Mcbrien, "Academic Freedom in Catholic Universities: The Emergence of a Party Line," *America*, December 3, 1988, 545–58, and David L. Schindler, "The Catholic Academy and the Order of Intelligence: The Dying of the Light?" *Communio* 26 (1999): 722–45.

25. Thomas A. Mulkeen, "Books on Education," *America*, September 10, 1988, 142–46.

26. See Patrick H. Byrne, "Paradigms of Justice and Love," *Conversations on Jesuit Higher Education*, spring 1995, 5–17.

27. Frank H. T. Rhodes, "The Mission and Ministry of Jesuits in Higher Education," *America*, July 29–August 5, 1989, 54–60.

28. Interview with Mary Flick, St. Louis University, May 1996.

29. This tension was the theme of the National Conference on the Commitment to Justice in Jesuit Higher Education held at Santa Clara University, October 5–8, 2000. For updates, see www.scu.edu/BannanInstitute/Index Conference.html.

30. See Charles Zech, "The Faculty and Catholic Institutional Identity," *America*, May 2, 1999, 11–15.

31. Rhodes, "The Mission and Ministry of Jesuits in Higher Education," 59.

32. For a helpful stock taking, see William C. McFadden, S.J., ed., *Georgetown at Two Hundred* (Washington, D.C.: Georgetown University Press, 1990).

33. Charles F. Donovan, S.J., David R. Dunigan, S.J., and Paul A. FitzGerald, S.J., *History of Boston College: From the Beginnings to 1990* (Chestnut Hill, Mass.: University Press of Boston College, 1990).

34. See Paul G. Scherrish, "Finding God in Some Things: Unintended Consequences for the Academy of the Faith That Does Justice," *Conversations in Jesuit Higher Education* 19 (2001): 21–27.

35. See, for example, Bishop Donald Wuerl, "The Institutional Identity of a Catholic University," *Origins* 29 (September 23, 1999): 232–35.

36. The reference is to Richard P. Mcbrien, "Why I Shall Not Seek a Mandate," *America*, February 12, 2000, 14–16. Among other things, McBrien argued (p. 14) that "Catholic higher education in this country is already suffering enough from all the charges, leveled without persuasive evidence, about the alleged erosion of Catholic character in our Catholic colleges and universities. (Jesuit schools, for some reason, come in for special condemnation, even though they are not only the most numerous, but also generally the best—and I say this as a non-Jesuit!)."

37. See Ernest L. Boyer, *Scholarship Reconsidered: Priorities of the Professoriate* (Princeton, N.J.: Carnegie Foundation for the Advancement of Teaching, 1990), and Alan Wolfe, "Catholic Universities Can Be the Salvation of Pluralism on American Campuses," *Chronicle of Higher Education*, February 26, 1999, B6–B7.

38. Isaiah Berlin, *Russian Thinkers* (London: Penguin, 1978).

39. See Paul Wilkes, "Catholic Spoken Here: A Report from the Academic Front," *America*, May 1, 1999, 13–18.

40. See David Hollenbach, S.J., "Is Tolerance Enough? The Catholic University and the Common Good," *Conversations on Jesuit Higher Education* 13 (1998): 5–15.

41. See "Centered Pluralism: A Report of a Faculty Seminar on the Jesuit and Catholic Identity of Georgetown University," November 1996.

42. See Robert N. Bellah, "Is There a Common American Culture?," *Journal of the American Academy of Religion* 66 (1998): 613–25, and Jeffrey C. Isaac, *Democracy in Dark Times* (Ithaca, N.Y.: Cornell University Press, 1998).

43. John Courtney Murray, S.J., *We Hold These Truths: Catholic Reflections on the American Proposition* (New York: Doubleday, 1964). See also Patrick W. Carey, ed., *American Catholic Religious Thought* (New York: Paulist Press, 1987).

44. Francis X. Clooney, S.J., "Goddess in the Classroom: Is the Promotion of Religious Diversity a Dangerous Idea?" *Conversations on Jesuit Higher Education* 16 (1999): 29.

45. Compare Franklin I. Gamwell, "Speaking of God after Aquinas," *Journal of Religion* 81 (2001): 185–210.

46. See David Solomon, "What Baylor and Notre Dame Can Learn from Each Other," *New Oxford Review*, December 1995, 8–19.

47. Compare William B. Scott and Peter M. Rutkoff, *New York Modern: The Arts and the City* (Baltimore: The Johns Hopkins University Press, 1999); see also Peter Conrad, *The Art of the City: Views and Versions of New York* (New York: Oxford University Press, 1984), and William R. Taylor, *In Pursuit of Gotham: Culture and Commerce in New York* (New York: Oxford University Press, 1992).

48. See Philip Gleason, *Contending with Modernity: Catholic Higher Education in the Twentieth Century* (New York: Oxford University Press, 1995), and the review by Richard H. Passon in *Commonweal*, May 18, 1996, 28–29.

49. See Patrick W. Carey, "College Theology in Historical Perspective," in Sandra Yocum Mize and William Portier, eds., *American Catholic Traditions: Sources for Renewal* (Maryknoll, N.Y.: Orbis Books, 1997), and Patrick W. Carey and Earl C. Muller, S.J., eds., *Theological Education in the Catholic Tradition* (New York: Crossroad, 1997).

50. A potential model is Thomas Aquinas College set in a small town in California; see *Thomas Aquinas College Newsletter*, winter 1998–1999. The Web site is http://www.thomasaquinas.edu.

51. See Michael J. Hunt, C.S.P., *College Catholics: A New Counter-Culture* (New York: Paulist Press, 1993).

52. See Michael Hechter, *Principles of Group Solidarity* (Berkeley and Los Angeles: University of California Press, 1987).

53. Because most Jesuit institutions of higher education are comprehensive colleges, smaller than research universities, with mostly local clienteles, it is plausible to treat them as roughly stand-alone units that engender a greater sense of belonging than what is typically found at the larger schools. At this intermediate level, methods of fostering religious identity and professional cohesion make some sense. See the case study (of St. Joseph's University in Philadelphia) by Nicholas S. Rashford, S.J., and David Coghlan, S.J., "Effective Administra-

tion through Organizational Levels," *Journal of Educational Administration* 30 (1992): 63–72.

54. The JSEA has periodically administered lengthy questionnaires to students, but these remain to be analyzed, partly because many of the questions themselves are poorly formulated. The results look like a hodgepodge. See *Student Profile Survey Booklet* (New York: Commission on Research and Development, JSEA, 1992). Assessing the attitudinal and behavioral effects of service learning and similar programs is challenging at any level, whether among high school or college students. See Diana Owen, "Service Learning and Political Socialization," *PS: Political Science & Politics* 33 (2000): 639–40.

55. See *The Alumni of 1965 Report Back: A Study of 3,722 Alumni of Jesuit High Schools of the Class of 1965* (Washington, D.C.: Center for Applied Research in the Apostolate, 1974), and Patrick H. McNamara, *Conscience First, Tradition Second: A Study of Young American Catholics* (Albany: State University of New York Press, 1992). The former study was conducted under the direction of the sociologist Joseph Fichter, S.J.

56. See Alice Gallin, *Negotiating Identity: Catholic Higher Education since 1960* (Notre Dame, Ind.: University of Notre Dame Press, 2001). Compare Frank H. I. Rhodes, *The Creation of the Future: The Role of the American University* (Ithaca, N.Y.: Cornell University Press, 2001).

CHAPTER 10

1. See Ernst Gellner and John Waterbury, eds., *Patrons and Clients in Mediterranean Societies* (London: Duckworth, 1977).

2. See Ronald Modras, "The Spiritual Humanism of the Jesuits," *America*, February 4, 1995, 10–32, and "Rooted in the Renaissance: The Jesuit Mission at Saint Louis University," *Conversations on Jesuit Higher Education* 18 (2000): 25–31. It is a measure of how far the Jesuits have come that such appointments are no longer rare, provoking little more than the occasional raised eyebrow.

3. See Robert N. Bellah, "Religion and the Shape of National Culture," *America*, July 31–August 7, 1999, 9–14.

4. Compare Elizabeth Weiss Ozorak, "The Power, but Not the Glory: How Women Empower Themselves through Religion," *Journal for the Scientific Study of Religion* 35 (1996), 17–29, and Kenneth L. Woodward, "Gender and Religion: Who's Really Running the Show," *Commonweal*, November 22, 1996, 9–14. See also Aurora G. Morcillo, *True Catholic Womanhood: Gender Ideology in Franco's Spain* (DeKalb: Northern Illinois University Press, 2000).

5. Peter McDonough, "Metamorphoses of the Jesuits: Sexual Identity, Gender Roles, and Hierarchy in Catholicism," *Comparative Studies in Society and History*, April 1990, 325–56.

6. See John Paul II, "Apostolic Letter on Ordination and Women," *Origins* 24 (June 9, 1994): 49–52. Compare Joseph Blenkinsopp, "Sacrifice and Social Maintenance: What's At Stake in the (Non-)Ordination of Roman Catholic

Women," *Crosscurrents* 45 (1995): 359–67, and Kelley A. Raab, *When Women Become Priests: The Catholic Women's Ordination Debate* (New York: Columbia University Press, 2000).

7. Aside from the statistical documentation, see James F. Keenan, S.J., "Joseph Fuchs and the Question of Moral Objectivity in Roman Catholic Ethical Reasoning," *Religious Studies Review* 24 (1998): 253–58.

8. The men were presented with ten-point scales, running from "dissatisfied" (0) to "satisfied" (10) and asked the following questions: "Overall, how satisfied or dissatisfied are you with the direction that the institutional church has taken over the past few years?" and "And how satisfied or dissatisfied are you, in general, with the direction that the Society of Jesus has taken over the past few years?"

9. See figure 6 for the statistical data.

10. The relevant data are given in table 9.

11. Among former Jesuits, the correlation is .34; among Jesuits it is an even stronger .41.

12. The correlation between positions on moral-sexual issues and evaluations of the Society of Jesus is a statistically insignificant .18 for both Jesuits and former Jesuits. The correlation between progressivism on social-political issues and approval of the Society among former Jesuits is also insignificant (.08). Among Jesuits themselves, however, it reaches a hefty .39.

13. The phrase is from Nathan O. Hatch, *The Democratization of American Christianity* (New Haven, Conn.: Yale University Press, 1989), 208.

14. See John W. Padberg, S.J., "The Society True to Itself: A Brief History of the 32nd General Congregation of the Society of Jesus (December 2, 1974–March 7, 1975)," *Studies in the Spirituality of Jesuits* 15 (May–September 1983).

15. An important qualification to the compatibility between the social agenda of the Jesuits and the designs of Rome should be noted, however. Jesuits and former Jesuits who define themselves as conservative on the social-political issues are more likely than social progressives to view the institutional church in a favorable light. For Jesuits and former Jesuits, the correlations between social-political conservatism and approval of the institutional church are .30 and .33, respectively. This connection is surprising only if it is supposed that support for the papacy should go hand in hand with the advocacy of the progressive economic and social platform set forth in recent encyclicals. In fact, the pattern hints at a broader alignment between the generally conservative thrust of John Paul II's regime and conservative donors and assorted economic viziers behind the financial recuperation of the Gregorian University and other bastions of Catholic tradition, such as Opus Dei. From this angle, the papacy is seen as the supreme defense against moral decay and not as a proponent of radical economic reform, even if it serves as a social conscience against the worst excesses of materialism. The Society is liable to run up against a distinct lack of enthusiasm from these quarters as it presses its social agenda. See R. Scott Appleby, "The Neo-Americanist Center and the Limits of Conservative Dissent," *U.S. Catholic Historian* 17 (1999): 13–27, and Jean-Guy Vaillancourt, *Papal Power: A Study of Vatican Control over Lay Catholic Elites* (Berkeley and Los Angeles: University

of California Press, 1980). See also Brian Murphy, *The New Men: Inside the Vatican's Elite School for American Priests* (New York: Grosset/Putnam, 1997).

16. The First Vatican Council took place from December 1869 to October 1870 in Rome and ratified, among other things, the infallibility of the papacy's teaching office.

17. One of the most interesting is the Christo Rey middle school project in Chicago, directed at poor students. There are similar "Nativity School" operations in other provinces.

18. See Colin J. Davis, "'Launch Out into the Deep and Let Down Your Nets': Father John Corridan, SJ, and New York Longshoremen in the Post–World War II Era," *Catholic Historical Review* 86 (2000): 66–84.

19. William F. Buckley, Jr., *Nearer, My God: An Autobiography of Faith* (San Diego: Harcourt Brace, 1997), 12.

20. Compare Richard A. McCormick, S.J., "Some Early Reactions to *Veritatis Splendor*," *Theological Studies* 55 (1994): 481–506.

21. Compare Mark Chaves, "Secularization as Declining Religious Authority," *Social Forces* 72 (1993): 749–74, and Jeffrey Stout, *Ethics after Babel: The Languages of Morals and Their Discontents* (Boston: Beacon Press, 1988).

22. Compare Penny Edgell Becker, *Congregations in Conflict: Cultural Models of Local Religious Life* (Cambridge: Cambridge University Press, 1999), and Peter-Hans Kolvenbach, S.J., "Faith and Justice in Jesuit Higher Education" (lecture presented at the conference on the Commitment to Justice in Jesuit Higher Education, Santa Clara University, Santa Clara, California, October 6, 2000).

23. Compare Michel Chaouli, "A Vast Unravelling," *Times Literary Supplement*, February 26, 1999, 14–15.

24. Compare Irving Kristol, "Faith à la carte: Religion and Politics in an Era of Good Feeling," *Times Literary Supplement*, May 26, 2000, 14–15.

CHAPTER 11

1. See Jeffrey von Arx, S.J., ed., *Varieties of Ultramontanism* (Washington, D.C.: Catholic University of America Press, 1998); J. Brian Hehir, "Catholicism and Democracy: Conflict, Change, and Collaboration," in John Witte, Jr., ed., *Christianity and Democracy in Global Context* (Boulder, Colo.: Westview Press, 1993); and A. James Reichley, *Religion in American Public Life* (Washington, D.C.: Brookings Institution, 1985).

2. See Carolyn M. Warner, *Confessions of an Interest Group: The Catholic Church and Political Parties in Europe* (Princeton, N.J.: Princeton University Press, 2000).

3. See Roger Haight, S.J., "The Logic of Christology from Below" (available at http://www.bostontheological.org/colloquium/haight).

4. For a more hopeful diagnosis, see Paul Philibert, O.P., "Toward a Transformative Model of Religious Life," *Origins* 34 (May 20, 1999): 9–14. See also James Heft, ed., *A Catholic Modernity?* (New York: Oxford University Press, 1999).

5. Joseph Fitzmyer, S.J., is a biblical scholar on the faculty of Catholic University of America in Washington, D.C. The oblate is Tissa Balasuriya, O.M.I., who was excommunicated in the late 1990s for his controversial theological writings, then "de-excommunicated." See "Statement by Sri Lankan Theologian," *Origins* 26 (January 30, 1991): 532–36, and Joseph A. Fitzmyer, S.J., *Scripture: The Soul of Theology* (Mahwah, N.J.: Paulist Press, 1993).

6. Pierre Teilhard de Chardin, S.J. (1881–1955) was a French archaeologist and theologian whose views on evolution became well known in the United States around the time of Vatican II. The "omega point" refers to the culmination of the evolutionary process—according to Teilhard, the final spiritualization of the universe. *Parousia* is a Greek word meaning "arrival" or "presence." The reference is to the second coming of Christ. See Michael Glazier and Monika K. Hellwig, eds., *The Modern Catholic Encyclopedia* (Collegeville, Minn.: Liturgical Press, 1999).

7. The theologian is apparently referring to the papal curia, not the staff at the headquarters of the Society of Jesus in Rome.

8. Compare James Q. Wilson, *The Moral Sense* (New York: The Free Press, 1993).

9. See Avery Dulles, S.J., "Orthodoxy and Social Change," *America,* June 20–27, 1998, 8–17.

10. Compare Lisa Fullam, "Juana, SJ: The Past (and Future) Status of Women in the Society of Jesus," *Studies in the Spirituality of Jesuits* 31 (November 1999).

11. On reading this passage, another Jesuit commented, "I'm thinking JP II has tough competition! Alexander VI had beautiful youths of Rome gilded, to stand along his coronation parade route. Then some (many?) fell dead because the gold sealed their pores." See E. R. Chamberlin, *The Bad Popes* (New York: Dorset, 1986), and Eamon Duffy, *Saints and Sinners: A History of the Popes* (New Haven, Conn.: Yale University Press, 1997).

12. Divergent views about the role of the papacy have surfaced among leading Jesuits. For a critical perspective, see John W. O'Malley, S.J., "The Millennium and the Papalization of Catholicism," *America,* April 8, 2000, 8–16. For a supportive view, see Avery Dulles, S.J., "The Papacy for a Global Church," *America,* July 15–22, 2000, 6–11.

13. Compare Ronald Inglehart and Wayne E. Baker, "Modernization, Cultural Change, and the Persistence of Traditional Values," *American Sociological Review* 65 (2000): 19–51.

14. Compare Thomas Landy, "Myths That Shape Us," *Studies in the Spirituality of Jesuits* 26 (November 1994).

15. See J. Brian Hehir, "Murray's Contribution," *Church,* spring 1997, 46–49.

16. Compare Elaine Sciolino, "Cleric Uses Weapon of Religion against Iran's Rulers," *New York Times,* September 18, 2000, and Robert Mickens, "Cardinals Press for More Sharing in Church Governments," *The Tablet,* June 2, 2001, 812–13.

17. Edward Song, "The Democratic Ideal: A Brief Review," *Hedgehog Review* 2 (2000): 140–55.

18. This is a variation on the "strict churches prosper" argument. See Laurence R. Iannaccone, "Why Strict Churches Are Strong," *American Journal of Sociology* 88 (1994): 1180–1211, and Rodney Stark and William Sims Bainbridge, *Religion, Deviance, and Social Control* (New York: Routledge, 1997). Compare Irving A. Kelter, "The Refusal to Accommodate: Jesuit Exegetes and the Copernican System," *Sixteenth Century Journal* 26 (1995): 273–83.

19. See Samuel P. Huntington, *The Third Wave: Democratization in the Late Twentieth Century* (Norman: University of Oklahoma Press, 1991).

20. See, however, John Dryzek, "Political Inclusion and the Dynamics of Democratization," *American Political Science Review* 90 (1996): 475–87, and Charles Taylor, "The Dynamics of Democratic Exclusion," *Journal of Democracy* 9 (1998): 143–56.

21. See Alfred O. Hirschman, *Exit, Voice, and Loyalty: Responses to the Decline in Firms, Organizations, and States* (Cambridge, Mass.: Harvard University Press, 1970).

22. Compare Guillermo O'Donnell, "Delegative Democracy," *Journal of Democracy* 5 (1994): 55–69.

23. See Eugene B. McCarraher, "The Church Irrelevant: Paul Hanly Furfey and the Fortunes of American Catholic Radicalism," *Religion and American Culture* 7 (1997): 163–94, and Joseph M. Schwartz, *The Permanence of the Political: A Democratic Critique of the Radical Impulse to Transcend Politics* (Princeton, N.J.: Princeton University Press, 1995).

24. See, however, Michael W. Cuneo, *The Smoke of Satan: Conservative and Traditionalist Dissent in Contemporary American Catholicism* (Baltimore: The Johns Hopkins University Press, 1998).

25. See Michael J. Baxter, C.S.C., "Catholicism and Liberalism: Kudos and Questions for Communio Ecclesiology," *Review of Politics* 60 (1998): 743–87; Thomas Langan, *Catholic Tradition* (Columbia: University of Missouri Press, 1998); and Richard A. McCormick, S.J., "The Church and Dissent," *Commonweal*, February 27, 1998, 15–20.

26. Compare Roger Finke, "An Orderly Return to Tradition: Explaining the Recruitment of Members into Catholic Religious Orders," *Journal for the Scientific Study of Religion* 36 (1997): 218–30.

27. See John P. Beal, "The Exercise of the Power of Governance by Lay People," *Jurist* 55 (1995): 1–92.

28. See Thomas P. Faase, "Bulwark Catholics and Conciliar Humanists in the Society of Jesus," *Sociological Quarterly* 21 (1980): 511–27.

29. Compare Josef Cardinal Ratzinger, *Salt of the Earth: Christianity and the Catholic Church at the End of the Millennium* (San Francisco: Ignatius Press, 1997), and Walter E. Wyman, Jr., "Revelation and the Doctrine of Faith: Historical Revelation within the Limits of Historical Consciousness," *Journal of Religion* 78 (1998): 38–63.

EPILOGUE

1. Bertrand M. Roehner, "Jesuits and the State: A Comparative Study of Expulsions," *Religion* 27 (1997): 165–82. See also Constance Jones Matthews,

"Early Spanish Qualms about Loyola and the Society of Jesus," *The Historian* 53 (1991): 679–90.

2. See Francis Fukuyama, *The Great Disruption: Human Nature and the Reconstitution of Social Order* (New York: The Free Press, 1999), and William Fine and Nancy Love, "Fighting for the Sixties," *Polity* 32 (1999): 285–99.

3. See George B. Wilson, S.J., "The Priest Shortage: The Situation and Some Options," *America*, May 31, 1986, 450–53.

4. Steven V. Monsma and J. Christopher Soper, *The Challenge of Pluralism: Church and State in Five Democracies* (Lanham, Md.: Rowman & Littlefield, 1997).

5. See David N. Power, O.M.I., "Theologies of Religious Life and Priesthood," in Paul K. Hennessy, C.F.C., ed., *A Concert of Charisms* (New York: Paulist Press, 1997), and Seán D. Sammon, F.M.S., "The Transformation of U.S. Religious Life," in Paul J. Philibert, O.P., ed., *Living in the Meantime* (New York: Paulist Press, 1994).

6. See Richard M. Gula, S.S., "The Law of Virtue," *Church* 15 (1999): 7–11; Karl Rahner, S.J., "Experiences of a Catholic Theologian," *Theological Studies* 61 (2000): 3–15; Luke Timothy Johnson, "So What's Catholic about It? The State of Catholic Biblical Scholarship," *Commonweal*, January 16, 1998, 12–16; and John Witte, Jr., *From Sacrament to Contract: Marriage, Religion, and Law in the Western Tradition* (Louisville, Ky.: Westminster John Knox Press, 1997). Compare John A. Hall, "A View of a Death: On Communism, Ancient and Modern," *Theory and Society* 27 (1998): 509–34; Michael Ignatieff, "The Era of Error," *New Republic*, August 9, 1999, 37–40; and Paul Lauritzen, "The Knowing Heart: Moral Argument and the Appeal to Experience," *Soundings* 81 (1998): 213–34.

7. Compare George Aschenbrenner, S.J., "The Presumption of Priestly Permanence," *Human Development* 19 (1998): 38–44; David Coffey, "The Common and the Ordained Priesthood," *Theological Studies* 58 (1997): 209–36; and Michael Purcell, "On the Ethical Nature of the Priesthood," *Heythrop Journal* 39 (1998): 298–313.

8. For a relatively sanguine prognosis, see Kenneth Untener, "Is the Church in Decline?" *Church* 15 (1999): 5–10. Untener, who is bishop of Saginaw, Michigan, writes, "Actually, the last thing we need to worry about in the church is the future of religious life. . . . We are witnessing not the death of religious life, but the end of religious life as a labor force to perform the regular tasks that we create for them" (p. 7).

9. See Paul Bernadicou, S.J., "Spiritual Direction Today," *Human Development* 18 (1997): 8–11; Joseph A. Tetlow, S.J., "The Experience of God in Consecrated Life during the 20th Century," *Review for Religious* 57 (1998): 491–512; and Owen C. Thomas, "Interiority and Christian Spirituality," *Journal of Religion* 80 (2000): 41–60.

10. Two qualifications to this difference between Jesuits and former Jesuits bear repeating. First, we lack firm information about what contributes to the difference aside from the sheer fact of being a Jesuit and the suggestion that sticking with service tends to be fulfilling. Second, the slightly greater satisfaction reported by Jesuits does not signify that they are actually more effective at what

they do. On the other hand, it would be churlish to deny the importance and legitimacy of work satisfaction, as if psychic rewards were irrelevant to getting the job done.

11. Compare Francis George, "Episcopal Conferences: Theological Bases," *Communio* 26 (1999): 393–409, and William J. Rewak, S.J., "The 'Gag Rule' and the Church," *America,* May 1, 1999, 21–22.

12. See Tony Judt, "Holy Warrior," *New York Review of Books,* October 31, 1996, 8–14; Brian Loveman, *The Constitution of Tyranny: Regimes of Exception in Spanish America* (Pittsburgh: University of Pittsburgh Press, 1993); and Claudio Véliz, *The Centralist Tradition of Latin America* (Princeton, N.J.: Princeton University Press, 1980).

13. See Kevin Wildes, "In the Name of the Father," *New Republic,* December 26, 1994, 21–25; compare Walter L. Adamson, *Hegemony and Revolution: A Study of Antonio Gramsci's Political and Cultural Theory* (Berkeley and Los Angeles: University of California Press, 1980); H. E. Chebabi and Juan J. Linz, eds., *Sultanistic Regimes* (Baltimore: The Johns Hopkins University Press, 1998); William Kornhauser, *The Politics of Mass Society* (Glencoe, Ill.: The Free Press, 1959); and Alan Wolfe, "Liberalism and Catholicism," *American Prospect,* January 31, 2000, 16–21.

14. Compare Ann Seleny, "Old Political Rationalities and New Democracies: Compromise and Confrontation in Hungary and Poland," *World Politics* 51 (1999): 484–519.

15. See Michele Dillon, *Catholic Identity: Balancing Reason, Faith and Power* (Cambridge: Cambridge University Press, 1999), and Philip S. Kaufman, *Why You Can Disagree and Remain a Faithful Catholic* (New York: Crossroad, 1991).

16. See, for example, Lawrence J. Engel, "The Influence of Saul Alinksy on the Campaign for Human Development," *Theological Studies* 59 (1998): 636–61, and T. Howland Sanks, S.J., "Globalization and the Church's Social Missions," *Theological Studies* 60 (1999): 628–51.

17. See Jacques Gernet, *China and the Christian Impact: A Conflict of Cultures* (Cambridge: Cambridge University Press, 1985); compare Charlotte Allen, "Confucius and the Scholars," *Atlantic Monthly,* April 1999, 79–83.

18. See Gavin Hyman, "Towards a New Religious Dialogue: Buddhism and Postmodern Theology," *Heythrop Journal* 34 (1998): 394–412, and Wade Clark Roof, "Religious Borderlands," *Journal for the Scientific Study of Religion* 37 (1998): 1–14.

19. See Ann Carey, "An Ignatian Retreat?," *Our Sunday Visitor,* June 27, 1999, 5; Howard J. Gray, S.J., "Being Catholic in a Jesuit Context," *America,* May 20, 2000, 23–26; Aristide Tessitore, "The Perspective of an American Catholic," *Furman Studies* 39 (1997): 63–89; and Charles Zech, "The Faculty and Catholic Institutional Identity," *America,* May 22, 1999, 11–15.

20. See Daniel Harris, *The Rise and Fall of Gay Culture* (New York: Hyperion, 1997).

21. Compare Randall Collins, "Emotional Energy as the Common Denominator of Rational Action," *Rationality and Society* 5 (1993): 203–30.

22. Compare Roger Finke and Patricia Wittberg, "Organizational Renewal

from Within: Explaining Revivalism and Reform in the Roman Catholic Church," *Journal for the Scientific Study of Religion* 39 (2000): 154–70.

23. Compare James Davison Hunter, *Culture Wars: The Struggle to Define America* (New York: Basic Books, 1991).

24. Compare Michelle Dillon, "The Catholic Church and Possible 'Organizational Selves': The Implications for Institutional Change," *Journal for the Scientific Study of Religion* 38 (1999): 386–97.

25. The typology is not very discriminating with regard to types of democracy. It has little to say about the debate between Catholic advocates of liberal (procedural) and communitarian democracy. See R. Bruce Douglass and David Hollenbach, S.J., eds., *Catholicism and Liberalism: Contributions to American Public Philosophy* (Cambridge: Cambridge University Press, 1994).

26. See Paul Veyne, *Bread and Circuses: Historical Sociology and Political Pluralism* (London: Penguin, 1992).

27. Political scientists will recognize pastoral hierarchy and combative democracy as variations, respectively, on *dictablanda* and *democradura* styles of soft authoritarian and hard democracy. See Richard Joseph, "The Reconfiguration on Power in Late Twentieth-Century Africa," in Richard Joseph, ed., *State, Conflict, and Democracy in Africa* (Boulder, Colo.: Lynne Rienner, 1999), and Lucian Pye, "Political Science and the Crisis of Authoritarianism," *American Political Science Review* 84 (1990): 3–19.

28. See Peter Augustine Lawler, "Francis Fukuyama as Teacher of Evil," *Modern Age* 42 (2000): 89–101.

29. See William P. Loewe, "From the Humanity of Christ to the Historical Jesus," *Theological Studies* 61 (2000): 314–31.

30. See Valerie Bunce, "Lessons of the First Postsocialist Decade," *East European Politics and Societies* 13 (1999): 236–43; compare Jack A. Goldstone, "Ideology, Cultural Frameworks, and the Process of Revolution," *Theory and Society* 20 (1991): 405–53, and Andrew M. Greeley, "The Revolutionary Event of Vatican II: How Everything Changed," *Commonweal*, September 11, 1998, 14–20.

31. Compare Robert H. Bates, "The Economics of Transitions to Democracy," *PS: Political Science & Politics*, March 1991, 24–27.

32. The indispensability of institutionalized rules that may benefit from but need not count on goodwill is the focus of Archbishop John R. Quinn, "The Exercise of the Primacy: Facing the Cost of Christian Unity," *Commonweal*, July 21, 1996, 11–20; see also Quinn, *The Reform of the Papacy: The Costly Call to Christian Unity* (New York: Crossroad, 1999).

33. See George B. Wilson, S.J., "'Dissent' or Conversation among Adults?" *America*, March 13, 1999, 8–12, and Ladislas Orsy, S.J., "Who Are the Bishops?" *America*, October 9, 1999, 8–11.

34. Compare Terence L. Nichols, "Who's Afraid of Hierarchy?" *Commonweal*, April 7, 2000, 16–18, and Hermann J. Pottmeyer, "Fallibly Infallible? A New Form of Papal Teaching," *America*, April 3, 1999, 10–13. See also Michael Novak, "Liberal Ideology, An Eternal No; Liberal Institutions, A Temporal Yes? And Further Questions," *Review of Politics* 60 (1998): 765–74.

35. See Eugene C. Bianchi and Rosemary Radford Reuther, eds., *A Demo-*

cratic Catholic Church: The Reconstruction of Roman Catholicism (New York: Crossroad, 1992).

36. See, for example, Anthony Black, *Monarchy and Community: Political Ideas in the Later Conciliar Controversy, 1430–1450* (Cambridge: Cambridge University Press, 1970); Dennis M. Doyle, "Henri de Lubac and the Roots of Communion Ecclesiology," *Theological Studies* 60 (1999): 209–27; Ad Leys, "Structuring Communion: The Importance of the Principle of Subsidiarity," *The Jurist* 58 (1998): 84–123; Ladislas Orsy, S.J., "Lay Persons in Church Governance? A Disputed Question," *America*, April 6, 1996, 10–13; and Carl F. Starkloff, S.J., "Church as Structure and Communitas: Victor Turner and Ecclesiology," *Theological Studies* 58 (1997): 643–68.

37. Compare Francis Fukuyama, "The Primacy of Culture," *Journal of Democracy* 6 (1995): 7–14.

38. See, for example, Jack Goody, "Comparing Family Systems in Europe and Asia: Are There Different Sets of Rules?," *Population and Development Review* 22 (1996): 1–20, and Lucian W. Pye, "Civility, Social Capital, and Civil Society: Three Concepts for Explaining Asia," *Journal of Interdisciplinary History* 29 (1999): 763–82.

39. See Hermann J. Pottmeyer, "Primacy in Communion," *America*, June 3–10, 2000, 15–18, and Carl F. Starkloff, S.J., "The Church as Convenant, Culture, and Communio," *Theological Studies* 61 (2000): 409–30.

40. Unpredictability is not all democracy induced. The status quo itself is unstable. Regardless of the pace of internationalization, autocracies themselves are notoriously prone to shocks and surprises brought on by the caprice or the incapacity of isolated leadership.

41. For a start, see Robert O. Keohane, "Governance in a Partially Globalized World," *American Political Science Review* 95 (2001): 1–14.

42. See Margaret O'Gara, "Shifts below the Surface of the Debate: Ecumenism, Dissent, and the Roman Catholic Church," *The Jurist* 56 (1996): 361–90.

43. Compare Richard Posner, "The Moral Minority," *New York Times Book Review*, December 19, 1999, 14.

44. See Russell Hardin, *One for All: The Logic of Group Conflict* (Princeton, N.J.: Princeton University Press, 1995).

45. Ken Jowitt has made a similar diagnosis of the impediments to collective action in communist and postcommunist societies: "As long as the socialist state was minimally able to compel external obedience, a weak social 'we' psychologically opposed an organized political 'they.' However, with the collapse of the party-state, the heteronomous social 'we' has become an unorganized collection of monadic 'me's distrustful of large collectivities . . . the true transition in most of these countries has been from We vs. They to Me vs. We" ("Challenging the Correct Line," *East European Politics and Societies* 12 [1998]: 96).

46. Compare Mark Regnerus and Christian Smith, "Selective Deprivatization among American Religious Traditions: The Reversal of the Great Reversal," *Social Forces* 76 (1998): 1347–72.

47. The other potential source of change, which we have mentioned only in passing, is concerted action on the part of lay interests; see Mary Fainsod

Katzenstein, *Faithful and Fearless: Moving Feminist Protest inside the Church and Military* (Princeton, N.J.: Princeton University Press, 1998). See also James Carroll, "The Wrong Side of History," *American Prospect,* January 31, 2000, 22.

48. See Rodney Stark, "Religious Effects: In Praise of 'Idealistic Humbug,'" *Review of Religious Research* 41 (2000): 289–310.

49. See Ann Swidler, "Cultural Power and Social Movements," in Hank Johnston and Bert Klandermans, eds., *Social Movement Culture* (Minneapolis: University of Minnesota Press, 1995).

50. Compare Margaret Weir, "Ideas and the Politics of Bounded Innovation," in Sven Steinmo, Kathleen Thelen, and Frank Longstreth, eds., *Structuring Politics: Historical Institutionalism in Comparative Perspective* (Cambridge: Cambridge University Press, 1992).

51. William V. D'Antonio et al., *Laity: American and Catholic* (Kansas City, Mo.: Sheed & Ward, 1996).

52. Compare Martin Shefter, *Political Parties and the State: The American Historical Experience* (Princeton, N.J.: Princeton University Press, 1994), xi.

53. See Sandra M. Schneiders, I.H.M., *Finding the Treasure: Locating Catholic Religious Life in a New Ecclesial and Cultural Context* (Mahwah, N.J.: Paulist Press, 2000).

54. Alexis de Tocqueville, *On Democracy, Revolution, and Society: Selected Writings,* ed. John Stone and Stephen Mennell (Chicago: University of Chicago Press, 1980), 230. Tocqueville continues: "Only consummate statecraft can enable a king to save his throne when after a long spell of oppressive rule he sets to improving the lot of his subjects. Patiently endured so long as it seemed beyond redress, a grievance comes to appear intolerable once the possibility of removing it crosses men's minds. For the mere fact that certain abuses have been remedied draws attention to the others and they now appear more galling; people may suffer less, but their sensibility is exacerbated."

NOTES ON METHODOLOGY

1. Besides Jesuits and former Jesuits, we spoke or corresponded with over 100 lay colleagues in institutions (mostly high schools and colleges) affiliated with the order. The sample is small and unsystematic. These materials are used mainly in chapters 8 and 9 devoted to ministry.

2. A revealing though time-consuming test of the supposed bias against pastoral Jesuits would be to tally how many of them get elected as representatives to province and general congregations of the Society. Our impression is that, at least until very recently, these men have been underrepresented. Another factor operating to lower the returns in the pastoral sample might be the men themselves, who are probably less given to answering questionnaires than the "armchair guys" in the schools.

3. For an example of this sort of approach, without the explicit sampling design, see Martha Nussbaum, *Cultivating Humanity: A Classical Defense of Reform in Liberal Education* (Cambridge, Mass.: Harvard University Press, 1997).

4. Opinions on moral-sexual and social-political issues are sufficiently dis-

tinct to warrant treating them separately, but they are strongly associated. Among former Jesuits, the correlation is .45; among Jesuits, it is .60. This means that men who are progressive on social-political issues are also likely to be progressive on sexual issues and vice versa.

5. Christopher Morash, quoted by Cormac Ó Gráda, *Black '47 and Beyond: The Great Irish Famine* (Princeton, N.J.: Princeton University Press, 1999), xii.

6. See Neil McInnes, "'Orientalism,' the Evolution of a Concept," *National Interest* 54 (1998–99): 73–81.

7. See William F. Powers, *Free Priests: The Movement for Ministerial Reform in the American Catholic Church* (Chicago: Loyola University Press, 1992).

8. Compare Nancy Scheper-Hughes, *Saints, Scholars, and Schizophrenics: Mental Illness in Rural Ireland* (Berkeley and Los Angeles: University of California Press, 1979).

9. Compare Wendy Ewald, *I Wanna Take Me a Picture: Teaching Photography and Writing to Children* (Boston: Beacon Press, 2001), and David Coghlan, S.J., and Teresa Brannick, *Doing Action Research in Your Own Organization* (London: Sage, 2001).

10. "Introduction," in Tobias Wolff, ed., *The Vintage Book of Contemporary American Short Stories* (New York: Vintage Books, 1994), xiv–xv.

apostolate: noun referring to ministerial activity, as in "the social apostolate," "the educational apostolate," and so on.

apostolic: refers to active religious ministry as distinct from the lifestyle of mainly contemplative religious—for example, the Carmelites or Trappists.

assistancy: regional grouping of provinces—for example, the North American Assistancy, the South Asian Assistancy.

consecrated life: religious life according to the rules of a religious order or congregation. "A religious" takes the three vows of poverty, chastity, and obedience.

cura personalis: personal care.

Ex Corde Ecclesiae: "From the Heart of the Church," apostolic constitution (papal directive) promulgated in August 1990, on the identity and mission of Catholic higher education.

examen: examination of conscience.

extern: non-Jesuit, outsider (obsolete).

formation: "training," usually with reference to Jesuits not yet ordained. "Ongoing formation" refers to the continuous nature of the spiritual life.

general, superior-general: head of the Society of Jesus elected for life at a general congregation of the order. Father-general resides in Rome with his curia (staff).

general congregation: calls representatives from the Society worldwide to Rome to elect a father-general or to legislate on important issues and set priorities for Jesuits. The Thirty-fourth General Congregation (1995–96) did not elect a new general, but it issued documents concerning the life and apostolates of Jesuits.

Ignatian: inspired by the life of Ignatius Loyola, first superior-general of the Society of Jesus, as in Ignatian spirituality. Frequently used in distinction to the more organizational and clerical connotations of "Jesuit."

magis, the magis: literally, "the more," greater effort, going the extra mile.

magisterium: teaching authority of the church.

mandatum: mandate, "license."

novice, novitiate: candidates to the Society usually spend two years as "novices," mostly in spiritual training.

Ours: a term, now less common, used by Jesuits to refer to fellow Jesuits. Opposite of "extern."

provincial, provincial superior: Jesuit director of, for example, "the New England province."

regency: period of training, usually two years, often spent in teaching high school.

religious: as a noun, refers to members of orders and congregations who live in community, compared to, for example, "secular" or "diocesan" clergy, who do not belong to religious orders.

scholastic: as a noun, refers to Jesuit in training.

socius: executive assistant to the provincial superior.

Spiritual Exercises: a thirty-day retreat according to a plan devised by Ignatius. The small book of *Exercises* is divided into four "weeks." The retreatant is led through a process of personal discernment and decision making in keeping with Christian theology and gospels. The *Exercises* are also adapted to shorter time periods and to diverse lifestyles.

synod: periodic conclave of bishops instituted by Vatican II.

theologian: Jesuit student of theology or, less often, professor of theology.

the works: ministries, usually institutional.

FIGURES

1. Jesuits and former Jesuits from comfortable or well-off families by year of entry into the Society   49
2. Religious devotion of mothers and fathers of Jesuits and former Jesuits by year of entry into the Society   50
3. Average perceptions of the church and the Society of Jesus by Jesuits and former Jesuits   241
4. Types of Catholicism   296
5. Total membership in United States of the Society of Jesus and cumulative number of departures, 1960–2000   308
6. Satisfaction among Jesuits with the church and with the Society of Jesus by age cohorts   323

TABLES

1. Distribution (%) of former Jesuit and Jesuit samples by province   310
2. Distribution (%) of former Jesuit and Jesuit samples by age cohort   311
3. Occupational distributions (%) of former Jesuits and Jesuits   311
4. Jesuit manpower distribution, three provinces, 1966, in percentages   312
5. Jesuit manpower distribution, three provinces, 1976 and 1986, in percentages   313
6. Jesuit manpower distribution, six provinces, 1996, in percentages   314

7. Jesuit manpower distribution, South Asian Assistancy
(India), 1996, in percentages   315

8. Average scores on sexual-moral and social-political issues,
when entering Society and today, by former Jesuits and
Jesuits   321

9. Average evaluations of the church, of the direction of the
Society, and of Jesuit ministries, by Jesuits and former
Jesuits   322

10. Correlations between opinions on sexual-moral and
social-political issues (and satisfaction with work) and
perceptions of the church, the direction of the Society of
Jesus, and the performance of Jesuit ministries, among
former Jesuits and Jesuits   324

INDEX

All index entries concern American Jesuits. **Boldface page numbers indicate material in tables or figures.**

abortion, 77
absolute truth, loss of confidence in, 289–90
Africa, Jesuits in, 273
AIDS, 340n3
AJCU. *See* Association of Jesuit Colleges and Universities
Alinski, Saul, 199
ambiguity, acceptance of, 117–23
annulments, marriage, 77. *See also* marriage
apostolates. *See* ministry, Jesuit
Arrupe, Pedro
  feelings toward, 265, 268
  on high schools, 217
  historical background, 4, 5, 352n28
asceticism, 24–25
Assembly '89, 215, 353n5
Association of Catholic Colleges and Universities, 234
Association of Jesuit Colleges and Universities (AJCU), 213, 214, 222–23, 230, 354n6
attrition rates, 335n33. *See also* leaving and staying in the Society
Augustine, 75, 89, 155, 335n30
autonomy. *See* individualism

Balasuriya, Tissa, 361n5
becoming a Jesuit. *See* entrants
Benedictines, 110
Berrigan, Daniel, 5, 223

Berry, Thomas, 110, 113
Bianchi, Eugene, 325
biblical scholarship, 153–54
birth control, 38–39, 76
Boston College, 222, 224–25, 229
Brown University, 229
Buddhism, 124, 126, 152, 154, 155, 335n30
Bultmann, Rudolph, 155
bureaucracy. *See* Catholicism; ecclesiastical authority

calling. *See* divine calling
Campbell, Joseph, 152
Carroll, John, 4
Carter, Jimmy, 222
Catholic University of America, 224
Catholicism. *See also* ecclesiastical authority
  church and state, 3, 281–82, 288–89
  during the Depression years, 51–54
  dualism, 335n30
  and finding God, 122
  historicity of, 153
  internationalization, 301–2
  as an intricate ecosystem, 272–74
  perceptions of, 239, 240–41, **241**, **242**, **322**, **324**, 359n8
  reforming, 1, 297–304
  sexual policies, 75–79, 86
  as a subculture, 46
  types of, 295–97, **296**
  Vatican II's effect on, 48–51

celibacy
   advantages of, 72, 82, 83, 88–93,
      341n9
   belief vs. behavior, 93–97, 341n12
   change in thinking on, 65, 98
   date of requirement, 288
   decline in advantages of, 107–8
   effects of, 75
   as a gift, 74, 80
   quandaries regarding chastity, 97
   as a reason for leaving the Jesuits, 23,
      35–36, 145
   as sacrifice, 62
   survival of the priesthood and, 251,
      281, 289
change in the Society of Jesus
   ambivalence toward, 267–72
   controlling, 285–86
   factors subduing, 283–85, 286, 304–5
   future conditions for, 302–3
   nature of, 1–3
   organizational options, 305–6
   since Vatican II, 6–9
charismatic influences, 121–22, 126, 158
chastity. See celibacy
Christology, 298. See also Jesus Christ
church and state, 3, 281–82, 288–89
Clark, Keith, 103
colleges. See also education; universities
   Boston College, 222, 224–25, 229
   Thomas Aquinas College, 357n50
combative democracy, 297. See also
   Catholicism, types of
commitment to religious life. See entrants,
   motivations of; leaving and staying
   in the Society
communist societies, 366n45
community, life in, 160–84
   age groups, 174, 180, 181
   changing nature of, 162–63, 166, 172,
      291
   competitiveness, 166–67, 173
   decline in sense of community, 101,
      104, 148
   difficulties, 168–69, 180–81
   expectations, 162, 163, 181
   in formation communities, 160–61,
      164–66, 348n2
   friendship, 21, 161, 171, 172, 173–74,
      182–83, 349n21
   homosexuals as a subgroup, 176–79
   importance of, 149–51, 342n16
   individualism and, 98, 101
   intimacy and, 20–21, 31, 34–35, 163,
      167–68, 174
   metaphorical dispersed communities,
      164, 169–71, 176, 183

professionalization and, 163–64,
      167
   reasons for staying, 20–21, 34–35,
      175–76 (See also leaving and stay-
      ing in the Society)
   subgroups, 161, 169, 172, 176–79,
      182
Company (magazine), 336n33
compartmentalization, 9–10, 207–8,
      264–65, 272
complaint, culture of, 23–24
Congregation for Catholic Education,
      224
Conversations on Jesuit Higher Educa-
      tion, 215
conversion experiences, 22, 147. See also
      redemption
CORPUS, 325
countercultural motivations for entrants,
      46–47, 62–63, 337n14
countercultural movements, 65, 99–100,
      292–94. See also Eastern reli-
      gions; faith-and-justice movement;
      homosexuality; neoconservativism
creation theology, 110, 113, 116
Crossan, John Dominic, 352n29
cultural revolution of the 1960s, 98

Decree on Religious Liberty, 263. See
      also Vatican II
democratization
   in Catholicism, 283, 297–98,
      365n25, 365n27
   in education, 217, 232–33
   in the Society of Jesus, 248
demographics, family, 48–51
Depression, Catholic family life during,
      51–54
Dezza, Paolo, 330n12
Dignity (gay support group), 102,
      343n26
dilemmas. See problems currently facing
      the Society
diocesan priests, 163, 348n7
dispersed community, 164, 169–71, 176,
      183
divine calling, 22, 25, 27–29, 45, 145,
      334n19
divorce, 59–60, 76–77
doctrinal-ideological reasons for leaving,
      19, 38–39
dogmatism. See ambiguities, accep-
      tance of
Donne, John, 111
dualism, 335n30
Duke University, 224, 229
Dulles, Avery, 140

Eastern religions. *See also* Buddhism
 acceptability of, 126, 157–58, 293
 attraction of, 99, 335n30
 impact of, 294
ecclesiastical authority. *See also*
 Catholicism
 attitudes toward, 9–10, 123, 148, 153,
 253, 264–72, 279–80
 in democratic nations, 263
 forces operating on, 8–9, 274–76
 leadership succession, 284
 nature of, 237, 287–88, 291–92
 reason for leaving the Jesuits, 37–39
 and sexuality, 64, 75–79, 82–83, 86
 and social justice, 243–45, 359n15
eclecticism
 charismatic influences, 121–22, 126,
 158
 evangelical influences, 126, 158
 identification with peripheral communities, 138–41, 142–43
 individualism and, 133–37
 and the institutional church, 141–42,
 158
 in spirituality, 117–19, 124–26, 156–
 57
 studying outside the Christian canon,
 151–58
ecumenism, 117–18, 124–26
education, 211–36. *See also* colleges;
 universities
 academic excellence, 212, 227–30
 Assembly '89, 215, 353n5
 Association of Catholic Colleges and
 Universities, 234
 Association of Jesuit Colleges and Universities, 213, 214, 222–23
 boards of trustees, 212, 216
 Congregation for Catholic Education,
 224
 *Conversations on Jesuit Higher Educa-
 tion*, 215
 decline in Jesuit numbers, 185–86,
 350n3
 democratization, 217, 232–33
 faculty, academic excellence of, 212
 funding, 214, 221–22, 354n1
 goals and vision, 212–13, 215
 governance, 232–33
 higher education, 222–24, 224–26,
 227–30, 236, 357n53
 humanities, decline of, 196–98,
 351n19
 incorporation, 212, 216
 influencing federal legislation, 214, 222
 integrating faith-and-justice agenda,
 219–20, 227–30, 245–46

Jesuit Educational Association, 213
Jesuit Secondary Education Association, 213–14, 216, 217, 236,
 358n54
 Land O'Lakes statement, 212–13, 216
 lay participation, 216–17 (*See also*
 marketization)
 ministry, sense of, 198–202
 mission statements, 231
 National Defense Education Act of
 1963, 221
 National Seminar on Jesuit Higher
 Education, 214–15, 354n6
 pluralism, 230–34, 235
 and postmodernism, 233
 professional schools, 197
 role of Jesuits, 4, 98, 211, 233–34
 safeguarding religious identity, 224–26
 secondary education, 215–20, 235–
 36, 245–46, 358n54
 secularization, 234–35
 students, background of, 6, 354n7
 success of schools, 186, 235–36,
 358n54
 Vatican strategies toward, 224, 234–35
Eliot, T. S., 155
entrants, motivations of, 43–63. *See also*
 divine calling; leaving and staying
 in the Society
 career alternatives, 45–46
 comparing time periods, 43–44,
 47–48
 countercultural, 46–47, 62–63,
 337n14
 declining number of reasons, 60–63
 during the Depression, 55–57
 family backgrounds, 48–51
 interaction of, 47
 neighborhood backgrounds, 51–57,
 342n16
 post-Vatican II, 57–60
 self interest, 44
 service, 44, 62
epicureanism, 157
Eucharist, 143–44, 155
evangelical-charismatic influences, 121–
 22, 126, 158
evangelism, 205
Ex Corde Ecclesiae
 avoiding secularization of schools, 234
 controversy over, 214, 223, 229, 230,
 251
 failing to measure up to, 235
exit option, 283–84. *See also* leaving and
 staying in the Society
exodus of the 1960s and 1970s, 20, 94,
 156

faith-and-justice movement
  church hierarchy and, 243–45,
    358n15
  declining membership and, 249–50,
    259
  education and, 6, 219–20, 227–30,
    245–46
  giving meaning and direction, 202–3,
    204–6, 293–94, 337n14
  opinions about, 66, 321, 324
  and satisfaction with the Society of
    Jesus, 242–43, 359n12
  sexual-moral views and, 367n4
family background of Jesuits
  comparison of pre- and post-Vatican II,
    48–51
  during the Depression, 51–57
  devotion of parents, 50
  financial status, 49
  post-Vatican II, 57–60, 338n29
fantasy life, 90. See also sexuality
Fichter, Joseph, 341n5
Fides et Ratio, 126
First Vatican Council, 360n16
Fisher, James T., 351n8
Fitterer, Jack, 222–23
Fitzmyer, Joseph, 265, 360n5
formation communities, 160–61, 164–
    66, 348n2
Freud, Sigmund, 154
friendships
  outside, 21, 171, 172, 173–74
  particular, 182–83, 349n21
  vs. community, 161, 174

gay Jesuits. See homosexuality
General Congregations, 331n24
  Thirty-second General Congregation,
    242, 353n37
  Thirty-fourth General Congregation,
    268, 270, 353n37
George, Francis Cardinal, 341n9
Georgetown University, 4, 215, 229,
    349n15, 354n5
GI Bill of Rights, 4, 196, 221
gnosticism, 157
God
  changing understanding of, 114–16
  and the church, 122
  and Eucharist, 143
  glory of, 175
  knowing, 146
  as love, 120
  in relationships, 149–50
  role in the Society's survival, 277
  as a terrifying deity, 60
  will of (See divine calling)

Golas, Thaddeus, 151
grace. See divine calling
Greene, Graham, 15
Gregorian University, 234, 359n15

Hamill, Pete, 332n36
Harvard University, 5, 224
Haught, John, 146
Healy, Timothy, 224
Hellwig, Monika, 229
hierarchy. See Catholicism; ecclesiastical
    authority
historicity of Scripture and of church, 153
Holy Spirit, 115, 118
homosexuality
  ascent of, 87–88, 341n3
  and becoming a Jesuit, 48, 343n25
  and community, 176–79
  as counterculture, 100–107, 108–9,
    138–41, 142–43
  and identity, 65, 98–99, 292, 294,
    337n14
  opinions about, 35–36, 77–78, 90,
    261
Hsia, R. Po-chia, 330n19
Humanae Vitae, 38, 66, 76, 153, 223
humanities, decline of, 196–98, 351n19

IAF (Industrial Areas Foundation), 199
identity
  homosexuality and, 65, 98–99, 292,
    294, 337n14
  Jesuit, 6, 88, 97–100, 288, 289,
    331n24
  renovated Catholic, 158
Ignatian Associates, 305
Ignatian Lay Volunteers, 305
Ignatian spirituality. See spirituality
Ignatius of Loyola
  and action, 26
  and discernment, 146
  encouraging written accounts, 15
  and humiliation, 276
  importance of, 150
  and individuality, 111
  and obedience, 332n37
  retreat plan (See Spiritual Exercises)
India, Jesuits of, 5, 6, 126, 273, 312–13,
    315
individualism
  and community, 98, 101
  emphasis on, 133–37
  and organizational purpose, 20–21,
    246–49, 284, 292
  in spirituality, 111, 119
Industrial Areas Foundation (IAF), 199
informality in religious observance, 113

Institute of Jesuit Sources, 354n6
institutional church. *See* Catholicism;
    ecclesiastical authority; Vatican
internationalization, 301–2, 305
intimacy
    and community, 20–21, 31, 34–35,
        163, 167–68, 174
    and homosexuality, 103
    as a reason for staying in or leaving the
        Society, 20–21, 23, 30–32, 34–
        39, 40–41
irenic democracy, 296. *See also* Catholi-
    cism, types of
Islam, 152

James, William, 118, 331n31
Jesuit Conference Board, 354n6
Jesuit Educational Association, 213
Jesuit Secondary Education Association
    (JSEA), 213–14, 216, 217, 236,
        358n54
Jesuit spirituality. *See* spirituality
Jesuit-Vatican relations. *See* ecclesiastical
    authority; Vatican
Jesuits (Society of Jesus). *See also other*
    main entries
    distinctiveness, 130
    endurance of, 9–10
    engagement in the world, 25–26, 28,
        111
    future of, 10–12
    historical background, 3–6, 129–30,
        287, 288
    mission of, 24, 185, 187, 202
    organizational purpose vs. individual
        autonomy, 20–21, 246–49, 284,
        292
    perceptions of, 240, 241–42, 322,
        324, 359n8, 359n12
    as a professional association, 130
    three-tiered hierarchy, 7–8, 290–91
Jesus Christ
    appreciation of, 115
    Christology, 298
    divinity of, 116, 151
    and Eucharist, 143–44, 155
    and the Holy Spirit, 118
    relationship with, 114, 115–16, 137,
        142, 143–47, 175
    resurrection, 155
John Paul II
    and contemporary culture, 83, 84
    on economic justice, 66
    governance, style of, 5, 8, 296
    neoconservatism, 48
    opinions about, 240, 268, 270, 275,
        276

prohibiting discussion on women's
    ordination, 239
John XXIII, 268
joining religious life. *See* entrants
JSEA. *See* Jesuit Secondary Education
    Association
Judaism, 152
Jung, Carl Gustav, 152

Kelly, James, 79
Kinerk, Edward, 203–4
Kolvenbach, Peter-Hans, 5, 215, 264,
    295
Krammer, Fred, 349n20

Lacey, Michael, 221
laity, ministry of
    authority of, 277–78, 285–86, 287–
        88
    collaboration with the Jesuits, 10,
        202–4, 209, 291, 298, 352n28
    in education, 216–17
Land O'Lakes statement, 212–13, 216
leaving and staying in the Society, rea-
    sons for, 17–42. *See also* entrants,
    motivations of
    ambivalence, 18, 20–21
    attrition rates, 336n33
    celibacy, 23, 35–36, 145
    church bureaucracy, 37–39
    complaint, culture of, 23–24
    cultural transformation and, 36–37
    divine calling, 22, 25, 27–29, 45, 145,
        334n19
    doctrinal-ideological reasons, 19,
        38–39
    exit option, 23, 283–84
    grace, 22 (*See also* divine calling)
    intimacy vs. community, 20–21, 23,
        30–32, 34–39, 40–41, 175–76
    joining the exodus, 20
    marriage vows, similarity to, 32, 36
    multiplicity of reasons, 18–19, 30, 33,
        36, 41–42
    personal costs vs. rewards, 19, 20, 22–
        25, 26, 30, 42
    prayer, 32–34, 40
    reluctance to speculate on, 17–18
    role of the priesthood, 24, 39, 41
    summary, 18, 41–42
legislation, influencing federal, 214,
    222
Leo XIII, 224
liberal arts. *See* humanities
Little, Arthur D., 246
love-it-or-leave-it syndrome, 293–94
Loyola University, 353n1

magis, 175
marginal people. *See* peripheral
   communities
marketization, 9, 90–91, 235
marriage, 77, 251, 252, 253
Marx, Karl Heinrich, 188
Mary (mother of Jesus), 115
McBrien, Richard P., 229, 356n36
McDonough, Peter, 325
membership, declining
   consequence of Vatican II, 289
   conservative viewpoint on, 254–57
   coping with, 187, 290–94
   in education, 185–86
   effect on other issues, 249–54
   numbers, 307, 308
   progressive viewpoint on, 249–54
   shortage of manpower, 6
methodology, 307–28
   biases, 325, 326
   confidentiality, 326
   emphasis on Jesuits in the United
      States, 11–12
   essay questions, 319–20
   feedback, 327
   interview guide, 317–19
   membership numbers in the Society
      of Jesus, 307, 308
   openness of responses, 14–16
   sampling, 12, 309–17, 331n30
      accuracy and limitations, 314–17
      distribution by age, 311
      distribution by occupation, 311,
         312, 313, 314, 315
      distribution by province, 310
Metts, Ralph E., 355n16
militant hierarchy, 296. *See also* Catholicism, types of
ministry, Jesuit, 185–210
   collaboration with laity, 10, 202–4,
      209, 291, 298, 352n28
   compartmentalization of, 9–10,
      207–8, 264–65, 272
   in education, 196–202 (*See also*
      education)
   faith-and-justice agenda, 202–3, 204–
      6, 293–94, 337n14
   and ordination, 200–202, 208–9, 210
   as personal service, 188–91
   satisfaction in, 186, 206–7, 350n7,
      351n8, 353nn35–36, 353nn
      37–38
   strategies, 194–96, 209
   traditional vs. therapeutic model,
      191–94
   trends, 8, 185–88
mission statements, 24, 187, 202

missioning, 247
Murray, John Courtney, 4, 156, 216,
   232, 281–82

National Catholic Reporter, 325, 341n5
National Defense Education Act of 1963,
   221
National Seminar on Jesuit Higher Education, 214–15, 354n6
neighborhoods, Catholic, 51–57, 165
neoconservatism, 48
neopaganism, 157
Newman, John Henry Cardinal, 118
Nietzsche, Friedrich Wilhelm, 154
nineteenth-annotation retreat, 351n23
Nixon, Richard, 222
nongeographical communities, 164,
   169–71, 176

O'Callaghan, Jack, 354n6
O'Keefe, Vincent, 354n6
O'Malley, John, 132–33
omega point, 267, 360n6
Opus Dei, 305, 359n15
ordination, 200–202, 208–9, 210, 251,
   281
organized religion, distrust of, 112

Padberg, John, 354n6
Pagels, Elaine, 352n29
parish workers, 186
particular friendships, 182–83, 349n21
pastoral and parish workers, 186
pastoral hierarchy, 296–97. *See also*
   Catholicism, types of
Paul (Saint), 155, 200
Paul VI, 268
Pell Grant program, 222
Perekkatt, Varkey, 315
peripheral communities, identification
   with, 138–41, 142–43
personal autonomy. *See* individualism
pluralism, 135–36, 230–34, 238, 282,
   294, 330n16
politics, 5, 262–86
prayer, 32–34, 40, 113, 334n24
priesthood, 185–210
   ordination, 200–202, 208–9, 210,
      251, 281
   role of, 39, 41, 43, 257, 290
Princeton University, 5
problems facing the Society, 237–64
   declining membership, 185–86, 249–
      57, 289, 307, 308
   organizational problems, 240–43
   organizational purpose vs. individual
      autonomy, 246–49

overview and degrees of severity, 237–40, 258–61, 282, 287–90
social justice and church hierarchy, 243–45
social justice and educational priorities, 246–49
viewpoints
ambivalence toward change, 267–72
Catholicism as an intricate ecosystem, 272–74
compartmentalization, 9–10, 207–8, 264–65, 272
following a traditionalist line, 265–67, 272
resignation to extinction, 277–81
traditional authority vs. cultural change, 274–76
professional schools, 197
professionalization, 163–64, 167
psychology
displacing of religion by, 259–60
therapeutic model of ministry, 9, 191–94

Quinn, John R., 365n32

Rahner, Karl, 122, 132, 156
Ratio Studiorum, 221
Ratzinger, Cardinal, 211, 223, 265, 268
Reagan, Ronald, 222
redemption, 25. See also conversion experiences
Reinert, Paul, 221, 355n19
Religion and Self-Acceptance (Haught), 146
religious job market, 9, 90–91, 235
retention. See leaving and staying in the Society
retreats, 111, 352n23
Rhodes, Frank, 225
Riis, Jacob, 53
Rome. See Vatican
Roof, Wade Clark, 346n13

Saint Louis University High School, 203
salvation, 41–42
Santa Clara University, 349n15
Schmidt, Robert, 315
School of the Americas, 214
schools. See colleges; education; universities; and names of individual institutions
Scripture, historicity of, 153
Second Vatican Council. See Vatican II
seeker-style evangelicalism, 346n13
self-determination. See individualism
self-sacrifice, 24–25, 193

Sertillanges, A. G., 154
sexual-moral issues
abortion, 77
birth control, 38–39, 76
correlations with other issues, 239, 240, 324, 358n12, 367n4
divorce, 59–60, 76–77
importance of, 251, 298
viewpoints, 259, 321
sexual orientation, 100. See also homosexuality
sexuality, 64–86, 341n4
behavior vs. belief, 69, 74–75, 79–85, 86
beliefs, 66–69, 87, 89–90
and cultural norms, 72–73, 77–78, 83–84
and ecclesiastical authority, 64, 75–79, 82–83, 86
fantasy life, 90
in innocence, 69–71
obsession in, 75–76
satisfaction, 73–74
Shadowbrook, 164
social justice. See faith-and-justice movement
Society of Jesus. See Jesuits
Southeast Asian candidates, 337n18
Spiritual Exercises (Ignatius)
contents, 332n37, 343n11, 351n23
and prayer, 40
rediscovery and rejuvenation of, 121, 125, 158, 167, 187, 245, 291
and relationship with Jesus, 114, 115, 116
and therapization, 9
spirituality, Ignatian, 110–31
affections over understanding, 112, 120–21, 122, 124–26
ambiguities in, 117–23
eclecticism, 113, 117–19, 124–26
epiphanies, 127–28
and organized religion, 112, 113, 123, 129–31
personalizing, 111–12
rediscovery, 26, 187, 290–91
retreats, 111, 351n23
Seminar on Jesuit Spirituality, 354n6
Studies in the Spirituality of Jesuits, 215
traditional, 335n30
value of, 128–29
staying, reasons for. See leaving and staying in the Society
Studies in the Spirituality of Jesuits, 215
subgroups, 161, 169, 172, 176–79, 182
syncretism, 113, 124, 125

Teilhard de Chardin, Pierre, 4, 267,
  361n6
therapeutic model of ministry, 9, 191–
  94
Thirty-second General Congregation,
  242, 353n37
Thirty-fourth General Congregation,
  268, 270, 353n37
Thomas Aquinas, 154, 335n30
Thomas Aquinas College, 357n50
Tip O'Neill Library, 222
To Turn the Tide (Reinert), 221
Tocqueville, Alexis de, 306, 367n54
Tripole, Martin, 205

universities. *See also* education
  Association of Catholic Colleges and
    Universities, 234
  Association of Jesuit Colleges and Uni-
    versities (AJCU), 213, 214, 222–
    23, 230, 354n6
  Brown University, 229
  Catholic University of America, 224
  Duke University, 224, 229
  Georgetown University, 4, 215, 229,
    349n15, 354n5
  Gregorian University, 234, 359n15
  Harvard University, 5, 224
  Loyola University, 354n1
  Princeton University, 5

Santa Clara University, 349n15
Yale University, 5, 197, 224
Untener, Kenneth, 363n8

Vatican, The, 8, 89, 223
Vatican I (1869–1870), 360n16
Vatican II (1962–1965)
  change point for Jesuits, 4, 39, 46, 289
  changes for Catholics, 43, 61
  and ecumenism, 124
  end of formalism, 162
  and homosexuality, 101
  importance of, 1, 285
  opinions about, 121, 131, 132–33,
    268
  and sexuality, 85, 107, 341n12
vow of chastity. *See* celibacy

WIN, 199
withdrawal from religious life. *See* leaving and staying in the Society
Wojtyla, Karol. *See* John Paul II
women
  relationships with, 67, 73, 94–97
    (*See also* sexuality)
  role of, 10, 239, 251, 252, 275

Yale University, 5, 197, 224

Zen, 124, 154, 155. *See also* Buddhism

Compositor: G&S Typesetters
Text: 10/13 Sabon
Display: Sabon
Printer and Binder: Haddon Craftsmen